PSYCHOPOLITICAL ANALYSIS

PSYCHOPOLITICAL
ANALYSIS
Selected Writings of
NATHAN LEITES

Edited by
ELIZABETH WIRTH MARVICK

SAGE Publications

Halsted Press
JOHN WILEY & SONS
New York - London - Sydney - Toronto

Distributed by Halsted Press, a Division of
John Wiley & Sons, Inc., New York

Printed in the United States of America

Library of Congress Cataloging in Publication Data

Leites, Nathan Constantin, 1912-
    Psychopolitical analysis.

    Includes bibliographical references.
    1. Political psychology—Addresses, essays,
lectures. I. Title.
JA74.5.L44   320'.01'9   77-2972
ISBN 0-470-99058-9

FIRST PRINTING

CONTENTS

For L. F. S.
in friendship

PART I.

EDITOR'S INTRODUCTION

PSYCHOPOLITICAL ANALYSIS AND THE CONTRIBUTION OF NATHAN LEITES

*P*sychoanalytical study of political behavior has reached a certain age. Inaugurated by Freud in 1921, with *Group Psychology and the Analysis of the Ego,* its agenda was laid out by Harold Lasswell in 1932 with "The Triple Appeal Principle: A Dynamic Key."[1] Since then the bibliography of its literature has grown to a size meriting sub-headings in indices of social science literature—a sure sign of majority, if not of senescence.

In this literature the work of Nathan Leites holds a special place. His contribution is outstanding on two counts: it has great importance for policy analysis, and its method is distinctive. It is proposed here to describe the ways in which these two features make his contribution outstanding. This will be done in a brief overview of the work of which this volume is designed to be a representative sample. Thereafter, the influence of his contribution will be discussed. Last, the potential significance of his contribution will be considered in the context of psychopolitical studies in general.

I

For more than three decades Leites' publications have described the *weltanschauungen* of those who move and shake the earth—the world's political and intellectual elites. No one's attention has ranged more widely. Only partly represented in this volume, it has extended from first-century Christian theologians to Mao Tse-tung and his companions-in-arms; from Charles de Gaulle to the post-1940 psychoanalytical Establishment. His focus has been unique: he considers the moral perspectives of these influential persons: their realism and their truthfulness, their dispositions towards cruelty and violence, their tolerance for opposition and dissent.

Moral perspectives are internalized social norms. Leites' work has therefore stressed group orientations: elite feelings of responsibility to moral standards independent of themselves, concern with the well-being of others both within their own groups and outside them. He has analyzed these dimensions of dispositions and beliefs in the context of public documents produced by leaders as they actually engage in decision-making. In this way he has aimed at improving our capacity for predicting and controlling the forces that rule our world.

Typically, Leites studies the beliefs of elites concerning what constitutes right and wrong conduct, and the expectations and feelings supporting those beliefs. As a Freudian, he sees these group norms originating in the experience of individuals from earliest childhood. As a social scientist, he sees this experience patterned by group culture, as it is transmitted to members from generation to generation. Political behavior is shaped by such regularities of experience.

People act and speak in response to the world around them by selecting, partly unconsciously, from the store of resources with which their experience has supplied them. The political process is therefore an interaction between the manifest environment of adults, visibly shaped by recorded history, and the latent motives and predispositions of those adults as these are formed by the culture in which they have been reared. Leites' aim is to relate the latent motives and predispositions of groups to their members' behavior in the manifest environment.

To study the link between personal experience and political behavior, Leites uses psychoanalytic theory and method. To do this he not only applies Freudian hypotheses concerning the genesis and dynamics of the human personality, but also applies the Freudian technique of interpreting word-associations. With few exceptions (among them "Violence as Strategy in Rebellion Situations," in this volume,) his attention is on the manipulation of symbols—usually words. Treating communications as though they were the utterances of patients, he seeks in the association of words what is both distinctive and apparently charged with meaning for the communicator—listening, as Theodor Reik described it, with a "third ear."

In three important ways, however, Leites' role diverges from the psychoanalyst's. First, the therapist, interested in curing his patient, considers of secondary interest the context in which the patient acts. For Leites the primary concern *is* contextual: how does the environment act on the communicator, and what effect does he, in turn, have on his environment? The social context of the communications studied is always in the foreground; usually, it is specified in considerable detail.

Second, the psychoanalyst is interested mainly in the personal life of his patient; he considers primarily personal, private communications from him. While Leites uses personal as well as public documents, the former are examined *only* for their relevance to a political context. Letters, memoirs, interviews, and biographies are scanned in the same way as speeches, novels, proverbs, tracts—only for their evident association with or their meaning for the communicator's orientation to his social milieu.

And third, the psychoanalyst, required to show moral neutrality towards his patient's behavior, is little concerned with the ethical content of what he hears except as it bears on symptoms. For Leites, on the other hand, psychoanalytical theory contributes to political knowledge by making it possible to understand the history, organization, and tendencies of value systems and moral feelings.

In one of the papers in this book Leites notes that "the empirical study of morality has hardly begun."[2] Part of his own work does constitute a major beginning, however. Freud's great discoveries concerning personality development made it possible to trace the formation of human values from infancy to adulthood. In his early *Group Psychology and the Analysis of the Ego* Freud himself applied his theory to a case of "dysfunction of the conscience." In that essay he describes situations in which a group delegates some of its superego functions to a leader, thus relieving members of feelings of moral responsibility. But until Leites, few other psychoanalytic inquiries have focussed on the vicissitudes of guilt feelings and beliefs about right and wrong in the political culture of groups. Since the early 1940s Leites has monitored trends in these feelings and beliefs. Briefly tracing this theme through some of his writings gives an overview of his work.

In the important paper of Kris and Leites, "Twentieth Century Propaganda Trends" (chapter 3), the authors identify an interwar trend in the Western world away from appeals to conscience and impulse and towards ego appeals. They explain the shift by tendencies towards privatization, arising out of spreading mutual mistrust.

In a subsequent article Leites carries further his own investigation of the alternative modes of validation which in those years seemed to be replacing moral justifications. In "Recent Trends in Moral Temper" (chapter 4), he finds the existentialist literature especially to reflect this atrophy of moral standards, thus culminating a two-century-long decline in religious belief.

The political significance of a trend towards amorality is that it augurs erosion of the basis of societies that require moral consensus. Leites has pointed to the likely consequences of declining belief in immortality in an article not presented in this volume. Discussing the point of view presented by Camus' hero in *The Stranger* he there observes that "If death is annihilation, life—all we have—is infinitely precious." This, he notes, represents "a resurgence of the *carpe diem* theme in highbrow speculation which has often accompanied the breakdown of civilizations."[3]

The "breakdown of civilization" phrase becomes an explicit warning about a particular civilization in "Political Democracy and Personal Destructiveness" (chapter 9). Writing this essay at a time when he saw many social psychologists and international relations specialists pooling their resources to combat "tensions" and "aggressiveness" in social relations, Leites observes that measures designed to achieve this purpose by changing patterns of child-rearing do not seem—so far—to have been effective. Instead it might be more to the point to consider the effects on democratic practices of moral atonia: "The dysfunctions of the conscience may be one of the major studies of the scientists of democracy."

As a scientist of democracy, Leites has given the dysfunctions of the conscience a large share of his attention. The contexts he has chosen for its study have ranged widely. In the earliest of his papers included in this volume, "German Attitudes and Nazi Leadership" (chapter 13), he speculates (with Paul Kecskemeti) that the prominence of the "might makes right" doctrine in German attitudes could be traced to those anti-paternal tendencies that aroused excessive guilt in the child and mobilized corresponding defenses against it. The willingness of Nazi leaders to commit unconscionable acts in the name of authority derived in part from the feeling that it was a compelling duty to obey the strong. Cruelty became, so to speak, a moral obligation.

In his most recent work, Leites still focusses on the political consequences of such dysfunctions. In the essay about Vietnam, presented here (chapter 18), he shows the disadvantage South Vietnamese leadership incurred by failing to set the high moral example modelled by their counterparts in the Viet Cong.

His Russian work includes *A Study of Bolshevism, The Operational Code of the Politburo* (a short monograph which is a partial skeleton of the larger work), *The Ritual of Liquidation* (with Elsa Bernaut), and a series of articles and monographs, some still unpublished. This whole body of work may be characterized as his inquiry into the vicissitudes of the conscience of Soviet leaders since Lenin. Several of his fundamental hypotheses—formed in the course of this inquiry—are well elaborated in selections in this volume.

Thus Leites suggests that Russian culture burdens the typical individual with strong feelings of guilt arising from early experience of destructive impulses towards other family members, especially the mother. What happens to these guilty feelings tells much about the course of Russian history in the past few decades. He demonstrates how the old Russian culture resolved guilt in a variety of ways, some of them exalting and humane. The typical Soviet solution, however, has been to project guilt onto others, defined as enemies of the Party, and to convert one's own latent fears of being overwhelmed by destructive forces into a systematic, ever more ruthless and violent eradication of opposition—real or imagined.

Leites considers the whole panoply of intellectual justifications for the course Soviet policy has taken under Lenin and Stalin. He finds a wide but predictable set of strategies from which the Bolshevik leaders select particular decisions. Following the varieties of policy since Stalin's death, he sees a new pattern emerging: an increasing tendency towards realism by the Soviet elite. Illustrated in detail in the concluding essay of this volume, the pattern confirms a trend in Politburo thinking which Leites, in earlier writings, hypothesized would occur. This is a decline of faith, at the highest levels, in the exoteric ideology of Bolshevism. In this respect the Soviet elite seems to be experiencing a progressive "moral atrophy" which parallels that in the West.

In his studies of post-war French political culture, Leites' perspective has also led him to search for the presence of formerly unperceived tendencies. It was once, for example, a truism of French republican studies to observe that an unbreachable ideological chasm separated the French Left from the Right. Among Leites' contributions to this field of inquiry is his discovery, presented with Constantin Melnik in *The House Without Windows,* that this conception of rigid French political division is belied by the facts.[4] In their formulation and in Leites' subsequent development of it, there existed under the Fourth Republic a wide consensus on general political principles. As a set, they constituted the "rules of the game" of democratic politics in France. They postulated, for example, a priority of self-interest over public interest from the point of view not only of the individual legislator, but also on the part of the legislature, as an in-group, vis-à-vis the country as a whole.

From Leites' later works on France, three of which are represented in this volume, we gain further insight into the tendency of Frenchmen—politicians and ordinary citizens alike—to view their leaders as self-interested and faithless and to see the public as abandoned or excluded from consideration by the powerful.

II

This brief summary of more than thirty years of scholarly analysis and documentation has been intended to give an idea of Leites' approach to political behavior. By using psychoanalytic understanding in the analysis of elite symbolism, he alerts us to the significance of variations in it which are not otherwise seen as important. Under his scrutiny, new dimensions of political conduct emerge which bear directly on policy. To illustrate the practical importance of such an approach only a few examples need be cited.

Whether Soviet strategists will decide flatly to deny a fact or whether they will elaborately rationalize a denial becomes, in Leites' analysis, important from the point of view of those affected by the regime. It reflects the state of defensiveness in which Soviet leaders find themselves. Likewise, underlying trends in realism of this elite are made manifest by examining whether and when Soviet spokesmen baldly falsify facts. New dimensions of political behavior emerge that a more superficial approach could not conceptualize, much less explain.

As one of these new dimensions consider the threat that Leites shows to be so conspicuous in pre-revolutionary Russian literature—the chiliastic hope that mankind will experience a sudden transformation in its nature, that humanity will experience a general reconciliation in a "universal embrace." How may we explain that even the analogous political transformation in Marxist doctrine—the "withering away of the state" and the achievement of universal harmony—itself withered and was lost in the course of Soviet history? Leites' demonstration in Soviet texts of a specific Bolshevik anxiety about seductive overtures and dangerous offers of "kisses" by the enemy reveals, as a less penetrating construction would never do, how Soviet leaders fight off what they feel to be dangerous impulses in themselves to surrender to forbidden homosexual desires. The many years when Politburo strategy puzzlingly rejected one apparent chance after another to take advantage of opportunities offered by the West and the tendency for the Russian leaders to "harden their hearts" when we "softened" ours become explicable with Leites' presentation.

As Leites' work on Bolshevik perspectives has always been oriented to trends in policy, so also does his vision of the Chinese political culture relate directly to policy questions. In the unpublished monograph excerpted for the present collection, Leites describes competing trends in Chinese thought that bear directly on decisions of Chinese leadership. If one trend dominates, Mao's successors might decide to subdue militancy towards the United States or Russia or both, in the belief that reprisals will be more serious if the enemy is provoked; if the other, they would believe it necessary to maximize aggressiveness towards hostile powers, on the grounds that these are, in any case, resolved on one's total destruction.

Also directly relevant to policy is Leites' unpublished work on De Gaulle (a small part of which is presented in chapter 7). This general was at once representative of and antagonistic to the political culture of traditional republican France. How did he succeed in turning its symbols to the advantage of a reform in the system? Why was he disposed to and how was he able to break the taboo, imposed by the rules of the game, against appealing directly to the public? How was he able so to reduce French popular skepticism of their leaders' intentions as to succeed in founding a new and more viable regime?

Conventional studies of the French republics, because they have dealt only with interaction of forces in the manifest, adult environment, lack the power to conceptualize political problems in such a way. Leites conceives the political process as the product of leader and public responding to one another in terms of each one's childhood experience as it interacts with adult environment. The two parts of the culture present in any political decision-making are linked by psychoanalytic understanding, as are the two relevant actors—communicator and audience.

Consider the promise of this approach to such a present-day problem as the chronic crisis state of Italian democracy. Comparing the dimensions Leites considers for France with the same ones for Italy would seem worthwhile. With similar institutional and social problems, the Italians, in Mussolini, acquired a leader whose aims and appeals not only resembled but, still more significantly, differed from De Gaulle's. What is lacking (or present) in the Italian political culture which accounts for this? To describe the Italian counterparts of those cultural traits Leites shows us in France should help explain why the political problems of post-war Italy are apparently so much more intractable than those of France.

III

Comparable considerations seem also to have been uppermost in Clyde Kluckhohn's mind when, in a review hailing the importance of Leites' first two major works on Bolshevism, he predicted it would found a school of political inquiry. Calling *A Study of Bolshevism* "a work of gigantic stature," he forecast that it was "likely to *faire école* in politics and the other behavioral sciences for many years to come."[5]

This has not happened. In fact, in 1970 an article on Soviet elite perspectives and policy could actually appear in a respected American professional journal which made no reference to any of Leites' bench mark studies.[6] It seems worthwhile to investigate why. Despite Kluckhohn's reasonable prediction, attention to Leites' work, its application to current problems in the behavioral sciences, and the replication of its designs in other studies have so far been quite limited.

In attempting to answer this question two difficulties posed by particular characteristics of Leites' method will first be considered. Next three problems in his work which are common to psychocultural analysis in general will be examined.

The limited influence Leites' work has so far had in attracting followers may be attributed first to an important characteristic of his method. He does not outline a scheme for conducting psychopolitical analysis. Instead he simply demonstrates a model for performance. Leites' performance is an act hard to follow because it depends on an unusual combination of skills, sensibilities, and motivations.

It has become a cliché of behavioral science that those barriers erected between "fields" by academic institutions are irrelevant to social inquiry. In fact, however, it is rare to find individual investigators who are equipped to breach very many of them. It is obvious that multidisciplinary skills are required in order to replicate Leites' analytical approach. To begin with, his method calls for psychoanalytical experience and training to be coupled with extensive studies in politics and social theory.

Leites has observed the pointlessness in separating that part of the human sciences which begin with the word-part "psych-" from the others comprising political science, sociology, anthropology, and economics.[7] In practice, however, psychoanalytical insight and training seem often to vary inversely with formal preparation in other kinds of social analysis. This was the complaint of critics who, in the 1940s, charged those newly engaged in the psychocultural analysis of politics with being ignorant of the history, economics, and political institutions of the countries they studied. Leites came to the defense of the group criticized—mostly anthropologists associated with Columbia University—with the observation that it was a fallacy frequent in the human sciences "to believe that if somebody at a certain moment talks about the importance of factor A, he is running down the importance of factors B, C. . . ."[8] Logically this is indisputable. Nevertheless Leites himself is well aware of the fact that if estimates are to be made of the importance of factor A—or even of its relevance at a given time—a good deal must be known about factors B, C, D, and so on.

In Leites' own case this awareness is combined with an undisputed ability to weigh factors A to Z. A classical *Gymnasium* education followed by a doctorate in economics preceded his preparation in psychoanalytic skills. Long experience and study of European politics had accompanied this formal training. Professional preparation in American political science followed. As a result, familiarity with the political and social setting of psychological data is reflected in the distinctive contextual emphasis that, as we have noted, is a feature of his work.

Facility in the human sciences is not the only one required to emulate the model Leites demonstrates. Of the skills necessary for his type of psycho-political analysis, none is more important than semantic and linguistic understanding. Listening with the third ear for the distinctive, highly charged, and significant word combinations in a communication requires not only familiarity with the political and social context and with the theory and practice of psychoanalysis, but also a sure knowledge of the meanings of words. Leites' range of cultural studies also requires a multilingual capacity. But even within a single culture the ability to discriminate between slight nuances of meaning, to apprehend with certainty when a word is used in an atypical sense, are necessities for psychocultural analyses of the kind Leites makes. Furthermore, such discrimination between words may not be the product of formal training; it may require apperceptive powers more akin to aesthetic sensibility than to intellectual discipline.

In addition to requiring uncommon skills and sensitivities, Leites' method seems to depend on personal motivation of a distinctive kind. The detailed semantic analysis characteristic of his work calls for special tastes and tolerances. These, one suspects, are more often found among natural scientists—and perhaps also among those in humanistic studies—than they are in the social sciences. The massiveness of the literature to be treated taxonomically may make replication of Leites' analyses too arduous, too painstaking, too boring for most social scientists to consider. For Leites, evidently, the differences in meaning conveyed by small differences in the use of words have an interest that sustains him in his efforts to reveal their significance to others.

While emulating Leites' model requires special skills and propensities, this does not of itself explain the relatively limited scope of his influence until now. For the same skills and propensities that are required to be a producer do not apply to consumers of this product.

Thus, a psychoanalytical orientation and training are not necessary in order to evaluate the propositions in Leites' work. No one is less prone to jargonizing than he. Furthermore, habitually he avoids typologies that add nothing to evidence, and routinely he presents all of his evidence so that the reader may form his own judgments as to its significance.

To know, for example, that those German cultural traits which Leites and Kecskemeti show to be conspicuous correspond with psychoanalytic descriptions of a compulsive character type is not essential in order to understand that the persistent presence of these traits in combination is important. Similarly, when Leites shows changing themes in recent Bolshevik propaganda, it is not necessary to appreciate that the newer symbolic arrangements are interpretable as characteristic of anal modes of thought, while older forms seem rather to call up fears and wishes originating in what are considered oral and oedipal phases of development. To be sure, the significance of these changing symbols might be greater for a reader who knew something of the clinical literature; certainly the empirical patterns are made more suggestive if one has knowledge of psychoanalytical findings concerning the etiology of character traits. Chinese imagery prominently features the notion of being torn to pieces by wild beasts; this suggests preoccupations associated with an oral sadistic stage of maturation. Leites is no doubt aware of this but he does not point it out. Instead, he scrupulously presents his material in context and allows it to speak, as much as possible, for itself. While he may listen with the third ear, his conclusions routinely are based only on what all may hear.

It is not necessary to be able to imitate Leites' methods in order to be influenced by them, nor to share his perspective in order to appreciate the value of his findings. Other reasons must be found to explain why his influence so far has been relatively unlimited.

To some extent the explanation may lie in those resistances that are encountered by psychoanalytic work of any kind. The psychopolitical inquirer, like the psychoanalyst, may find he is the bearer of unwelcome news. Thus Leites' readers, like patients in analysis, may resist uncomfortable truths by opposition or incomprehension.

Opposition is more likely when "the patient" reviews a book about himself. This was the case with the reception given by psychoanalysts as a group to a book Leites wrote about them. In *The New Ego,* Leites analyzed the concepts of "identity," "identification," and "ego" as they have been developed in the literature of recent "meta-psychological" psychoanalysis.[9] In the vast web of terminology that some psychoanalysts had spun around these terms since 1940, he found a morass of tautology and redundancy and a paucity of fact statements that could be empirically tested. Observing trends in the development of this terminology and considering its position in the context of intellectual commerce, he suggested motives for what could be called a "pathology of language." Psychoanalytical writers, by spinning webs of "statements about words," managed to evade their responsibility to make actual propositions about real behavior. The unconscious motive was to gain "respectability" for psychoanalysis. This could be done by sacrificing some of those methods and interests that differentiated it from (and made it unacceptable to) other psychological approaches.

At the same time, Leites found, analysts kept a toe in the water by proposing more daring hypotheses. By entertaining at once an "extreme" and a "moderate" meaning for such words as projection, introjection, or identification, the writers could have their cake and eat it as well. That is, they could reduce the resistance, hostility, and skepticism with which the psychoanalytic movement continues to be met, and at the same time they could enjoy the same sense of intellectual adventure, bravery, and esoteric camaraderie for which their forerunners had paid a high price.

Leites' work, with its great import for intellectual and professional ethics, was published in 1971 but was not reviewed by any professional journal of psychology or psychoanalysis until 1976. When a first review, by a psychoanalyst, finally appeared, though not entirely unfavorable it accused Leites of citing "very brief excerpts out of context" and of "having substituted words and left out qualifications," thus unfairly converting a reasonable statement of psychoanalytical literature into a "ridiculous assertion." Without providing one actual example of such a misrepresentation, nor indeed even of a specific case where inadequate contextual description was supplied, the reviewer suggested that the "slices of material" Leites presented were often "too minute to permit a clear judgment with regard to the intent of the author. . . ." [10] Aware of Leites' scrupulous care in correctly representing both context and quotations, one waited in vain for the reviewer's own "slices of material," minute or otherwise. If a practicing psychoanalyst, trained in introspection, can defend himself against discussion of unpleasant propositions about his own group by using such a patently projective device, it cannot be surprising if less schooled readers offer unconscious resistance to psychopolitical observations!

Indeed, however, Leites' psychocultural inquiry does not encounter resistance only from the butterflies which happen to be pinned down. His work has occasionally met incomprehension or misunderstanding by persons whose interests are not obviously jeopardized. A rather amusing example appeared in a review, again largely favorable, of one of the early works on Bolshevism. A political scientist complained mildly that some material cited by Leites as illustrative of a certain mode of Bolshevik rationalization was actually rational and obvious. [11] In this category the reviewer placed Leites' references to Lenin's recurring dictum, repeated frequently also by his successors and followers, "If I pursue an enemy who does not move in a straight line but zigzags, then I too must zigzag in order to reach him." [12] Lenin's comment seems like a bizarre refusal to recognize a well-known physical law about the shortest distance between points, yet it did not seem so to the American professor of politics. Many other cautionary observations made by Leites must also be lost on those in the Pentagon and the State Department who might do well to note them.

A second feature of psychopolitical inquiry tends to make the scope of its influence self-limiting. This has to do not with resistance by consumers but more with serious production problems that arise directly from the dualistic nature of psychoanalytic principles.

Psychoanalysis offers propositions about psychic development which imply dynamic concepts of personality. That is to say, human behavior is seen at any given moment as the outcome of a temporary balance of forces operating in different directions. Impulses are met by inhibitions, phobias by counter-phobias, depression by mania, and so forth. Which response will be "triggered" by a given stimulus?

Psychoanalysts themselves do not routinely focus on this central question. In his monograph on psychoanalytic theory, Leites observed that literature on ego responses to outside stimuli sometimes sees "total relinquishment of objects," at other times "partial renunciation," and on yet other occasions responses not involving object relations at all. Therefore he emphasized, "the point would seem to be to learn more about the conditions making for each of these configurations." [13] A central point of *The New Ego* was that psychoanalytic authors were very often satisfied with simply having once more formulated the problem, rather than with making attempts to resolve it.

One must presume that clinical practitioners of psychoanalysis do, however, attempt to resolve this problem in individual cases. But the psychoanalyst's focus on the subjective state of his patients generally prevents him from formulating systematic and general propositions about the contextual patterns that trigger certain psychic mechanisms. One must assume that the psychoanalytic artisan will stick to his last and continue to supply the social scientist with more and more examples of particular cases. Formulating propositions about *which* psychological mechanisms, while constrained by any particular social context, determine *what* kinds of political behavior will remain largely the problem of the social scientist.

From the beginning Leites has been aware of the need for a clear focus on this problem. In an essay included here (chapter 2), he notes two different psychic mechanisms are apparently at work in a cultural contrast between Americans and Britons made by Mead and Bateson:

> In the American case there is adult continuation of certain childhood behavior patterns, in the British, an assumption of the adult role which one had first

perceived (but not adopted) in childhood. What are the conditions making for invariance in the one case and change in the other? (That is, what are the conditions making for the choice of different "psychological mechanisms"?) Psycho-dynamics and psycho-cultural analysis have during the last fifteen years enriched our inventory of "solutions" which human beings find in given situations. The 1950s will presumably more systematically attempt to enrich knowledge about the conditions fostering or hampering the adoption of any given solution.[14]

While Leites' optimism about what the next decade would bring was perhaps not justified, his own concentration on these problems yielded fruitful results.

Leites has been consistently alert to the conditions fostering or hampering adoption of any given psychic solution. His attention, as we have seen, to the context of political pronouncements, geared as it is to policy outcomes, aims almost always at answering the question: "what determines that one psychic mechanism will be invoked rather than another?"

Usually he formulates the problem dualistically. Thus, in De Gaulle's eyes, France is "great France; Eternal France" and De Gaulle himself is the great man above the human crowd; on the other hand, France may appear to him as full of levity, indolence, and shiftlessness and he himself as poor, shy, isolated, ordinary. Under what conditions will De Gaulle's less grandiose image of France and himself be evoked? Again, the Bolsheviks sometimes indicate that they are strong enough to be proof against infiltration by Western businessmen and intellectuals; on other occasions they will express the fear that even the tiniest penetration from the outside is a dangerous threat that could corrupt the whole. What promotes feelings of Bolshevik intrepidity in the face of internal dissent and external influence? What fosters their anxiety? As Leites formulates the problem for Politburo policy choice, "when the operational code permits the application of two or more contrasting rules to a certain situation, what are the factors determining the choice?"[15] The Chinese, believing that the enemy is unremittingly murderous in intent, may nevertheless on some occasions show they believe those hostile to them can be propitiated by their own "good" behavior. When does each response occur?

The selections in this book have all been made with the intention of showing how, to a great extent, Leites can answer these questions. By identifying the mechanisms "triggered" when one side or the other of each dichotomy is dominant, and by using available evidence on the etiology of characteristic mechanisms invoked, he is quite often able to provide us with an understanding of what forces are at work, when, and why.

However, it is admittedly one thing to understand and another to predict. In the policy sciences, as in the natural sciences, the central objective is to predict with confidence that when a given stimulus is applied a certain response will be evoked. If mankind is to control the future, it needs to "understand" before, and not just after, the fact.

Leites' own batting average in this respect is high. In effect, for example, he and Kecskemeti counselled the policies that were to prove reasonably effective in allied military occupation of Germany, in changing German behavior patterns to fit democratic objectives. He predicted France's withdrawal from the North Atlantic Treaty Organization under De Gaulle's leadership. He also anticipated the warning that would cause Khrushchev to withdraw rather than resist in the Cuban missile crisis.

Yet, in every case, the problem of predicting future events depends on accurately weighing the relative force, under varying sets of conditions, of operative motives and mechanisms. Leites' predictive ability may be due to intuitive appraisal of many unspoken variables rather than to close reckoning. Nor is he infallible; *Du malaise politique en France* did not explicitly predict the fall of the Fourth Republic; changes in the trend of Soviet policy after Stalin are not anticipated in the early works on Bolshevism. In any case he does not give his readers a comparable predictive ability. His analysis is mostly not formulated in quantitative terms that would make it replicable.

Again, Leites is well aware of the importance of quantitative judgments. In the first essay in this selection he notes the difficulty of predicting whether particular psychic or other variables will be operative in a given situation. In any case, he concludes,

> Most disagreements about "degrees of importance" of various factors are at present undecidable in this research area, as the term "degree of importance" itself usually does not receive a sufficiently precise definition.[16]

Nearly three decades of multivariate analysis, not to mention the development and application of other quantitative techniques for analyzing symbolic behavior, have gone over the dam since he wrote this appraisal. Still largely unchanged is our capacity to estimate weights for the converging vectors of forces in a given situation with sufficient accuracy to anticipate specific behavior.

Robert Stoller has remarked that psychic material seems intractable to quantitative investigation. "There are very few discoveries indeed in human psychology that have been made by statistical techniques; on the record so far their generative power is low."[17] "Still," he continues, they "act as a marvelous conscience." Leites does not, as a rule, provide us with this palliative, although he professes to expect that someone will do so—or at least that they *should* do so.

Thus, in a passage prefatory to a discussion of the importance, "in a certain type of Russian family," of the thought that one member may damage another, Leites notes that he is alluding, in referring to such qualities as " 'intense' emotions," "to frequencies and degrees of certain feelings and acts which would have to be more specifically indicated for purposes of validation."[18]

Yet, despite the apparent promise of his line of inquiry, few have followed in Leites' wake to provide the quantitative base that would act as a "marvelous conscience." In the absence of this base, the nature of psychoanalytic hypotheses about political behavior raises a bothersome and recurrent question: to what extent does an apparent group stress on a psychic trait reflect a common distinctive early experience, or to what extent is it better explained by the "adult environment"?

This question is recurrent because psychoanalytic principles deal with developmental phases common to all human personalities. Hence, for example, every human being has no doubt had the childhood experience of feeling abandoned when a parent was absent—or even absent-minded. Leites demonstrates impressively that the equation "absence-desertion" was prominent in the French legislature under the Fourth Republic. Even a casual acquaintance with American congressional debate is enough to confirm an appraisal (as a plausible comparison) that there is relatively slight American emphasis, in the same context, on this form of "dereliction." However, perhaps the political emphasis is not explained by a relatively greater personal preoccupation with absence as abandonment, but because institutional arrangements, under the Fourth Republic, made personal attendance about the only visible public function a French legislator—or even a cabinet minister—was expected to perform. Congressmen, presumably, have more effective *legislative* ways they can hope to influence policy. Did the emphasis disappear under the Fifth Republic, after constitutional reforms made the government as a whole less manifestly impotent? Are American politicians perhaps as sensitive to absence from committee sessions as French ones were to absence from the Chamber? And what kind of quantitative test would serve to validate or refute the myriad variables involved in making such comparisons?

Awareness has increased that psychopolitical description of symbolic material is exceptionally intractable to quantitative analysis. In the past few years it has become more obvious that the significance of communications often eludes the quantitative techniques devised to capture it. This is, for example, the case with communications of a popular leader to his public: a key word used once in a particular context may be the important message for an audience, while measurement techniques of most kinds will make the emphasis seem to lie elsewhere—and leave the quantitative investigator up a blind alley. A like handicap applies to quantitative inquiries about communications to and within elites. Social scientists who were at first concerned with the frequency of symbols transmitted with the aim of "getting messages" to, say, a chief of state, have lately become sensitive to the fact that such a figure may fail to register a symbol not because it figures insufficiently in the messages he receives, but because the context in which it would become significant for him is lacking. The context that would make it meaningful may well be found in his personal motivation—what he wanted to do in the first place—and might bear no relationship to the form in which the message is presented.

These problems of validating quantitative statements about psychic processes through measuring symbolic data are not peculiarly relevant to the methods employed by Leites. Nor are they peculiar to psychopolitical inquiry in particular nor even to social science in general. On the contrary, their discussion is intended to suggest that, those who seek, by disciplined use of the intellect, better to understand their environment, would be ill-advised to dismiss as "unscientific" formulations that merely lack the "proper" array of tables and computations. In this common search for understanding few intellects have seemed as powerful, as productive, or as disciplined as that of Nathan Leites.

Elizabeth Wirth Marvick
Paris

NOTES

1. Harold D. Lasswell, "The Triple-Appeal Principle: A Dynamic Key," *American Journal of Sociology*, XXXVII (1932), 523-528.
2. "Recent Trends in Moral Temper," chapter 4.
3. Nathan Leites, "Trends in Affectlessness," *American Imago*, IV (1947), 96.
4. Constantin Melnik and Nathan Leites, *The House Without Windows: France Selects a President* (Evanston, 1958).
5. Clyde Kluckhohn, "Politics, History and Psychology," Review article in *World Politics*, VIII (1955), 117.
6. W. Zimmerman, "Elite Perspectives and the Explanation of Soviet Foreign Policy," *Journal of International Affairs*, XXIV (1970), 84-98.
7. In "Political Democracy and Personal Destructiveness," chapter 9.
8. In "Psychopolitical Analysis of Cultural Data," chapter 2.
9. Nathan Leites, *The New Ego: Pitfalls in Current Thinking about Patients in Psychoanalysis* (New York, 1971).
10. Nathan Schlessinger in *The American Journal of Psychoanalysis* (1976), 662.
11. Charles E. Merriam in *The American Journal of Sociology*, LVII (1951); 290.
12. Nathan Leites, *The Operational Code of the Politburo* (New York, 1951), 33.
13. *The New Ego*, 98.
14. "Psychopolitical Analysis," see chapter 2.
15. *Operational Code*, xiii.
16. "Psychopolitical Analysis," chapter 2.
17. Introduction to *The New Ego*, 37.
18. "Bolshevism and Russian Violence," chapter 10.

EDITORIAL NOTE

The editor's aim has been to make Nathan Leites' work accessible to more readers by presenting a wide array of the subject matter he has investigated. This has generally involved a difficult choice. On the one hand, one could extract a very wide assortment of hypotheses, presenting his work in skeletal form without the citations and illustrative material so important to his method. Or one could select very sparsely from among his writings and represent those chosen rather fully. Because his unique contribution depends very largely on contextual elaboration, for the most part the latter course has been followed. For this reason no selection appears here from what is, perhaps, Leites' most widely read book *The Operational Code of the Politburo*. Because that short work is already condensed into essential propositions, it does not lend itself to the editing principles followed here.

Even so, however, the reader is advised that not all citations and illustrative material in the original writings have been reproduced. For these he should consult the original versions.

More important, the reader should not suppose that all, nor even most, of the interesting propositions put forth by Leites on any given topic will be found in these few selections. Leites has a horror of redundancy and rarely repeats himself. If he did, an editor's task would be easier but more dispensable. As it is, a selection of his work can only be a sample, not an adumbration, of his major contributions.

—E.W.M.

PART II:

ANALYTICAL PERSPECTIVES

Chapter 2

PSYCHOPOLITICAL ANALYSIS OF CULTURAL DATA

EDITOR'S NOTE: During the course of World War II, a number of anthropologists turned their attention to modern cultures with a view to applying their techniques to nations then active in international power struggles. Already experienced in psychocultural research, Leites was aware of the temptations psychoanalytical insight presented to engage in "wild" interpretations of national behavior. He was also aware of the kind of untenable propositions that were being attributed to the new practitioners by more conventional specialists in political investigations. Here he seeks to forestall both developments by clarifying the implications of the new approach and the premises on which it rests. He goes on to show how psychocultural research can help in understanding the meaning of political acts by providing knowledge of the genesis of cultural patterns in childhood experience. He illustrates by applying findings on Burmese culture to Burmese attitudes towards the political use of violence. He further suggests that insight into the personal dynamics characteristic of a culture will help predict such political behavior patterns as the Japanese ones of submission and revolt.

From "Psycho-Cultural Hypotheses about Political Acts," World Politics *I (1948), 102-119.*

$\mathcal{D}$uring recent years there has been a noticeable rise in the production of, and interest in, a relatively new kind of analysis of political behavior. Anthropologists had become increasingly concerned with describing and explaining the entire way of life of the non-literate societies they were studying. Some of them came to believe that cultural anthropology should return to home, i.e., that the methods of observation and recording, and also the theories which they had developed on so-called primitive material should be applied to our own society and other large and complex groups. At the same time, psychologists and psychiatrists had become increasingly interested in describing and explaining the entire way of life, subjective and behavioral, of the individuals they were studying. They tended to be particularly interested, on the one hand, in the broad varieties of human nature ("character types" and "defense mechanisms") and, on the other, in the unique structure of each case. But some of them came to be interested in ascertaining the psychological regularities, if any, in large groups. The confluence of these two developments in the human sciences led to the emergence of what we may call psycho-cultural analyses of social events.

As in many other instances of intellectual change, this development provoked both intensely friendly and hostile reactions. While those involved in the discussion tended to be either "for" or "against" the kind of analysis in question, there was often insufficient clarity and agreement about what the specific points of contention were. In view of this situation, I propose to examine with some explicitness a number of the general aspects of the psycho-cultural analysis of political acts. I shall do so by recalling particular representative statements without trying to be systematic or exhaustive.

I. WHAT IS AND WHAT IS NOT
REQUIRED OF PSYCHO-CULTURAL HYPOTHESES
ABOUT POLITICAL ACTS

One set of relevant propositions is concerned with how culturally typical political acts are related to the past life experiences of those who perform them. They thus correspond, in the formulation of Heinz Hartmann and Ernst Kris, to the "genetic propositions" in psychoanalysis which indicate "how any condition . . . has grown out of an individual's past."[1] One major general hypothesis in this area runs as follows: if children adopt a certain reaction in certain emotionally important—usually, but not always, familial—

situations, they are later on apt to adopt a similar reaction in structurally analogous political situations. *[This is obviously an incomplete hypothesis. Clearly it is not always true (see below), and clearly it is sometimes true. (Hence, stated without qualifications, it is false.) The question is: under what conditions are adults apt to continue (in a way) certain patterns? This is the type of question which is now beginning to become central as will be seen later here.]*

According to the Kluckhohns, there is a relationship between the American orientation on "effort and optimism"—presumably an important one in American political behavior—and the following fact: the mother in America offers her love to the child on condition of his fulfilling certain performance standards which the child has a good chance of reaching.[2] According to Benedict "the will to achieve . . . has little place with Rumanians" whose view of the universe attributes a dominant role to "luck." These adult feelings and behaviors—of obvious political relevance—are related to the fact "that the Rumanian child did not have to earn as a youngest child his mother's unconditional pleasure in him; with the birth of a next child it was . . . lost . . . ; his mother punished him according to her own mood of the moment. Rewards, either from the mother or from other persons, were not given for specific approved acts or for achievements . . . even to 'think' praise was supposed to cast the evil eye. The child did not know what he could do to earn approval."[3]

Statements of this kind raise many questions, such as the following:

(1) If one wants to be very "precise," it is necessary to indicate more specifically under what conditions we will choose to say that the "will to achieve" (or the "orientation on effort") have "little" or "much" place in the life of an individual and of a culture. In both cases we are presumably dealing with continua: the intra-individual continuum ranging from "no" to "total" orientation on effort; the inter-individual continuum ranging from the complete absence of "highly" effort-oriented individuals in a culture to a situation in which all members of a culture are so oriented. When we speak of "high" or "low" in either case, we introduce arbitrary cuts in these continua. That is, we decide to say that a society is "highly" effort-oriented if more than a specified number of its members (we may add, members in such and such positions of influence) are "highly" effort-oriented; and we may decide to say that an individual is "highly" effort-oriented if more than a specified number of his acts of certain emotional weight are undertaken with some sense of strain and are intended to produce ulterior results. This, of course, leads to further definitions of "act," "emotional weight," "sense of strain," "intended" (consciously and/or unconsciously?), and so forth. All these definitional operations are required if and only if one wants to make the proposition involved capable of full empirical proof or disproof. The practical

difficulties one encounters are not different from those one meets in making any proposition operational which refers at least in part to subjective events.

(2) Suppose we had evolved all the definitions which may be required—i.e., suppose we had translated our hypothesis from "theoretical" into "empirical" language—we would then come up against the next obstacle: the appropriate observations have been not at all or only insufficiently made and recorded. The "translation" I spoke of would furnish a statement of the *required* evidence. Its very statement would make it plain that the *available* evidence falls far short of it.[4]

In the current discussion of the kind of statements I am concerned with in this paper one can frequently discern an objection against the utterance (particularly in printed form) of statements for which only quite insufficient evidence is available in proper records. (I am talking here not about the researcher's degree of subjective certainty about how the records would look if they existed, but only about whether they exist.) The answer to the question—which statements should or should not be "admitted" as members of the class of "scientific" statements?—is presumably a decision rather than a factual (true or false) statement. This decision need not be the same in the following two cases:

(a) statements for which available evidence is low, and which are presented without an explicit indication of this;

(b) similar statements which do explicitly indicate the gap between required and available evidence.

Presumably many human scientists object to (a) without objecting (with the same intensity) to (b). Many object to the kind of hypotheses dealt with in this paper because they regard them as falling within class (a). Do we really know scientifically that the Rumanian degree of effort-orientation is significantly lower than the American one? *[Propositions about national differences are of course subject to the suspicion of being derivatives from stereotypes which in their turn may be connected with nationalist reactions.]*

In part, a failure of communication seems to occur here. My guess is that most of the statements involved are meant by those who advance them as statements of class (b). Possibly those who propose them are rather sure about the outcome of an adequate collection of comparative data concerning Rumanian and American effort-orientation (and may therefore not want to spend too much time on collecting them). But they agree, I think, that, while their points are based on already collected data, sufficient data have not yet been collected. In other words, they advance their statements as hypotheses, often with a high expectation-of-full-verification feeling about them. It may be that the expressions of this feeling prevent many critics from perceiving that everybody agrees on the lack of full evidence.

Both critics and advocates of current psycho-cultural hypotheses about social behavior might, I propose, accept the current usefulness of publicly communicating "mere" hypotheses. Such a communication may foster their fuller disproval, or proof, and promote the invention of other hypotheses, with similar consequences. We are at present still hampered by a lack of explanatory hypotheses about social behavior.

(3) Suppose the difficulties mentioned under (2) had also been resolved: i.e., suppose we had fully established the asserted Rumanian-American differences in (a) child-training patterns (b) adult behaviors. What about the relationship between them? The transition from "correlation" to "causation" implies a "universal proposition" of the logical form "if a, then b." What is the particular universal proposition implied in our instances? In the present style of psycho-cultural analysis this premise is often not stated explicitly— another instance of the elliptic mode of expression already discussed under (2). It is some such sentence as this (I am simplifying it for the purposes of this discussion): if a child is rewarded for efforts undertaken he is *(caeteris paribus)* more likely to show high effort-orientation as an adult than if he is not so rewarded. (This would be a member of the class of statements affirming the transfer of patterns of feeling and behavior "learned" in early intimate relations to adult social relations.)

Hence, the degree of confirmation of a psycho-cultural statement such as the one I choose as an example will depend in part on the degree of confirmation of the implied universal proposition. This will usually be one from "dynamic psychology." Frequently, of course, this premise itself is not yet fully proved. However, here again explicitness about what the premises are and what their present scientific status is would fulfill one version of the requirements of "science." In addition the present status and rate of progress of dynamic psychology are viewed by a number of specialists in a rather favorable light.

According to Gorer and Benedict, Japanese adults issue complicated and heavily sanctioned prescriptions to the child as to how and where he may or may not move around the house (in American terms, they behave as if most of the house were composed of radiators and as if they were set upon punishing the child for having touched hot radiators). This childhood experience has, it is asserted, an adult sequel which has been of considerable military significance in the late war: Japanese are much disoriented if they find themselves without preparation in an unknown environment; hence the intense striving to "learn" new environments one goes into. Available Rorschach performances indicate that "unforeseen situations, which cannot be handled by rote, are frightening."[5]

A statement of this kind raises the three issues already discussed with the aid of our previous example, and others (which were equally present though not discussed) such as these:

(4) It is not implied that the peculiar Japanese treatment of early loco-motion is the sole cause of adult Japanese preferences for situations believed

to be thoroughly known. Frequently, of course, similar cultural results are produced by various combinations of various factors. Other childhood experiences—in this case, for example, certain aspects of sphincter training—probably contribute to the same adult trait.

The type of communication failure mentioned under (2) operates here, too. Critics of a particular psycho-cultural hypothesis frequently assume that the condition-factor focussed upon is asserted to be the *sole* cause of the phenomenon. Usually this will not have been meant by the researcher who put the hypothesis forward, though he may not have stated this qualification explicitly. It is a frequent fallacy in the human sciences to believe that, if somebody at a certain moment talks about the importance of factor A, he is running down the importance of factors B, C. . . . *[Most disagreements about "degrees of importance" of various factors are at present undecidable in this research area, as the term "degree of importance" itself usually does not receive a sufficiently precise definition.]*

(5) It is not implied that only intimate ("psychological") childhood events determine adult behavior to the exclusion of various wider ("economic," "political," "social," etc.) aspects of the adult environment. On the contrary, the presumption is that any adult act is related to (a) the predisposition of the individual—which in its turn is connected with his previous experiences from birth (at least) to the present moment; (b) the (human and non-human) environment which contains "stimuli" evoking the act involved.[6]

One may expect an adult's reaction to any given social environment to vary with his predisposition. The close and comparative examination of any given act-in-situation will show that other persons (groups) have responded differently to a similar situation, revealing another of the many potentialities of "human nature." The differences in response can often be related to differences in predisposition rather than to nuances in the current environments which almost always leaves "choices" open. If two culturally contrasting groups are faced with overwhelming odds, one may tend recurrently to submit, the other to fight it out. We may find a link between such propensities and the ways in which parents expected their children to behave in fights with other children.

While predispositions are "important," it is equally true that we may expect the reactions of a number of adults with similar predispositions to vary according to the situations in which they find themselves. Thus, it is entirely compatible with the hypothesis stated above to assume that adult Japanese preferences for known routines are (also) related to the tradition and presence of a socio-political order rewarding (on the whole) compliance with very specific and differentiated rules applying to one's status.

(6) While psycho-cultural analysis of adult political behavior thus does not imply that "childhood" is "all-important," it does—as already conveyed by the examples quoted—affirm that it is "important." In doing so, it can—apart

from the specific evidence of an increasing number of particular propositions—refer to the following general points: [7]

(a) Acts called political begin to occur (in Western culture at least) late in
childhood or even later.

(b) It is a fundamental truism much confirmed by 20th century research
that act patterns arising as "late" as that in life are very apt to be noticeably
influenced by what happened earlier. Thus, the intimate (and to the adult
often "trivial") experiences of the child with the few persons who begin his
socialization are apt to influence (mostly unconsciously) the adult when he is
concerned with local, regional, national, and world politics.

(7) While patterns of child training are regarded as important in the
explanation of political behavior, it is not implied that these patterns in their
turn are uninfluenced by such behavior. *[Psychocultural analysis in the late
1930s and 1940s has largely taken child training patterns as given and
focussed on the investigation of their consequences. It is to be expected that
the 1950s will drop this limitation and attempt to develop a richer set of
propositions about culture change (including zero change).]* On the contrary,
it is assumed that the behavior of adults towards children is influenced not
only by the adults' childhood[8] but also by their current life experiences; and
these include politics, or politically determined events (in our culture, increasingly so). Thus the stimulation of competition among siblings by parents may
derive in part from the competitive acts of the parents outside the family. In
the previously mentioned instance, Japanese parents may model their imposition of rules within the home on their own subjection to political rules
outside the home. Also, while Japanese parents *"exaggerate* the dangers of
the house [i.e., the danger of the child's spontaneous movements damaging
the house], it is true that Japanese houses are so constructed that "when
children can walk they can do a lot of mischief."[9] *[This leads to the further
question: what factors have determined the choice of such a fragile house
structure? Presumably they were not all "environmental." Little systematic
speculation (and less research) has as yet been done on questions of this kind,
as implied above.]*

It is common knowledge that in recent Anglo-American inter-personal
relations on various civilian and military levels Americans not infrequently
exhibited a type of behavior which Britons called "boasting," while Britons
frequently impressed Americans as being "arrogant." Many political scientists
with appropriate experiences in the late war would probably agree that this
was a politically relevant situation. According to Bateson and Mead this is
related to certain differences in childhood experiences in the two cultures:
"In Britain . . . Father . . . exhibits to his children: he is the model for their
future behavior. Father does the talking . . . before a very quiet and submissive audience, in accordance with the . . . ethical disapproval of overuse of
strength. He underplays his strength, understates his position, speaks with a

slight appearance of hesitation in his manner, but with the cool assurance of one who knows. . . . At the American breakfast table, it is not Father but Junior who talks, exhibits his successes and skills, and demands parental spectatorship and applause with an insistence that can be clamoring and assertive because . . . he is speaking from weakness to strength." In adulthood "an American spoke . . . as he had learned to speak when he was small . . . a Briton spoke . . . as he had heard his father and other elders speak . . ." [10] *[In the American case, there is adult continuation of certain childhood behavior patterns, in the British, an assumption of the adult role which one had first perceived (but not adopted) in childhood. What are the conditions making for invariance in the one case and change in the other? (That is, what are the conditions making for the choice of different "psychological mechanisms"?) Psycho-dynamics and psycho-cultural analysis have during the past fifteen years enriched our inventory of "solutions" which human beings find in given situations. The 1950s will presumably more systematically attempt to enrich knowledge about the conditions fostering or hampering the adoption of any given solution.]*

This statement raises the issues (1) through (7) discussed above, and also some others (equally applicable to our previous examples):

(8) It is not implied that all Britons (Americans) exhibit adult understatement (overstatement) to the same high, or to any high, degree at all periods. Nor is it implied that all Americans (Britons) have been equally vocal (silent) at their early breakfast tables (which stand, of course, in Bateson-Mead's language for a large number of childhood situations). It is implied that these are "typical" patterns; the existence of "idiosyncrasies" is not denied, nor their possibly vast consequences. We are confronted here with one of those statements which may need greater precision in the fashion discussed under (1). I shall not repeat that discussion, but only add some specific points.

(a) When current psycho-cultural hypotheses imply (or state explicitly) that a certain act is "typical" in a certain culture at a certain time, they do not imply (nor do they deny) that this act is equally typical at other times. Psycho-cultural analysis does not "deny history." On the contrary, it is particularly apt to take account of history as it focusses on the causal role of life experiences rather than of hereditary endowment. (Thus when a probably inexpedient term like "national character" is used by the researchers here discussed, it carries no connotations of national biological peculiarities.)[11]

What is meant then, is, Junior talks more and is louder at breakfast tables today in this country than, say, three generations ago. Psycho-cultural analysis is interested in whether this is so, why, and what of it.

(b) When it is asserted that a certain behavior is "typical" in a given culture at a given time, it is not implied that it is equally frequent and emphasized in all sub-groups of this culture. (I am not interested in making the definition of "culture" more precise at this point. I am using the term in a sense which allows us to talk about "American culture," "British culture,"

"French culture," "Great Russian culture.") It is entirely compatible with psycho-cultural analysis to assume considerable differences, in child training patterns and adult experiences, between various "social classes," regions, ideological groups, or any number of other sets of persons who are all members of a given culture. [12] As the pertinent data are at present largely uncollected [cf. (2) above], it is impossible to say how large these intra-cultural differences are in any given case; presumably cultures vary widely in their degree of internal homogeneity. Some researchers have been impressed by the plausibility of the guess that the various Western national cultures have a higher degree of internal homogeneity than was assumed in previous decades under the influence, e.g., of Marxist hypotheses. Sometimes these researchers have been misunderstood to imply that such an assumption—it is no more than that at the present moment—is, as it were, an axiom of psycho-cultural analysis. It is, of course, just a special (though a major) hypothesis to be "processed" like any other hypothesis. It is in this fashion that one might interpret a point of Benedict's. One's property, she suggests, is felt as very close to the core of one's self in Dutch culture, "whether the individual belongs to court circles or can only say in the words of a proverbial expression: 'If it's only a penny a year, lay it by.' " On the other hand, one's property is felt as remote from the core of the self in Rumanian culture: "An upper class person may be . . . a pensioner of a wealthy man without loss of status or self-confidence; his property, he says, is not 'himself.' And the poor peasant argues that, being poor, it is futile for him to lay anything by. . . ." [13] In either case the position of a culture on this variable may have politically relevant consequences, e.g., as to reactions to politically induced property loss. *[Thus a somewhat fuller explanation of the political impact of, say, the agrarian changes in Rumania after the first world war might be obtained.]*

(c) When it is asserted that certain behaviors are "typical" in a certain culture, it is not denied that certain subgroups of this culture may show substantial similarities with corresponding subgroups in other cultures. One may choose the use the term "national character" to refer to similarities between members of a subgroup of Western culture called a class. Thus certain aspects of the life of a *petit bourgeois* in Tours may be referred to in a "national (French) character" proposition; and others (or sometimes the same?) in a "class (lower middle) character" proposition. The question has often been asked: do people have more in common with other members of their nation or with the members of some trans-national group, e.g., class? To this one may reply that (1) "more in common" has not yet been well defined, operationally; (2) the pertinent data have not been collected; (3) if they were, the answer would presumably be different in different cases; (4) this question does not seem urgent if we want to decide on the next steps in research.

(d) When it is asserted that a certain behavior is "typical" in a certain culture, it is not implied that there is no other culture in which it is, at the same or some other time, equally "typical." What has hitherto turned out to be rather unique is the syndrome of each culture (the ensemble of its regularities), but not each element of this syndrome. The conscious aversion against hitting the fellow who has already fallen down may be typical in both British and American culture; but it is in each of these cultures related to other distinctive reactions towards violence.

II. ILLUSTRATIONS OF GENETIC INTERPRETATIONS

As stated above, the propositions hitherto examined were largely concerned with the continuation of certain childhood patterns in adult political activities. There are of course many other and more complex interrelations between early private life and later public life. I shall mention some, with the aim of illustrating current work rather than of being systematic and complete. *[A complete and systematic typology would presumably be isomorphic with one of relationships established in dynamic psychology.]* Take the following two points.

According to Gorer, in contemporary America "custom and votes, other things being equal, go to the man who most adequately demonstrates friendly interest." He relates this to the fact that Americans are "insatiable" in their demands for "the signs of friendship, of love." This in turn is related to the fact that "any occasion on which they are withheld raises the . . . doubt that maybe one is not loveable." [14] And this doubt goes back to the "conditional" character of paternal love already mentioned above.

As to destructiveness, according to Gorer, Burmese admire intensely "successful daring and ingenuity" in exploits of violence; the dacoit (outlaw) who specializes in such acts is highly esteemed. The aims for which violence is being used are less stressed: "the Burmese dacoit is to be admired for his violence as such"; various violent Burmese movements had "no program"; "two Burmese policemen . . . quarrelled about the merits of two . . . *danseuses* . . . the crowd, relishing the absurdity of the thing, backed up the quarrel with such energy . . . that . . . a ward in the infirmary was filled." Further, "the use of violence for long-term ends (such as railroad sabotage to produce a bottleneck twelve months hence) would probably seem nonsensical and repulsive to the Burmese." Violence tends to be accompanied by looting. There is a tendency to use violence also in situations "with no hopes of success." Violence tends to be set off with little premeditation: "accidentally, usually in a crowd, a spark will set off a fight which will sweep like a forest fire through the people present"; "folk tales and plays are full of situations in which a character feels a sudden desire to commit some unlawful act . . . and immediately proceeds to commit the act"; Burmese quite consciously entertain "the belief that temptation is irresistible." There is a pattern of "running amok." "Drunken Burmese are said to become aggressive." In addition, "Burmese violence is easier to start than stop." As a counterpart to these traits "there are practically no professional criminals." In the case of adult outbursts of criminality "no explanation is apparently given or required."[15]

This adult handling of violence is related to various experiences of the Burmese child. "The preponderant relationship in childhood is between the boy and his mother." There is evidence for "the Burmese woman's unwilling-ness to bear children." "The nursing situation is unemotional . . . the mother talking or transacting her other business while the infant suckles." During the first years of life the Burmese mother, "firm and business-like," gives her child "good-humored, cool, rather impersonal efficient succorance." "Most of the time baby does not get much attention . . . most of the time he will be left alone . . . near to mother." After a long nursing period, the child is weaned, usually at the birth of the next sibling: "The child is apparently just pushed away, perhaps with some verbal admonitions. . . . A period of crying and babyish behavior is expected from the weaned baby . . . nothing is done about this; the child is just left to recover." Similarly, as to the frequent temper tantrums of the male child, set off by maternal refusal to accede to the boy's demands: "The mother does nothing in the face of these temper tantrums, waiting for the child to recover its equanimity without action or consoling word . . . the boy will be allowed to kick and scream until he exhausts himself." However, "there are no situations in which it is permissible to answer back at or interrupt . . . [the] parents, much less show any overt aggression."[16]

While, thus, the Burmese mother usually exhibits little affection towards her young child, she will sometimes become "intensely . . . affectionate, playing with the child, tickling it . . . nuzzling it. . . . Very often in these bursts of loving the mother will massage the baby all over with oil . . . even playing with the baby's genitals." At other times "she will tease the child . . . 'making him cry and lose control'." The mother acts as her "whim" suggests it. Transitions between these various rather contrasting behaviors are apt to be sudden and quick; the length of each spell short, irregular, unpredictable.[17]

What are the relationships between these various aspects of Burmese child training and the adult Burmese handling of violence? They are probably manifold and require for their elucidation—in the fashion discussed under (3)—a number of special propositions of dynamic psychology. Space, and the purpose of this paper, preclude a full statement of this matter.

First, the previously illustrated pattern of continuing early reactions is present here, too: some aspects of Burmese adult violence may be continua-tions of early temper tantrum behavior. As temper tantrums made no impres-sion on mother, adult tantrums may be gone through "with no hopes of success."

Second, another type of relationship involved here is as follows: adults are apt to react in wider relations in ways in which adults had acted towards them when they were children, in intimate relations. The Burmese mother does not explain the deprivations she inflicts on her child. The Burmese man does not explain acts of violence.

Third, the following relation seems to be involved: adult (political) behavior may in part act out infantile strivings which had been interfered with, or not sufficiently gratified.

The insatiable love demand of the American child may thus be striving for satisfaction when it is desired that "the smallest purchase should be accompanied by a smile ... [and that] the weightiest business or political conference ... [should] start with those greetings and anecdotes which demonstrate that the conferers like one another."[18]

The Burmese mother presumably arouses intense rage towards her in her child in a variety of ways. *[I am now adding some specific hypotheses about the interrelations between Burmese childhood and adulthood to Gorer's points.]* She also promotes intense repression, by the child, of his own rage by her impassivity (invulnerability) and by prohibiting overt aggression against herself (both of these behaviors also contribute to the intensity of the child's rage). At the same time her erratic and (to the child) unloving behavior hampers the development of strong powers of reason and conscience in the child. (The "weak" role of the Burmese father in the family works in the same direction.) Hence, the Burmese adult is able to go through with acts of destructiveness not so much when reason and conscience can be brought to approve them as when these restraints can be put out of action: in a crowd, in a fugue state, under alcohol. The connection between the seizure of somebody else's property (in kleptomania or looting) and rage about unsatisfied early love-demands is well established. The "close shave" reduces anxiety about retaliation (I made it) and alleviates guilt (I exposed myself).

A fourth type of relationship can be illustrated by the following point. According to Erikson one of the major aspects of the image of Hitler in Nazi Germany was that of "an adolescent who never gave in." This is related to idiosyncratic aspects of Hitler's life and fantasy and to typical aspects of life and fantasy in German middle class youth in the first half of the 20th century.

In *Mein Kampf,* "Hitler spends a considerable and heated portion of his first chapter in the description of how 'no power on earth could make an official' out of him.... This was his father's greatest wish...." He did not become a *Beamter.*

In his *Sturm und Drang* phase "the German boy would rather have died than be made aware of the fact that ... [his rebellion] would ... lead to exhaustion. The identification with the father which had been ... established in childhood would come to the fore. In intricate ways *Fate* would ... make a

Buerger out of the boy—a 'mere citizen' with an eternally bad conscience. . . ."[19]

This represents a type of proposition related to that discussed just before: somebody else's (here a leader's) adult political behavior may in part act out strivings of the self which had been interfered with, or not sufficiently gratified; and this may foster positive reactions towards that other person.

To state a fifth type of relationship, Loewenstein's discussion of anti-semitism suggests the following sequence (in the terminology of psycho-analysis): the power-relations between the diaspora Jews and their human environment may have reinforced those aspects of Jewish child-training which in their turn induced a Jewish "compulsive character . . . based on . . . the repression of aggressive impulses." The "contemporary German compulsive character . . . based on 'sphincter morals' [i.e., the repression of 'anal' rather than 'sadistic' strivings]" used the Jews as targets for the re-projection, and subsequent destruction, of its superego: "Jews have represented for the Nazis . . . those who repress aggression and, like Christ, suffer for the faults of others. They are the incarnation of the tendency of their own superego to repress aggression."[20]

This represents a type of proposition related to that discussed just before. In contrast to the preceding proposition it is concerned with inter-cultural rather than intra-cultural relations; and with the basis of negative rather than positive interpersonal reactions.

III. INTRODUCING A DYNAMIC FACTOR

The propositions discussed hitherto were all, as indicated above, concerned with relationships between the present and an ostensibly remote and irrelevant past. Besides such "genetic" statements there are "dynamic" ones which, in the words of Hartmann and Kris "are concerned with the interaction . . . of forces within the individual and with their reaction to the external world, at any given time or during brief time spans."[21]

Thus, Gorer and Benedict recall the polarized reactions, in pre-occupation Japan, towards the Emperor (against whom no negative reactions were expressed) and other members of the political elite (against whom such reactions were easily, frequently, and intensely expressed). They also recall the Japanese propensity to consider as hostile towards the Emperor behaviors which were ostensibly either slips (e.g., in the ceremonial readings of Imperial rescripts) or unrelated to the Emperor (e.g., a railway man temporarily and without consequences misplaces a signal while the Imperial train is somewhere within the wider area). As to polarized reactions to the political elite apart from the Emperor, these authors mentioned the coexistence of "fanatic discipline" and gross insubordination towards military authorities.[22]

This entire pattern of submission-revolt is related to the presence of intense, and intensely warded off, hostilities towards authority figures, dealt with by the mechanisms (among others) known in the language of psychoanalysis as reaction-formation (going to the opposite of an objectionable striving) and decomposition of ambivalence (splitting up the mixed feelings towards a given object between at least two).

A special set of "dynamic" propositions in psycho-cultural analysis indicates those interrelations between culturally typical acts which are in themselves culturally typical. An instance of this was the proposition just mentioned that the Japanese "choice" between available "psychological mechanisms" prefers (though, of course, not exclusively) reaction formation and decomposition of ambivalence.

Another instance would be the previously implied proposition that the Japanese "choice" between available life aspects stresses the continuum submission-revolt (Japanese acts cluster towards both ends of this continuum). [Compare Bateson's formulation: "We shall not describe varieties of character in terms of . . . (their) position on a continuum between extreme dominance and extreme submissiveness, but we shall instead try to use . . . some such continua as 'degree of interest in . . . dominance-submission.' " 23]

Available "genetic" propositions in psycho-cultural analysis—which formed the bulk of the examples in this paper—almost always deal with the interrelations within a very limited set of acts which is usually much smaller than the list of variables we are interested in. (While we may have some hypotheses about the interrelations between Japanese reactions to the Emperor and to the "rascals around the throne," we may not have any hypotheses about the interrelations between these reactions and those, say, of an employer towards his employees.) The advance of psycho-cultural research may furnish more genetic explanations of more complicated dynamically explained syndromes.

NOTES

1. Heinz Hartmann and Ernst Kris, "The Genetic Approach in Psychoanalysis," *The Psychoanalytic Study of the Child,* I (1945), 11.

2. Clyde and Florence R. Kluckhohn, "American Culture: Generalized Orientations and Class Patterns," *Conference of Philosophy, Science and Religion* (New York, 1946), 106-128. This point was also conveyed by Margaret Mead, *And Keep Your Powder Dry* (New York, 1942), 90f.

3. Ruth Benedict, "Rumanian Culture and Behavior," (mimeographed document of the Columbia University Institute for Intercultural Studies, New York, 1943), 54.

4. Paul Kecskemeti and Nathan Leites, "Some Psychological Hypotheses on Nazi Germany," *Journal of Social Psychology,* XXVI (1947), 143.

5. Geoffrey Gorer, "Themes in Japanese Culture," *Transactions of the New York Academy of Sciences,* V (1943), 106-124; Ruth Benedict, *The Chrysanthemum and the Sword: Patterns of Japanese Culture* (Boston, 1946), 10.

6. This point has been formulated with particular clarity and force by Harold D. Lasswell, *The Analysis of Political Behavior: An Empirical Approach* (London, 1948), 195-234.

7. See Harold D. Lasswell, *Psychopathology and Politics* (Chicago, 1930).

8. This is not a logically circular, but factual "feedback" system; cf. Gregory Bateson, "Morale and National Character," in Goodwin Watson (ed.), *Civilian Morale* (Boston, 1942), 71-91.

9. Benedict, *The Chrysanthemum and the Sword*, 260.

10. Margaret Mead, "The Application of Anthropological Techniques to Cross-National Communication," *Transactions of the New York Academy of Sciences,* Series II, IX (1947), 136-138.

11. Thus Gorer states, "I have assumed . . . that the genetic peculiarities of the Japanese do not involve any . . . psychological differences from other groups of human beings." Gorer, "Themes in Japanese Culture," 10.

12. See Clyde Kluckhohn and William H. Kelly, "The Concept of Culture," in Ralph Linton (ed.), *The Science of Man in the World Crisis* (New York, 1946), 87f.

13. Ruth Benedict, "The Study of Cultural Patterns in European Nations," *Transactions of the New York Academy of Sciences,* Series II, VIII (1946), 277f.

14. Geoffrey Gorer, *The American People: A Study in National Character* (New York, 1948), 133f.

15. Geoffrey Gorer, "Burmese Personality," (Columbia Institute for Intercultural Studies, New York, 1945), 38-61. On destructiveness see also Talcott Parsons, "Certain Primary Sources and Patterns of Aggression in the Social Structure of the Western World," *Psychiatry*, X (1947), 167-182.

16. Gorer, "Burmese Personality," 29-33.

17. Ibid., 32.

18. Gorer, *The American People*, 133.

19. Erik H. Erikson, "Hitler's Imagery and German Youth," *Psychiatry,* V (1942), 477-480.

20. Rudolph M. Loewenstein, "The Historical and Cultural Roots of Anti-Semitism," *Psychoanalysis and the Social Sciences*, I (1947), 345f.

21. Hartmann and Kris, "The Genetic Approach," 11.

22. Gorer, "Themes in Japanese Culture," 106-124; Benedict, *The Chrysanthemum and the Sword.*

23. Bateson, "Morale and National Character," 80.

Chapter 3

TWENTIETH CENTURY PROPAGANDA TRENDS

(with Ernst Kris)

EDITOR'S NOTE: In this essay Leites and Kris identify a major difference in propaganda appeals between the two world wars. The change is interpreted in terms of Freud's tri-partite concept of personality: the authors find a shift from morally or emotionally highly charged symbolism to matter-of-fact, ego-oriented language. They suggest this trend away from appeals to conscience and impulse may be explained by important cultural changes in the Western world towards increased privatization and political mistrust.

From *"Trends in Twentieth Century Propaganda,"* Psychoanalysis and the Social Sciences *I (1947), 393-409.*

*I*n speaking of propaganda, we refer to the political sphere and not to promotional activities in general. We define acts of propaganda, in agreement with H. D. Lasswell, as attempts to influence attitudes of large numbers of people on controversial issues of relevance to a group. Propaganda is thus distinguished from education which deals with non-controversial issues. Moreover, not all treatments of controversial issues of relevance to a group fall under the definition; they are not propaganda if they aim at the clarification of issues rather than at the changing of attitudes.[1]

In the following, we deal mainly with propaganda by agents of government and exclusively with propaganda using the channels of mass communication, i.e., principally print, radio, and film.

However, neither the potentialities of any one medium, nor the variety of promotional devices used by all will be discussed here. We are concerned with the place of propaganda in Western civilization. Our general hypothesis is that responses to political propaganda in the Western world have considerably changed during the last decades; and that these changes are related to trends in the sociopsychological conditions of life in the twentieth century.

We shall not be able to offer conclusive proof for the points we wish to make. We do not know of the existence of data comprehensive and reliable enough to demonstrate in quantitative terms broad hypotheses about changes in responses to propaganda. We start out from changes in content and style of propaganda, assuming that they reflect the propagandist's expectation as to the response of his audience. The propagandist may be mistaken in his expectations, but finally he will be informed to some extent about his audiences' response, and adapt his output, within limits, to their predispositions.

We choose two situations in which propaganda was directed towards comparable objectives: the two world wars.

Wartime propaganda is enacted in a situation with strictly limited goals. Under whatever conditions, the objective of propagandists in wartime is to maximize social participation among members of their own group and to minimize participation among members of the enemy group.[2] Social participation is characterized by concern for the objectives of the group, the sharing of its activities, and the preparedness to accept deprivations on its behalf. High "participation" is therefore identical with high "morale." Its psychological dynamics are mutual identifications among group members, and identification of individual members with leaders or leading ideals of the group, strong cathexis of the goal set by the group, and decreased cathexis of the self; processes that at least in part are preconscious and unconscious. Low participation may manifest itself in two ways: first, participation may be shifted partly or totally from one group to another. In this case, one may speak of a split in participation. Second, low participation may manifest itself as a withdrawal of individuals from the political sphere; in this case, we speak of privatization. *[Two kinds of decreased participation in the direction of privatization can be distinguished: first, a decrease of active attitudes towards the political sphere, in favor of passive or merely adjusting attitudes—in this case one must speak of a decrease of attitudinal participation; second, a decrease of the actual sharing in political action—in this case one might speak of a decrease of behavioral participation.]*

The psychological dynamics of a split in participation are obvious: one set of identifications and objectives has been replaced by another. The only dynamic change consists in the fact that, as a rule, the old group has not lost its cathexis, but has become the target of hostility.

The dynamics of privatization are more complex: withdrawal of cathexes from the group of its objectives leads to a process comparable to, but not identical with a narcissistic regression. Concern with the self becomes dominant. Since the striving for individual indulgence is maximized, the individual becomes exceedingly vulnerable to deprivation.

Modern warfare is distinguished from older types of warfare by the fact that it affects larger numbers of individuals. In total war "nations at arms" oppose each other with all their resources. Hence participation becomes increasingly important. To the extent that preparedness for war infringes upon life in peace, the problem continues to exist in peacetime.

Participation of whole nations was more essential during World War I than during any previous war; and yet it was somewhat less essential than during World War II; the first world war, especially at its onset, was "less total" than the second. On the other hand, the media of mass communication were less developed; radio and film had hardly been tested. Three areas of difference between the propagandas of the two wars seem particularly relevant in our context:

(1) Propaganda during the second world war exhibited, on the whole, a higher degree of sobriety than propaganda during World War I; the incidence of highly emotionalized terms was probably lower.

(2) Propaganda during the second world war was, on the whole, less moralistic than propaganda during the first world war; the incidence of preference statements as against fact statements was probably lower.

(3) Propaganda during the second world war tended to put a moderate ceiling on grosser divergences from presently or subsequently ascertainable facts, divergences that were more frequent in propaganda during the first world war. Also, propaganda during the second world war tended to give fuller information about relevant events than propaganda during World War I.

In summarizing the psychological aspects of these differences, we might say that propaganda appeals were less frequently directed to id and superego, more prominently to the ego.

In this respect, these areas of differences are representative of others. At least two qualifications to the points mentioned above are essential: first, most of the differences we stress became ever clearer the longer the second world war lasted; second, they were more accentuated in the propaganda of the Western democracies than in that of Germany and Russia. In the following analysis, we shall in the main limit ourselves to examples from American, British, and German propaganda, and to some data on response; information on reactions of Russian and Japanese audiences is not accessible.

The use of emotionalized language was, at the outset of World War II, almost completely absent in British propaganda. When, in the autumn of 1939, Mr. Churchill, then First Lord of the Admiralty, referred to the Nazis as "Huns," thus using the stereotype current during World War I, he was publicly rebuked. Basically, that attitude persisted throughout the war in Britain and the United States. "We don't want to be driven into hate" was the tenor of opinion. There were modifications of this attitude: in the United States in regard to Japan, in Britain after the severe onslaught of bombing. However, hate campaigns remained largely unacceptable. In Germany, a similar attitude persisted: attempts of German propaganda to brandish the bombing of German cities by British and later by American planes as barbarism, to speak of the crews of these planes as "night pirates" and of German raids against British as retaliatory largely failed to arouse indignant hate.

The waning power of *moral* argumentation in propaganda is best illustrated by the fact that one of the predominant themes of propaganda during World War I played no comparable part in World War II. The theme "Our cause is right; theirs is wrong" was secondary in the propaganda of the Western powers; its part in German propaganda was limited; only in Russian propaganda was its role presumably comparable to that it had played in World War I propaganda. In the democratic countries and in Germany, the moral argumentation was replaced by one in terms of indulgence and deprivation (profit or loss): "We are winning; they are losing"; and: "These will be the blessings of victory; these the calamities of defeat." There is evidence indicating that both in the democracies and in Germany this type of appeal was eminently successful. In other words: success of propaganda was dependent on the transformation of superego appeals into appeals to the ego.[3]

The third area of difference, the increased concern for some agreement between the content of propaganda and ascertainable facts, and the increased concern for detailed information was to some considerable extent related to technological change. Thus, during the first world war, the German people were never explicitly (and implicitly only much later) informed about the

German defeat in the battle of the Marne in September 1914. A similar reticence during the second world war would not have proved expedient, since in spite of coercive measures, allied radio transmissions were widely listened to by Germans. However, technological progress was not the only reason for the change. The concern with credibility had increased, independently of the technology of communication. The tendency to check statements of one's own against those of enemy governments existed both in Germany and in the democracies; while it was limited in Germany, it was widely spread in Britain and the United States.

The differences of propaganda during World Wars I and II are epitomized in the treatment of a theme related to all three areas discussed—enemy atrocities. As far as we know, only Russian propaganda on German atrocities, and German propaganda on Russian atrocities gave to this theme about the same importance in World War II that all propagandists had given it during World War I. But German reports on allied atrocities were rather timid, if compared to the inventiveness of German propaganda in other areas; and German propaganda about Soviet atrocities was largely designed to create fear and defensive combativeness rather than hate and indignation. In the democracies, however, the "playing down" of reports on enemy atrocities was a guiding principle of propaganda, at least until 1945. While during World War I, allied propagandists did not refrain from exaggerating and even inventing atrocities, uncontestable evidence of enemy atrocities was, for a long time, withheld during World War II. It is needless to say that the atrocities to which this documentation referred and which, at the end of the war and after the war became manifest to the soldiers of armies traversing Europe, were of a kind totally different in horror from anything the world of the earlier twentieth century had known. The purposeful reticence of the democratic governments becomes thereby even more significant.

No adequate understanding of these propaganda trends is possible unless we take two closely related trends in the predispositions of the public into account. Our thesis is that the differences between the propaganda styles during both world wars are largely due to the rising tendencies towards *distrust* and *privatization*—tendencies that we believe to have existed in the Western democracies as well as in Germany.

Distrust is directed primarily against the propagandist and the authority he represents, secondarily also against the "suggestibility" of the "propagandee."[4]

The first mentioned manifestation of distrust can be traced back to the last war. Propaganda operated then on a new level of technological perfection; the latent possibilities of the mass communication media became suddenly manifest; in all belligerent countries, outbursts of enthusiasm for war occurred. Propagandists, like children playing with a new toy, charged their messages with many manufactured contents. After the war, they reported on their own achievements—sometimes exaggerating the extent to which they had distorted events. These reports helped to create the aura of secret power that ever since has surrounded propagandists. In Britain and the United States, some of this prestige was transferred from the propagandist to the public relations counsel; some of the men who had successfully worked in government agencies became pioneers of modern advertising. Beliefs in the power of propaganda led to a phobia of political persuasion; propaganda became "a bad name," an influence against which the common man had to guard himself.

The political and economic failures of the postwar era, the futility of the idealistic appeals which had helped to conclude the first world war, reinforced this distrust. Its spread and influence on the political scene, however, was sharply different in different areas. In Germany, the distrust of propaganda was manipulated by the nationalist, and later, the national-socialist movement. Propaganda was identified with those allied propaganda efforts that had accompanied German defeat.[5] While distrust was directed against one side, nationalist and national socialist propaganda could operate more freely under the guise of anti-propaganda. In the Western democracies, the propaganda phobia rose during the Great Depression. It became a lasting attitude both in the United States and, possibly to a lesser degree, in the United Kingdom, and it took years of experience to discover a propaganda style that would at least not provoke distrust. While the disdain of propaganda had been initiated by the upper strata, it was during the second world war more intense with lower socioeconomic groups.

At this point, it becomes essential to supplement our analysis of the distrust of propaganda by a discussion of contemporary privatization tendencies. Many motivations contribute to such tendencies. Some of them are not taken up here. *[For instance, we do not propose to discuss how privatization is related to changes in values (see "Recent Trends in Moral Temper," chapter 4).]*

Individuals in the mass societies of the twentieth century are to an ever increasing extent involved in public affairs; it becomes increasingly difficult to ignore them. But "ordinary" individuals have ever less the feeling that they can *understand* or *influence* the very events upon which their life and happiness is known to depend.[6] At the same time, leaders in both totalitarian and democratic societies claim that decisions ultimately rest upon the common man's consent, and that the information supplied to him fully enables him to evaluate the situation. The contrast between these claims and the common man's experience extends to many areas. Thus in economic life ever more depends upon state interference. But, on the other hand, people increasingly regard economic policy as a province in which the professional specialist is paramount and the common man incompetent. The increasing "statification" of economic life has been accompanied by a rising mass reputation of scientific economics as a specialty. The emotional charges of simple economic formulae such as "free enterprise" or "socialization of the means of production" seem to have decreased (one might speak, at least in certain areas, of the silent breakdown of "capitalism" and "socialism" as ideologies). While the economic specialist is to fulfill the most urgent demand of the common man, that for security of employment, the distance between him and his beneficiary grows; he becomes part of a powerful elite, upon which the common man looks with a distrust rooted in a dependency.

This is but one instance of the experience of disparity—of insight as well as power—between the common man and the various political organizations into which he is integrated. That disparity counteracts the feeling of power which accompanies the manipulation of increasingly effective machinery, whether of production or destruction: the common man is usually acutely aware of the fact that the "button" he is "pushing" belongs to an apparatus far out of the reach of any unorganized individual.

This feeling of disparity greatly affects the common man's attitude to foreign policy: The potential proximity of total war produces situations that not only seem inherently incomprehensible, but that he, the common man, feels cannot be made comprehensible to him by his government. "Security considerations," he infers, are the reason why the "real dope" is kept away from him. Thus the distance between the common man and the policy maker has grown to such an extent that awe and distrust support each other.

The common man feels impotent in a world where specialized skills control events that at any moment may transform his life. That feeling of impotence bestows upon political facts something of the solidity of natural events, like weather or hurricane, that come and go. Two attitudes result from this feeling: first, one does not inquire into the causation of the events thus viewed; second, one does not inquire into their morality. *[American soldiers during the second world war were frequently explicitly opposed to discussion of its causation: going into its pre-history was apt to be regarded as futile and somewhat "out of this world."]*

The feeling that politics as such is outside the reach of morals is an extreme form of this attitude. Probably moral indignation as a reaction to political events has been declining since the turn of the century. One may compare the intense reactions to injustice against individuals under comparatively stable social conditions—the Dreyfus affair, the cases of Ferrer, Nurse Cavell, Sacco and Vanzetti—with the limited reactions to Nazi terror and extermination practices as they gradually became notorious. In the case of the Nazis, public reaction went through a sequence of frank disbelief, reserved doubt, short-lived shock, and subsequent indifference.

The psychological dynamics operating the interplay of distrust and privatization can now be formulated more sharply. We here distinguish, in the continuum of distrustful attitudes, two cases: one we call critical distrust, the other projective distrust.[7] In the child's development, the former arose not independently from the latter. Critical distrust facilitates adjustment to reality and independence; it is at the foundation of scientific thought and is an essential incentive in the battle against what Freud called the prohibition of thinking in the individual. Critical distrust has gained a decisive importance in modern society, since technology has played havoc with many kinds of magic. Projective distrust, on the other hand, is derived ultimately from ambivalence; it is an expression of hostility, in which aggressive tendencies against others, frequently against authority, are perceived as tendencies of others, frequently as attitudes of authority.

We allude to these complex questions only in order to round off our argumentation: in the world of the twentieth century, the exercise of critical distrust by the common man meets with many obstacles; it is at the same time increasingly stimulated and increasingly frustrated. He therefore regressively turns to projective distrust: he fears, suspects and hates what he cannot understand and master.

Privatization is, amongst other things, a result of the hostility between the individual and the leadership of the group: we mentioned that it is comparable to what is known as a narcissistic regression. In order to maintain this attitude in which self-interest predominates over group interest—the self in this case may include "primary" groups such as the family—projective distrust is set into operation. Scepticism becomes the guarantor of privatization: scepticism here acts as a defense. If the individual, for instance, were to accept available evidence on atrocities, his emotional involvement in politics might rise; he might hate or experience enthusiasm. Thus privatization could not be maintained. The propagandist's concern in wartime is therefore to reduce such scepticism.

That concern, we said, was more clearly expressed in the democracies than in Germany or Russia. In order fully to understand this difference, we turn to a more detailed discussion of the relationship between propagandist and "propagandee." Every propaganda act occurs in such a relationship; in the case of propaganda by agents of governments, it is the relationship between the individual and his government.

We discuss this relationship in regard to two types of political organization: the totalitarian state with the charismatic leader and democracy. In both cases, the propagandists speak for the leaders, who are the chief propagandists. In both cases, propaganda presupposes, and attempts to strengthen identifications of the propagandees with, the propagandists. These identifications, however, have a different character under the two regimes.

In a totalitarian state these identifications concern, to a large extent, id and superego functions. These identifications facilitate the gratifying completion of impulses, as superego functions have been projected upon the propagandist, and as he is idealized in an archaic sense: omnipotence, omniscience, and infallibility are attributed to him.

In democratic states, the corresponding identifications concern, to a large extent, ego functions which are delegated to the propagandist. Amongst these functions, the scrutiny of the existing situation and the anticipation of the future are of predominant importance. While the propagandee relies upon the propagandist for the fulfillment of these functions, he retains a critical attitude in relation to him.

Superego and ego identifications, of course, constantly interact. The distribution of their intensities, however, is clearly dependent upon the institutionalized relationship between propagandist and propagandee. In this sense, we may say that the one is typical of totalitarian, the other of democratic propaganda relations.

That difference is reflected in the devices of propaganda. Totalitarian propaganda·tries to sway the audience into participation; its preferred setting is the visible leader talking to the masses; it is modeled after the relations between the hypnotist and his medium. Democratic propaganda gives weight to insight as basis for participation; it is to a greater extent modeled after the principles of guidance or education.

The nature of the two propaganda situations accounts for the fact that for each of the two kinds of propagandists different goals are difficult to reach. The totalitarian propagandist finds it arduous to stimulate initiative among his followers. When German propaganda was faced with the task of stimulating cooperative action "from below" among the citizens of bombed towns, that difficulty became apparent: the devices then adopted were plain imitations of the techniques of British propagandists in a similar situation. Democratic propagandists meet a comparable difficulty when faced with the task of manifestly denying information on reasons for government action, that is, of demanding implicit trust for a limited time. The impasse in which allied leadership found itself when faced with a public demand for the opening of a second front, especially in 1943, is an example.

The two types of propagandists react to the impact of distrust and privatization in different ways; these tendencies show a different incidence under the two political orders. In a totalitarian state, privatization grows with deprivation. Then the latent cleavage of the totalitarian state becomes manifest, the cleavage between the faithful, from whose ranks elite and sub-elite are recruited, and the indifferent, who are controlled by the faithful. Their mounting privatization renders this control more difficult. Superego identifications cease to function with ever more individuals, and finally they function only with the fanatics. When that situation crystallized in Germany with the approach of defeat, two devices were adopted: first, a gradual revision of propaganda policy. Appeals to superego identifications became less and less important and increased weight was given to the stimulation of fear: ego interests should now motivate continued allegiance. But this did not prevent further privatization. Thus the central method of all totalitarian social control was applied ever more consistently: violence. In its last phases, Nazi propaganda hardly fulfilled the purpose of gaining participation in the present; building the Nazi myth, it addressed its appeals to future generations.

Democratic propaganda is better equipped to deal with the tendency towards privatization, since it puts greater emphasis on the creation of insight. Its appeals are better in tune with a high level of distrust. In totalitarian regimes, there is a polarization between the politicized and the privatized, which is, however, difficult to perceive from the outside. In democratic states, tendencies towards privatization are clearly perceptible but their distribution within the society is less clear-cut.

There are periods when this tendency decreases: in America after Pearl Harbor, in Britain after May 1940. While enthusiasm was kept at a low level, determination prevailed and sacrifice was willingly sustained.

What was the part of the propagandist in such situations? It may be illustrated by turning to one specific situation, in which democratic propaganda reached its greatest success.

We refer to Churchill's propaganda feat during the spring of 1940. The series of speeches he made in May, June, and July of 1940 are remembered for the singular depth of feeling and the heroic quality of language. But these qualities were only accessories to the major political impact of these speeches. Their function was a threefold one—to warn Britain of the danger, to clarify its extent, and to indicate how everyone could help to meet it. In order to illustrate this point, we refer to one topic only: the announcement of the Battle of Britain.

The first intimation was made on May 12th, three days after Churchill's appointment, when the Battle of Flanders had not yet reached its climax. After having described the battle on all fronts, Churchill added that "many preparations had to be made at home." On May 19th, after the surrender of Holland, and during the climax of the Belgian battles, he devoted well over one-third of his speech to announcing "that after this . . . there will come the battle for our island." And after demanding full mobilization of production, he gave for the first time the "box score": he reported that the R.A.F. had been downing three to four enemy planes for each of their own. This, he inferred, was the basis of any hope. On June 4th, in his famous speech after Dunkirk, the theme was taken up anew, and an elaborate account of the chances of the fighter force in a battle over the homeland was given. Churchill went into technical details; at a time when France seemed still vigorously to resist, he acquainted the British people with the chances of their survival. While the enemy had broken through the allied front with a few thousand armored vehicles, he forecast the future by saying: "May it not also be that the course of civilization itself will be defended by the skill and devotion of a few thousand airmen." And while he discussed the necessity of ever in-creasing production, he spoke at this time of imminent defeat of "the great British armies of the later years of war."

In the later speeches of that unforgettable spring, he elaborated on the subject. Everyone could understand how his own behavior was related to the total situation, and how this situation was structured; how supplies were needed for the repair and construction of fighter planes, and how in this matter every detail, even the smallest one, could contribute to the final result. All this information was released well in advance of any German attack.

Thus Churchill had not only given the "warning signal" and mobilized "emergency reactions." His detailed analysis of the situation also contributed to the prevention of an inexpediently large and rapid increase in anxiety: unknown danger was transformed into a danger known in kind and extent. He fulfilled those functions of leadership that can be compared to those fulfilled in the life of the individual by the organization of the ego.[8] At the same time, Churchill offered his own courage as a model: "If you behave as I do, you will behave right." He not only spoke of Britain's "finest hour" but was careful to add that in this hour "every man and woman had their chance."

The propagandist thus seems to fulfill a double function: first, that of structuring the situation so that it can be anticipated and understood, and second, that of offering himself as a model.

It is essential to understand the difference between the democratic leader who functions as a model and the charismatic leader.[9] The latter offers himself as an object that replaces superego functions in the individual. The model function of leadership implies that in identifying with the leader, the individual will best serve the ideals he shares with him. But the understanding of the situation is a precondition for such moral participation.

The general problem which we here finally approach concerns the relation between ego and superego functions. One might tentatively formulate the hypothesis that in a situation in which the ego functions smoothly, the tension between ego and superego is apt to be low. In fact, we find in the study of superego formation in the child some evidence in support of such a formulation.[10] However, other evidence is contradictory. Frequently, suc-cessful ego performance is accompanied by intense conflicts between ego and superego. We therefore reject this formulation and substitute another: unsuccessful ego functions endanger the positive relationship between ego and superego. They tend to encourage regressive trends. Individuals who feel impotent in the face of a world they do not understand, and are distrustful of those who should act as their guides, tend to revert to patterns of behavior known from childhood, in which an increase of hostility against the adults and many neurotic or delinquent mechanisms may develop. The incidence of such maladjustments may increase in a society in which privatization tendencies have become dominant. *[We here note that the traditional discussion of the applicability of "individual" psychological hypotheses to social events lacks substance, since events dealt with in the empirical analysis of human affairs, "psychological" or "sociological", occur individuals. We deal with frequencies of incidence.]*

Little can be said here about what conclusions can be drawn for the future of democratic propaganda from these considerations. They clearly point to the desirability of sharp and wide increases of insight into events in the world at large among the citizens. Briefly, the trend towards distrust and privatization among the audience of the propagandist should be turned into a trend towards increase of insight. That trend would find a parallel in changes of related techniques: psycho-therapy and education, largely under the influence of psychoanalysis, have substituted or are substituting insight for pressure. If the appropriate education, on a vast enough scale and at a rapid enough rate is not provided for, the distrust and privatization of the masses may become a fertile soil for totalitarian management.

NOTES

1. Harold D. Lasswell, *Propaganda Techniques in the World War* (New York, 1927).

2. Hans Speier and M. Otis, "German Radio Propaganda to France during the Battle of France," in *Radio Research, 1942-43*, ed. by P. F. Lazarsfeld and F. N. Stanton (New York, 1944), 208-247.

3. Jules H. Masserman, *Principles of Dynamic Psychiatry* (Philadelphia, 1945), 219. He makes a similar point, speaking of "resonance with personal incentives."

4. Ernst Kris, "The Danger of Propaganda," *American Imago*, 2 (1941), 1-42; Ernst Kris, "Some Problems of War Propaganda: A Note on Propaganda, Old and New," *Psychoanalytic Quarterly*, II (1943), 381-399.

5. For the question of the actual contribution of propaganda to this defeat and generally for the question of the limited influence of propaganda on warfare, see E. Kris, H. Speier, et al., *German Radio Propaganda* (New York, 1944).

6. Karl Mannheim, *Man and Society in an Age of Transformation* (London, 1940); Paul Kecskemeti and Nathan Leites, "Some Psychological Hypotheses on Nazi Germany," (Washington, D.C., 1945). [See selection in this volume, chapter 13.]

7. On their genetic interrelation and pathological manifestations, especially in obsessional neuroses and paranoid syndromes (not discussed in detail here), see Helene Deutsch, "Zur Psychologie des Misstrauens," *Imago*, (VII (1921), 71-83. A fuller treatment would also have to consider the question of retaliatory and self-punitive distrust.

8. Ernst Kris, "Danger and Morale," *American Journal of Orthopsychiatry*, XIV (1944), 147-155.

9. Fritz Redl, "Group Emotion and Leadership," *Psychiatry*, V (1942), 573-596.

10. K. Friedlander, "Formation of the Antisocial Character," *Psychoanalytic Study of the Child*, I (1945), 189-204.

Chapter 4

RECENT TRENDS IN MORAL TEMPER

EDITOR'S NOTE: Continuing his inquiry into twentieth century cultural changes, Leites presents in this essay a "reading" of the large body of existentialist literature which had been produced since the 1930s. He perceives in it evidence of an atrophy of moral feeling and an absence of religious belief qualitiatively different from the perspectives of typical nineteenth centural "amoralists" and atheists. By analyzing the form in which the new loss of feeling and belief is expressed, and by describing adaptations and reactions to the loss characteristic of such writers as Sartre and Camus, he anticipates trends which have since become major tendencies in popular culture in the western world.

From "Trends in Moral Temper," American Imago *V (1948), 3-37.*

To make guesses about contemporary developments in moral temper is risky for various reasons. First, the pertinent data are mostly not yet gathered, as the empirical study of morality has hardly begun. Hence every statement to be made is only a tentative hypothesis. Second, a reasonably complete picture would show a complicated structure of tendencies and counter-tendencies, within and between individuals and groups. Almost all broad statements would have to be qualified according to class, character structure, region, age, ideology, etc. Third, it is one of the trends to be discussed that contemporary moral changes proceed rather covertly and unobservedly—"not with a bang but with a whimper," if I may use this familiar quotation. Fourth, in the presence of these difficulties, speculation is apt to be distorted by the moral preoccupations of the person who engages in them. He may, for instance, be inclined to exaggerate the occurrence of his own predicaments in others. I shall not burden every guess set forth below with a repetition of these qualifications.

What follows refers only to the non-totalitarian part of western culture, and more specifically to the metropolitan areas of North America and Western Europe.

This paper deals mainly with directions of current changes. It does not deny that older and well-known patterns persist. As to current changes, I shall deal particularly with disintegration, rather than re-integration.

The data mentioned below (particularly the literary and philosophic ones) are illustrative, i.e., not designed to prove my general statements. Philosophic statements are mainly viewed in this paper as expressing feelings of those who create and accept them rather than as describing the world.[1]

I. THE DECLINE IN MORAL CERTAINTY

In previous periods the feeling of certainty about some moral statements (e.g., those condemning the indefinitely protracted torture of others) was probably as "absolute" as the feeling of certainty about immediate sense data (this table is brown) or about logical-mathematical statements (two plus two is four). I am not concerned here with the epistemological relevance, or lack of relevance, of such certainty feelings, but only with the feelings themselves.

Many people, of course, felt such an absolute certainty only for some of their ethical beliefs and not for others. In addition there were in the course of western history increasing disagreements about the content of the absolutely certain ethical norms. But a certain core remained untouched.[2]

In the second quarter of the twentieth century two long prepared events emerged on a large scale, one by now common-place, the other less so. First, the core of moral agreement tended to vanish as western culture split into a totalitarian and a non-totalitarian part. Second, the degree of felt certainty in moral reactions, of whatever content, tended to decline in the non-totalitarian part. A moral statement began to seem by its very nature incapable of the massive certainty of statements about facts.

With this, there was a decline in the feeling that ethical statements could be as conclusively proved as statements about facts. In the older image of a dispute about ethics there were two possible outcomes: either the right side won by the cogency of its arguments, or the wrong side refused to accept the truth, governed by uncontrolled passions. In the newer image of such a dispute both sides become aware of the impossibility of proving their points. "Rational" persuasion in moral matters has become less conceivable. The older attitude could be accompanied by the desire to coerce those who refused to be instructed. (Hitler still spoke of "die Unbelehrbaren.") The newer attitude tends to look for extra-verbal means of resolving a verbal deadlock. Such means may range from silence to violence. The decrease in public discussions of ethical problems is related to this.

The philosophic counterparts of these feeling trends can be found in logical empiricism (the rage of the thirties) and existentialism (the rage of the forties). *[Precursors of "existentialism," such as certain variants of German "phenomenology" in the twenties, had shown the increasing precariousness of ethical feelings by an extreme denial of that precariousness. They put unusual stress on the assertion that the goodness or badness of an event is a property of this event comparable in its objectivity to, for instance, sensory qualities of things.]*

Radical empiricism—so often approached in the history of western philosophy—was never fully formulated before the middle thirties. Take the "Vienna Circle" and its Anglo-American sequels. In the twenties this group insisted on the distinction between "meaningful" (logical-mathematical and empirical) statements and "meaningless" (metaphysical) ones. It did so with a feeling-tone which took for granted some superiority of science over metaphysics. At the same time this group insisted on the arbitrariness of preference statements. *[It is, again, significant that the full statement of the logical "No bridge" relation between statements of fact and of preference was delayed until this century. We are now for the first time mastering the skill of*

"...parting
All that we feel from all that we perceive,
Desire from Data"

(W. H. Auden).]

But, as I just noted, a preference statement in favor of science as against metaphysics was at least suggested in the way in which the distinction between "meaningful" and "meaningless" sentences had been formulated. This was increasingly recognized in the thirties, and the last preference residue eliminated. "Positivists" renamed themselves "logical empiricists." Some proposed to replace the preferential terms "meaningful" and "meaning-less" by such terms as "connectible with scientific language" or "uncon-nectible" with it.[3] I can be a metaphysician *and* a logical empiricist.

Jean-Paul Sartre tells about a young man who saw his past life as a series of failures:

> He judged . . . this as a sign that he was not destined for secular triumphs, that only religious triumphs . . . were accessible to him . . . and he took orders. Is it not clear that he himself decided the meaning of this sign? One might have inferred . . . from this series of failures . . . that he should have become a car-penter or a revolutionary. . . .

In a more general vein:

> What proves that it is my task to impose my conception of man . . . on humanity? I shall never find any sign which could convince me. . . . If I consider this act as good, it is I who choose to say that it is good rather than bad.[4]

The disappearance of ethical certainty may be followed by a fading out of the ethical dimension of feeling. In the past some deviants had denied ethical certainty in a milieu which possessed it. Ethics preoccupied them probably more than it did the conformists. They denied, often with effort (expressed in elation or cynicism, for example) a certainty which remained emotionally conceivable or even plausible to them. The same holds true for anti-religious and anti-metaphysical activists of the "heroic period" of struggle against dominant religious and metaphysical beliefs.

Now perhaps a new type of "tabula rasa" man is appearing for whom earlier "live options" have died. During the last generations there were more and more who, religiously "color-blind," had lost empathy with religious feeling. In their wake there was an increasing number who had lost the sense of metaphysical experience. And finally now those may be appearing who find it difficult to understand what the pros and cons of ethics are all about. *[The decline of the conscious conscience is of course accompanied by a rise in the role of social anxiety. Various intermediate forms short of a complete carrot-and-stick orientation become prominent. In one such form I may still feel that my moral standards are my own, but also that I myself am unable to judge my performance in relation to those standards.]*

II. MORAL FEELINGS AND RELIGIOUS BELIEFS

There is probably a direct relationship between the weakening of religious and metaphysical beliefs and the decline of ethics. This assertion is both highly familiar and somewhat new. It has been a stock polemic weapon of conservatives during the last five hundred years. Its denial has been an only slightly less standard polemic tool of innovators who stressed their ethical respectability. Thus the implicit formula of French anti-clericalism under the Third Republic was: "Nothing changes if God does not exist."[5]

If traditional moral attitudes depend on traditional attitudes towards religion and metaphysics, the late nineteenth and early twentieth centuries were living, morally, off their inherited religious-metaphysical capital. There was a lag between the decline of religious-metaphysical certainty and that of ethical certainty. The morally respectable "agnostics" or "atheists" of that time had mostly been raised by religious parents and teachers.

The recent catching up of ethics in the general decline of non-empirical certainties leads to a reconsideration of beliefs about the independence of ethics and religion. In part, the various views designated as "existentialism" are attempts at such a reconsideration. References to the existence or non-existence of God had become almost impolite in philosophic discussions of the preceding period. More and more people had come to *feel* that the existence of a God was implausible if not impossible. But elaborate atheist *ideologies* became a rarity (the very word "atheism" is now dated). *[I shall point to an inverse relationship between the diffusion of a feeling and of its symbolic elaboration at other places in this paper. In these cases a minority position fosters, and a majority position renders obsolete, the expression of feeling by idea.]*

Now Sartre states that

> existentialism is nothing but an attempt to draw all the consequences from a coherent atheist position. . . . God does not exist . . . *all* the implications of this must be made explicit. . . . Existentialists oppose a certain type of secular ethics which would like to eliminate God with a minimum of cost.[6]

The elimination of God affects ethical attitudes in at least three ways: as the elimination of the creator of ethical norms; as the elimination of the being who punishes their violation and rewards conformity; and as the elimination of after-life. Beliefs in the second function of God had probably decreased earlier and more rapidly than beliefs in the first and third. The contemporary discussion is therefore largely centered on these two.

If my immediate certainty about whether I agree with a moral norm declines, I will be more dependent on external grounds for such a certainty— e.g., the belief that the norm has been set up by a God. Similarly, I will depend more on critics of the arts if I feel little immediate certainty about beauty and ugliness. Those who are not sure what they feel about a radio symphony rely on the intermission commentator to tell them how good it is. Generally, as immediate certainty about values declines, it becomes crucial to know the brand and the endorsers. This is part of the current trend toward externalization.

Thus moral norms are threatened from two sides. While immediate certainty about them is declining, beliefs about their maker are also weakening. The result may be complete uncertainty:

> It is very embarrassing that God does not exist, for with Him the possibility disappears of finding values in a Heaven of Ideas . . . Dostoievski wrote: 'If God did not exist everything would be permissible.' This is a starting point of existentialism.[7]

In Sartre's play *The Flies*, the hero says: "Freedom crashed down on me. There was nothing left in heaven, no Right or Wrong."[8]

Even if I still believe in the existence of extra-natural creators of norms, my doubts may be displaced to my relation with them. Sartre takes up Kierkegaard's discussion of "Abraham's anxiety": When an angel orders the patriarch to sacrifice his son, how can he be sure that it really was an angel, that the message was intended for him, that it really said what he thought it said?

Camus says: "Man-aware-of-absurdity could accept only one ethic, namely one which would not be separated from God, one which would be dictated." However, looking at the world, he exclaims: "The earth! in this vast temple deserted by the Gods, all my idols have feet of clay."[9]

In describing the hero of Camus' *The Stranger,* Sartre adds to Dostoievski's point:

> Man-aware-of-absurdity experiences the divine irresponsibility of one condemned to death. Everything is permitted as God does not exist and as one dies.[10]

Presumably the forecast of one's death as annihilation has been steadily gaining in frequency and emotional certainty during the past decades. This is one of the least observed and most influential events in recent cultural history. It evokes a variety of reactions to be discussed below. I shall deal at this point only with the impact of the disappearance of after-life ethics.

Against the horizon of my impending annihilation all ethical alternatives may appear as equivalent since they lead to the same terminal state. Thus the hero of *The Stranger,* awaiting execution, feels:

> Nothing, nothing, had the least importance, and I knew quite well why. . . . From the dark horizon of my future a sort of slow, persistent breeze had been blowing

towards me, all my life long. . . . And on its way that breeze had leveled out all the ideas that people tried to foist on me. . . . What difference could . . . (it) make . . . the way a man decides to live, the fate he chooses, since one and the same fate was bound to 'choose' not only me but thousands of millions of . . . people. . . . All alike will be condemned to die one day. . . . And what difference could it make if . . . he [the prison chaplain instead of the hero] were executed since it all came to the same thing in the end.11

However, this twentieth century indifferentism is not nineteenth century satanism:

Awareness of absurdity . . . does not recommend crime; that would be childish. . . . If all experiences are indifferent, conforming to one's duty is as legitimate as anything else. One can be virtuous by caprice.12

Closely related to this experience of universal equivalence is the feeling of pointlessness of a life rushing towards annihilation—including the pointlessness of ethics. Sartre describes Camus' feeling of absurdity this way: "Absurdity . . . is . . . the discrepancy . . . between man's surge towards eternity and the finite character of his existence. . . ."13 Camus himself speaks of "the profound uselessness . . . of an individual life." "In the deadly light of this destiny [death] uselessness appears. No ethic and no effort are a priori justifiable in view of the bloody mathematics of our condition."14

Similarly the hero of Sartre's Le mur, a Spanish anarchist awaiting execution feels this:

I had the impression that my whole life was before me and I thought: It's a darned lie. It wasn't worth anything as it's finished now. I asked myself how I had been able to go for walks, to have fun with girls. If I had known that I was to die like this I wouldn't have moved my little finger.

He observes the Franco officers who are his jailers:

These two dressed-up fellows with their whips and riding boots were after all human beings who would die. A bit later than I but not much. And they were busy looking for names in their files, running after other people to imprison or liquidate them. They had opinions on the future of Spain and other subjects. Their little doings appeared to me shocking and burlesque—they seemed mad.15

The life of others appears particularly pointless as the impact of death is reenforced by lack of empathy. Thus Camus tells us:

human beings secrete . . . inhumanness. In certain lucid moments one perceives how their mechanical gestures, their meaningless pantomimes render their entire surroundings silly. A man is phoning behind a glass door. I don't hear him. I see the incomprehensible faces he makes. I am asking myself why he should be alive.16

In this context also belongs Sartre's intense aversion to those who "try to show that their existence is necessary whereas it is actually utterly contingent." He calls them *les salauds*.[17]

III. DEATH-ORIENTED ETHICS AS A RESPONSE TO THE DECLINE OF MORAL CERTAINTY AND RELIGIOUS BELIEF

Moral certainty and religious belief served as protections against anxiety and depression associated with thoughts of death. Thus the ideological muteness of contemporary atheism may be related to the fact that it is largely a *depressed* abandonment of the wish to believe. "The existentialist . . . thinks it is very embarrassing that God does not exist. . . . Man is condemned to be free." [18] Camus reflects,

> To look for what is true is not to look for what is desirable. If it were necessary to accept illusions in order to avoid [Kierkegaard's question] "What would life be [if the void were hiding beneath things]. . .?" the man-aware-of-absurdity prefers . . . Kierkegaard's answer: "Despair."[19]

For Camus has become unable to accept Dostoievsky's fallacy: "If belief in immortality is so necessary to man" as a defense against tendencies towards suicide "then human immortality doubtlessly exists."[20]

The depressed feeling-tone of Camus' reluctant atheism is also expressed in his identification with Ivan Karamasov, whose exclamation "Everything is permitted!" he describes as

> not a cry of joyous delivrance, it is a pained statement. A God who would make life meaningful is much more attractive than the impunity of wrongdoing. . . . But there is no choice. Here bitterness begins. . . .[21]

In earlier periods atheism had often *proudly* disposed of God as not only impossible but undesirable. The depressive feeling-tone of contemporary atheism is in its turn reenforced by its muteness. It lacks the relief which may come with the verbalization of a distressing feeling, particularly if the words dramatize the predicament of the sufferer.[22]

As long as death was not predominantly felt as annihilation, it was speakable. It was then often one of the major themes of serious discourse. When in the later nineteenth and twentieth century the belief in death as annihilation increased, two extreme reactions developed. On the one hand there was the tendency to eliminate death from consciousness, on the other hand a tendency to be overwhelmed by the awareness of death.

The elimination of death from consciousness by repressive and phobic devices has been accomplished with varying degrees of success. [23] It has often been noted that America has gone particularly far in this respect—cf. the U.S. morticians' industry or the invulnerability of the Hollywood thriller hero who maintains his body intact through repeated fierce beatings and in the midst of a mounting pile of corpses.

It was not only the awareness of death which tended to decline, but also the variety of feelings about it.

> The poverty of our thoughts on death amazes me again and again. In other subjects we are rather inclined to complicate matters.[24]

A major contemporary alternative to repressive and phobic reactions toward death is concentration on it as "the only reality."[25]

I may attempt to transform distress about death into elation. Various contemporary philosophers console their audiences—whether with conscious intent or not—that if there were no death it would have to be invented. Heidegger has often been understood to say that the limitation of time at my disposal may confer intensity upon every moment. Death sets the pervasive deadline which makes my life during this instant urgent and hence enjoyable. Eternal life may then appear dull.[26]

Another defense against death-anxiety is to force oneself to face death. One inoculates oneself and one's self-esteem is heightened because of the feat one performs. This is a major attitude of Camus.[27]

Camus presents man-aware-of-absurdity as the new type of human being who has shed all previously indispensable illusions.

> In Italian museums there are little painted screens which the priest held in front of the faces of those about to be executed in order to prevent them from seeing the scaffold. The [metaphysical] leap . . . , the surrender to the illusions of everyday life . . . , all these screens conceal absurdity.

Death as something else than annihilation was "the great cry of hope which has been heard in so many centuries and animated so many hearts, except that of the man-aware-of-absurdity."[28]

"Death" and "absurdity" tend to become equivalent terms for Camus. In *The Brothers Karamasov*

> it is not the acceptance of Christianity which contradicts the awareness of absurdity, but the annunciation of an after-life. One can be a Christian and aware of absurdity. There are Christians who do not believe in an after-life.

Sartre presents his views as implications of the statement that God does not exist. Camus offers his as implications of the statement that death is annihilation "I know a . . . true statement . . . which says that man is mortal. Very few have drawn all its consequences."[29]

Camus prefers a counterrepressive and counterphobic reaction to the realization of one's death. He contrasts the nineteenth century "search for oblivion" with his "obstinate testimony to a life without consolation,"[30] his aspiration for the "words which would express precisely—in a mood compounded of terror and silence—the conscious certainty of death without any hope." Thus lucidity about death should dominate life.

> Man-aware-of-absurdity turns his mind entirely towards death. . . . He feels detached from everything except his passionate concern. . . . To live a destiny . . . means to accept it fully. Hence we cannot live our destiny, which we know to be absurd, without doing everything to keep this absurdity constantly in front of us. . . . To be alive is to make our absurdity come alive; that is, first of all, to look at it.[31]

The differences between human beings and the changes through time which matter for Camus concern the degree of man's lucid orientation towards his own death. As to secular trends, "the only progress of civilization . . . is to create conscious deaths."[32] As to Camus' place of origin, the nature of Algiers

> requires an act of lucidity, corresponding to the act of faith which people make. . . . This people (of Algiers) throws itself entirely into the present. It lives without myths and consolations. It has staked everything on this earth, hence it is defenceless against death.[33]

As to the typical development of a life, Camus believes in two peaks of death anxiety:

> That is youth, that hard-to-face encounter with death, that physical fear of the animal which loves the sun. . . . At the end of their life human beings worthy of that name (sic) return to this face to face encounter with death."[33]

However, this counterphobic reaction does not suffice for Camus. He adds to it a turning of destructive tendencies against the event to which his distress is attached, namely death. He prefers that the unmitigated contemplation of death be accompanied by a mood of a "revolt." Man ought to be replete with

> the certainty of a crushing destiny minus the resignation one would expect. . . . The point is to die unreconciled. . . . The only truth of man-aware-of-absurdity is defiance.[34]

This revolt expresses itself in the abuse of death. "The ultimate end . . . is despicable." Death is "a horrible and dirty affair."[35]

> The cemeteries covering Europe . . . are hideous. We make beautiful only what we
> love, and death repels and fatigues us. . . . It is a sign of Western courage to have
> made the places where death is supposedly honored so ugly. . . . Death is the
> supreme abuse.[36]

Camus attributes a decisive value to this attitude, and here he may express
covertly fantasies of omnipotence-by-protest.

> This revolt gives life its worth. If extended over the whole length of a life, it
> restores greatness to this life. . . . The spectacle of human pride is incom-
> parable. . . . Tenacious revolt against this condition is man's only dignity. . . . Any
> destiny can be overcome by contempt for it.[37]

This is achieved by a minimum of overt behavior. Silence is the expression
of contempt (and contained panic) towards death which Camus favors. He
takes the motto for *Noces* from Stendhal's *La duchesse de Palliano:*

> The executioner strangled Cardinal Cerafa with a silk cord which broke. It was
> necessary to begin all over again. The Cardinal looked at the executioner and did
> not deign to say a word.

Camus' revolt against death may be a last residue of a traditional world
view which he otherwise renounces. It probably involves, unconsciously,
anthropomorphic or even theistic beliefs. It may express accusations against
parent figures for putting us into an intolerable position of helplessness. You
can do with me as you please, but don't deceive yourself: I despise your
methods and only give in to overwhelming force.

IV. MORAL FEELINGS AND DETERMINISM

A third major change related to the decline of ethics is the growing feeling
that human behavior is determined. The nineteenth century produced numerous general deterministic formulae which were popular among the high-
brow. But it probably largely maintained on the level of feeling a sense of the
"freedom" of human behavior. Philosophic determinism is now less prevalent.
However, the sense of freedom is presumably weakening—under the impact,
among other things, of anti-individualistic trends in social structure and of
contemporary psychology. For the first time we are acquiring some skill in
predicting scientifically how a certain person is likely to feel and act under
certain conditions. Of course knowledge of this kind is still in its beginnings.
But its existence—as distinct from mere announcements of a deterministic
psychology yet to be constructed—has made it much more convincing that
human events may be as "determined" (or undetermined) as non-human
events.

To my mind "determinism" in the science of human affairs does not logically preclude "absolute" moral norms. But the psychological impact of the awareness that this or that human act is "determined" has probably been to weaken ethical feelings. One reason for this is, of course, that traditional ethics affirmed man's "freedom." Conversely the "natural" events which we are accustomed to treat as "determined" are also the ones to which we do not apply ethical norms. The animal world is called to mind. The latter part of the nineteenth century was full of affirmations that human and non-human animals are essentially alike. But the prevailing feeling-tone was still that there was an abyss between them. This was probably so not only in the rear-guard actions in which the essential identity between man and animal was anxiously denied, but also in the avant-garde actions in which it was, with a now dated elation, affirmed. In the middle twentieth century formal discussions on these points are rare. The previous avant-garde view has become commonplace not only intellectually but also emotionally. One of the themes of current literature is the transformation of a man into a disgusting animal. In Franz Kafka's *Metamorphosis* a man awakens one morning as a large bug. Similar themes have been used by David Garnett, Maurice Sandoz, Sartre, and others. It is emotionally no longer entirely self-evident why stockyards and extermination camps should be utterly incomparable.

The same holds true for human artefacts. The tendency is fostered to at least want to react to a misbehaving person as we spontaneously do to a misbehaving car.

At the same time various factors make for an opposite, indeterministic orientation. Predictability in human affairs has increased mainly in the small world of one or a few intensively studied individuals. On the other hand, large-scale events seem much more unpredictable than a generation ago. The discontinuity of the public surface of happenings has become greater. The vast prognostic schemes of the late nineteenth and early twentieth century, such as Marxism, seem less adequate now.

My dismay in thinking of my own life as entirely determined may be enhanced if I feel stuck in personal or professional ruts which make me predictable and which are as unsatisfactory as they seem unavoidable. I will then also resent it if any aspect of my life is treated as a "mere" instance subsumed under a general law. This predicament is currently expressed in the violent antideterminism of some "existentialists." According to Sartre the existentialist who describes a "coward" in a novel "says that this coward is responsible for his cowardice. . . . The coward whom we show is guilty of his cowardice. . . . It is possible for the coward to cease being cowardly." For "there is no human nature"—which presumably means that there are no ascertainable laws of feeling and behavior. Everything is possible at every moment. Sartre does not indicate how this affirmation is compatible with contemporary psychology.[38]

V. ADAPTATIONS TO MORAL DECLINE

I shall now discuss some less extreme aspects of moral disintegration, and defenses against it. *[Ironically, our capacity to feel indignation about overt and large-scale destructiveness has decreased at a time when our sensitivity to covert destructive tendencies in the small world of personal relations has increased.]* These trends concern, first, moral feelings; second, formal characteristics of moral judgments; third, their context.

I spoke above of the loss of the sense of moral experience. Short of this there may be a decline in moral revulsion at events which violate my norms, and a decline in moral indignation against those who have committed these violations. *[Revulsion at immoral acts and indignation against immoral persons are psychologically related. But their intellectual contents are rather divergent. Moral indignation against wrong-doers attributes to them a "freedom" of choice which science disputes. Moral revulsion at wrong acts does not carry such an implication.]* In many cases even the person or group that has suffered at the hands of others is incapable of reacting with much moral feeling. There is probably also a decline in moral concern about this decline in moral concern: "Our growing insensitiveness has escaped our own attention."[39]

A related trend is this: The violator of an ethical norm tends to feel his act as less alien to his central self. This is shown, among other things, by changes in the style of neuroses. A relevant distinction is that between neurotic symptoms (such as hysterical conversions, compulsions and obsessions, anxiety states and phobias), which the person experiences as intruding foreign bodies, and non-symptomatic neurotic acts (such as expressions of "undesirable" character traits), which the person feels to belong to the core of his self. The relative frequency of non-symptomatic neurotic acts, as against symptomatic ones, has been and probably still is increasing.

Conversely, conscience reactions are increasingly felt as alien to the core of the self. It happens more frequently that I conform to a moral norm not so much because I fully accept it—I may regard it as absurd—but rather because I predict that I will hate myself in the morning if I violate this norm. I may regretfully view such guilt-like discomfort as a fact to be reckoned with—just as I may accept my propensity to develop a certain absurd obsession and try to know and avoid the conditions under which it occurs. The conscience becomes a symptom. *[This is fostered by the tendency of "virtue" to decline more rapidly in emotional convincingness than "vice." An increasing number of persons can achieve little more than absence of conscious guilt. Regarding oneself as "good," or being thus regarded, may become slightly shameful.]* Nineteenth century theories of human behavior, now obsolete, developed elaborate pleasure-pain calculations. The contemporary behavior pattern which I just described calls them to mind again.

Also, I may act morally in a near-compulsive way: I find myself acting morally without knowing why. Thus the Spanish anarchist who is the hero of Sartre's *Le Mur* refuses to purchase his life by telling the whereabouts of a comrade (though the indication which he gives to mislead his jailers turns out to be correct):

> I should have liked to understand the reason for my behavior. I preferred to die rather than to betray Gris. Why? I didn't love Ramon Gris anymore. My friendship for him had died together with my wish to live. Of course, I still respected him. . . . But it was not for that reason that I chose to die in his place. His life wasn't worth more than mine. No life was worth anything. They were going to put a man against the wall and shoot at him until he died. It did not make any difference whether it was Gris or somebody else. I knew that he was more useful to Spain than I, but I didn't care a damn for Spain or anarchism. Nothing mattered anymore. And nevertheless, there I was, I could save my skin by betraying Gris and I refused to do it. I thought that was rather funny. What obstinacy![40]

In *Lettres a un ami allemand,* first illegally published during the war, Camus points out that many Frenchmen felt impelled almost automatically to resist the Nazis, but that they also felt the lack of a convincing set of moral norms to support this reaction.

Thus the writers discussed here deal with people who behave well, in traditional terms, without feeling too good about it (cf. the instances just mentioned); or who behave badly without feeling badly about it (cf. the hero of *The Stranger*); or who behave badly and feel badly about it (cf. the male figure in Sartre's *In Camera*). What is lacking is behaving well and feeling good about it.

Another adaptation to the decline of moral certainty is the tendency to set up moral norms not for all men and all times, but—in the extreme case—for myself alone, or even for a unique situation in my unique life. This is a major expression of the trend towards privatization, the counterpart of the increasing involvement of the individual in large organizations. It is probably also an attempt to counteract the decline of moral certainty. Traditional moral norms were formulated as universal statements, that is, as statements applying to an indefinite number of actions at any time, in any place. (Traditional moral norms had this much in common with scientific laws.) Conscious as I am or should be of my future as a corpse, moral standards can scarcely be timeless: "What would I do with a truth which does not rot?" asks Camus; "It wouldn't fit me."[41] A moral norm which claims validity only for a limited set of familiar persons and events may at present often be able to arouse more conviction. The different variants of "existentialism" are all in favor of non-universal norms.

In relation with this there is a tendency to feel that my moral norms are valid only for me, whether they are universal or not. Thus there is an indefinite number of equally valid moral perspectives on the world, each corresponding to a unique standpoint, i.e., to a certain life situation of a certain individual. This view applies to morality an attitude which has long been current in aesthetics (there is no disputing about taste). Here again there is probably an attempt to counteract moral uncertainty. If my choice is either to affirm the absolute validity of my norms as against any others or to deny validity to them altogether, I may feel forced to do the latter. The pluralism which I just mentioned may be an emotionally tenable middle position.

Sartre shows in a fashion characteristic for this age the conflict between the traditional attribution of validity to one moral system and the newer desire for an indefinite number of equally valid moral systems. He starts his argument with the second position: "Every time a man chooses to commit himself in all sincerity and in all lucidity, whatever the project may be, it is impossible to prefer another one to it." [42] But then it suddenly appears that "sincerity" and "lucidity" had been implicitly defined in such a fashion that only one "commitment" is compatible with them: that of maximizing my "freedom" and that of others. However, "freedom" is in its turn so defined that almost any more specific moral system is compatible with it, provided it is antideterministic and felt as created by myself.

For in connection with the point just discussed there is the tendency to regard myself as creating my moral norms (and as continually recreating them if I hold them through time), rather than merely discovering them. Sartre insistently denies the contention of *l'esprit serieux* that moral norms are "given," "a priori," outside of myself.

> There are no signs in the world. . . . Neither behind us nor in front of us are there any justifications. . . . No a priori value determines my choice. . . . Man chooses without basing himself on pre-established values. . . . Life has no a priori meaning. Before you live, life is a nothing. . . .

Conversely, "it is up to you to give life a meaning . . . namely value. . . . There is no other legislator than man himself."[43]

This view, too, is in part a defense against the threatening collapse of moral feelings. First, it assimilates moral reactions to aesthetic reactions. Aesthetic reactions had seemed less sure than moral ones to previous generations, but may now appear more certain. The earlier emancipation of aesthetics from pre-established rules—formerly felt as a source of aesthetic uncertainty—becomes a model for morals:

> Moral choice must be compared with the construction of a work of art. . . . Has anybody ever reproached a painter for not having been guided by a priori rules? (sic) Has anybody ever told him which picture to paint? (sic). . . . It is generally understood that aesthetic values are not a priori, but appear after creation has been completed. . . . Art and morality have creation and invention in common. We cannot decide a priori what to do.[44]

Second, this view is designed to maintain morality despite the disappearance of God. The premise is that "man is forsaken, as he finds nothing within or outside him to cling to.... We are alone.... Man is without any support and without any aid." More specifically, there is unfortunately no God who could create a priori moral norms. "There can be no a priori good as there is no infinite and perfect consciousness to think it.... There are only human beings." Thus there are only two possibilities: either there are no moral norms, or man creates them. Sartre in his restitution attempt takes the second option as a lesser evil.

> One objection to existentialism runs: ... values are not serious as you choose them. To this I answer, I am very sorry that this is so. But if I have eliminated God the Father, I need somebody to invent values. Let us face the facts.[45]

The eighteenth century motto "if God did not exist, we would have to invent him," is thus changed into this formula: as God does not exist, we have to invent his creations.

The plausibility of this attitude is enhanced by man's rising omnipotence feelings in relation to nature and his own body and mind. We take it for granted that we can, now or in some near future, make rain, visit the moon, produce homunculi in the shape of ever better thinking machines, prolong life, "beautify" bodies, and "adjust" minds. We receive advances along these lines with a minimum of surprise and elation. It is rather the delay of an advance, as in the case of cancer therapy, which occasions raised eyebrows. *[At the same time there is less of a feeling that such discoveries or inventions will produce a heaven on earth. This earlier forecast is too massively contradicted by the various hells on earth of the middle twentieth century— Auschwitz, Hiroshima, and places in between. Our optimism about our skills tends to become unlimited. So does our pessimism about the ways in which these skills will be utilized by them—those in control in relation to whom everybody else feels increasingly impotent.]*

Another defense against the decline of moral feelings is the tendency to reduce the content of moral norms to a minimum in the hope of reaching a core of certainty. The moral norms which are then put forward appear on closer examination to be almost empty, i.e., compatible with almost any behavior. I mentioned Sartre's norm of "freedom" as an instance of this. Another instance is Camus' advocacy of the maximization of experience, in connection with his preferences for lucidity about death and revolt against death.

> The point is not to live best but to live most.... On the one hand awareness of absurdity implies that all experiences are equivalent. On the other hand, it asks for the maximization of the number of experiences.... Premature death ... is the only obstacle.... Thus man-aware-of-absurdity would prefer forty years of

consciousness and sixty (sic) years of lucidity to any depth of experience, any emotion, any passion, any sacrifice.

In the face of death he acts according to Nietzsche's point that it is not eternal life which matters but eternal liveliness.[46] He tries to snatch a few experiences in the face of death:

Awareness of absurdity is, at the end of the last thought of the man about to be executed that shoe-string . . . which he sees at a distance of a few feet on the edge of his dizzy fall.[47]

Camus does not point out in detail how a Total Life Experience Index could be constructed which would enable us to assign a numerical value to any given life, or at least to decide which of any two lives ranks higher than the other. His only suggestion is to give weight to the diversity of experiences. (The relation of this point, as well as of the maximization point itself, to the weakening of moral feelings is clear. It is no more evident that one kind of life is morally superior to another. Hence the only affirmation which remains plausible is that the more you get of various kinds of life, the better.) Thus "Don Juan realizes an ethic of quantity." Similarly actors "act man in the diverse ways in which he can exist and does exist," which brings them into conflict with the Catholic Church: "There can be no compromise between 'everywhere' and 'always'." Like travelers—another type of life maximizers—actors "exhaust any given experience and ceaselessly search the earth for more."[48] The traveling actor with a girl in every town would thus seem to be the caricatural version of the ideal proposed here.

The life maximization norm excludes suicide but little else. *[The initial question of* Le mythe de Sisyphe *is: Do I have to kill myself right now if I know that I will be annihilated sooner or later? It is this context that gives a contemporary slant to Camus' nineteenth century revolt against the traditional values of the French church and bourgeoisie. He thus presents a combination of older and very new ideas that is characteristic of much in France today.]* It seems compatible with any kind of destructive behavior short of killing. In his gallery of life diversifiers Camus does not include the concentration camp commandant who "unceasingly searches" his imagination and that of his assistants for new nuances of destructiveness. Nor does he include the type of collaborationist who—concurring with Camus' preference for life against death—feels that it is better to be a living slave than a dead free man and who is willing to purchase life at any price of abjectness. It is indeed striking that the types of life maximizers whom Camus does mention are relatively harmless according to traditional moral standards. But, as I have just tried to show, they need not be. Thus Camus' master norm is rather empty of content.

It should be noted that Camus believes mistakenly that his *preference* statement in favor of "living most" as against "living best" is a fact statement. (People who were highly certain about their preference statements in the past were often under the illusion that they were fact statements. Usually people were not aware of, or not interested in, the distinction between these two classes of statements.) Thus he says:

> I don't have to ask myself whether it is vulgar or disgusting, elegant or regrettable to want to live most rather than best. Once and for all value judgments are eliminated in favor of fact statements. . . . Where lucidity rules a hierarchy of values becomes unnecessary.[49]

Nevertheless it is still a moral norm. In other cases the core of certainty, when finally reached, may not even be *moral*. It may be simply the *factual* denial of a pervasive sense of unreality. The "neurotic" doubt about preferences then recedes as the "psychotic" uncertainty about facts becomes dominant. Thus the hero of Camus' *The Stranger* attains just before his execution a state of exaltation in contemplating the Facts of Life and Death:

> It might look as if my hands were empty. Actually, I was sure of myself, sure about everything, far surer than he [the prison chaplain], sure of my present life and the death that was coming. That, no doubt, was all I had; but at least that certainty was something I could get my teeth into—just as it had got its teeth into me.[50]

Similarly Heidegger's first

> principle . . . is . . . the naked 'factness,' that is what remains of life when . . . its entire traditional content has been eliminated. The term which expresses the notion of factness in *Sein und Zeit* is 'existence'. *[Some awareness of the relative emptiness of the moral systems here discussed expresses itself in the frequent use of "bareness" and "nakedness" terms. According to Hermann Rauschning, SS intellectuals in the thirties were impressed by an apocryphal remark of Marshall Tukhatshevski: "The world must become naked again."]* This refers not to what a being is . . . but to the very fact that a being *is*. . . . This fundamental point of existentialism makes a supreme problem . . . out of something which appears obvious. This in its turn implies . . . that all the traditional contents of life have lost their substance.

Hence the peculiar nature of Heidegger's influence at the University of Freiburg in the Weimar period:

> The principal point of his impact on his disciples was not their expectation of a new system, but, on the contrary, the indeterminacy of the content of his philosophy and . . . his concentration on 'the only thing which is necessary' . . . sheer decidedness, without an indication of its objectives. One student invented this witticism: I am decided, only I don't know about what.[51]

The witticism just quoted recalls that the reaction to an almost empty norm is apt to be ambivalent. One of the factors fostering current disaffection from traditional moral systems is, in fact, the growing awareness that they do not enable us to decide many conflicts which we encounter. Sartre presents at length the predicament of a man confronted with mutually exclusive obligations towards his mother and his nation. *[Sartre argues incorrectly in an all-or-none fashion. He affirms that it is not feasible to construct a set of general norms which would decide every case which will come up—a point known from Anglo-American jurisprudence and the* Freirechtschule. *He infers from this that a set of general norms can decide nothing. This he wants to prove for the purpose of his contention that man can not avoid creating his own norms.]* He gives this old story a somewhat new twist by stressing that none of the traditional moral systems has anything to say about what he should do.[52]

Sartre probably expresses here a frequent contemporary attitude. Reading Kant today one is apt to feel that certain specific norms (e.g., in favor of keeping promises) are not derivable from the categorical imperative. Kant argued that a society in which immoral behavior, in traditional terms, is universal, would provoke panic in everyone and expose everyone to heavy losses. We have in the meantime become increasingly inured to a dog-eat-dog situation. Many trust their skill in inventing techniques of survival. Some are confident they will be top dogs.

There is probably a mounting wish for a full rather than an empty set of moral norms. But this wish comes up against the difficulties of producing certainty feelings about specific norms. Thus it is common to almost all variants of "existentialism" to use words like "substantive," "concrete," "particular," "specific" as positive terms in ethical theory, and "formal," "abstract," "universal," "general" as negative ones. But, as I have tried to show, usually existentialists do not declare norms which possess those characteristics they regard as desirable.

If the content of norms obstinately remains dubious, there will be inducement to revive the *credo quia absurdum* defense against ethical collapse. One stresses the act of accepting a norm rather than the norm itself. This may be done in a number of ways. The act of acceptance may be felt as a moment of ecstasy when barriers against belief suddenly break down (cf. Kierkegaard). The lingering feeling that the norm, though accepted, remains unconvincing ("absurd") may appear as the indispensable sign of its validity. What is easy to believe can't be right.

Another attempt to counteract the threatening collapse of ethical feelings is to insist that every moment counts. In Sartre's *In Camera,* whose scene is laid in hell (a drawing room in Second Empire style), a man looks back over his life and tried to avoid believing in his cowardice: "I died too soon ... I wasn't allowed time ... to do my deeds." But another character answers:

"One always dies too soon—or too late. And yet one's whole life is complete at that moment, with a line drawn neatly under it, ready for the summing up."[53]

This attitude of living morally as if this moment were my last is related to various current trends of feeling. First, the greater awareness of death as annihilation tends to minimize the feeling of distance between this moment and the last moment of my life. Second, it becomes more plausible that violence will cut my life short. When this forecast is not faced directly it may be evaded by "living in the moment." Third, beliefs in "Progress" are yet more weakened and replaced by feelings of the unpredictability of everything, if not by pessimism. It becomes increasingly difficult to look at one's life as an ingredient to be thrown into a vast and time-consuming enterprise.

At present the personal planning of most people does not include the probability that the rest of our lives will be influenced—quite short of war—by a state of Permanent Atomic (and Virus, etc.) Alert. Presumably the minority that faces this fairly realistic forecast contains a high percentage of people with rather severe neurotic trends. Most people would, of course, find it difficult to take account of this forecast in their behavior even if they kept it in mind. The probability of future acute international crises is of course now widely taken for granted intellectually, but the conscious emotional reactions to this forecast are rather low. In contrast, in the thirties, war appeared intellectually more avoidable, but the forecast of its imminent possibility evoked more intense emotional reactions. Consider, for example, Toynbee's overemphatic description of an atmosphere in the autumn of 1937:

> We live in daily dread of catastrophe. . . . It would hardly be an exaggeration to say that the shadow of this fear [of war] that now lies athwart our future is hypnotizing (sic) us into a spiritual paralysis that is beginning to affect us even in the trivial avocations of our daily life.[54]

Similarly, Decline-of-the-West theories are probably less in vogue in the forties than they were in the twenties, though so much of intervening history can be taken as a confirmation of such views. To the extent to which they are in vogue, they may take a milder form: Spengler did not give us a chance, Toynbee does—although on extra-empirical grounds.

A similar point can be made for the development of Brave New World forecasts. Blueprints for totalitarian transformations are now issued in limited editions or as "classified" documents by practicing administrators, rather than as semi-bestsellers by unconventional novelists. Similarly predictions of total destruction are now expressed in bare and unemotional abstractions by physicists rather than in dramatic visions by novelists.[55]

It is in this context that we may view Sartre's recommendation of "action-with-despair."

I must commit myself . . . and act according to the old formula: hope is not
necessary for activity. . . . I shall be without illusions and . . . do what I can. For
example, when I ask myself whether there will be a general nationalization [of
economic activities], the answer is that I don't know anything about that. I only
know that I'll do everything I can to make this happen. Outside of this I can't rely
on anything. 56

An attitude of this kind admits of two variants. First, I may act without
any regard for the predictability of the outcome or for the success of the
collective operation in which I participate. Such an attitude may accompany
a pervasive sense of my annihilation through death and of the annihilation of
life on earth by virtue of the second law of thermodynamics. Hence Camus'
counsel "to create without considering any tomorrow." A creator ought to be
able "to see his work destroyed a day after its completion and be aware of
the fact . . . that building for centuries to come isn't any different." Still
more, "as I know that no cause is victorious [as everything dies], I like lost
causes." 57

Another possibility is this: I may be willing to act in a collective enterprise
only if at least some short-run predictions can be made and if they are not
too unfavorable. *[I shall not discuss here feelings that my acts will not make
any difference in the outcome of the collective undertaking.]* In the first case
I am willing to act even in utter darkness or hopelessness—or I even regard
such conditions as inevitable. In the second case I require at least a flashlight
lighting up some of my immediate surroundings and revealing not too
unfavorable terrain.

The late nineteenth and early twentieth century political activists—e.g.,
many Marxists—felt that they acted in full daylight and saw wide and
agreeable prospects. They relied on themselves (implicitly) and on the Historical Process (explicitly). Sartre, befitting the temper of the age, with-
draws the second support. But befitting the temper of early post-libera-
tion France, he substitutes for this loss the reliance on the present activities of my organization:

I will rely on my comrades-in-arms to the extent to which they are involved
together with me . . . in a party or group which I can more or less control, i.e.,
whose active member I am and whose activities I am always acquainted with. . . .
But I can't rely on human beings I don't know. I must limit myself to what I see.
I can't be sure that future comrades-in-arms will take up my effort after my
death. 58

This view is weakened by the powerful trends which make the individual
feel increasingly helpless and in the dark in relation to the organizations he
belongs to. 59 I am less apt to feel that "I can more or less control" my
organizations; that "I am always acquainted" with their activities; that I
"see" these organizations. It is not only the future which appears invisible.
Kafka's castle, existing in the present, is equally invisible.

Hence, a tendency towards extreme positions. To state this exaggeratingly: either I accept participation in collective action in utter darkness. Or I privatize myself. That is, I rely only on myself and, at the most, a few others whose reactions I can calculate by familiarity or enforce; and I only go in for brief undertakings. An instance of this is the predominant hero type of the Hollywood melodrama in the forties. He moves about a strange city at night, aware of unknown enemies, suspecting the motives of those who seem friendly, uncertain whether any move will bring him nearer to his goal or lead to beatings and death. His more delicate counterpart is the student of Sartre who had to choose between making his mother unhappy and remaining passive in the second world war:

> He was aware of the fact . . . that his relationship to his mother had an assured effect. He helped her to keep alive. Any attempt to leave (France) and to fight (in the Free French Forces) was an ambiguous act which could well get lost in the sands . . . , could well be interrupted before completion.[60]

Feelings of this kind currently lead to a revaluation of small-scale activities by people who previously felt the need to relate themselves as directly as possible to the Historical Process. A preoccupation with the next phase of World Capitalism may give way to concern for this year's building projects of the local school board.[61]

I discussed before the attitude of getting a favorable moral score right now. Concentration on this moment may of course also take the hedonistic form of "carpe diem." This is an implication of Camus' life maximization norm which I discussed above. "The present moment and the succession of present moments before a ceaselessly conscious consciousness—that is the ideal of man-aware-of-absurdity." "I obstinately refuse any 'later on', as I do not want to renounce the richness of the present moment." Don Juan leads "a life oriented on joys without any tomorrows." And actors

> draw the best conclusion from the truth that everything dies. . . . A writer preserves some hope of future repute even if he is not appreciated. The dead actor leaves us nothing of his essential qualities. *[It is interesting that contemporary methods of permanent auditory and visual recording have not entered the world image of this French writer who is in such close rapport with the Zeitgeist in non-technological respects.]* [62]

The hero of Camus' *The Stranger* awaiting execution, attempts to get rid of the intruding prison chaplain: "I'd very little time left and I wasn't going to waste it on God."[63] In the final scene of the pre-war French film *Port aux brumes* the hero lies fatally wounded on the street as his girl friend runs toward him. He indicates impatiently that she should kiss him quickly: he has so little time left to enjoy her kiss. In the post-war French film *Jericho,* hostages in occupied France spend the night in a church awaiting their execution at dawn. The collaborationist among them mounts the pulpit and delivers a sermon: Let us try to purchase life at any price. If we die, a monument in our honor will in due time be unveiled one sunny afternoon on the main square of the town. Who will drink the beer, flirt with the girls, walk in the sun that afternoon? Not we. We will have ceased to be. What will it matter to us?

Related to the point that every moment counts morally is the affirmation that only completed overt actions are morally relevant, not subjective preparations for them. I mentioned before that in Sartre's *In Camera* a man in hell tried to avoid believing in his cowardice. He had been a Brazilian pacifist for many years. When war came he attempted to flee the country to evade conscription, was caught and executed after collapsing in front of the firing squad. In hell he asks:

Can one possibly be a coward when one has deliberately courted danger at every turn? And can one judge a life by a single action?

Another character answers:

Why not? For thirty years you dreamt you were a hero and condoned a thousand petty lapses—because a hero, of course, can do no wrong. . . . Then a day came when you were up against it, the red light of real danger,—and you took the train [sic] to Mexico. It's what one does and nothing else, that shows the stuff one's made of. (Seuls les actes décident de ce qu'on a voulu.) You are—your life, and nothing else.[64]

In general terms:

Only action is real. . . . Man is . . . nothing but his actions taken together, nothing but his life. There is no artistic genius except that which expresses itself in works of art. . . . Outside of this, there is nothing. . . . Mere dreams expectations, hopes make a man a disappointed dream, an abortive hope, a useless expectation. . . . Man is but a series of enterprises.[65]

This emphasis on the exclusive moral relevance of actual accomplishments is probably in part an attempt to compensate for the fragility of moral feelings. In addition, recent developments in psychology have made subjective states increasingly unsuitable for a central place in ethics. First, many attribute a greater "freedom" to overt action than to subjective events. We are often held "responsible" not for our feelings and thoughts but for "acting them out." Second, many tend to infer the seriousness of an intention from the vigor of the action expressing it. The feeling is spreading that any given conscious content may have a number of unconscious meanings. The ensuing action then becomes the only practicable way (short of a psychoanalysis) of deciding what any such conscious intent "really means." In the nineteenth century and in the early twentieth century much emphasis was put on *Gesinnungsethik*. There may now be a swing back to *Erfolgsethik*.

VI. POLITICAL TRENDS AND MORAL TRENDS

A further adaptation to the decline in ethical feelings is the tendency to confine them to an ever smaller area. Spheres which were previously invested with strong ethical feelings are now being more or less divested of them. One instance is politics. Presumably the amount of attention to the moral aspect of political events has been declining. This is related not only to the decline in moral certainty, but also to a number of other rising trends of feeling: the feeling that politics, in and between wars, is "too big" to be viewed morally; that the individual is in any case powerless in this area which is, in addition, increasingly unintelligible; that huge violations of traditional moral norms are by now "fixtures" in politics. During the twentieth century there has been a steady rise in the level of political immorality, in traditional terms, which has been taken for granted. How puny the moral enormities of the first world war appear today!

There are almost no new norms to transform these old-style violations into new-style conformities. For example, political acts increasingly disregard any moral obstacles in the path of what seems to be maximum efficiency. But the doctrine that the end justifies the means does not spread correspondingly. Similarly, there is a growing tendency to do to the political enemy what he (atrociously, we said at the time) did or planned to do to us. But there is no movement towards an explicit "an eye for an eye" doctrine. Totalitarian practices spread more quickly than totalitarian ideas. This lag fosters the tendency to take morals out of politics.

One mechanism is for us (any political group) to exaggerate the extent to which the sufferings of others are the "natural" consequences of past events rather than the results of acts of our own which we experienced as free when we committed them. Western "public opinion" did not argue that it was morally just to inflict such and such sufferings on Germans through the Potsdam agreement. It minimized the impact of the agreement and presented German distress mostly as an inevitable consequence of the second world war. Similarly some progressive educators disguise punishments of their pupils as "functional" consequences of the pupils' misconduct. (You had better stay in from the playground so you can finish the work you didn't do during the work period.)

Another expression of this tendency is the decrease in the intensity with which political ideologies are held. A comparison of the ideological atmospheres in and around the two world wars could illustrate this point. The official ideological documents of the western powers in the first war roused more feeling, held attention longer, and were to a higher extent viewed as yardsticks for behavior than twenty-five years later.

A related trend is to take for granted "jobs" which have somehow become part of one's life routine, i.e., to exempt them from any moral evaluation. *[This is not the same as the pattern aimed at by totalitarianism in which I morally approve all jobs assigned to me through proper channels.]* The development of the figure of the private detective in mystery stories may be a case in point. Agatha Christie's detective, Hercule Poirot, is repeatedly confronted with the request to stop searching for the murderer. Somebody tries to convince him that the removal of the victim was to everybody's advantage. Poirot, representing the older attitude, habitually answers that he disapproves of murder under whatever circumstances. In contrast to this is the typical reaction of the private detective in the 1946 Hollywood movie *Nocturne*. The heroine appeals to him "as a human being" to stop tracking down the murderer of a man who has caused suffering to everyone he knew. The detective remains blank. He answers that it is his job to deliver the murderer. Whether the murderer afterwards gets the chair or a public vote of thanks is, he says, no concern of his. Also related to the tendency to exempt many events from moral consideration is the tendency to avoid the moral evaluation of an action by viewing it entirely as a means to an end. For example, reverence for Scientific Truth—as distinct from the appreciation of the usefulness of scientific truths—has decreased. Camus expresses the view as follows:

> Galileo abjured most easily the important scientific truth he had found as soon as it endangered his life. In a certain sense he was right. This truth wasn't worth the stake. Whether the earth turns around the sun or whether it's the other way around, is profoundly indifferent.[66]

In the past a downward swing in the significance attached to empirical Truth was apt to be accompanied by an upward swing in the status of Superempirical Truth. Now they are both declining. "For Chestove reason is vain but there is something beyond reason. For man-aware-of-absurdity reason is vain and there is nothing beyond reason."[67]

Expediential rather than moral justification is particularly striking when an action is justified by expediency though it could easily be regarded as good in itself. Take the truth value of western propaganda in the two great wars. The degree of truthfulness in the "output" of the second war was well above that of the first war. The "Strategy of Truth" became a rule to which more than lip service was paid. But its main justification was by expediency. It became a standard point in the training of propagandists to affirm that it does not pay to lie. The Truth with a capital T invoked, e.g., in the Dreyfus affair, had become just a device.

Similar attitudes appeared when in 1945-1946 rations in the western zones of occupied Germany were sometimes above a near-starvation level. Official statements repeatedly explained that this was a matter of expediency for the occupants—to avoid epidemics, riots, a "collapse" with its inconvenient consequences for reparations and occupation costs. Moral considerations, whether beneficient or punitive, had become almost unspeakable.

NOTES

1. "The following pages deal with a feeling of absurdity which one finds here and there in this age. They do not state a philosophy of the absurd." Albert Camus, preface to *Le mythe de Sisyphe* (Paris, 1942). Translations from this essay are the author's.

2. "Before 1914 . . . when . . . [politicians] were guilty of hypocrisy . . . , it was the same God whose name they took in vain." T. S. Eliot, preface to *The Dark Side of the Moon* (London, 1946).

3. Cf. Richard von Mises, *Kleines Lehrbuch des Positivismus* (The Hague, 1939).

4. Jean-Paul Sartre, *L'Existentialisme est un humanisme* (Paris, 1946), 48f., 30f; translations from this essay are the author's.

5. Ibid., 35.

6. Ibid., 94, 33f.

7. Ibid., 33-36.

8. Jean-Paul Sartre, *The Flies*, trans. by Stuart Gilbert (London, 1946), 96.

9. Camus, *Le mythe de Sisyphe*, 94; Camus, *Noces* (Paris, 1939), 123 (the final sentence of the essay). Translations are the author's.

10. Jean-Paul Sartre, *L'Explication de l'Etranger* (Paris, 1946), 10 (author's translations).

11. Albert Camus, *The Stranger*, trans. by Stuart Gilbert (New York, 1946), 152.

12. Camus, *Le mythe de Sisyphe*, 94.

13. Sartre, *L'Explication de l'Etranger*, 6.

14. Camus, *Le mythe de Sisyphe*, 158, 30.

15. Jean-Paul Sartre, *Le Mur* (Paris, 1939), 25, (author's translations).

16. Camus, *Le mythe de Sisyphe*, 29.

17. Sartre, *L'Existentialisme*, 84f.

18. Ibid., 33-37.

19. Camus, *Le mythe de Sisyphe*, 61.

20. Ibid., 149.

21. Ibid., 94

22. Nineteenth century atheism, insofar as it was depressed, often had these compensations. Cf. James Thomson's *City of Dreadful Night* (London, 1932).

23. "One can never be adequately amazed about the fact that everybody lives as if nobody 'knew'." Camus, *Le mythe de Sisyphe*, 30.

24. Camus, *Noces*, 44. George Orwell recently commented, "Since the decay of the belief in personal immortality, death has never seemed funny. . . . Hence the disappearance of the facetious epitaph, once a common feature of country churchyards. I should be astonished to see a comic epitaph dated later than 1850." *Tribune*, London (February 14, 1947).

25. Camus, *Le mythe de Sisyphe*, 81.

26. Cf. Paul Kecskemeti and Nathan Leites, *Some Psychological Hypotheses on Nazi Germany* (Washington, D.C., 1945), 7-9.

27. Camus opposes those whom he calls "existential philosophers" for attempting to turn panic into elation: "They deify what crushes them and find reason for hope in what deprives them. . . . The important thing . . . is not to get well, but to be able to live with one's pains. Kierkegaard wants to get well." *Le mythe de Sisyphe,* 51, 58.

28. Ibid., 124, 59.

29. Ibid., 151, 33.

30. Ibid., 130, 84.

31. Camus, *Noces,* 41.

32. Camus, *Le mythe de Sisyphe,* 82, 76.

33. Camus, *Noces,* 44, 55, 77, 42f.

34. Camus *Le mythe de Sisyphe,* 77, 79.

35. Ibid., 106; Camus, *Noces,* 41.

36. Camus, *Le mythe de Sisyphe,* 122.

37. Ibid., 78, 156, 166.

38. Sartre, *L'Existentialisme,* 59-62, 52. The passages quoted refer presumably to characters in various works of Sartre, such as Garcin in *In Camera* and Mathieu in *The Age of Reason.*

39. Victor Gollancz, *Our Threatened Values* (London, 1946), 27.

40. Sartre, *Le mur.*

41. Camus, *Noces,* 120.

42. Sartre, *L'Existentialisme,* 79.

43. Ibid., 47, 37, 74, 89, 93.

44. Ibid., 74-77.

45. Ibid., 36-38, 35f., 89.

46. Camus, *Le mythe de Sisyphe,* 84-88, 113.

47. Ibid., 77f.

48. Ibid., 100f., 109, 113, 109.

49. Ibid., 84-87.

50. Camus, *The Stranger,* 151.

51. Karl Loewith, "Les implications politiques de la philosophie d'existence chez Heidegger," *Les Temps Modernes,* II (November, 1946), 347.

52. Cf. Sartre, *L'Existentialisme,* 77f., 85f.

53. Jean-Paul Sartre, *In Camera,* trans. by Stuart Gilbert (London, 1946), 163.

54. Arnold J. Toynbee, *A Study of History* (Oxford, 1939) VI, 314.

55. Cf. as an example of the new style Edward Teller, "How Dangerous are Atomic Weapons?"

56. Sartre, *L'Existentialisme,* 54.

57. Camus, *Le mythe de Sisyphe,* 154, 118.

58. Sartre, *L'Existentialisme,* 51-53.

59. Cf. Kris and Leites, "Twentieth Century Propaganda Trends," in this volume (chapter 3).

60. Sartre, *L'Existentialisme,* 40f.

61. Cf. Granville Hicks, *Small Town* (New York, 1946).

62. Camus, *Le mythe de Sisyphe,* 88, 40, 105, 108.

63. Camus, *The Stranger,* 150.

64. Sartre, *In Camera,* 153.

65. Sartre, *L'Existentialisme,* 55, 58.

66. Camus, *Le mythe de Sisyphe,* 15f.

67. Gollancz, *Our Threatened Values,* 22-27.

PART III

IMAGES OF AUTHORITY

Chapter 5

POLITBURO IMAGES OF STALIN

(with Elsa Bernaut and Raymond L. Garthoff)

EDITOR'S NOTE: In this selection an unpromising sample of apparently little-differentiated extravagant praise of Stalin is made to yield subtle contrasts. Among birthday messages sent to Stalin by a group of Soviet leaders, the authors distinguish two styles of commendation. There is the "old Bolshevik" style that sees Stalin as subordinate to the communist movement, and there is a newer "popular image" that sees Stalin as possessing superior personal qualities. The authors find the different symbolic emphases to be associated with the position of the praisers in the Politburo hierarchy: the top leaders are more apt to use the older form of praise. Presumably also the difference in stress is related to the various roles played by different members in the "court politics" of Stalin's Kremlin. This presumption is given more weight by Soviet history since Stalin's death. Of the roster studied here, those who had the most influential subsequent careers were Khrushchev, Bulganin, and Kosygin. It may be significant that their words, of all the group, were most free of the "old Bolshevik" praise terms.

Reprinted from World Politics *III (1951), 317-339. The authors are indebted to Hans Speier, Victor M. Hunt, and Joseph M. Goldsen for a number of points and formulations.*

*H*ypotheses regarding differences (or lack of differences) in policy-orientation or in degrees of influence between the various members of the Soviet Politburo have always been of great interest to students of politics. Thus there have been frequent speculations regarding alleged differences in foreign policy lines and on the problem of succession. The absence of confirming or disconfirming data for any of these hypotheses is striking, and obvious in view of the secrecy that enshrouds the internal operations of the Politburo. Published statements of any kind by members of the Politburo have become infrequent in recent years. Such statements as are available for analysis have usually dealt with different subjects and have been made at different dates, so that they were difficult to compare from the point of view of testing hypotheses regarding differences in policy or influence. Through Stalin's seventieth birthday, December 21, 1949, however, a rare opportunity for comparative analysis did occur. *Pravda* published articles by Politburo members Malenkov, Molotov, Beria, Voroshilov, Mikoyan, Kaganovich, Bulganin, Andreyev, Khrushchev, Kosygin, and Shvernik (in this order), preceded by a joint message to Stalin from the Central Committee of the Party and the Council of Ministers of the U.S.S.R. These articles were reprinted in *Bolshevik,* the Party organ, and the Soviet press in general. *[As far as is feasible, quotations are given from the translations in Volume I, No. 52, of* The Current Digest of the Soviet Press *(hereafter cited as* Digest*). Other passages have been translated from December 1949, No. 24,* Bolshevik. *All italics, unless otherwise indicated, are by the authors of this paper.]* In addition, the anniversary issue of *Pravda* (but not *Bolshevik*) contained two articles on Stalin by persons who are not members of the Politburo, M. Shkiryatov (a Party Secretary) and A. Poskrebyshev (presumably Stalin's personal secretary), thus treating their statements on a par with those made by the members of the Politburo. This body of materials will be examined as to what it may reveal regarding the distribution of influence and attitudes within the Politburo.

While all the statements mentioned appear at first glance to express the same adulation of Stalin, they do contain nuances in style and emphasis. These nuances could more easily be dismissed as matters of individual rhetoric, of little relevance to political analysis, if the statements had been made by Western statesmen. But nuances in the political language used by members of the Politburo when talking about Stalin are of a different nature. Stalinism is not afraid of monotony and does not shun repetitiveness. Lack of complete uniformity of language is therefore possibly of political interest. It is worth while to examine the materials intensively in order to determine whether or not the differences in language, however subtle, fall into any patterns, and to explore the meaning of differentiations between groups or individuals in the Politburo. It seemed especially useful to approach the material with a view to investigating the degree of maintenance (or disuse and replacement) of earlier Bolshevik terms and themes.

Two major types of statements about the image of Stalin which can be discerned in the articles are analyzed in this paper. The accompanying table gives the total frequencies of statements *[A "statement," for the purposes of this table, means each incidence of an explicit idea and may vary from a phrase to a paragraph. The examples cited in the text should clarify this point.]* concerning these ideas: first, Stalin in comparison to Lenin, and second, characterizations of Stalin's dominant role, as "perfect Bolshevik" or "ideal Father." A third image, "Stalin" as person or symbol, is not presented in this table or discussed in detail because the difference between images is a more qualitative classification derived from analysis of the context within the articles; it is briefly discussed at the close of this article.

TABLE 1

REFERENCES TO STALIN IN THE
BIRTHDAY SPEECHES OF DECEMBER 21, 1949

Politburo Member	Stalin: Lenin's Pupil or Equal?			Stalin: Perfect Bolshevik or Ideal Father		
	Bolshevik Image	Ambiguous	Popular Image	Bolshevik Image	Ambiguous	Popular Image
Molotov	5	1	0	12	3	0
Malenkov	4	0	2	11	3	0
Beria	13	3	1	15	1	2
Shvernik	4	0	5	2	2	2
Voroshilov	0	0	1	1	2	4
Mikoyan	2	2	9	3	0	5
Andreyev	1	0	2	3	0	15
Bulganin	0	1	6	0	0	3
Kosygin	1	0	3	0	0	8
Khrushchev	0	1	4	0	0	7
Kaganovich	0	3	6	0	3	21
Shkiryatov	0	3	6	0	0	6
Poskrebyshev	2	1	3	0	0	10

The source used in this compilation is Bolshevik, No. 24, December 1949

The frequencies of statements, when read across, indicate the weight within an article given by the Politburo member to the "Bolshevik image" relative to the weight given to the "popular image" of Stalin. *[The groupings within the Politburo are self-explanatory; Shkiryatov and Poskrebyshev are separated from the "bottom group" because of their non-Politburo status.]* The articles were not uniform in length: Malenkov's article was approximately 3,500 words; those of Shvernik, Andreyev, Kosygin, Khrushchev, and Shkiryatov were each about 2,500 words; the others were each approximately 5,000 words. However, since the relative weight given to characterizations within each article is the subject of our attention here, no "weighing" of frequencies has been made in the table, and absolute figures have been used.

From this table it is evident that the "top group" (Malenkov, Molotov, and Beria) uses language closer to the older Bolshevik ideology than do the rest; the other two groups use language which resembles more closely that of Soviet synthetic folklore dealing with Stalin.

I. STALIN: LENIN'S PUPIL OR LENIN'S EQUAL?

In current Soviet public discourse, the "great" Lenin is not called "greater" than the "great" Stalin; nor is it affirmed explicitly that Lenin and Stalin are equal in "greatness." It is, however, possible to adopt formulations that suggest the former or the latter of these emphases.

In the articles on Stalin's birthday, the differences of stress fall into the pattern of tendencies toward what we have termed the "popular" and the "Bolshevik" images of Stalin; the popular image emphasizes Stalin's equality (and in some instances even primacy) in relation to Lenin, while the Bolshevik image lays more stress on Stalin as Lenin's "pupil," or the "continuer" of his work and ideas. *[The longest* Pravda *article on the occasion of Stalin's fiftieth birthday, December 21, 1929, was by Stalin's old friend and later victim, Abel Yenukidze. Instead of presenting the couple Lenin-Stalin, he told about the activities of Stalin-Yenukidze. And to Stalin himself, Yenukidze said: "it is difficult to write about him. He always was and will remain to the end of his life, a real Bolshevik."]*

In the treatment of this point, the Bolshevik image characterizes the articles of the top group of the Politburo—Malenkov, Molotov, and Beria. In a "middle" position, using both images, are the joint article of the Central Committee and the Council of Ministers and Shvernik's article. Tendencies toward the popular image are expressed by Kosygin and Voroshilov (each of whom makes only two comparisons), Andreyev, and Poskrebyshev. The popular image is most frequently and clearly presented by Mikoyan, Kaganovich, Bulganin, Khrushchev, and Shkiryatov.

Beria uses the Bolshevik image, illustrated in the following examples, most frequently:

Even during Lenin's lifetime and *under* his leadership . . . Comrade Stalin emerged as Lenin's closest *pupil,* the most loyal of his *followers* and as the greatest theoretician, organizer and builder of our party *after* Lenin. [*Digest,* p. 11.]

From his first steps of revolutionary activity Comrade Stalin stood unwaveringly *under* Lenin's banner. He was Lenin's true and devoted *follower.* He made his extremely valuable contributions to *Leninist* development of the Marxist Party's . . . tenets. [*Digest,* p. 12.]

Establishing and developing *Leninism* and relying on *Lenin's instructions [uka- zaniya],* Comrade Stalin developed the *tenets* of . . . industrialization. *[Digest,* p. 12.]

There are other instances where Beria states that "Comrade Stalin developed *Lenin's instructions" (Digest,* p. 13) and "developed *Lenin's teaching* on the Party" (*Digest,* p. 12), but this quotation is especially significant since Stalin is in Soviet writing almost universally credited with the decision to collectivize and industrialize the country at a rapid tempo. There are many other references to Stalin's "arming the Party with Leninism," or "defending" or "advancing" Leninism, but these are not real comparisons.

There is one statement of equality on a situation (the conduct of the Civil War) concerning which Stalin has credited himself with a role possibly higher than Lenin's, so that equality in this respect would belong to the Bolshevik image.

During the difficult Civil War years *Lenin and Stalin* led the Party, the State, the Red Army and the country's entire defense. [*Digest,* p. 12]

Beria even makes one statement about the "the introduction of the *Leninist-Stalinist national* policy" (*Digest,* p. 13) dealing with the one matter attributed to Stalin's own authorship prior to the middle twenties.

Beria also mentions Stalin's investiture by Lenin—a theme that is rarely touched upon:

Lenin proposed that the Central Committee of the Party elect Comrade Stalin General Secretary of the Central Committee. Comrade Stalin has been working in this high post since April 3, 1922. [*Digest,* p. 12.]

As Lenin proposed, in 1923, that the Party consider the "removal" of Stalin from this "high post," Beria's reference is unusual. (So are references to any date, in the statements here analyzed, except the dates of the revolution, of the beginning and the end of the past war, and of some of Stalin's writings.)

Beria also makes two statements less clearly expressive of this image, in one of which he praises Stalin's Bolshevik virtues, thrice interjecting "like Lenin" (*Digest,* p. 15), and in the other of which Stalin joins Marx, Engels, and Lenin "among the names of the greatest geniuses of mankind" (*Digest,* p. 11).

Molotov also expresses the Bolshevik image of Stalin in comparison to Lenin, emphasizing his theoretical continuation rather than personal discipleship, as Beria does. Both mention the fact that after Lenin's death, Stalin headed the Communist Party. Molotov goes on, however, to state:

> Comrade Stalin upheld and developed *Lenin's theory* of the possibility of victory of socialism in one country.... [*Digest*, p. 7.]

> ... the victory of socialism in one country, which was *first* raised *by Lenin* and found a profound scientific basis in the works of Stalin.... [*Digest*, p. 10.] *[When Stalin put forward this new position in the middle twenties, it was, of course, necessary for him to present it as one already taken by Lenin. The top group in the Politburo preserves this line after a quarter of a century; the others do not deny it but stress it less and even tend to imply Stalin's creativeness in this matter.]*

> As the ... representative of creative Marxism, Comrade Stalin has highly developed the *Leninist* principles of strategy and tactics of our party.... [*Digest*, p. 10.] *[December 21, 1929, Molotov wrote more specifically that Stalin had been a "man of practice"* (praktik i organizator) *up to Lenin's death, after which he became a "theoretician." Even in 1949 Molotov has not quite suppressed his tendency to deny that Stalin was manifestly perfect from the start. He begins his speech by saying: "It is* now *particularly clear how very fortunate it was ... that after Lenin the Communist Party of the USSR was headed by Comrade Stalin."* (Digest, p. 6.) *In the Bolshevik atmosphere of veiled language, this is bound to be understood, to some extent, as conveying: It was not* always *clear.]*

Molotov also expresses the Bolshevik image of Stalin as the successor to Lenin in his capacity as "head of the Party" and the preserver of its monolithic character, and says:

> As the great *continuer* of the *cause* of immortal Lenin, Comrade Stalin stands *at the head of* all our socialist contruction.... [*Bolshevik*, p. 22]

Similarly he describes how *"Stalin and the Stalinist leadership"* kept the Soviet people "on the path indicated by the great *Lenin" (Digest*, p. 6), and how Stalin, as Party chief, overcame "anti-Leninist vacillations" (*Digest*, p. 7). (The term "anti-Stalinist" is not even found in the popular image; it is too strong.)

Malenkov also stresses the Bolshevik image (despite two statements of apparent equality concerning their role in the Revolution).

> He [Stalin] has defended and developed *the Leninist theory* of the possibility of socialism in one country. [*Digest*, p. 3.]

> Better than anyone else, Comrade Stalin profoundly *understood Lenin's* inspired *ideas* on a new-type Marxist party. [*Digest*, p. 3.]

A middle position, using both images frequently, is noticeable in the joint C.C.-Council of Ministers message, and in the article by Shvernik, entitled "Comrade Stalin—*Continuer* of the Great *Cause* of Lenin."

In addition to the title of his article, Shvernik makes three weaker Bolshevik image references to Lenin and Stalin, such as the one cited below.

From the first steps of his revolutionary struggle, Comrade Stalin was pervaded with a boundless faith in *Leninist* genius, and went on Lenin's path as the most loyal of his *pupils* and companions-in-arms. [*Bolshevik*, p. 91.]

On the other hand, he expresses the popular image four times, writing "together with Lenin, Comrade Stalin" (*Bolshevik*, p. 91, twice) and "Lenin and Stalin" led the working-class to victory (*Bolshevik*, p. 91), and finally, in words borrowed from Mikoyan, he says: "Stalin—that is Lenin today" (*Bolshevik*, p. 95).

Poskrebyshev (Stalin's secretary, and possibly a future member of the Politburo) also expresses a mixed attitude on this question, with three unequivocal statements of equality, three as "continuer of the cause of Lenin," and two as teacher-pupil.

Kosygin, Andreyev, and Voroshilov employ the popular image more frequently than the Bolshevik but do not compare Lenin and Stalin often. Thus Kosygin writes: "The ideas of *Lenin-Stalin* have triumphed. One-third of the population of the globe has entered firmly onto the path indicated by Lenin-Stalin . . ." (*Bolshevik*, p. 89), and later "path of socialism, indicated by *Lenin-Stalin*" (*Bolshevik*, p. 90). Kosygin even omits the name of Lenin in a passage where one might have expected to find it:

With the name of Stalin is indissolubly connected the creation of our Communist Party and of the first Soviet socialist state in the world. . . . [*Bolshevik*, p. 86.]

Andreyev employs the Bolshevik image in one passage but uses the popular one in his other two comparisons (and in other ways). Thus:

The great Lenin charted the basic means of putting the peasantry on the path of socialist construction . . . Comrade Stalin brilliantly worked out this plan and put it into practice. [*Digest*, p. 28.]

But:

The Bolshevist Party, led by *Lenin and Stalin,* carried out the century-old hopes of the village by transferring all the land to peasant use. . . . But an *even more profound* revolution was carried out by the Bolshevist Party, *under Comrade Stalin's* leadership, in the collectivization of the countryside. . . . [*Digest*, p. 28.]

Just as Andreyev's article was predominantly devoted to agricultural matters, Voroshilov's article was concerned with military affairs, more specifically the strategy and conduct of the Great Fatherland War.

In addition to two references to "the Party of Lenin and Stalin" he makes only one comparison, expressing equality.

> During the years of the heroic struggle and labor [the Revolution], the Soviet people under the leadership of the Party of Bolsheviks, under the guidance of the great leaders *Lenin and Stalin,* secured a world-historical victory. [*Bolshevik,* p. 35.]

The popular image is clearly dominant, and frequent, in the articles of Mikoyan, Kaganovich, Bulganin, Khrushchev, and Shkiryatov.

Thus Mikoyan states:

> Stalin not only fully mastered the entire scientific heritage of Marx, Engels and Lenin . . . [he "defended" and "brilliantly interpreted" it]; he also enriched Marxism-Leninism with a number of great discoveries, and further developed the Marxist-Leninist theory. In the words of Comrade Stalin Leninism is raised to a new, *higher* historical plane. . . . The Marxist-Leninist philosophy, which is transforming the world, has reached its *apex* in the works of Comrade Stalin. (*Digest,* p. 19.) *[Although Molotov and Beria both praise Stalin as the theorist, they do not state explicitly (or clearly implicitly) that Stalin is as great a theorist as Lenin, to say nothing of the statement that "Marxist-Leninist philosophy has reached its apex" in Stalin's work.]*

Kaganovich is even more devoted to the use of the popular image, representing Stalin as equal to (or in rare instances even superior to) Lenin. There are no clear uses of the Bolshevik image in his article, which abounds in comparisons.

> Comrade Stalin did not *simply* defend and safeguard the Leninist theory of the possibility of the victory of socialism in one country, but on the foundation of rich experience of the struggle, he *creatively augmented* and *enriched* the theory. . . . [*Bolshevik,* p. 59.]

In one place Bulganin credits Stalin with the distinction between just and unjust wars ("as Stalin teaches . . ."), without any mention of Lenin, who first made this distinction, and until now has been generally so credited in the Soviet Union (*Bolshevik,* p. 70).

Khrushchev also uses the popular image, with one possible exception, in all his comparisons of Lenin and Stalin. In addition to five references to "the x of Lenin and Stalin" (x = Party, teaching, idea, cause, and banner), he makes three statements of clear equality and one which may even attribute superiority to Stalin.

Herein lies Comrade Stalin's tremendous and invaluable service. He is the true friend and *comrade-in-arms* of the great Lenin. [*Digest*, p. 30.] ... Stalin, who *together with Lenin* created the great Bolshevist Party, our socialist state, *enriched* Marxist-Leninist theory, and *raised it* to a new, *higher* level. [*Bolshevik*, p. 80.]

Shkiryatov also expresses the extreme image most frequently, stating only three times that Stalin is continuing the "cause" or "banner" of Lenin, while using the phrase "the teaching of Lenin and Stalin" four times, and making six comparisons of Lenin and Stalin, in all of which they are clearly represented as equal.

Reviewing the treatment of this theme we see that there emerge rather distinctly a Bolshevik image and a popular image, in the treatment of the relative standing of Lenin and Stalin by Politburo members.

The "Bolshevik image" is most prominent in the articles of the top sector—Beria, Molotov, and Malenkov (in that order). It represents Stalin as the pupil of Lenin, his follower, and his continuer; as Lenin's successor, who continued to implement, defend, and elaborate Leninism. He appears as the most loyal of Lenin's followers and the one who best understood his ideas. Stalin is not considered as Lenin's peer (with the single exception of Malenkov's treatment of the October Revolution).

The "popular image" of Stalin is predominant, in varying degree, in the words of all the others, especially Kaganovich, Khrushchev, Mikoyan, Bulganin, and Shkiryatov. It represents Stalin as the equal of Lenin, also in situations where this was obviously not the case. In rare instances, Stalin even appears greater than Lenin.

II. STALIN: THE PERFECT BOLSHEVIK PARTY LEADER, OR THE IDEAL FATHER

The Bolshevik image is employed by Beria, Malenkov, Molotov, and to a lesser degree by Shvernik and Mikoyan. Stalin appears as the great "leader" and "teacher," but by implication the Party is superior to him. He possesses a very high degree of Bolshevik virtues.

The perfect Bolshevik takes it for granted that his life is dedicated to the advancement of communism, at whatever deprivations to himself. He regards it as improper to talk about ultimate values and personal sacrifices; attention, he feels, should be concentrated on discerning the correct line and carrying it through. The traits ascribed to Stalin by Beria, for instance, are almost all means to this end and are presented as such. A positive evaluation of a Bolshevik commends him for having made himself an effective tool in correct directions.

The popular image of Stalin—given much more profusely—does not present him as a Party leader impersonally fulfilling the moral obligation to render service to the proletariat by providing a correct policy line. It shows him as a People's Leader in the Soviet Union and in the rest of the world, bestowing boundless paternal solicitude *(zabota)* on the "simple people." The people, overwhelmed by surprise at finding such freely tendered goodness in one of their very own *(rodnoi)* on high, work harder and better for him in loving gratitude. While the aim of the Party leader is to realize communism in the future, at the cost of current hardships, the solicitude of the Leader of the People aims at satisfying human needs now. This he does, not only by laying down over-all policy, but also by innumerable concrete actions. In all this, Stalin possesses the virtues of an ideal father (sometimes brother and friend) which his children do not strive to equal. Stalin tends to become the creator of all good things.

The use of the Bolshevik image by the top group in this respect is far from excluding the use of elements of the popular image. Nevertheless, there is a differentiation, which we shall endeavor to show.

1. One of the aspects of the Bolshevik image of Stalin is his endowment with a very high degree of Bolshevik virtues. The implication is that these distinctive virtues should be emulated by less perfect Bolsheviks and that, although the chances of attaining Stalin's degree of perfection are slight, the model is clear, and there is no predetermined limit to advance. *[On the other hand, when someone who exhibits a predilection for the popular image attributes to him Bolshevik traits, there is often an allusion to the impossibility of imitation. Thus Mikoyan says: "The power of Stalinist (Stalin's) foresight of revolutionary events is most uncommon, and is one of the basic qualities of our great leader"* (Bolshevik, p. 46). *"It is impossible not to wonder at the wise patience, the temperance and the inimitable endurance and boldness displayed by Comrade Stalin in his appraisal of facts and events . . ."* (Digest, p. 20). *There is, for those accustomed to older Bolshevik language, a jarring note in the juxtaposition of the classical Bolshevik stress on "the appraisal of facts and events" with largely non-Bolshevik virtue-words.]*

For example, Beria says:

Comrade Stalin's whole life and work are a great *inspiring example* of fidelity to Leninism and unbounded love of Lenin, an example of self-sacrificing service to the working class and to all working people, to the cause of freeing humanity from oppression and exploitation. [*Digest*, p. 16.]

Our leader's genius is combined with his simplicity and modesty, with an extraordinary personal charm, with implacability toward the enemies of communism, with considerateness and paternal concern for individuals. He possesses extreme clarity of thought, calm greatness of character, scorn and intolerance of all boastfulness and outward effect. [*Digest,* p. 16.] [*"Extraordinary personal charm" belongs to neither the Bolshevik nor the popular images. "Considerateness"* (chutkost') (*The Digest's* translation of this word has been altered) *and paternal solicitude* (otecheskaya zabota) *are popular image traits.*]

In Comrade Stalin the Soviet people saw even more clearly and distinctly the features of his great teacher, Lenin. They saw that our army and people were led into battle against a brutalized enemy by a tested leader who, like Lenin, was fearless in battle and merciless toward the enemies of the people; like Lenin, free of any semblance of panic; like Lenin, wise and bold in deciding complicated questions; like Lenin, clear and definite, just and honorable, loving his people as Lenin loved them. [*Digest,* p. 15.] [*"Loving his people" also belongs to the popular image. These occasional popular image terms in a moderate picture may be the effect of reverse seepage of exoteric propaganda into the constantly assaulted esoteric integrity of the top group.*]

Molotov also stresses Stalin's Bolshevik traits in several passages, some outstanding examples of which follow below.

The works of Stalin are now appearing, containing his works from 1901. It is impossible to overestimate the theoretical and political significance of this publication. Before our eyes, stage by stage, there unfolds the picture of the inspired creative work of the great Stalin, in all its diversity and spiritual wealth. Here all the diverse practical questions of the work of the Bolshevist party and the international communist movement and, together with this, complex scientific problems of history and philosophy, are treated in the light of the ideas of Marxism-Leninism. . . . [*Digest,* p. 9.]

A profound knowledge of the history of nations, the versatile experience of leader of the international Communist movement, the ability to fathom and to discern in time the strategic plans and tactics of individual states, the boldness and flexibility of decisions in complicated international affairs, which are so characteristic of Comrade Stalin, determined the decisive successes of the foreign policy of the Soviet Union. [*Digest,* p. 8.]

In most cases, popular image characterizations are admixed with Bolshevik statements showing Stalin as "leader" and "teacher." Of all the statements by the top group in the popular vein, only one (by Molotov) communicates a feeling or judgment by the speaker himself; all the other instances allege judgments or feelings of the *people.*

Comrade Stalin is rightfully considered a great and loyal friend of the freedom-loving peoples of the countries of people's democracy. . . . [*Digest,* p. 3.]

That is why the peoples of the Soviet Union and the whole of progressive mankind see in the person of Comrade Stalin their recognized leader and teacher. That is why today they express their love and devotion to Comrade Stalin with especial warmth, take note of his great services in the struggle for happy lives for the people for peace among nations. [*Digest,* p. 3.]

In addition to stressing his Bolshevik virtues, the Bolshevik image presents Stalin as leader in three forms: political strategist, teacher, and Party executive. We shall examine these in turn.

2. According to the Bolshevik image, Stalin's main role is to make a diagnosis and prognosis of the political situation and to derive the correct line from it. In the popular image of Stalin this is stressed much less. This aspect of the Bolshevik image is conveyed particularly by Molotov, as the examples below indicate.

> ... [Stalin's] ability ... to show the Party the true way and to lead it to victory. [*Digest*, p. 11.]

> In order that the anti-Hitler three-power coalition might be created during the war, it was necessary first to thwart the anti-Soviet plans of the governments of Britain, France.... Comrade Stalin discerned in time the ... Anglo-French intrigues ... enabling us ... to bring the developments of events to a point at which the governments of Britain and the U.S.A. were faced with the necessity of establishing an Anglo-Soviet-American ... coalition.... [*Digest*, p. 8.]

3. Related to this in the Bolshevik image is Stalin's function in "teaching" the Party rules of organization, strategy, and tactics. This is another point less stressed in the popular image of Stalin. But it is one of the main emphases of Malenkov (who may expect to take over this function). The following citations from his speech are but a few of many.

> Comrade Stalin *teaches* that the Bolshevist Party is strong because ... it multiplies its ties with the broad masses of the workers. [*Digest*, p. 4.]

> Comrade Stalin *teaches* that without self-criticism we cannot advance ... Comrade Stalin *teaches* that ... Comrade Stalin *teaches* that ... Comrade Stalin *teaches* that.... [*Digest*, pp. 4-5.]

> Comrade Stalin *educates* the cadres of our Party.... [*Digest*, p. 5.]

> Comrade Stalin constantly *warns* that not conceit but modesty adorns a Bolshevik.... [*Digest*, p. 5.]

Molotov and Beria emphasize Stalin's character as the "continuer," "defender," and "developer" of Leninism more than this teaching role, but they often do refer to Stalin as "leader and teacher." (This standard phrase is also found in the popular image, but less frequently and prominently.)

4. The top-level statements frequently present as the major acting force not Stalin but the Party (or, sometimes, the "Soviet Union," or the "Soviet people"), while other members of the Politburo stress the personal role of Stalin by omitting references to the Party. The Party is even credited with those services most often credited to Stalin by most of the others—inspiring,

mobilizing, organizing. The term "leadership of the Party" clearly refers to others besides Stalin—in fact, to the speaker himself. Thus in the following passage, Malenkov mentions the Party eight times, and Stalin only once.

> The friendship among peoples which is firmly established in our country is a great *achievement of the leadership* of the Bolshevist *Party. Only* the Bolshevist *Party* could forge the indissoluble fraternity among the peoples—the Bolshevist *Party* which consistently carries forward the ideas of internationalism. . . . [The recent war] was a most serious one for the Bolshevist *Party* itself. The *Party* emerged from this test a great victor . . . following the instructions of Comrade Stalin, our *Party* constantly inspired the people and mobilized their efforts in the struggle against the enemy. The *Party's* organizational work united and directed. . . . Again the unsurpassed ability of the Bolshevist *Party* to mobilize the masses under the most difficult conditions was demonstrated. [*Digest*, p. 4.]

On the other hand, the image of Stalin as the People's Leader (the popular image) shows him acting directly, without using the transmission belt of the Party. Occasionally the "top-group" and the "middle-group" members use this image in topics intended for mass consumption:

> *All who desire to fight* against the instigators of a new war know . . . that they will not err in rallying around Comrade Stalin. . . . [Molotov, *Digest*, p. 3.]

> . . . Stalin's voice in defense of peace . . . has penetrated throughout the world. . . . *All simple and honest people* responding to his appeal group themselves into powerful columns of fighters for peace. [Voroshilov, *Digest,* p. 19; *Bolshevik*, p. 44.]

The popular image of Stalin, as we have indicated previously, does not stop at the limits which mark the Bolshevik characterization described above. Indeed, it very rarely uses them at all, except for casual and occasional reference to the standard term "leader" and "teacher."

The articles of Kaganovich, Khrushchev, Shkiryatov, Poskrebyshev, Bulganin, Kosygin, and Andreyev, in roughly that descending order, are most expressive of the popular image, in the aspects presently under review. Mikoyan and to a lesser degree Shvernik also use it, but there are a number of mixed and even Bolshevik statements in their articles. On the other hand, the seven writers listed above have only four Bolshevik image statements in all their articles. Voroshilov is a special case; in his introduction and conclusion he makes a number of statements in the popular image.

1. In the popular image Stalin is characterized as the "father" of his people, who constantly helps them because of his "paternal solicitude" for them. (This is sometimes weakened to a "friend" relationship, and sometimes intimate relationship terms are not employed.) "The simple people" are grateful, loving, and industrious in return. For them Stalin is *rodnoi*, meaning "one's very own," and connoting familial intimacy.

Each of the members of the "bottom group" uses this description (to varying degrees, of course, as shall become evident). The following examples are by no means exhaustive of the instances used.

Kaganovich depicts Stalin in this manner in the following passages:

> Comrade Stalin displays *exceptional solicitude* regarding miners and the alleviation of their labor. . . . The glorious army of railway workers responds to Comrade Stalin with *warm love, devotion,* and with a growing and improving transport [system] for his *paternal warmth and solicitude.* . . . The systematic increase of wages [etc.] . . . all these are the results of the *constant solicitude and attention* of *our very own [rodnoi]* Comrade Stalin, whom the people *lovingly* call *father* and *friend. [Bolshevik,* pp. 60-61.]

> . . . all the toiling people of our Motherland, *with all its heart, warmly love* and praise Comrade Stalin for the fact that *he is always with* the working class, *always with* the people, at the head of the people both in *its hardest hour [tyazhkaya godina],* in days of great difficulties, trials and sufferings, and in the days of joy and victory. [*Bolshevik,* p. 56.]

Bulganin develops a similar image:

> Comrade Stalin *always* displayed and displays up to the present time a *constant paternal solicitude* for the *bringing up* [*vyrashchivani;* used in the phrase "bringing up one's children"] of military cadres, *educating* them in the spirit of supreme fidelity to the Bolshevist Party, in the spirit of self-sacrifice in the service of the people. . . . [*Bolshevik,* p. 67.]

Khrushchev similarly states:

> Lenin and Stalin stood at the cradle of each Soviet republic, they guarded it from menacing dangers, *paternally [po-otecheski]* helped it to *grow* and become strong. . . . This is why all the peoples of our land, with the uncommon *warmth and feeling* of *filial love,* call the great Stalin *their very own [rodnoi] father.* . . . [*Bolshevik,* p. 81.]

> Today the peoples of the great Soviet Union and all advanced progressive humanity *from their heart* salute *their very own [rodnoi]* Comrade Stalin . . . Praise to *our very own father,* wise teacher, gifted leader. . . . [*Bolshevik,* p. 85.]

> *Attentively, paternally,* daily leading and *watching over* affairs on the collective farms . . . [is] Comrade Stalin. [*Digest,* p. 29.]

The two non-Politburo members, Shkiryatov and Poskrebyshev, both use this aspect of the popular image frequently. Poskrebyshev even titled his article "*Beloved Father* and Great Teacher."

Shkiryatov writes:

> The peoples of our country grow and become stronger like one *family,* and glorify Comrade Stalin—*father* and *friend* of all peoples of the USSR. [*Pravda,* p. 11.]

Stalin, our *father* and *friend*, instills in us a love for all that is *ours, native*—in science, in culture, in production, and *educates* into the Soviet people a *warm devotion* to its Motherland. . . . [*Pravda*, p. 11.]

2. As has already become evident, the popular image pictures Stalin as the People's Leader, as contrasted to the emphasis on the Party and Stalin as Party leader in the moderate view. There are several aspects to being "People's Leader," and one which has been suggested in several of the quotations already cited shows Stalin as an opponent of "bureaucracy." In his concern for the welfare of the simple people, he must overcome the inefficiency, selfishness, and malice of the bureaus standing between him and the people. Bulganin makes this almost explicit:

Comrade Stalin always paid great attention to the welfare of soldiers and sailors. He was interested in food standards, the quality of uniforms, and the weight of arms carried by soldiers. Comrade Stalin frequently pointed out in his orders that concern for the soldiers.' . . . welfare was the sacred duty of the commanders, that they must see to it most strictly that soldiers received all the food due under established standards, that the troops were given well-prepared warm meals in good time. . . . Due to the constant solicitude of Comrade Stalin for the supplies of the troops our front fighters were well fed and comfortably and warmly clad. [*Digest*, p. 28; *Bolshevik*, p. 71.]

Many other examples could be cited to demonstrate this aspect of the popular image.

The popular image of Stalin shows him, by implication, almost as a one-man Party-government-and-army apparatus. The previous quotations have pointed out this characterization of Stalin in situations where the welfare of the people required it. But this does not exhaust the range of his actions, and Kaganovich and Bulganin in particular extend Stalin's active personal role to rather extreme lengths. According to Kaganovich:

. . . while . . . the countries of Europe, and the U.S.A., first of all, are slipping toward a crisis, here in the Soviet Union the socialist economy improves constantly. . . . We are obliged for this to the superiority of the socialist system of economy, and *above all to Comrade Stalin's great energy, initiative and organizing genius.* [*Digest*, p. 25.]

Further, Stalin's "initiative" was responsible for the development of coal production before the war, and he gave "specific attention" to its restoration afterwards. His "initiative" has "established" new oil districts. He "ascribes particular significance" to ferrous metallurgy, gives "constant attention" to electrification, and "special attention" to the production of the means of production, and

. . . everybody knows how high Comrade Stalin has *raised the significance* of transportation as a whole and of rail transport in particular. [*Digest,* pp. 24-25.]

Bulganin concerns himself with Stalin's role during the war, where Stalin performed an apparently prodigious amount of diverse labors constantly. Already in the Civil War,

> Comrade Stalin was the creator of the most important . . . strategic plans and the *direct leader* of the decisive battle operations. . . . At Tsaritsyn and Perm, at Petrograd and against Denikin, in the West against the Poland of Pans, and in the south against Wrangel—*everywhere* his iron will and military genius secured *[obespechivali]* the victory of Soviet forces. [*Bolshevik,* p. 66.]

And in the recent war,

> *All operations* of the Great Fatherland War were *planned by Comrade Stalin and executed under his guidance.* There was *not a single operation* in the working out of which he did not participate. Before finally approving a plan . . . Comrade Stalin subjected it to thorough analysis and discussion with his closest companions [an unusual statement] . . . Comrade Stalin *personally directed the whole course* of *every* operation. Each day and even several times a day *he verified the fulfillment* of his orders, *gave advice,* and *corrected the decisions* of those in command, if there was need of this. [*Bolshevik,* p. 69.]

> *Every operation . . .* was marked by originality of design and creative uniqueness in execution. *Each time* Comrade Stalin knew how to find methods . . . best corresponding to . . . the situation and . . . unexpected by the adversary. [*Digest,* p. 27.]

Bulganin describes Stalin's wartime habit of "personally visiting the fronts to verify on the spot the preparedness of the armies" (*Digest,* p. 27).

This image of Stalin as omnipresent and competent in every matter—an image never presented by the Politburo top group—is developed to a still further extreme by Poskrebyshev:

> Attentively supervising the work of the leading *Michurinists* [the new geneticists], headed by Comrade Lysenko, Comrade Stalin gave them *daily assistance by his advice and instructions.* . . . Comrade Stalin must also be noted as a scientific innovator in specialized branches of science. . . . Among the old specialists in agriculture it was considered firmly established that the cultivation of citrus crops could not be extended on a wide scale in the region of the USSR Black Sea coast. . . . *Having for many years engaged in the cultivation and study of citrus crops in the region of the Black Sea coast,* Comrade Stalin proved in practice that it is possible to produce types of citrus crops . . . adapted to the climatic conditions of the Black Sea coast. . . . *Comrade Stalin's decisive role is well known* in the matter of *planting eucalyptus trees* on the Black Sea coast, *cultivating melons* in the Moscow region and extending the cultivation of *branched wheat.* [*Digest,* p. 34.]

III. STALIN: PERSON OR SYMBOL?

In our material, "Stalin" often refers to more than the man, J. V. Stalin. The boundary between references to Stalin the person and, as might be said, Stalin the symbol is blurred, probably on purpose. The top group, however, is more careful than the other to distinguish between these two images, and to lay stress on Stalin the person.

One way of indicating that Stalin is being referred to as a symbol is by speaking of his "name" or actually declaring his name to be a "symbol." Thus Beria states in his introductory paragraph:

> Since the great Lenin there has been no *name* in the world so dear to the hearts of millions of working people as the *name* of the great leader, Comrade Stalin. [*Digest*, p. 11.]

And Molotov tells us that for "the world movement for peace"

> ... the *name* of Stalin is its great banner. [*Digest*, p. 9.]

Malenkov also states this:

> The *name* of Comrade Stalin has long since become a *banner* of peace in the minds of the peoples of all countries. [*Digest*, p. 3.]

> *Through the voice* of Comrade Stalin *the whole of the Soviet people declares* unconditionally that the USSR is against military adventures. ... [*Digest*, p. 4.]

And Bulganin writes:

> The *name* of Stalin became for the Soviet troops the *symbol of the greatness of our nation* and its heroism. They went into battle with the slogan: "For Stalin, for the Motherland!" [*Bolshevik*, p. 71.] *[These examples were drawn at random from the large number used by the top group.]*

Another way of differentiating between Stalin the person and Stalin the symbol is by making explicit the *personal* character of the reference. In the birthday articles, Molotov, Shvernik, and Bulganin use this mode of expression most frequently. Although many other references which do not specify that Stalin the person is meant probably do mean this, the method remains, when used by the top group, an indication of instances where Stalin's personal role is held to be highly significant. Malenkov uses a different method of achieving a similar effect. Although he refers to Stalin an average number of times (average number, 59; Malenkov's total, 60), a disproportionately large number of the references are to the effect that "Stalin teaches that . . ." or "as Stalin said," etc. Consequently, he says relatively less about other accomplishments of Stalin.

A technique used to transform "Stalin" from the person into the symbol is to employ the adjectival form of the word, "Stalinist." *[For analysis of this term, the* Current Digest *translation should not be used, as the Russian* stalinski *is frequently translated by them as "Stalin's" or "Stalin" (Constitution, etc.). The Foreign Languages Publishing House in Moscow also translated this term as "Stalin's" in some instances.]* The Bolshevik image usually reserves the term "Stalinist" to describe the achievements of Stalin's regime rather than his personal accomplishments. The popular image is, on the whole, lax about this differentiation, and apparently allows personal and impersonal meanings to be given to "Stalinist," as well as to "Stalin."

The proportion of uses by the top group (Molotov, Beria, and Malenkov) of "Stalinist" as meaning "Stalin's" personally is only two out of a total of twenty-seven, in contrast to the very frequent use of the term in this meaning by all the others (excepting only Voroshilov's account of Stalin's role in the recent war). Very often statements are made describing "the Stalinist, Soviet path," "Soviet, Stalinist military science," and the like, inferring clearly that the term in these instances indicates merely "under the present regime" or "in a Bolshevik manner."

The relatively impersonal meaning of the adjective "Stalinist" is particularly evident in such passages as the following. Molotov, affirming that the Soviet Union has gained in strength over the last quarter of a century, says:

> This is a very great service of Comrade *Stalin and of Stalinist leadership.* [*Digest,* p. 6.]

Presumably, "Stalinist leadership" here refers to Party leaders other than Stalin, and becomes a synonym for "Party." This is shown when Kaganovich, in a rare formulation, says:

> A decisive condition for the victory of socialism was the incessant struggle of Comrade *Stalin and of the united collective Stalinist leadership* . . . for the realization of the general line of the Party. [*Bolshevik,* p. 63.]

IV. CONCLUSIONS

Two main conclusions emerge from this study of the birthday articles:

1. Despite many individual differences among these articles and despite the variations within each of them, two major images of Stalin may be constructed, toward which each article is oriented to its particular degree. Briefly, these images are Stalin the Party Chief and Stalin the People's Leader. The Party Chief is a very great man; the People's Leader stands higher than

any man. The Party Chief is characterized by Bolshevik traits; the People's Leader by constant and boundless solicitude for the welfare of all. We have referred for the sake of brevity to the first as *"the Bolshevik image,"* and to the second as *"the popular image."*

2. Three groups within the Politburo can be distinguished in terms of using these images. Malenkov, Molotov, and Beria, who presumably are the most influential members of the Politburo, stress the Bolshevik image of Stalin more than the other members, although indications of the popular image are not totally absent from their statements. Kaganovich, Bulganin, Khrushchev, Kosygin, and to a lesser degree Mikoyan and Andreyev, occupy positions near the popular image (as do Shkiryatov and Poskrebyshev). Shvernik and the joint Party-government address occupy a middle position. Voroshilov is a special case, presenting the popular image of Stalin in his introduction and peroration, but a very moderate Bolshevik image in terms of specific military operations (in contrast to Bulganin).

These two images of Stalin can now be reviewed with two questions in mind: (1) To whom is either image addressed? Is there a preferred audience for the popular image and another such audience for the Bolshevik image? (2) What political significance can be attached to the finding that the Bolshevik image is stressed by the "top group" in the Politburo, while the popular image is used most freely by the "bottom group"?

Concerning the first question, it should be remembered that all statements analyzed in this paper were published; they were not made in private. As public statements they were not primarily, or at any rate not exclusively, addressed to Stalin. It is reasonable to assume that the "masses" of the Soviet population were meant to be the consumers of the popular image, whereas the Bolshevik image was offered primarily for adoption by communists, i.e., a small segment of the population. It is characteristic of Bolshevism, though paradoxical to Western thinking, that the symbols of nearness and intimacy ("father," "solicitude," etc.) appear most frequently in the popular image of Stalin and are stressed for that audience which is far removed from Stalin. Those closer to Stalin politically are permitted to speak of him in terms of lesser personal intimacy ("leader of the party"). This paradox results partly from the merely instrumental use in Bolshevik language of words indicating personal nearness, and partly from the Bolshevik deprecation of such nearness in political relationships. The ideal Party member does not stress any gratification he may derive from intimacy with others, much as he may use such intimacy for political ends.

.For this reason it is difficult to answer the second question with certainty. It cannot be ruled out that the Politburo—or a leading group within it, or Stalin personally—decided to use both images of Stalin in the birthday statements and to adopt a certain distribution of roles among its members in presenting them. (Such a decision may have taken the form of an editorial scrutiny of each statement, in the course of which the differentiation of language was imposed.)

However, the assumption that there was a decision within the Politburo on the use of different images of Stalin does not preclude certain tentative conclusions about the status of the groups within the Politburo. The emphasis on the Bolshevik image by a few members of the Politburo and on the popular image by others not only reflects the Bolshevik evaluation of the Party as distinguished from, and superior to, the masses at large, but also indicates the relative distance of the speakers from Stalin. In the situation under review, it is a privilege for a member of the Politburo to refrain from using the crudest form of adulation, words signifying personal intimacy and emotions; that is, private rather than political words. Given the Bolshevik evaluation of political as against private life, the use of the Bolshevik image indicates higher political status. Hence, a planned distribution of roles in using the two images of Stalin on the occasion of his birthday would still indicate a political stratification of the Politburo, though not necessarily political antagonism within it.

Unless one were to make the somewhat absurd assumption that the roles to be performed on this occasion were distributed by lot, or the improbable assumption that they were assigned for the purpose of concealing the real stratification within the Politburo, those members who stress the Bolshevik image could be assumed to be politically closer to Stalin than those who do not.

The assumption that there had been a decision of some kind on the use of the two images would appear more plausible if either image were used by certain members of the Politburo without the admixture of elements taken from the other. As it is, the difference between the "top group" and the "bottom group" is one of *emphasis* in imagery. For this reason, we are inclined to regard the differentiation of political language discussed in this paper as the result of individual choices rather than of a central decision. However, in this case we may assume that the stress—whether conscious or not—of any given Politburo member on the one or the other image of Stalin was related to his status in the Politburo in the fashion indicated above.

Chapter 6

A FRENCH VIEW OF
LEADERS: ABANDONMENT

EDITOR'S NOTE: Leites sees a preoccupation with abandonment in French political culture. "Those in charge" are suspected of indifference to their responsibilities, deserting their posts, running away, or excluding those who have a right to be present. He hypothesizes the source of this concern in certain French child-rearing practices. He then examines evidence of stress on these themes in political commentary and in literature. Finally he considers some characteristic French political behavior patterns which seem to be adaptations or reactions to fears of abandonment.

From Images of Power in French Politics *(RAND report RM-2954-RC, June 1962), I, 313-390.*

*T*he noun "abandonment" and the verb "to abandon" can be employed in the mildest and gravest circumstances alike. "You've been abandoned," smilingly exclaims a shopkeeper who has let a customer wait. (To be abandoned is thus not so terrible a thing.) On the other hand, a historian recalls the day his unit was encircled in the 1940 campaign:

> I had just tried to get general headquarters on the telephone. I admit that it was only after trying several times that I fully realized the abandonment implied by the tragic words: "a surrounded army."[1]

An area of national life whose situation seems unfavorable is readily regarded as abandoned. Under the Fourth Republic, the achievements of the public sector of the economy were often regarded as brilliant, but the headline of an article by a specialized journalist in a distinguished newspaper proclaimed: "The nationalized industries, 'lost children' of the French economy." On another occasion the same paper affirmed that: "Trade appears to be a poor relation of the economy,"[2] while, according to Paul Gerardot, a former commanding officer of the air force, the civil aviation firms regarded themselves as the "poor, neglected and misunderstood relations" of the air force.[3] On the other hand, according to an ace flier who had evolved into a deputy (Edouard Corniglion-Molinier),

> All the airmen and members of the ground crews of the Air Force . . . think they are the victims of an ever-increasing abandonment. . . . They consider themselves the poor relations of the army, which is, or should be, one big family.[4]

The great expression that is used to stigmatize a policy that favors or simply accepts the independence of an area outside the home country is "policy of abandonment," one of the strongest terms used in public life in the 1950s.

I. FRENCH CHILDHOOD EXPERIENCE AND ABANDONMENT

The tendency to believe that the other person is in the process of abandoning me and to fear lest he do so is probably linked with certain experiences of childhood.

In various social groups it is not unusual for parents to separate from a child early and for a rather long time. The child is put out to a *nourrice* or sent to live with its grandparents or other relatives. Parents give many reasons for doing this: they are going on vacation (in which case there may be sudden weaning); living space is short; the mother has to work; or she has a new baby, and during the first few months after the baby is born she has no time for the other child. Then comes boarding-school (particularly for children who live in small towns or in the country).

Many parents think that this kind of thing is not very painful to the child. They consider chiefly the demands of the difficult situation in which they find themselves and may content themselves with seeing to it that the child whom they have decided to send away receives satisfactory treatment in physical respects.

Robert's *Dictionary* gives an "abusive" meaning of the noun "courage": "hardness of heart." He gives the following example: "He had the courage to abandon his children," and adds the following quotation from Jacques Chardonne: "One must have the courage to abandon one's children. . . ."

It need hardly be said that the person who has this kind of "courage" is likely to feel rather hostile to his victim, and guilty, too. Even when separation becomes necessary for external reasons, the presence of a desire on the part of the parents to lessen their contact with a child probably creates in them an uneasiness that is likely to be communicated to the one who is to be sent away.

It is also probable that the child will react acutely to abandoning, though the parents may manage not to notice.

In these conditions separations that are much less radical—and even less peculiar to France than those cited—can assume some importance. Many middle- and upper-class parents (that is, those who have adequate housing facilities) insist that, at certain times of the day at least, their children stay in the part of the home assigned to them, thus attempting to exclude them from the area in which the parents want to live their own lives. The children may, more or less consciously, feel expelled, chased away.

Many parents prefer that their children not always be at home. It is not unusual for the arrival of vacation periods or even other school holidays to provoke rather mixed reactions among adults who are responsible for children. There were times in the 1950s when many parents seemed obsessed by the fear that there would be no room for their children in schools after the summer holidays. Parents who had had enough of their offspring during the long vacation were afraid that they would continue to have them on their hands.

These various moves of adults are, to be sure, generally presented to the children, with more or less sincerity, as being inspired by a concern for their welfare—or at least as not doing them any harm. Such justifications are often received with a scepticism, either at the time they are given or in retrospect. In films, there recurs a scene in which young parents, who suddenly have a desire to make love, announce to the little nuisance: "You can hardly keep your eyes open!" The child obeys; he has understood.

Separation is not only an expedient imposed by necessity or that serves the parents' convenience; it is also threatened and employed as a punishment. To begin with, there is the removal that is meant to establish solitude: the guilty child is sent into a corner, to his room (when he has one), to the stairs (the service stairway, if there is one), to the *cagibi,* a dark and perhaps dirty place where discarded objects are kept.

Added to these are threats that would be difficult to carry out but that are nevertheless impressive. When the family is about to leave on vacation, the parents may say to a child: if you don't behave, we'll go without you. Or, when they are away and are about to return home: I'll leave you here!—or: I'll put you on the train alone!

Parents also threaten children with the bogeyman or other imaginary characters. (This is not the place for analyzing in detail the various figures in this category.) Real characters may also be drawn upon: the policeman (who may actually be in cahoots with the parents in order to make his supposed role more convincing); a neighbor with a reputation for wickedness; the next man we see in the street; the big dog; the big cat.

And there is also the quite real possibility of being sent away to some disagreeable place such as a boarding school. When things go badly, the tendency of parents to get rid of their children may often be served by the widespread belief that a separation (and the placing of the guilty youngster in the hands of presumed specialists of reform) will arrange matters.

Nor is the child safe in school either. There, too, he can be threatened with being sent away. Many parents and children believe that a student may be dismissed from a lycée in some unforeseeable and incomprehensible way for unavowable or petty reasons—"for any kind of small misdeed."[5] It seems possible to be dismissed almost without warning. From time to time, there occurs a suicide of a schoolchild which seems to be associated with such practices or apprehensions.

There is also the idea of the definitive abandonment of a child, as in the case of the parent who commits the offense of abandoning his family or the one who treats the child in such a way that it is taken away from him by the authorities.

While "There are at least four times as many families wanting to adopt children as there are 'free' babies,"[6] stories of abandoned children are prominently before public attention so much that any case of a parent's heroic love for a child may seem, above all, to be a refutation of the suspicion that the tendency to abandon prevails. In one such case, a mother insisted that one of her kidneys be removed so that it could be grafted on to her son. For a few days, she received enormous attention. Doctors deplored the publicity given to the case, but *Le Monde* explained the phenomenon:

The public, which reads many more stories about unworthy parents and abandoned children, could hardly be indifferent to Madame Renault's gesture.7

In novels, plays and films, the contrast between those who abandon their children and those who merit the title of parent by wanting or agreeing to adopt them is an effective theme (for example, in Marcel Pagnol's trilogy and in Jacques Duval's *Mademoiselle*). A sketch in a literary cabaret may present a number of married couples, each of whom loses their children at a railway station. In another sketch about a father and son who do not recognize each other after a long absence, a member of the cast who is planted in the audience cries out from his seat, "I didn't pay 900 francs to see this kind of drivel! Who ever heard of such a thing happening in real life?" Another accomplice in the audience replies, "I find the scene very true to life. When I was twelve years old, my father lost me in a department store!" The exodus in the spring of 1940 stimulated fantasies of children being abandoned by their parents (for example, in Jacques Laurent's *Le Petit Canard*) or left in a state of abandon by their death (in the film *Jeux Interdits*).

The authors of a best-selling collection of odd items found in the press and elsewhere claim to have seen the following classified advertisement in a detective-story magazine: "Will exchange my first child (to be born shortly) for a small house."8

In family life, allusions to abandoning a child are fairly common in jokes and threats: "Do it or mama will disown you!"; "We must have taken the wrong baby!" Friends or waitresses go into ecstasies over a pretty child: "She's so cute! We're going to keep her! You'll stay with us, won't you?"

The threat that, as far as "my little kitten" is concerned, is merely a friendly joke, becomes a reality for actual kittens. *Le Monde* announced: "An undertaking of the Society for the Prevention of Cruelty to Animals to remedy the abandoning of pets during the summer holidays" and explained:

The tragic abandoning of so many animals during the summer holidays has led the Society for the Prevention of Cruelty to Animals to create a vacation service for pets. . . . The service has issued an urgent appeal to all persons who can take care of an animal for a given period.

But a literary critic in the same paper points out that supposed helpers can become murderers. Addressing those persons who would like to adopt an abandoned animal, he observes:

They should think carefully before deciding. The worst possible thing is the kind of sentimentality that will lead them to take care of an animal only to regret their generosity after a month and to abandon it again.9

It is reasonable to suppose that the body of practices, threats and beliefs which I have just indicated creates in many children a fear, usually unconscious, of being abandoned, a fear which may persist into adulthood.

Any normal and temporary absence of another person may then obscurely revive the idea of a definitive desertion. This is expressed in the following imaginative exaggeration:

> I no longer see anything without mistrust. Such and such a creature was there, present, two minutes ago. He is no longer there. He is absent. Words rang out in the room three minutes ago. They will never ring out again.[10]

After all, it is not uncommon for a mother to adopt the expedient of sneaking off on tiptoe after promising that she would not, thus avoiding the painful scene of an unconcealed departure.

In contemporary French sensibility the following aspect of the human condition seems to be stressed: not all the feelings of parents regarding their children are favorable. The parent's behavior is often thought to reflect hatred for or indifference to the child.

"From his exasperation one might have thought he was the father of five children," says Montherlant of one of his characters.[11] To be a parent is to expose oneself to the likelihood of being annoyed, irritated, and exasperated by one's children, often without wanting to be, to rail against faults or misbehavior which, to the observer, do not always seem commensurate with the reactions they provoke. The child is then likely to be called, at least momentarily, "unbearable" or "hateful," if not unworthy or inferior. The child may seem to the parents an obstacle to their enjoyment of life—a further aspect of the human situation which perhaps assumes particular importance for certain Frenchmen.

When one has to deal with children, one has to spend time wiping their noses, time that could otherwise be turned to better account. Children disturb their parents' affairs in both the literal and figurative sense of the word. They tend to stick their noses into everything, they upset things that were in order, they are in the way. They are nuisances and encumbrances. (I need hardly say that in speaking of certain disagreeable features of their presence, I am not denying—it would be absurd to do so—that parents also have kindly reactions towards their children.) In speaking of a young girl, Montherlant expresses this feeling in so excessive a way that one can easily reject what he has to say, though without robbing it of the significance for which I quote it here:

> What I like about her is that spontaneous and ingenuous taste for happiness, the conviction that life is meant only for happiness and that whatever is not happiness is horrible. At the age of sixteen, she already looks forward with terror to the time when her mother will be old and a burden to her; she shudders at the

thought twenty-five years in advance. . . . And she vigorously . . . thrusts aside the thought of having a child later on, because of the trouble it may cause her. . . .[12]

The parent frequently desires that the child conclude that manifestation of his existence by which he pesters the adult at a given moment: "Stop that!" "Are you going to stop that?" "Are you going to stop pestering me?" "Well? Have you finished?" The well-behaved child is, to put it with exaggeration, the child who plays dead.

It is also part of the human situation for parents to feel from time to time, with regard to their child: why did I ever have to have him; if only I could get rid of him; I'm fed up with him. At times: we had him too soon; it was an error in calculation. These universal reactions, too, seem to leave a distinctive mark in French sensibility, even though their incidence may not be distinctive.

When expressed in a jocular way, the idea of killing the intruder has a certain appeal. A Christmas issue of a weekly published an article by a fashionable young writer in which the author described Breughel's *The Census of Bethlehem.* He imagines that Breughel had organized a village fair with that theme. But then emerge the children "who had been left at home." Despite the parents' protests, they disturb the merrymaking:

Then arose a voice, perhaps that of Aloysius Tron the butcher:

—After all, since we've started, why not go the whole hog. What is it that comes after the census?

—No, no, protested Breughel weakly, in the tone of the sorcerer's apprentice who is unable to control the dark powers that he has unleashed. It was already too late.

—The Massacre of the Innocents is the tranquility of the parents! coldly muttered the one who embodied Herod, fitting the action to the word.

After resisting for a moment, Breughel felt it his duty to set this scene down, as he had the preceding one. And thus, almost one after the other and in much the same setting, two paintings came into being on the terrible square of the snow-covered little village.[13]

The murder of the child by its parents is one of the major themes of Montherlant's plays. In explaining the *Maître de Santiago,* he observes:

The sacrifice of Abraham is unquestionably an obsession in my plays! Alvaro accepts the risk of sacrificing Mariana . . . in the name of transcendence. Ferrante sacrifices Pedro to the welfare of the state *(La Reine Morte).* Georges sacrifices Gillou to his conception of man *(Fils de Personne).* At the end of *L'Exile,* Geneviève agrees to sacrifice her son if by this act she will regain her son's love.[14]

It is part of the human situation for relations between the mother and her children to slacken after birth. According to one hypothesis on French child-training, the mother often speaks in an earnest way in the presence of the nursling and even addresses it; when the child becomes capable of understanding and answering, she may become more distant. At the same time, the child thus deprived may become a witness of the privileges now granted to the next baby.

The feeling may then arise that parents, after having been close to the child at the beginning of its life, turn away from it gradually as it grows older, treating it somewhat as if it did not exist. The behavior of the chief character in *Demain il fera jour,* explains Montherlant, "is based on a postulate: he no longer loves his son." The author adds:

> Is such parental indifference after ardent affection plausible? Of course it is. One sees it all the time. . . .[15]

In the case of young people who become students, the abrupt transition from the strict discipline of the home and the secondary school to the independence of university life may create not only the feeling of having obtained freedom, but also that of having been abandoned. The young student may feel deprived of the contacts and advice which he desires and the need of which is sharpened by his lack of independence in a still recent past.

The child's impression that "they don't care" is thought to be frequent. So is the absorption of parents in their own concerns, their tendency to let things ride and to be absent in spirit even when they are with their children. The claim to the contrary may not be convincing. A novelist presents a mother meeting her daughter:

> "Did you behave?" she asked. The child bowed her head. Mme. Etchat's mind was already elsewhere.[16]

The covering-up of a fundamental indifference by a show of solicitude is a costly operation if it is not carried out lightly:

> The effort I made to seem to take an interest in that life which was so alien to mine exhausted me

says one of Montherlant's characters about his daughter.[17]

When a person is what in the French of the classical period was called "personal," he refuses to make this effort. Explaining the meaning of this adjective, Littré quotes Saint-Simon:

> M. de Gand was so personal a man that he never bothered about a single member of his family.

This image of the parent as indifferent to the child may be succeeded in the adult by a deep conviction regarding "others": they don't give a rap about me.

II. ABANDONMENT THEMES IN FRENCH POLITICAL AND LITERARY CULTURE

1. INDIFFERENCE

Chamfort reports an epigram about the fashionable world of his time:

Society would be a charming thing if people took an interest in each other.[18]

The feeling expressed in this remark remains very much alive. "Politeness," observes Valéry, "is organized indifference." [19] "At bottom, nobody gives a damn," is a ready diagnosis. "A France in which nobody gives a damn about anything, as the Stalinon affair (involving the faulty manufacturing of a drug) has shown": that was how *Le Canard Enchaîné* hailed the year in which the Fourth Republic died.[20]

Let us note (with Robert's *Dictionary*) the twofold meaning of "disinterestedness," "disinterested": "Altruistic, kind, generous, prodigal," but also "detached" and "indifferent." If the other person is not related to me in the pursuit of his own advantage, I can always hope that he will turn to me in a "disinterested" way. But should I not rather fear lest he "disinterest" himself in me? In explaining "to be disinterested," Robert gives the following example: "an unworthy father who is disinterested in his son."

"We are staggered when we see the selfishness of other people," observes Renard, "as if we alone had the right to be selfish." [21] "The self is hateful . . . that of others, of course" says Valéry. [22] In explaining the meaning of "indifference," Robert quotes from Julien Green's *The Closed Garden* about the shock one feels when one realizes the indifference of others towards oneself:

She suddenly felt something she had never experienced before, the complete indifference of everything regarding what was happening inside her, the indifference of that church and that square to her pain, the indifference of millions of people to her fate.

In exceptional but conspicuous cases evoked in literature, the horror changes to ecstasy (often accompanied by a keen attachment to what I think is indifferent toward me). Maurice Sachs writes:

Around three in the morning we stretched out on the ground for a moment. I cannot explain . . . the singular pleasure I took in the indifference of the stars, in the fact that their brilliance was unaware of me and that I was intensely aware of them.[23]

Baudelaire praises the woman who is indifferent to her lover; Montherlant exclaims in his journal: "Three cheers for the one who abandons me!" [24] He declares: "What we desire is that the others do without us as easily as we do without them"[25] and imagines as follows a mistress of whom his hero is very fond:

> She gave Costals what he asked of women: pleasure for both of them enveloped in indifference and absence.[26]

The extravagance of this attitude reveals the depth of the unhappiness it tries to cover.

The reactions of parents to their children often seem subject to broad and rapid fluctuations. Suddenly, in a way that the child can neither foresee nor understand (nothing in his own conduct seems to explain what is happening), a parent turns to him, then turns away from him, takes an interest in him, and then loses interest. "Obliviousness" can then, in the words of Salacrou, be "as strange, as rapid, as violent as love." [27] The effect may be deep and lasting, as Paul Valéry observes:

> Every man has latent within him something terribly somber, prodigiously bitter and hostile . . . the feeling of being . . . delivered up to a power . . . that gives and takes away, that engages us and abandons us. . . .[28]

In the effort to explain the fluctuations of parents, children—and adults— often arrive at interrelations centered around self-interest. The parent turns away from the child when he has had enough of him—a novelist puts the following in the mouth of a mother regarding her little boy:

> I would smother him with kisses and stuff him with chocolate for five minutes. Then he would annoy me and I would send him packing.[29]

—or when his own preoccupations rise to the surface again. In Jacques Duval's *Etienne,* a father calls a family meeting to deal with the misdeeds of his adolescent son. At that moment, he learns that he has just been awarded a decoration he has been wanting for a long time. He calls off the meeting: let us not strike a note of gloom on a day of glory! Inversely, in another successful comedy, Marcel Francks's *Isabelle et le pélican,* a father's indifference and even hostility toward his children changes into active solicitude when an unexpected event links his interest with theirs.

By the time I grow up I am supposed to have learned not to exclude the possibility that those who take an interest in me at a given time will drop me very shortly; the only faithful love, said Sacha Guitry, is self-love.[30]

It is indifference that lasts. Nothing sticks to a tree so well as a dead branch,

says one of Montherlant's characters, [31] and the author recalls the following war-time incident:

There is a village where we were received with open arms in the evening and that we left in the middle of the night without anyone's bothering about us, without anyone's even putting on a light. . . .[32]

The other person grants me his favors when he expects his benevolence to pay off in the immediate future. When he has no further need of me, he drops me at once.

In contrast with the expectation of being dropped, we find—in circumstances to be determined and with degrees of conviction to be analyzed—affirmations, exaggerated perhaps, regarding the "fidelity" of others to the collective self. This theme has been important in French images of France's position in her overseas territories and in the beliefs concerning France's cultural "radiation" in the world at large.

Chamfort relates the following:

In the past, the Epiphany cake was cut before dinner. M. de Fontenelle got the figurine and was king. As he neglected to serve the excellent dish that had been set before him, someone said to him, "The king is forgetting his subjects." To which he replied, "That's what we kings are like."[33]

"We kings" also means the leaders of the Republic. Old chestnut though it be, to call the Minister of Foreign Affairs the "Minister to whom affairs are foreign" rarely fails to raise a laugh. A popular collection of supposedly witty remarks includes the following:

M. de Selves . . . a minister of foreign affairs . . . took no interest in his functions, and it was for that reason that he was nicknamed "the minister to whom affairs are foreign."[34]

A prominent statesman of the Third Republic (Joseph Caillaux) relates the following opinion of him expressed by a colleague (Jean Jaurès) to a common friend (Ivon Delbos):

Now as to Caillaux. Imagine an excellent pilot. He has a knowledge of seamanship. He is familiar with the movements of the heavenly bodies. I even grant him a certain amount of genius. But if I have reason to fear that he falls asleep at the wheel, can I trust him with the job of steering the ship?[35]

Office-holders are so highly suspected of having no interest in their duties that they sometimes think it advisable to deny the charge. When challenged by a deputy (Frédéric Dupont) regarding the difficult situation of the veterans of Indo-China, a Minister of National Defense (Pierre Koenig), in whom simplicity went hand in hand with military glory, defended himself as follows:

> Mr. Rapporteur, I am certainly not disinterested in the situation of the demobilized soldiers. I am very fond of them, and you know it.[36]

When a member of Parliament engages in wire-pulling (which takes up a good deal of his time), his aim is supposedly often to demonstrate his solicitude—to refute the suspicion that he takes no interest in such and such a voter—rather than to obtain tangible advantages for his constituents.

The average pre-1914 deputy could say to himself:

> Although my errands are fruitless, although my promises are always vain and my letters never achieve anything definitive, that has only relative importance.

For

> The voter who requests a favor does not even always want it to be done. He wants: a) to show his importance; b) to receive letters.[37]

A former Minister of National Education (Jean Zay) recalls the kind of thing that went on between the two wars:

> At the time of examinations, competitions and the granting of scholarships, several typists would be busy sending out answers to the thousands of requests for intervention—not all of which, far from it, were from deputies. Here was a typical case of improper and—even more so—useless recommendations. Everyone knew it. At bottom, all that the writers asked was to be informed of the result of the examination in order to communicate it to the interested party and thereby prove that they were concerned about him rather than that they had been able to exert pressure.[38]

A speech in Parliament may not only have the same aim, but may even flaunt it. "In coming to the speaker's platform," said a former Minister of Veterans' Affairs (Emmanuel Temple) during a discussion concerning North Africa, "I shall address not only the Assembly, but also my former fellow-fighters in the Army of Africa." He explained why:

> If I had remained silent, my silence would have been interpreted by them as—if not an abandoning of them—at least a sign of indifference.[39]

2. DEPARTURE AS ABANDONMENT

According to a widespread suspicion, authorities are inclined to slip away or stand off when there is trouble and try to save their skins when there is a catastrophe for which they are probably responsible and in which it is certainly their duty to act. "For almost twenty-two days," observed *Le Canard Enchainé* during a long ministerial crisis, "the man in the street has been repeating that we are without a government. . . . The brutal fact is . . . that if trouble arose there would be nobody of any importance to beat it to Bordeaux."[40]

This feeling seems confirmed by historical memories or myths. According to a man of the extreme right, a "collaborator," most of the officers did not stay with their men during the 1940 retreat:

> In the cars and trucks were colonels. But among the tens of thousands of poor devils on foot . . . who were moving in front of us, we did not see a single officer. Not one. Nobody will ever believe that they were all killed in the front lines.[41]

Sir Edward Spears agrees:

> There must, of course, have been cases when officers did remain with their men, and this was certainly so with many armored formations, but these were the exceptions. . . .[42]

In a speech to the National Assembly in Vichy on July 10, 1940, Pierre-Etienne Flandin had the same to say about the civilian authorities:

> I have come from the Yonne . . . and have spent the last few weeks in contact with the German authorities. . . . If the government does not act without delay, we shall witness a complete nazification of our people. They lack everything, and the Germans are supplying them with what they need. They are substituting for the French authorities who have fled. There is no longer any representative of the French government. On the other hand, the German military authorities are making every effort to provide food and to organize help.[43]

Jacques Benoist-Méchin recalls that

> The walls of the occupied cities were covered with posters showing a German soldier carrying a child in his arms. The poster bore the inscription: "Abandoned population, have confidence in the German soldier."[44]

A leftist historian seems to confirm the words of the rightist leader:

> I know a certain industrial center in which, when the German columns approached, the top-ranking directors hastily abandoned their factories without even seeing to it that the workers were paid.

He adds:

Who of us did not encounter on the highways, amongst the lines of evacuated persons, troops of firemen perched on their municipal firewagons![45]

The man who was Prime Minister at the time of the battle of Dien-Bien-Phu alleged the following about the high command in Indo-China:

Generally speaking, the high command did not have a sufficient experience of the battle of Dien-Bien-Phu. . . . It is regrettable that General Cogny did not think it necessary to leave his headquarters in Hanoi to visit the defenders of the fortified area. . . . It is no less regrettable that on the eve of the attack General Navarre, instead of remaining in Saigon, was not transported to Hanoi to direct the battle there. . . . The command . . . remained too far away from the fighting men.[46]

When Charles de Gaulle withdrew from the government at the beginning of 1946, a high official made this note in his diary:

His opponents accuse him of running away. . . . His opponents who inveighed against him on the sly are the first to say "He let us down!"[47]

When, in the spring of 1953, the same leader withdrew from his party, *Le Canard Enchainé* entitled an article: "An unworthy father abandons his children.[48]

In view of this, any removal in space may arouse the suspicion—if not the certainty—of an abandonment. One of the meanings of the verb "abandon," according to Littré, is "to forsake, to desert," for example, "to abandon one's post"; another is "to leave." Littré quotes Fénelon:

As he had an extraordinary desire to know the customs of foreigners, he abandoned his country . . . in order to travel.

In the case of officeholders, the second meaning, which is harmless, tends to involve the first, which is not.

On June 13, 1940, the members of the French government were expecting a visit from Churchill, who was in France. As the result of a misunderstanding, he left for England without turning up for the engagement. According to Sir Edward Spears, the reaction of the French leaders was violent:

The bad impression and the ill-temper caused by the disappointment of not seeing Churchill . . . undoubtedly played its part in swaying the majority of the Cabinet towards surrender. To these . . . men, the picture of Churchill flying off to his own country without seeing them gave them a feeling of being abandoned.[49]

To go away is to desert! On June 21, Pierre Laval dared declare to the President of the Republic, who was thought to be planning to leave:

> When it becomes known that you chose to leave at a time when our country was
> in a very grave plight, a word will spring to everyone's lips: defection. . . . Perhaps
> a more serious word: betrayal. . . .[50]

Marshal Pétain declared at the same time:

> It is impossible for the government, without emigrating, without deserting, to
> abandon French territory.[51]

If a statesman claims that the country's interest requires that he depart, is
it not obvious—cannot one maintain that the country would regard it as
obvious?—that he is simply camouflaging—and camouflaging crudely—
personal motives? In June 1940, the departure for Morocco of a steamer
with a cargo of duputies was delayed by sailors who were reluctant to
evacuate runaways. At the meeting of the Cabinet on June 13, General
Weygand had, as it were, spoken for them:

> the ministers should . . . have the courage to remain in France, regardless of what
> might happen, in the first place because only at that price would Frenchmen
> accept the sacrifices they were being asked to make. When the President of the
> Republic interrupted me to say that the sacrifice of leaving the country's soil was
> even more cruel for the ministers, I replied that nobody would interpret it in that
> way. People would think that they were continuing, without any hope of
> resistance, to have our people killed, bombarded and burned after being careful to
> put themselves out of harm's way. . . .

Since the government's stay abroad was likely to last "several years,"

> Did they imagine that, after leaving France in the hands of the enemy, they would
> still have any authority [when they returned]?[52]

Indeed, the following was the "immediate reaction of Parisians to the
occupation":

> Because they resented those who were not there to share their danger and
> humiliation, they at first felt less resentment toward the invaders.[53]

These feelings impressed even the most tough-minded. One of the eighty
deputies who voted against Pétain's assumption of power (Jean-Paul Boncour)
recalled:

> I am . . . not sure that Mandel himself was not against the evacuation. That was a
> rather common complex among those who resisted. . . .[54]

This "complex" is easily observable in the case of Jules Moch, Mandel's
successor as Minister of the Interior at the time of the collapse of the next

republic. In June 1958, explaining his behavior of the month before, he stated that, if the Assembly had refused to induct De Gaulle, Paris would have been instantly "threatened, assailed or conquered" by the rebellious armed forces, that the government would then have "blown up" and "would have had to retreat towards the mines in the North." But "Legitimacy in retreat, even in exile, would have been only partial. . . ."[55] Although departure may border on treason, one can nevertheless try to justify it as an indispensable means of avoiding an even more glaring breach of duty.

When, at the beginning of May 1958, the Socialist Party decided not to be part of the combination that was to resolve the crisis begun on April 15, one could predict that Robert Lacoste, who had been Minister for Algeria since the winter of 1956, would not remain in office. On May 8, General Salan awarded him the Cross of Military Valor. The citation stated:

> On numerous occasions, without measuring the danger, he brought the fighting units the comfort of his presence. . . .

Lacoste left for Paris. Signs of imminent disorder in Algiers were accumulating. The Prime Minister, who had resigned but was in charge of current matters (Félix Gaillard), the one who had been designated by the President of the Republic (Pierre Pflimlin), the leader (Guy Mollet), and the governing board of his party (the Socialists)—all of them asked Lacoste to return to Algeria immediately. He refused. On May 12, he exclaimed in the corridor, "with the coarseness that is a specialty of his": "Return there? My ass!"[56]

On the evening of May 13, news of the insurrection reached the corridors:

> Where's Lacoste? In Algiers?
>
> —No, in the restaurant.
>
> —It's a desertion of post.
>
> —If we had a Clemenceau, he'd be in jail this evening.[57]

Almost two months later, Lacoste explained matters to his party. The conspirators in Algiers had insisted that he remain in order to participate in the insurrection. His abandoning of his post, he declared, was the necessary and sufficient condition for avoiding having to join the seditious group:

> I did not want to commit the crime of breach of duty. I did not want to violate the Constitution. I wanted to reconcile my duty to the Republic, the Party and Algeria. The "pro-consul" of Algeria refused to be the leader of an Algeria that was rising in revolt against the Republic.[58]

Doing his duty without choosing between desertion of post and going over to the insurrection? Defending with his authority and body the invaded building of the General Government? Too naive a solution even to be mentioned.

3. ABSENCE AS DEFECTION

Thus, persons in power often seem inclined to commit the sin of dereliction *(carence)*. In giving the analogical meaning of this noun—"situation of a person who is found wanting, who evades his obligations, who does not fulfill his task"—Robert offers the following example first of all: "The dereliction of the government, of the authority." According to a widespread notion, the authorities—be they parents or their successors—do not fulfill their duties of remaining in the presence of their charges.

In an Anouilh play, a young man who is about to stage a complicated pretence asks an old actress to impersonate his mother. In order to show her competence, she recalls that "in *La Grande Coupable,* I abandoned my baby on the steps of a church." To which the young man replies:

I mistrust . . . the bad mothers of the stage. They overdo things. If they had a real child, it wouldn't even have time to be unhappy. It would die or become an idiot immediately. Who would ever think of abandoning one's baby on the steps of a church when there are so many easy ways of abandoning a child, even while keeping it conveniently at home until it reaches its majority.

The mother that he wants the actress to impersonate is

the kind that little boys dream of when they sit in the kitchen with the maid, waiting for their mother to come home—reeking of perfume after her eternal afternoon shopping. Ah, a mother who had no shopping to do, no friends to see![59]

In the course of a ceremony at the monument to the war dead in La Rochelle on November 11, 1957, the prominent guests and the general public were surprised that the National Anthem was not played:

The members of the town orchestra who usually played it were present, but as private individuals. They had not brought their instruments. . . . On September 20, the twenty-five members of the town orchestra had submitted their resignation to the mayor. They simply accused their leader, M. Turandot, of not giving them sufficient attention. Nor did they forgive him for not having attended several rehearsals. M. Turandot is unquestionably an excellent musician, they said, but he forgets about us![60]

"There's only one evil—absence," says an adolescent in one of Montherlant's plays.[61] This feeling must be very intense if so exigent an author chooses so worn a formula.

In the case of the politician, too, absence seems a proof of indifference. According to a journalist of the Third Republic, this feeling leads to the "martyrdom of the deputy":

> Once he is elected, he has to leave for Paris. Taking advantage of his necessary departure, his enemies seize upon every opportunity to attack him. At local marriages, funerals and celebrations, they point out that the politician is absent, and they insinuate: "He's not interested in you."62

Under the Fourth Republic, Parliament was in session during a very large number of hours, often dealing at length with exceedingly special matters. Hence the number of legislators present at any given session was bound to be limited. This was yet another one of the numerous aspects of their life which politicians viewed not only as "normal," but also as scandalous. With more or less sincerity one could always charge others with absenteeism (one more penchant which the Fifth Republic has tried to check).

Even when one claims that the appearance of overworking in Parliament does not mask a fundamental idleness, one may have to grant that it suggests the intention of faking. (It is easier for adults to get out of doing something than it is for children, who are often really required to overwork.) "Last night," observed a deputy (Pierre Courant) "the Assembly met until 4:30 a.m. and decided to continue at 9:30." This raised the following question:

> In doing so, are we giving the impression that we are working a great deal or rather that we are working badly?

Among ourselves, we deputies know something of which the country may be less aware, to wit, that "it may not be the same deputies who are present night and day"—naturally, "which explains, to a large extent . . . absenteeism [in Parliament].63

One could always attack this absenteeism. Deputies felt so uncomfortable about it that they regarded silence as the best defense unless the charge was particularly violent or justification unusually easy. For example, early in the day on which the E.D.C. treaty was rejected, the chairman of the Foreign Affairs Committee (Daniel Mayer) made an unusual declaration:

> This is a morning meeting. I wish to say at the very beginning, for those newspapers that may speak of a form of Parliamentary absenteeism, that absenteeism in the morning is justified by the unusual number and length of the sessions, by committee work, by the practice of relaying one another. Hence, the press does not have the right to speak of absenteeism this morning.

This unexpected comment, which seemed to some deputies to conceal a maneuver directed against the treaty, aroused "various reactions" and "protests" among the proponents of the E.D.C.—which impelled the speaker to even greater frankness: "My dear colleagues, I am defending the entire Parliament against a public campaign."[64]

For absence creates a strong presumption of dereliction. The present writer recalls having been present at a meeting of the Assembly on a great occasion (the induction of Georges Bidault on June 10, 1953); he was sitting next to a priest whose sentiments were very far to the right. Almost every time a deputy in the center section just below us left the meetinghall during the discussion, my neighbor would exclaim in a low voice: "Ah, the bastard! They're all corrupt!" This enemy of the regime was merely adopting the attitude of a prominent Third Republic politician, André Tardieu, who— owing to illness, among other reasons—abandoned politics and the regime shortly before the collapse of 1940:

> The laws on which the country's life depends are discussed before empty benches. Among those who are present, a large number do not listen and attend to their mail. . . . Deputies put in an appearance at committee meetings rather than participate in them. The door is constantly opening and closing. People are continually going in and out.[65]

When one speaks of the absence of colleagues in the Assembly, one almost always expresses the hostile feeling I have just indicated.

In a debate on foreign policy, a leader, Georges Bidault, began his speech with the following words: "Ladies and Gentlemen, the debate that occupies the part of the Assembly present this morning. . . ." He observed, with regard to the line that France should follow:

> And if it has anything to say, when could it say it—I ask of the faithful who are here present at this hour *(smiles)*—when could it say it with less brio and waste of time than at this morning's session. . . ?[66]

In the discussion that ended with the ratification of the Common Market Treaty, a deputy spoke ironically of his colleagues' absenteeism:

> it is far less a matter of convincing the numerous legislators crowded on these benches *(smiles)*. . . .[67]

Another resorted to indignation:

> The inadmissible absenteeism that has made a caricature of this discussion and that has warranted the irony of the papers. . . .[68]

A third suggested to the President of the Assembly that he employ severe methods:

I should like to ask you whether it is not possible for you, when the debate is adjourned during lunch time, to assemble the Board of the Assembly so as to consult it regarding the possibility of continuing so important a discussion in the presence of so small a number of deputies.[69]

Addressing a sprinkling of deputies—as usual—a speaker reminded his listeners that civil servants were on strike that day:

On this morning of November 19, I think that the press will be able to conclude from the large number of deputies present that they should be classified as civil servants. . . .[70]

In the early hours of the morning, the Assembly voted, after a first reading, that various articles of the Constitution be revised. When the members came to the question of forbidding deputies to abstain from participating in a vote of confidence, even the vote-collectors of various groups had disappeared. Ushers replaced them—which was the practice in such cases.[71]

Under these circumstances, presence may by itself seem to be a meritorious act:

These problems, as you are well aware, my dear colleagues who are willing to be present at this somewhat thorny debate. . . .

said a deputy, speaking of a major project, the Common Market.[72] At the end of a debate on an important matter (the reorganization of the Ministry of National Defense), the chairman of the competent committee, Pierre Montel, expressed his thanks:

I would like . . . to ask you to be so kind as to join me in thanking our rapporteur who worked very hard during the last forty-eight hours. I also thank those of our colleagues who were so good as to participate in this discussion.[73]

"Objections are raised to the absenteeism of deputies," observed a leader who had been out of office for some time (René Pléven). "Is it not also true, all too often, that ministers are absent from the government bench when the time comes to answer oral questions?"[74] The deputies were not likely to forget this; the fact offered them a precious opportunity to be accusers rather than accused:

The Minister of National Defense, whom I am surprised not to see at his place during a discussion of this kind. . . .[75]

This is the type of stinging remark that was often heard and that could be developed, for example, in accordance with the pattern offered by a speaker during the discussion preceding ratification of the Common Market Treaty:

> The absence of M. Ramadier during the discussion of the Common Market greatly
> surprised and even shocked the National Assembly.... But the new minister
> Félix Gaillard is not present at this discussion either.[76]

In the case of ministers, too, absence denotes disinterest (whatever knowledge one may have of the "crushing burden" that weighs on them):

> In the absence of the Keeper of the Seals, whom this discussion does not seem to
> interest *(various reactions)* ...,[77]

said a deputy in commenting upon the special powers requested by the
government for the purpose of checking Algerian terrorism in Metropolitan
France. To be sure, it was an opponent who was speaking; it is possible that
he was not entirely sincere. Nevertheless, the fact remains that a charge of
this kind may be acceptable and even useful.

When the image of the statesman who cares little about his duties is not
fully developed, it may be so distinctly implied that the defense will be
explicit. "At a time when Parliament is deeply disturbed by matters affecting
North Africa," observed an enemy of Pierre Mendès-France (Pierre Montel),
"it is rather curious that the Prime Minister ... is not present at the opening
of so important a debate." The Minister of the Interior, Francois Mitterrand,
then replied:

> The Prime Minister will be present in a moment. It is not fair to say that at such a
> time the Prime Minister is not concerned with North Africa ... that he is not
> interested in the discussion at the National Assembly, whereas the fact is that in
> the course ... of so many sessions, everyone has seen him in his place listening to
> the various speakers and replying to them.[78]

At a difficult moment during the discussion of the W.E.U., the President
of the Assembly (André Le Troquer), who had left the meeting hall, was
replaced by a vice-president (Jules-Julien). The way in which the latter
conducted the discussion was not appreciated by everyone. Commenting on
the matter in the corridors, the deputies were of the opinion that the
President had abandoned his post at a critical moment. When he returned, he
felt obliged to declare:

> The Assembly will not assume for a moment that its President is not interested in
> its discussion (applause). I follow it with keen interest, even when I am working in
> my private office.[79]

To refute the ever-plausible hypothesis that I am remiss in my duty, the
best thing to do is to remind my hearers discreetly that what may seem at
first to be a matter of duty may also be regarded as one of interest:

> I intended to ask the Minister of National Defense when the French government was going to inform the Parliament ... of the policy it meant to follow henceforth,

said a deputy, Pierre de Chevigné, who continued as follows:

> But as the Minister of National Defense does not seem to be interested in his budget, I shall wait for a good opportunity in the near future to ask him this question.

The session was suspended until the arrival of the Minister, Jacques Chaban-Delmas. After excusing himself—"owing to ... a misunderstanding in the preparing of my schedule, I planned to be here at 4:15, at which time I thought that the discussion of the military budget was to be continued"—he made short work of the hypothesis of his "disinterest," in the sense of "no longer being interested in (someone or something)," by casting doubt on his "disinterestedness," in the sense of "detachment from any personal interest":

> None of our colleagues ... could have thought that I was disinterested in a discussion that concerns me so very directly.[80]

4. NO ANSWER: FAILURE TO PROTECT

The authority that loses interest in me neither helps me to satisfy my needs nor protects me against the many vicissitudes of life. It leaves me entirely on my own. It cares not a rap about what may happen to me, provided that it itself is not affected. It is often felt among leaders and the general public alike that a politician tends to evade his duties just as a criminal evades the police.

After the collapse of 1940, a great writer who was also a high official had the following to say about the rulers of the period between the two wars:

> Absorbed by war, by peace, by debts, by raw materials, by security, by all the accidents of life, they left France to itself. They let it find housing unaided, they let it amuse itself unaided, they let it invent the inventions of the century unaided, they let it wash itself unaided.

Thus, "our pre-war state was one of false sickness and true abandonment."[81]

In declaring to its subjects "do what you like, but don't bother me," the authority can try to indulge in the pleasures of inaction. "What we are not told," declares one of Salacrou's characters,

> is that, after creating the earth, the sun and human beings, God fell asleep. God is sleeping. It took a God to create the world; it took the sleep of God for unhappiness to be born there.[82]

Furthermore, people in office are supposedly absorbed in activities that promote their personal interests. Jules Renard recorded a conversation he had had with Lucien Guitry on July 9, 1900:

> We spoke about our ministers. This is one of our favorite subjects. He said to me that when Waldeck-Rousseau ... delivers a speech in a calm tone, he trembles inwardly and that he is dripping with sweat by the time his agenda is adopted. ... Their excuse is that they do not have time to bother about us.[83]

In both cases, the authority becomes inaccessible to his subjects. "If a Parisian," once observed the review, *Le Petit Crapouillot,* "picked up his telephone and dialed the letters: 'Good God,' the answer he got would surprise no one. It would be as follows: 'The number you have dialed does not exist.' " There we have the great theme: no answer.

Here, as elsewhere, the politician merely follows what is viewed as a normal human tendency. By virtue of the very nature of the disposition in question, he is not worried by the fact that, in his case, the universal tendency towards dereliction may have far wider consequences than in the case of those who occupy less influential positions.

Life abounds in situations in which one fears the refusal of help that one needs urgently. There is the great category of acts of non-assistance to a person in danger.

The following incident in the 1940 campaign is related by Montherlant. A detachment was going down a road strewn with the bodies of dead Frenchmen:

> "Look at that one," said a man. "He's still moving!" "He's still moving": that's what a Marseilles waiter says to you when he shows you the sole that's going to be cooked for you. Indeed, the body on the ground was still moving. As he went by, the person who had said "He's still moving" tossed away his cigarette, which hit the shoe of the wounded man. It came within a few inches of falling on the body itself. A small tank was moving behind us. The occupants repeated the words: "There's one that's still moving." Yet not a single one of them lifted the wounded person onto the tank. I turned around three or four times. I could see from the movement of people's heads and from their looks that they were passing on the words: "He's still moving." But until something or other that I no longer remember blocked the scene from view, nobody stepped out of the column—which was full of all kinds of vehicles—to try to save that living person from death.[84]

The following takes place in a military hospital:

> Someone groaning. —Shut up! You're keeping us from sleeping!
>
> —I'm going to die!
>
> —O.K., go right ahead!

—Do you think you'd talk like that if you were going to die?

—Just let us sleep, that's all we're asking you!

And what a tone! As if they were tearing his liver out of his body. During the night, he sends out calls in all directions, like a sinking boat sending out an S.O.S. "Paul! Jacques!" They sleep, or pretend to. And he is dying, surrounded by his fellowmen, by his brothers, by those whom he called by their first name, by the diminutives of their first name, and he was more abandoned than if he were alone in a desert; worse than abandoned; rejected and barked at.[85]

And here, according to the same author, is a street in peacetime:

A friend of mine, who is about sixty years old, fell down, for some reason that I have forgotten (he sprained his foot or had a dizzy spell), and remained lying on the sidewalk of a street in Paris without being able to get up. "I don't know how long I remained there. But I remember very well that the people going by looked at me and continued on their way without stopping. One man, in order to get by, even *pushed me aside with his foot*."[86]

A spectacular automobile accident may raise the following question: how many offenses of non-assistance to a person in danger did it entail? The following is the comment of a journalist about an accident that befell a popular writer:

So the entire world was staggered by what happened to Francoise Sagan. But the fact is that if the accident was not mortal . . . the whole world is not responsible for its not being so—the whole world represented by the few dozen motorists who blandly sped by the inanimate body of their idol without stopping, without informing themselves, without even informing the nearby police station. How many? There is no way of knowing. Some people have said that she lay there for forty minutes without being helped; the most reliable witnesses say that it was only ten minutes. But the time doesn't matter. Two days later, *Paris-Presse* undertook an enquiry. It reconstituted a similar accident and, despite the convincing staging (automobile smashed against a tree, girl lying on the grass, etc.), it saw streams of motorists racing by, glancing briefly at the "dying person" and going on their way without slowing up for a moment in order to maintain their average speed. Finally, someone stopped. It was an old man in an old-fashioned tin lizzie.[87]

An association of old people might launch a membership campaign with the slogan: "When you're old, you may be abandoned." The tendency of the general public and of the authorities not to help those who urgently need assistance is often supposed to manifest itself even at the expense of those whose merit and fate would seem to compel energetic action.

Witnesses of the 1940 campaign often declared that the country turned away from the retreating and disorganized army, an affirmation that was of course stressed by those who became enemies of the Resistance. A prominent writer, who was a "collaborator" described, in 1942, the arrival of his unit in the Perigord area:

> For the first time, entire towns displayed a compassion for which we were, on our part, begging. . . . In Sarlat, girls stood in the street offering us biscuits, chocolate and cigarettes. The men were dazzled. The worst grumblers from the North were beaming: "Can you imagine! I can't get over it. I sure will remember Sarlat!"[88]

In 1958, a man of letters who had been through the French campaign of 1940 and who remained faithful to Vichy remembered the day when Bordeaux was occupied by the Germans:

> while the population of Bordeaux, with an eagerness mingled with curiosity, fear and admiration, went to meet the enemy, we moved along . . . deserted streets . . . towards the wharves that were reserved for us[89]

a scene recalling unpublicized embarkations for Indo-China, one of the circumstances which gave the army during that war the feeling of being abandoned by the country, a feeling which significantly contributed to the insurrection of 1958.

In the late spring of 1956, a captain who was stationed in southern Morocco, Pierre Moureau, was kidnapped. In the winter of 1957, a number of prominent persons in the home country stated that the captain was alive and that members of the Moroccan "army of liberation" were dragging him through the South in order to display him "in chains, emasculated, with his eyes plucked out and his forearms broken, as a symbol of our decline." It was also alleged that the authorities had not done all they could have done to help him. Far from it. The captain was said to have been

> condemned to a torture greater than the physical torture he had endured, that of feeling he was alone, abandoned by his chiefs, his elders . . . abandoned even by a country that he had served so well."

What a contrast with the behavior of the foreigner:

> When a British officer was . . . kidnapped in Port Said, the English government demanded that he be sent back, and public opinion was not satisfied until the body of Lieutenant Moorhouse was returned to Great Britain.

But the French authorities were said to have responded to those who were worried about the captain with "a wall of silence and a wall of indifference." They were said to have chosen to "announce his death only because this reassured both their consciences and their apprehensions of a scandal."[90]

Of course this theme was developed particularly by certain right-wing groups within the framework of their propaganda against "the abandoning" of North Africa. But it was not only in this context that the suspicion or certainty of an "abandoning" appeared. A left-wing weekly published an article by a novelist who, beneath a big headline—"The Abandoning of Captain Moureau"—declared:

> Moureau had stopped thinking of his executioners long before his death. He thought of us. He called us cowards and hated us.[91]

The situation, from 1955 onward, of the French of North Africa who left for Metropolitan France was often described as one of people who had been "abandoned." According to a Moderate (Pierre André), in an address to the Assembly in the spring of 1957,

> close to a hundred thousand Frenchmen have taken refuge in the home country ... and they are ... reduced to having to appeal to public generosity in order not to die of starvation! I do not want to inflict upon you a reading of the appeals to public generosity that appeared in the Lyons and Marseilles newspapers with the approval of the local prefects. The French refugees from Tunisia and Morocco are relying on public charity to be housed and fed.[92]

An M.R.P. leader, Maurice Schuman; added at the same time, in the course of an important discussion in the Assembly, the following description of the situation of the French who had been expelled from Egypt after the Suez expedition:

> My dear colleagues, after the long speeches we have heard, I should like to address the Assembly briefly for the purpose of drawing the government's attention ... to the situation of many Frenchmen who have been expelled from Egypt. The Prime Minister is not unaware of their situation, since, immediately after the events of November, he took a very firm stand by declaring that he wanted all French citizens who had been evacuated from Egypt to be able to find employment in France and to be sheltered, housed, fed, and aided.

> Unfortunately, the commitments that were made in the government's name have thus far not been fulfilled.

> I shall not make any comparison between the situation of French citizens who were expelled from Egypt and the advantages granted to English citizens who were repatriated from Egypt. I merely point out that, apart from a daily allowance of 800 francs for adults and 400 francs for children under the age of ten, French citizens returning from Egypt have received no permanent aid and particularly no welfare assistance, no payment of pensions and life annuities due from the Egyptian government or its administrative offices, no grant for re-establishing themselves in France, no advance on sequestrated property and no aid or priority with regard to housing.

They have not received the benefit of any priority in employment, any effective and sufficient cooperation in resettlement or regarding scholarships, no loans. As for the French doctors who were expelled from Egypt, they are being blocked by a regulation of the Order of Physicians and they experience the greatest difficulties in establishing themselves and in practising their profession in France.

We know very well that M. Guy Mollet intends to respect the promise he made spontaneously, but thus far the instructions that have been given have not been applied and there has even been a tendency to what I shall euphemistically call a retraction.[93]

The Foreign Minister (Christian Pineau), "though recognizing the inadequacy of what had been done in the past," attempted to impress Parliament with a piece of good news, which actually did not indicate that any action was being taken. He made public the fact that during the preceding weeks

the President of the Association of French Property and Interests, who had a complete file concerning Frenchmen in Egypt, had been received at the Foreign Ministry. On the basis of the documents that he submitted to us, we requested all members of the government concerned in the matter—and, in view of the great sums required, not only the Foreign Minister—to try to settle the problem as soon as possible.[94]

Obviously, "as soon as possible" did not mean that the "problem" would be "settled" overnight. Meanwhile, yet another rather prominent parliamentarian (Edouard Bonnefous) exhorted his colleagues:

Let us not leave our fellow-citizens in a state of misfortune, discouraged, left to themselves; let them not see only this dismal aspect of France, which they left so long ago. . . . A country that allowed its citizens to be mistreated or that was disinterested in their fate would . . . lose face. We must not let our fellow-countrymen seek random solutions, unaided. . . .[95]

Was May 13, 1958, to some extent such a solution? According to a deputy who regarded himself as carrying on the great tradition of men like Ferry (Edouard Pisani), the "reflex" of the French from Algeria was

that of people of modest means who were informed of the fact that, despite fine promises, the home country was reserved for the artisans and farmers who had left Tunisia and Morocco.[96]

If an authority does actually concern itself with certain matters, there remains an apprehension: will it persevere? Will it not abandon its activity in mid-air? One of the meanings of the verb "to abandon" is "to renounce something," and Littré's dictionary gives the following example: "to abandon an undertaking . . . that has been begun."

In Montherlant's *Fils de Personne,* the chief character says to his fourteen-year-old son, a natural child whom he has not recognized and with whom he has lived very little:

> In the last analysis, what are you? You're an abandoned child. . . . Furthermore, most children in France are abandoned children. Either their parents do not look after them or if they do, they do so badly. Or else they look after them for a while in an intelligent way and then abandon them.[97]

A few weeks after the Hungarian revolution of 1956, a deputy (Robert Duron) examined the plight of the refugees who had arrived in France:

> There is a tendency of the French mind . . . which causes people to act in such a way that, after the welcome has been organized, after the frontier has been crossed, after the first food has been distributed, they have a feeling of virtue and tend to forget about those whom they first welcomed warmly.

Generally speaking,

> what I am always afraid of in France . . . is a tendency to be very generous, of course, but also to forget rapidly.[98]

In addition to the danger of lassitude are the limitations imposed by considerations of self-interest. If the other person helps me only as long as it serves his purpose to do so, he will drop me as soon as our needs cease to converge. This may happen at a moment when I am in a particularly difficult situation, when I depend on his support more than ever. Such is the law of the discrepancy of interests.

The beloved leader, the man to whom one devotes oneself, is, under these circumstances, generally represented as a man who cannot conceivably "abandon" his followers. I can count on his active solicitude; he is faithful, persevering. These traits were, for instance, major features of the official image of Marshal Pétain.

5. EXCLUSION AS DISMISSAL

If fantasies of abandonment contribute to the image of authorities who run away, those of dismissal probably contribute to the aversion for the ban, *l'exclusive,* the contemporary meaning of which word Robert's *Dictionary* illustrates by the following phrase: "Former minister who became the object of an *exclusive* of a majority party." To be subject to an *exclusive* seems, in an obscure way, like one of the many disadvantages of childhood that normally should disappear when one becomes an adult.

As a child, I may feel painfully excluded from my parents' intimacy, as the hero of a recent French novel is from the affair of his wife. He expresses the horror of remaining "outside" in front of others "who have already closed themselves off."[99]

As a politician, I like the "accessible ministers"[100] who replace the *exclusive* by inclusion. A prominent statesman of the Third Republic described as follows a politician of the period (Ferdinand Sarrien):

> What he liked particularly was to be approached familiarly by ministers or prominent men ... to be conspicuously drawn aside for some private discussion.[101]

I react sharply against those who, in trying to issue an *exclusive* against me, seem to be thrusting me back into childhood.

During the crisis of the spring of 1957, the Socialists announced that they were opposed to the awarding of certain posts to Moderates by the M.R.P. prime minister designate (Pierre Pflimlin). The following, according to a journalist, was the reaction of the leaders of the group thus attacked:

> They in turn went to see M. Pflimlin. Some of them were furious when they left his office, and others, such as M. Pinay, were very relaxed. The latter declared, "We asked M. Pflimlin whether he was aware of the Socialist Party's *exclusive* against us. . . . M. Guy Mollet had punished us and now was locking us up in the lumber room."[102]

The Socialist prime minister, Guy Mollet, excluded the "Poujadist" group from those whose representatives he was consulting. Whereupon one of the Poujadist deputies (Marcel Bouyer) addressed him in the following terms:

> When you set forth your program for an Algerian policy, you spoke about safeguarding the interests of minorities, the elimination of feudal practices. These words seemed odd to us, for you are automatically excluding those who are nevertheless grown up and can defend themselves.[103]

This is a curious argument which, however, reveals again the association between the *exclusive* and childhood.

The *exclusive* is permissible only as a response to an aggression prohibited by the rules of the game. (I may therefore fear the temptation of intransigence that may make me commit such an aggression and even provoke me to backslide into it; the fate of Pierre Mendès-France can serve as a warning.) One must at least pretend to cry out with Victor Hugo:

> Oh! let us exile no one!
> Oh! Exile is impious!

and to declare with Briand:

> I am not a man who closes the door of the Republic to anyone.[104]

It is often good form to show indignation at the issuing of an *exclusive* and almost always proper to deny that it has been issued. When the crisis of the spring of 1957 was in the process of being resolved, a representative (Aimé Paquet) of the Moderates addressed the prime minister designate (Maurice Bourgès-Maunoury) as follows:

> During this crisis we did not issue an *exclusive* against anyone. But you did![105]

A leader, François Mitterrand, who was said to have refused to belong to the new combination because the prime minister designate had not accepted the *exclusive* that he demanded (against Robert Lacoste) declared, in the name of his group:

> I want to make it quite clear that we have not issued an *exclusive* against anyone.[106]

The series of events that ended with the death of the Fourth Republic began with an *exclusive*. On May 8, 1958, certain groups (Socialists, Radicals, M.R.P.s) declared their opposition to the inclusion of a certain deputy (André Morice) in the cabinet of the prime minister designate (René Pléven). Representatives (Roger Duchet and Camille Laurens) of the Moderates close to the politician whose way had been barred protested:

> We are shocked that, at a time of the greatest peril, *exclusives,* which, be it added, do not affect us, have been issued.

The *désigné* gave up his efforts: "I had said . . . that I would accept no *exclusive*. . . ."[107] It was then Pierre Pflimlin's turn, and that of May 13, 1958.

The rejection of the *exclusive* in politics is matched, in other spheres, by the efforts to guarantee a situation that has been established—a characteristic that has often been regarded as typical of French law. If the child may feel threatened with being sent away from school or from home, the civil servant is strongly protected against dismissal and the tenant against expulsion.

> Is there anything that is not the result of expulsion? The mother vomits forth her child, thought expels phrases,

says Paul Valéry.[108] But since expulsion is also frightening, civilization offers protection against it.

The defense is precarious. The tendency to expel is always likely to prevail. Let us take an example at random: a leader (René Pléven) made the following proposal to the Assembly one year after the end of the Indo-Chinese war:

> If reserve officers and non-commissioned officers who have served as volunteers in Indo-China request to be enrolled in the active army and if their request is not granted, they are entitled to receive notice before being sent back to civilian life, such notice to be calculated at the rate of six months per year of service in Indo-China.

Why this precaution?

> A number of very painful incidents occurred recently. Reserve officers who had applied for admission to the regular army received, along with a rejection of their application, an announcement that they were being dismissed with twenty-four hours notice.[109]

At the end of the *exclusive* is solitude, a state that inspires terror of which one does not always seem to be fully conscious.

Jules Renard speaks of "the certainty of not being alone which is comforting even in a cemetery."[110] According to a contemporary writer "the terror of being alone" is the "chief motive of marriage."[111] As an observer at the front during World War I, Montherlant noted:

> The only soldiers of the Foreign Legion whom I ever saw go off by themselves . . . with . . . or without a book were Germans or Russians; the Frenchman . . . is *sociable.*[112]

We have already mentioned certain childhood situations in which the absence of persons about me is usually associated with anguish, which it heightens. We might also mention a kind of punishment that begets a feeling of dreadful solitude—in another sense of the word—in the very presence of those who are usually about me. A parent or teacher scolds me for something in front of everyone. The other adult members of the family, the other teachers, my brothers, sisters, schoolmates, neighbors, and even passers-by are all encouraged to become judges and executioners, a role which they often do not mind playing.[113]

To become an adult is also to acquire the means of avoiding solitude.

To be a child is to have to sleep alone, a sad thing indeed, as Mallarmé and Proust have noted in famous passages. In a popular comedy, a young man exclaims: "After all, at my age, I have the right not to sleep alone! I'm no longer a boy." "I don't want to sleep alone any more," declares a young husband in another play when his wife leaves him.

In a novel by Jean Freustué a man tries to find a way of seeing his mistress more often; he examines the obstacles:

> I said to her, "Can't your husband take a trip without you?" She answered, "Unfortunately, not! He's physically unable to sleep alone."[114]

A character in a play who, for the time being, lives alone, describes his impossible situation: "During the day, I don't mind. But at night, no. . . . When I think of all the nights of the coming winter!"

Jules Renard records a comment of his wife:

> "How," said Marinette, "could you go to Nevers in such weather and sleep in an icy room without your wife to warm you?"[115]

The horror of solitude seeps into politics. In Parliament every group knows that, by virtue of parliamentary "arithmetic," most of the others are "condemned" to "live" together with it. Nevertheless, one often suspects conspiracies with the intention of "isolating" such and such a group, a possibility that makes its members shudder—when it does not infuriate them.

The country itself seems threatened with solitude, to a degree that is perhaps not always justified by the realities of the situation. Replying to the opponents of the Common Market Treaty, a Minister of Foreign Affairs (Christian Pineau) asked:

> Why . . . bring up constantly the inevitable isolation of France . . . when nothing justifies such a fear?[116]

After the insurrection of May 13, 1958, the former Minister for Algeria (Robert Lacoste) tried to make citizens of the home country understand the reaction that the intentions ascribed to Pierre Pflimlin had aroused in Algeria:

> When mention was made of conferences on neutral ground for the purpose of agreeing to a cease-fire, the following count was immediately made: Morocco, Tunisia, the F.L.N., the U.S.A., England. That makes five participants at a round-table discussion against poor France alone. The reaction in Algiers was violent.[117]

Almost four years before, when Pierre Mendès-France asked the Assembly to decide upon the fate of the E.D.C. Treaty, he spoke at length of another round-table discussion (the Brussels Conference of August 1954) at which five participants had rejected the modification of the treaty proposed by France. There too the evocation of "France alone" was followed by a "violent reaction": the treaty was rejected. The threat or the fact of isolation (be it real or imaginary) is likely to arouse powerful feelings.

III. REACTIONS AND ADAPTATIONS

One of the major reactions to the feeling or danger of being abandoned is to retaliate. "Abandonment," says Littré, "has an active meaning and a passive meaning. The abandonment of friends can mean both that one abandons one's friends or that they abandon us."

Montherlant points out that abandonment is a two-edged sword:

We are surprised to see that certain painful moments in our lives mean little to our friends, men and women alike, and I am thinking of our true friends. . . . But when we ourselves see that friends are going through a difficult period, we do nothing for them. All we offer is a few words. And yet they are people whom we are fond of. But Pascal's reaction stops us short: "Our own affairs do not suffice; we concern ourselves with those of our friends, etc. . . ." We are abandoned by others, and we abandon them in turn. We do not interest them, and we are not interested in them.[118]

The act of abandoning may be felt to be a deep expression of the person who commits it. In Anouilh's *Roméo et Jeannette*, a young woman says to a man:

I've detached myself from you forever. The church ought to have included the sacrament of abandonment among the other sacraments.[119]

What a pleasure to drop someone! In Montherlant's *La Reine Morte*, the king declares:

Oh! don't think that it's bitter to cease to feel affection. On the contrary, you have no idea how good it is to feel that one no longer loves. I don't know which is better, to detach oneself or for the other person to detach himself from you.[120]

If La Fontaine says that "absence is the greatest of evils," he also observes that "Absence is a remedy for hatred as well as a device against love."

"Woe to the absent!" cried La Rochefoucauld [121] before Destouches observed that they are "always wrong." In illustrating the meaning of the verb "to abandon," Paul Robert, in his *Dictionary*, quotes Georges Duhamel: "As soon as he stops seeing people, he forgets them, he abandons them."

At the cabinet meeting of June 13, 1940, General Weygand examined the consequences of the government's departure for North Africa:

How long will they remain away? . . . Several years . . . and do they imagine that anyone will remember them?[122]

In opposing, toward the end of the Fourth Republic, a proposal to abolish by-elections, a Moderate deputy (Robert Bruyneel) reminded the Socialists that it was thanks to this institution that Léon Blum, who had been defeated in Paris in the general election of 1928, was able, shortly thereafter, to be elected in Narbonne. The abolition of by-elections, the speaker pointed out, was likely to eliminate first-class men for the entire term of an Assembly "and perhaps even forever, for people forget quickly" [123]—an apprehension that is perhaps unjustified but nevertheless important.

Often one affirms with intensity and delight that one does not have the slightest interest in such and such a person or affair. In expressing this attitude, one may take pleasure in using coarse language or making certain gestures such as that of "the hand in the air, a protestation of the most absolute, indifference."[124]

During the Fourth Republic, chansonniers—to the delight of audiences—harped on the theme of the ignorance of the citizens regarding political questions and personages. Even when one does recall a name, it still has to be associated with the right thing. Laniel? Is it the name of a brand of noodles? When Réné Coty became a candidate at the end of the long-drawn-out election for president of the Republic in 1953, an usher is reported to have said to a colleague: "Now they're starting to invent names!" The fact that people do not know the names of all the members of the cabinet often seems not evident (in view of their number and the limited functions of many of them), but shocking, perhaps because one feels so hostile to them. Thus, under the headline "Unknown People in the House" (a disturbing image) *Le Canard Enchaîné* asked its readers:

> Are you informed of the reality of M. Pic, M. Bordeneuve, M. de Felice, M. Pinton . . . regarding whom the Journal Officiel has been stubbornly attesting to the fact for the last fourteen months that they are something . . . in the Guy Mollet cabinet? No, obviously not. It can't be.[125]

One often declares very vigorously that one doesn't give a damn about what happens to so and so: "They may not bother about me, but if you think I've ever given a damn about them. . . !" In a successful comedy (Jacques Deval's *Frère Jacques*) the chief character greatly admires the behavior of a person who has escaped uninjured in a railway accident: instead of trying to help the victims, he goes to the nearest station and asks to be reimbursed. In the first place, I have every right not to bother about others. Is there anything that really obliges me to do so? In the same comedy, the hero explains why he simply walked away from the already mentioned accident: I'm neither a nurse nor a fireman nor a doctor nor obliging! After a childhood excessively filled with tasks imposed by adults who were often suspected of selfishness, the grownup insists on his privilege of not giving a damn, if such be his good pleasure, about anything that is not an obligation in a very narrow sense.

Added to this is the fear of seeming to be the kind of person who makes a great show of zeal. According to Montherlant, when a man falls in the street

> the passers-by stand around open mouthed, but as for making a gesture, not the slightest. And he sometimes does, although he might have been saved if someone had immediately taken him to a pharmacy. What immobilizes people is, I think,

not indifference, but, in part, human respect (if they intervene, they seem to be naive, to be over-zealous) and, in part, the fear of looking as if they were trying to show off.[126]

There is also the fear of getting involved, of not heeding the voice of prudence, which advises me not to intervene. Won't I later regret having succumbed to the folly that impels me to get stupidly mixed up in what doesn't concern me? Above all, I don't want to get involved! In any case, I have other things to do!

And besides, what do you expect me to do? Does not a realistic examination of the situation tend to demonstrate that there is nothing I can do for you? Am I even needed? Isn't the other person big enough to manage by himself? Isn't he exaggerating his difficulties or his dangers?

Do I even have a right to intervene? Does not respect for the other person's privacy oblige me to mind my own business? Parents vigorously object to the child's annoying tendency to stick his nose everywhere, to meddle in everything (although they themselves assume the right to interfere in his domain.)

Are the motives that impel me to concern myself with others as respectable as they seem at first sight? And are the consequences as beneficent? Let everyone sweep in front of his own door and mind his own business! *Le Canard Enchaîné* dares apply the French adage "Everyone to his trade and the cows will be taken care of" to a certain fifteenth-century shepherdess:

> and what if the English had conquered all of France? You don't think that a tiny island could have become the master of an entire continent? . . . France: capital, Paris; chief cities, London, Rouen, Edinburgh and Bordeaux. That's what you would have learned in school.[127]

Certain plays (for example, Saint-Granier's *Olga s'en occupe*) and films (such as *Marchandes d'illusions*) demonstrate the, to say the least, unexpected results that the over-zealous person is likely to cause.

In contrast with ordinary people who do not bother about what does not concern them are the originals who compensate for their feeling of having been abandoned, not by retaliating, but by helping other victims. Paul Léautaud and Louis-Ferdinand Celine, with their shelters and cemeteries for abandoned cats and dogs, illustrate this unusual behavior, their work furnishes ample testimony of their strong sense of having been abandoned.

If I am abandoned, I may abandon in turn, but I will not abandon myself. "It seems to me that to be intelligent . . . is never to abandon oneself," declared Paul Léautaud.[128]

To abandon oneself is to lose self-control. "This happy agitation, which gives me a delicious sense of abandon," said Casimir Delavigne, who is quoted by Littré to illustrate "abandon," a delightful but perilous state.

To abandon oneself is to surrender recklessly, to put oneself in the hands of someone else, unreservedly. That is what one must do with respect to God. "One must settle matters by abandoning oneself to God;" "the all-important thing is to be able to abandon oneself to God," says Bossuet, whom Littré quotes to illustrate "abandon" and "to abandon oneself." But it is equally important not to do the same with respect to men. "In speaking of women," says Littré, "to abandon oneself means to deliver oneself," and he gives the following example from Voltaire: "Anne Boleyn had the art of not abandoning herself entirely and of exciting the King's passion." Since, "despite the fact that one is two, love remains solitary,"[129] one must be careful to maintain a certain reserve, a certain "distance," even in very intimate relations. In the business of love, observes Montaigne,

> I did not let myself go entirely; I took pleasure in it, but I did not forget myself; I preserved entirely the little sense and discretion that nature has given me, . . . a little excitement, but no folly.[130]

To abandon oneself to someone is to have unlimited confidence in him. One of the meanings of "abandon," according to Littré, is "full confidence." For example: "He spoke to me . . . with utter abandon." Paul Robert quotes Roger Martin du Gard, who speaks of a character's "expression of abandon, of utter sincerity."

But to think oneself utterly secure is dangerous folly. "One's self, that unique place of our security," says Montherlant.[131] "Confidence," according to Paul Robert, "the security of one who trusts someone or something," evokes: misplaced confidence. "To deceive, to betray someone's confidence, to abuse someone's confidence. Abuse of confidence."

Well-placed confidence is rare indeed. Robert quotes André Maurois:

> Some of us have had the good fortune to meet a man (or woman . . .) who has never deceived us, who, in almost every circumstance, has acted exactly as we wished, who, in the most difficult moments, has never abandoned us. Such people know that wonderful feeling: confidence.

Short of such exceptional circumstances, the only safe attitude is expressed by the great commandment so often applied to innumerable circumstances of daily life: "Beware." Mistrust, says La Fontaine, is the "mother of safety." "I cannot imagine wisdom without mistrust," declares Chamfort.[132]

To abandon oneself is to expose oneself to severe blows: when the person to whom I have abandoned myself abandons me. If I do not abandon myself to God, I am in danger of being abandoned by Him, but if I refuse to abandon myself to men, their tendency to abandon me will not be increased thereby; on the contrary. And if they do abandon me, I am better prepared to deal with the situation. In placing limits upon my attachments, I also limit the suffering that those to whom I am attached may inflict upon me by dropping me.

Before I am abandoned—if I am to be—I shall then have delivered nothing on credit—but cash down:

> And I cast myself on the world only for the share of favor I get now. When I leave it, I shall hold it quits,

says Montaigne. [133] "Our existence each day is based on transaction," said Camille Chautemps, a prominent politician of the Third Republic. [134]

One of Montherlant's characters declares:

> There is, in sensual pleasure, something round, something achieved which never exists in tenderness. You have had pleasure; I have had pleasure; the circle is closed; no disappointment and no doubt. In tenderness there is almost always disappointment and always doubt. [135]

When passion is replaced by pleasure, the others become

> persons whom we joyfully grant the power of being agreeable to us, but whom we energetically refuse the power of making us suffer. [136]

In tragedy, and in passion, I abandon myself to a given person, and to that person only. And that is what leads to catastrophe. In comedy, and in the ordinary course of life, one can substitute, one can take one's pleasure where one finds it, thereby avoiding the disaster with which tragedy and passion conclude. The child's feelings remain confined to the family circle; those of the adult can reach out to all women, all men, and thus can avoid certain impossible situations.

On the one hand, there is the all-or-nothing, the reaction of Alceste with regard to Célimène in Molière's *Misanthrope*. On the other hand, escaping the blind alley into which this attitude leads me, I decide to take advantage of what every moment has to offer, even if it is less than and quite different from what I really desire. Marcel Proust describes in surprisingly simple terms the evolution that leads from intransigence to compromise:

> Certainly, in the past, even with a woman of whom I had merely caught sight on a road near Balbec, in a street in Paris, I had felt the individuality of my desire and that it would be adulterating it to seek to assuage it with another person. But life . . . had taught me that, when one partner is unavailable, one has to make do with another." [137]

"The obstinate heart" of which Jean Moréas speaks needs Queen Cleopatra, Helen of Troy, and Melusina. But "since Suzon comes along," "let us lie under the leafy bough. . . .[138]

If necessary, one can merge the idea of what one desires with the reality of what one has obtained. According to a familiar literary theme, a man for instance, imagines that he is making love to the woman he really desires when he is in fact doing so with the one who is available or the one he has to put up with.

If someone does not or no longer satisfies me because he stands aloof or abandons me, "I go elsewhere." Avoiding the catastrophe to which "immobilism" in the sphere of attachments is fated, I find what is known in politics as a "substitute solution." In Molière's *Misanthrope* Eliante would like to marry Alceste. When he refuses, she accepts the offer of Philinte, with whom she will be happy; they are both "tractable" individuals. The argument of the fifth act of Molière's *La Princesse d'elide* describes this process:

> He says to her that if she does not want him to belong to another, she must take him for herself.

It is thus that in Racine's *Bérénice* Arsace, who encourages Antiochus, sees Bérénice:

> Open your eyes, my lord, and think
> Of all the reasons why Bérénice is yours.
> Since Titus no longer tries to please her,
> Know that she must now wed you.[139]

Antiochus is impressed: "Great is my hope, Arsace."[140]

Attachment to a disappointing object is often vigorously rejected. With a sudden about-face after a long lamentation, Philippe Desportes says of the "cruel" woman:

> Let us therefore cease to love her, and,
> To turn our thoughts from her,
> Let us turn our steps elsewhere.[141]

Do I not exaggerate the difference between the various objects all of which can provide me with a certain pleasure? Several important clichés express this belief. It's not the bottle that counts, it's what's in it; for everyone lost, a dozen found.

Paul Léautaud contrasts this attitude with the opposite one, the dangerous consequences of which are to be avoided: on the one hand, "the most insignificant detail" can be decisive in a "physical meeting," but, on the other,

> The wise man says to himself that it is certainly agreeable to love and equally so to be loved or to think one is loved, but that if it were not this one and by this one, it would have been that one and by that one, and that there is therefore; no reason to get worked up. . . .[142]

The refusal to depend upon a single and disappointing object may be accompanied by pride. I overcome the temptation to suffer; I am shrewd enough to get satisfaction elsewhere—two movements whereby the adult improves upon the position of the child.

However intense may be my feeling for the creature who rejects or abandons me, if I am a spirited person I am capable of shaking it off:

> A sound mind
> Is never content with the other's refusal

says one of Moliere's characters and also: "He who suffers such scorn really wants to suffer it." [143] Hence, all that is required is the will not to want to suffer it. Montesquieu declares:

> It is very seldom true that the heart is meant only for a particular person and that one is fated for a particular individual, and that a bit of reason cannot destine you for another. [144]

Similarly Montherlant:

> It is only an illusion that makes us think that such and such a person is irreplaceable. Forty-nine individuals out of fifty are replaceable—and I would readily add: replaceable for the *better*—when one takes the trouble to find someone else. [145]

This is a serious attitude, the light version of which is given in Moliere's *La Princesse d'Elide* when the father of the princess announces to the two wooers that their suit has been rejected:

> I am afraid, Princes, that my daughter's choice is not in your favor, but there are two princesses who can console you for this little misfortune.

To which one of the princes replies:

> My Lord, we know what course to take, and if these kindly princesses are not too scornful of hearts that have been rejected, we can, through their favor, have the honor of being allied to you. [146]

Tragedy manifests the powerlessness of the will when it is confronted with abandonment; comedy, which expresses the aspirations, if not the reactions, of the average sensual man, reflects the sovereignty of the will in the fight against suffering and in the quest for pleasure.

NOTES

1. Marc Bloch, *L'Etrange défaite* (Paris, 1946), 33.

2. N. Jacquefont in *Le Monde* (June 26, 1955); José Lestours in *LeMonde* (November 13, 1954).

3. *Combat* (January 24, 1956).

4. Assemblée Nationale (AN) (February 28, 1958), *Journal Officiel (JO)*, 1148.

5. Henry de Montherlant, *L'Exil, Théâtre* (Paris, 1954), act II, scene VIII.

6. *Combat* (December 19, 1957).

7. *Le Monde* (January 29, 1953).

8. Albert Aycard and Jacqueline Franck, *La réalité dépasse la fiction* (Paris, 1955), 123.

9. *Le Monde* (July 3, 1954); Robert Coiplet in *Le Monde* (September 10, 1952).

10. Jean Dutourd, *Doucin* (Paris, 1955), 76.

11. Henry de Montherlant, *L'Histoire d'amour de la rose de sable* (Paris, 1954), 30.

12. Henry de Montherlant, *Carnets (1930-1944)* (Paris, 1957), 302.

13. Anthoine Blondin in *Arts* (December 25-31, 1957).

14. Montherlant, *Théâtre,* 660f.

15. Montherlant, *Demain il fera jour, in Théâtre,* 750.

16. José Cabanis, *Juliette Bonvielle* (Paris, 1954), 172.

17. Henry de Montherlant, *Le Maitre de Santiago, Théâtre,* act II, scene I.

18. Sébastien Chamfort, *Maximes et anecdotes* (Monaco, 1944), 214.

19. Paul Valéry, *Tel quel* (Paris, 1943), II, 51.

20. *Le Canard Enchaîné,* (January 1, 1958).

21. Jules Renard, *Journal* (Paris, 1960), 105.

22. Paul Valéry, "Mélanges," in *Oeuvres* (Paris, 1957), 325.

23. Maurice Sachs, *La chasse à courre* (Paris, 1949), 184.

24. Henry de Montherlant, *Carnets (XIX-XXI)* (Paris, 1956), 192.

25. Montherlant, *Carnets (1930-1944),* 131.

26. Henry de Montherlant, *Les lépreuses* (Paris, 1939), 129.

27. Armand Salacrou, *Histoire de rire* (Paris, 1941), act II.

28. Paul Valéry, *Mauvaises pensées et autres* (Paris, 1942), 60.

29. Jean-Louis Curtis, *Les justes causes* (Paris, 1954), 88.

30. Sacha Guitry, *Bibliothèque rosse* (Paris, 1953), 158.

31. Montherlant, *Demain il fera jour,* act I, scene I.

32. Henry de Montherlant, *Mors et vita* (Paris, 1954), 100.

33. Chamfort, *Maximes et anecdotes,* 113.

34. Michel Chrestien, *Esprit, es-tu là?* (Paris, 1957), 94.

35. Joseph Caillaux, *Mes mémoires* (Paris, 1947), 102.

36. AN (July 22, 1955), *JO,* 4075.

37. Robert de Jouvenel, *La République des camarades* (Paris, n.d.), 23.

38. Jean Zay, *Souvenirs et solitude* (Paris, 1945), 296.

39. AN (March 26, 1957), *JO,* 1863.

40. *Le Canard Enchaîné* (June 10, 19530.

41. Lucien Rebatet, *Les décombres* (Paris, 1942), 453.

42. Edward Spears, *Assignment to Catastrophe* (London, 1954), II, 319.

43. Quoted by Jacques Benoist-Méchin in *Soixante jours qui ébranlèrent l'Occident* (Paris, 1956), III, 176.

44. Ibid.

45. Bloch, *L'Etrange défaite,* 151.

46. Joseph Laniel, *Le drame Indochinois* Paris, 1956), 61.

47. Jacques Dumaine, *Quai d'Orsay, 1945-1951* Paris, 1955), 56f.

48. *Le Canard Enchaîné* (May 13, 1953).

49. Spears, *Assignment*, 260f.

50. Quoted by Benoist-Méchin in *Soixante jours*, II, 405.

51. Quoted by Robert Aron in *Histoire de Vichy* (Paris, 1952), 21.

52. Paul Weygand, *Rappelé au service* (Paris, 1950), 218.

53. Pierre Audiat, *Paris Pendant la guerre* (Paris, 1946), 12.

54. Jean Paul-Boncour, *Sur les chemins de la défaite* (Paris, 1946), 207.

55. *La Nef* (July-August, 1958), 12.

56. Claude Estier in *France-Observateur* (May 15, 1958). See also Jean Ferniot in *L'Express* (May 17, 1958); Georges Mamy in *Le Monde* (May 13, 1958).

57. *Le Canard Enchaîné* (May 16, 1958).

58. *Le Monde* (July 8, 1958).

59. Jean Anouilh, *Le rendez-vous de Senlis*, Théâtre, act I.

60. *Paris-Presse* (November 14, 1957).

61. Henry de Montherlant, *La ville dont le prince est un enfant, Théâtre*, act II, scene IV.

62. Edmond Wellhoff, *Autour d'un député moyen* (Paris, 1932), 14.

63. AN (March 11, 1958), *JO*, 1523.

64. AN (August 30, 1954), *JO*, 4456.

65. André Tardieu, *La profession parlementaire* (Paris, 1937), 163.

66. AN (December 18, 1956), *JO*, 6086.

67. Pierre-Olivier Lapie, AN (July 5, 1957), *JO*, 3314.

68. Pierre Naudet, AN (July 6, 1957), *JO*, 3411.

69. Raymond Triboulet, AN (July 6, 1957), *JO*, 3353.

70. Pierre André, AN (November 9, 1957), *JO*, 4856.

71. Claude Erraty in *Le Monde* (March 23-24, 1958).

72. Pierre André, AN (January 15, 1957), *JO*, 4868.

73. AN (June 24, 1955), *JO*, 3338.

74. AN (February 20, 1958), *JO*, 913.

75. Jean Chamant, AN (January 21, 1958), *JO*, 63.

76. Raymond Triboulet, AN (July 6, 1957), *JO*, 3353.

77. Roland Dumas, AN (July 17, 1957), *JO*, 3714.

78. AN (February 2, 1953), *JO*, 605.

79. AN (December 23, 1954), *JO*, 6808.

80. AN (December 12, 1957), *JO*, 5322-5324.

81. Jean Giraudoux, *Sans pouvoirs* (Monaco, 1946), 54f.

82. Armand Salacrou, *Le casseur d'assiettes, Théâtre*, I, 27.

83. Jules Renard, *Journal*, 593.

84. Henry de Montherlant, *La solstice de juin* (Paris, 1941), 144f.

85. Montherlant, *Mors et vita*, 129.

86. Henry de Montherlant, *Malatestiana*, in *Théâtre*, 572.

87. Morvau Lebesque in *Le Canard Enchaîné* (April 24, 1957).

88. Rebatet, *Les décombres*, 450.

89. Stephen Hecquet, *Les guimbardes de Bordeaux* (Paris, 1958), 37.

90. Le Colonel Bourgoin in *Le Monde* (March 16, 1957).

91. Pierre Moinot in *Demain* (March 21-27, 1957).

92. AN (May 21, 1957), *JO*, 2587.

93. AN (March 27, 1957), *JO*, 2587.

94. Ibid.

95. AN (March 22, 1957), *JO*, 1799.

96. Conseil de la République (CR) (May 16, 1958) *JO*, 884.
97. Henry de Montherlant, *Fils de personne, Théâtre*, act III, scene IV.
98. AN (December 18, 1956), *JO*, 6089.
99. Félicien Marceau, *L'Oeuf* (Paris, 1957), 98.
100. George Bonnefous, *Histoire politique de la Troisième République* (Paris, 1956), II, 81.
101. Emile Combes, *Mon ministère* (Paris, 1956), 233.
102. Georges Rotvand in *Bulletin du Centre d'Etudes Politiques* (June 5, 1957).
103. AN (May 2, 1957), *JO*, 2699.
104. Bonnefous, *Histoire politique*, I, 180.
105. AN (June 12, 1957), *JO*, 2699.
106. *Le Monde* (June 12, 1957).
107. Ibid. (May 9, 1958).
108. Paul Valéry, *Histoires brisées* (Paris, 1950), 76.
109. AN (July 23, 1955), *JO*, 4207.
110. Jules Renard, *Journal.*
111. Jean Bloch-Michel, *Journal du désordre* (Paris, 1954), 153.
112. Montherlant, *Mars et vita,* 101.
113. Lawrence Wylie, *Village in the Vaucluse* (New York, 1956), 84-87.
114. Jean Freustué, *Auteuil* (Paris, 1954), 92.
115. Jules Renard, *Journal.*
116. AN (July 6, 1957), *JO*, 3370.
117. Quoted by *Le Monde* (May 21, 1958).
118. Montherlant, *Carnets (1930-1944),* 341.
119. Jean Anouilh, *Roméo et Jeannette, Théâtre*, act IV.
120. Henry de Montherlant, *La reine morte, Théâtre*, act II, scene III.
121. La Rochefoucauld to the Countess of Clermont (September 24, 1669).
122. Aron, *Histoire de Vichy*, 22.
123. AN (April 9, 1957), *JO*, 2110f.
124. Jules Renard, *Journal.*
125. *Le Canard Enchaîné* (April 17, 1957).
126. Henry de Montherlant, *Service inutile* (Paris, 1935), 145.
127. *Almanach du Canard Enchaîné* (1956), 30.
128. Paul Léautaud, *Propos d'un jour* (Paris, 1947), 95.
129. Jules Renard, *Journal.*
130. Montaigne, *Complete Works,* trans. by Donald M. Frame (London, 1958), 680.
131. Montherlant, *Mors et vita,* 118.
132. Chamfort, *Maximes et anecdotes,* 36.
133. Montaigne, *Complete Works,* 614.
134. Quoted by Benoist-Méchin in *Soixante jours,* III, 541.
135. Henry de Montherlant, *Celles qu'on prend dans ses bras,* act II, scene I.
136. Montherlant, *Mors et vita,* 29.
137. Marcel Proust, *Remembrance of Things Past,* trans. by C. K. Scott-Moncrieff and Stephen Hudson (London, 1941), II, 191.
138. André Gîde, *Anthologie de la poésie française* (Paris, 1949), 624.
139. Racine, *Bérénice,* act III, scene II.
140. Ibid., act V, scene IV.
141. Georges Pillement, *Anthologie de la poésie amoureuse* (Paris, 1954), I, 148.
142. Léautaud, *Propos d'un jour,* 14f.
143. Molière, *Le Sicilien, ou l'amour peintre; Le dépit amoureux,* act IV, scene II.
144. Montesquieu, *Mes pensees,* in *Oeuvres complètes* (Paris, 1949), 1065.
145. Montherlant, *Carnets (1930-1944),* 357.
146. Molière, *La Princesse d'Elide,* act V. scene III.

Chapter 7

FRANCE AND ITS LEADER THROUGH DE GAULLE'S EYES: MEDIOCRITY AND GREATNESS*

EDITOR'S NOTE: Most of the selections in this volume concern themes in the political culture of groups—whether elites or broader strata. Leites is also the author of a major work on Charles de Gaulle; in it he shows the French leader interacting with his audience—exemplifying, evoking, and responding to distinctive features in French culture. By illuminating the link between de Gaulle and his public, Leites helps explain the effectiveness of one of the most prominent charismatic figures of our time.

In the larger work, Leites shows a broad range of tensions in the character of the founder of the Fifth Republic. De Gaulle's own words, presented in the context of the French political scene as it changed from the 1930s onward, are used to reveal the way his political behavior reflected these tensions—his aspirations for personal greatness and for France's greatness, as well as his misgivings about these aspirations. The balance this extraordinary leader struck between his own contrasting inclinations had important political consequences for France. The general's complex personal dynamics made it possible for him to act with authority and popular support, first to restore, then to nurture a democratic political system.

In the passages here, Leites uses de Gaulle's published statements on the qualities possessed by men in general and the French in particular: on French leaders, great leaders, and himself. The leader's own imagery shows a persistent demand for power, together with inhibitions against giving full play to this demand. In passing, Leites' analysis suggests the origins and dynamics behind this imagery.

AUTHOR'S NOTE: Since de Gaulle often refers to himself in the third person, I denote him by "G" when he himself speaks or acts. "De Gaulle" is one of the subjects of which he speaks. "The war" is that of 1939-1945.

Translated and abridged by the editor from "Médiocrité et Grandeur," mimeographed manuscript (Paris, 1961), 26-63, 201-236.

I. MEDIOCRITY

It is obvious that G entertains opinions of the French which he feels to be favorable. It is less clear that he also harbors somewhat qualified feelings about his countrymen. In this section some of the negative aspects of his reactions will be analyzed.

A comrade recalls, "They used to say in the RPF that General de Gaulle had a profound contempt for the motives which inspired human actions.[1] G. says to Marie Noel, "You've often raised me above life."[2] Real life, that is, actually goes on down below. The spontaneous actions of most humans—of that "crowd thick with mediocrities"[3]—are often stained with baseness. To be human is to risk being vile: "mud" is one of the chief components of the universe.

When G applies his standards to his own country, he often finds it gravely wanting. He perceives "all in its 'character' which is infirm."[4] He finds it in frightful situations: "We picked up the country in its surrender, we brought it out of the mud," he recalls after the war.[5]

1. UNWORTHY LEADERS

The elites produced in France tend to be bad. G expresses this belief with particular insistence when he is not in power. It is perhaps not entirely absent from his thoughts even when he is in command, for it resembles the "black myth" which French leaders often entertain about themselves.[6]

Corruption, even of the best, takes place simply by virtue of being in power. This maxim is illustrated by the degradation that took place over the years in the relations between G and Pétain. During the early period, the Marshall favored young G's non-conformity in matters of strategy and tactics. He even assigned him the task of writing a history of the French army. However, when G had fully developed his ideas, Pétain opposed them. When G wanted to publish *France and its Army,* Pétain made his consent contingent on inclusion of a dedication to himself, actually drawn up by himself. According to a friend of G, Pétain's version would have left "the unsuspecting public in no doubt that the author's role was only one of taking dictation." Before knowing the contents of the text in question, G accepted this condition. Eventually, however, he inserted a different dedication. Pétain's protest was so strong that "he only withdrew a threat of punishment when promised that the entire original text would be restored in the second edition." In the event, this was postponed by the war.[7]

During the war G claims that "the fourth French republic asked that she be served, and not that others make use of her."[8] But once the regime is installed, it resembles that "system which feudal lords used to exploit for their own advantage," which parties "constructed for their own benefit."[9] Those charged with the protection of the general interest readily sacrifice it for what they consider immediate personal advantage. Thus, those in power may be "those who try to hurt the country for personal reasons."[10]

Now, if it is to be "for their personal use," the regime can only be "confused and impotent."[11] De Gaulle thus recounts that after the Liberation

> All the feudal powers—and this is an old story in our French history—all those who had a fief in one of the parties, or anywhere in politics, or even in the newspapers or business or trade unions—were hostile to . . . France's renovation.

And later,

> All the organized groups in the nation were . . . hostile to me from the moment that it became a question of rebuilding institutions.[12]

As early as the summer of 1944 de Gaulle anticipated the resurgence of these vested interests:

> I know very well that as the danger recedes I will find that all the factions, all the ideologues, all the demagogues will revive their hostility to me.[13]

G was disappointed to find that after the liberation,

> I had to admit that the notion I had had of the stature and the rights of France found little support from most of those who tried to influence public opinion.[14]

Often the elites are easily reconciled to France's "throwing in the sponge." They even contribute to her doing so. In the days of Joan of Arc, as in 1941, most of the "higher ups collaborated with the enemy."[15] As for the politicians, "I find them to be only lukewarm to my main aim, which is to restore the power of France."[16] Thus did he find himself, in the affair of the Levant,

> destitute of effective support from most of those who played any public role. . . . Sometimes my tone inspired uneasiness and sometimes disapproval among all those of influence or position.[17]

When he develops, in the fall of 1945, the idea of a great "western grouping, having for arteries the Rhine, the Channel, the Mediterranean," once again he is disappointed in the French elites. While this "vast design"—this "great project of France"—seems to him to stir the fascinated attention of the other peoples concerned (the Belgians welcome it with "transports" when G outlines it to them), the

> leading French politicians have little . . . feeling for it. . . . Everything goes on as though my conviction that France has the opportunity to play an independent role and my attempt to lead her to it met universal suspicion from those preparing to represent the country.[18]

According to G, French elites sin not only in giving their personal interests preference over the general interest, but also by the triviality of their aspirations. Thus the system of "party rule" is one in which "each one of them cooks up his own little soup on a tiny fire in his own little corner." People in office like to

> stay where they are while waiting to be served. . . . They eat the soup. . . . They get along so well together. . . . It's so good to be on vacation—they believe it will last forever![19]

Imagining that it will last forever, they react to the mortal dangers threatening the country first with unconcern and then by improvising. Although the most elementary wisdom teaches that "everyone should be ready for anything," France over and over becomes the country where "neglect and easy-going just miss selling out the future." It is a country prone to "all those setbacks that improvisation brings."[20]

2. IMPERFECT FRENCHMEN

When G spells out the faults of elites he often contrasts these with the "good people." Thus, after the Liberation, when those in power turned away from him, "the people showed me their sympathy by thousands of stirring indications." One can overcome the feudal powers which "entrench themselves forcibly" if one "appeals . . . to the people."[21] Bad elites can apparently come from a people entirely different and who tolerate them despite fundamentally contrasting aims.

Sometimes this image of good people and bad elites seems useful and satisfying to G. But it does not express quite his whole thought on the subject of a people who tolerate evil-doing by their leaders.

After the Liberation G observes the "moral mediocrity and the . . . national flabbiness in which the French bathe far too often." Jacques Darnand, a hero of two wars, agrees to become chief of the rebellious militia because he is "fed up with the baseness, the pervasive softness." In Darlan's case, too, "almost his entire active life unfolded surrounded by the flabbiness of the nation."[22]

The same dangers seem to have beset G's own leadership. When he founded the RPF movement he affirmed, "we have become neither stupid nor lazy nor corrupt." Recalling its early history, however, he says, "The supports the ·nation was willing to offer me were becoming few and faltering." When the movement is losing its force he admits that "the regime" managed to worsen "the country's defects" and "aggravate" its "weaknesses."[23]

G speaks of an "encompassing flabbiness." In 1953 the climate of the only national election in which the RPF participates is one of "drowsy mediocrity." [24] The following year everyone is still in a "period of national listlessness," and the people "doze." A year later they are still "napping," having also been "asleep" eight years before.[25] In the year that was to see his return to power he claimed of this lethargy: "This situation could last thirty or forty years. . . . The startled awakening might not come for half a century."[26]

The mediocrity, baseness, and lethargy of too many Frenchmen puts France in mortal danger. A national ordeal is seemingly necessary. Such as they are, the French need the hardest possible lessons in order for them to understand and apply the most elementary wisdom. The people have a pernicious inclination to shirk the least effort.

"We can do marvelous things when we want to," G suggests at a university appearance. But we don't always want to? Obviously, for we are "the most capricious people in the world," the "most changeable and hard to manage." Visiting the place where the highly successful *Caravelle* airplane is manufactured, he declares, "It's a comfort to me to see on the spot what the nation can do when it gives itself the trouble."[27]

What is even more serious, while "the mainspring of a people is ambition," he finds the French people lacking in this essential motive: "In our day," he announces towards the end of the Fourth Republic, "collective ambition no longer exists."[28]

During the war G sees them shedding their apathy. He exalts the "rage, the good and fertile rage," that France feels towards the enemy—"this solid French rage." "The triumphant fury" of the great French Revolution, "the 'Marseillaise' is rage itself."[29]

Again, on the subject of the Algerian war, G alleges, "French public opinion accepts the sacrifices asked of her . . . with a spirit of greatness."[30]

To what extent is G himself convinced of this? May not this fervor ebb away? Indeed, do not the French show an inclination to abandon France? In leading circles in Paris, just before the start of the war, "people pretended to think" that we still had a "nation ready for sacrifices," while, in fact, there was already only "a nation prostrate."[31]

It is in this context that the insistence with which G proclaims the greatness of the country must be understood.

II. GREATNESS

1. FRANCE

Beyond Frenchmen—there is France.

"All my life I have had a certain idea of France," comments G in beginning his memoirs.[32] France remains noble even when Frenchmen are not. While they vary, she is immutable. They are many, she is one.

"Once more" declares the chief of state at a grave moment, "I call on all Frenchmen to rejoin France," because "we know that everything we do is something higher than ourselves and which is called France."[33] This object has characteristics independent of those of Frenchmen.

"Nations" explains G to the children of France during the war, "are like women—more or less beautiful, good, and brave. Well now, among 'My ladies the nations,' none has ever been more beautiful, better, nor braver than Our Lady France."[34]

France is Mother: "Our Lady, France," of whom everyone comprising the nation is a child. She is the mother who had, in 1918, "the great happiness to recover her dear Alsace and her dear Lorraine," and who, at the end of the war, "was not afflicted as deeply by her own wounds as by those of Brest, her beloved daughter."[35]

But mother risks finding herself now in magnificent condition, now in a frightful state—glorious at one moment, rolling in the mud of the abyss at another. In the only sentence where G speaks of his own mother he speaks of a similar tension in his image of her. He notes that her "intransigent passion for the country," (patrie), is equalled by her "religious piety."[36] Perhaps this conception indicates an atmosphere in which it was hard for young G to fuse the image of a sacred mother with that of a profane one.

France, G never ceases to affirm, has a vocation for grandeur. "We are made to be a great people." She wills it: "We are determined to be." She will be and she knows it: "You know that France will live and be great. . . . We all believe this." She has the wish to prove all this. "Our people . . ." has the "will to show once more that it is a great people." In short, France possesses it—greatness—it *is* a great people: "We are!" Thus does he address it, crying from time to time, "French people, Great people!"[37]

In general, greatness seems to require a certain amplitude of means, however difficult it may be for the country to acquire it. In fact, is it not necessary, in order to be great, to be in some way "colossal"?—a word which G does not hesitate to use in a favorable sense. Only after years have passed does G congratulate the English and French for having escaped that giddiness "which sometimes carriers away colossi."[38]

Because greatness—it goes without saying—is also and above all, potency. "The will . . . to see the influence and scope of the nation increase," G is supposed to have said during his second retirement, "truly, that's what Gaullism is!"[39]

2. GREAT LEADERS ARE INDEPENDENT

Great leaders are autonomous: they create themselves.

Great men ... are so for having willed it. Disraeli formed the habit from adolescence of thinking as though he were prime minister. ... While Foch was still obscure, the generalissimo in him shone through his teachings.[40]

In the book where these reflections are to be found, the future leader—himself also still obscure—presents himself at length as though he were already "the nation's guide." "The leaders of the Great War," he stresses, owed to no one but themselves "the genesis of their actions." "Their creative spark did not come from a rulebook," for "if received opinions and humdrum occupations suffice to shape most of us, the powerful ones form themselves."[41]

"I owe nothing to anyone," says G in speaking of political obligations.[42] Perhaps this phrase finds its echo in his very early thoughts, like that in which he notes an essential characteristic of the armored tank corps, championed by him from 1933 to 1940:

Nothing essential can be done until mechanized forces can act on their own and can be put in the service of decisive goals to be attained by their own actions.[43]

Since 1940 G has often admitted that France does not possess by herself all those means which she needs. It is obvious, he says during the war, "that the organization and activity of Free France cannot presently ... maintain itself without the support of the British government."[44]

But the point at which G ceases to recognize that France does not possess all those resources required for actions vitally needed becomes evident when one considers certain aspects of the liberation of Paris. From the moment planning began for the Allied landing in Europe, G began asking the Anglo-Americans to agree to make exceptions to the rule that foreseeable developments should be planned only on the basis of military necessity: "I held it to be essential," he writes, "that French arms show their power in Paris before those of the Allies." The Anglo-Americans then agreed that the "liberation of the Capital bears the mark of a French military and national operation" and not that of an enterprise of all the armies fighting the Germans.[45] Thus G's division was to be held in reserve until the moment to advance on the Seine; entirely fresh, it was to be the first to enter Paris. Under these conditions he reached the Hotel de Ville on August 25, 1945 and spoke thus of

> Paris . . . liberated by itself, freed by its own people with the cooperation of the armies of France, with the support and participation of all of France—of fighting France, the only France, true France, Eternal France. . . . The enemy who held Paris has surrendered into our hands.[46]

Only after having evoked this picture of a combat between France and Germany does he return to reality: "It is with the collaboration of our dear, admirable allies that we routed him from among us."[47] And it is not until four more days have elapsed that he speaks of the "allied armies . . . whose offensive permitted the liberation of Paris."[48]

However, the inclination to pretend he is completely autonomous, no matter what the reality, is variable in G. He becomes, for example, singularly weak in the course of those very satisfying trips which he takes in the spring of 1960. His words before the Queen show an unprecedented realism in recalling the war:

> The British people took upon themselves the whole burden of the war at a moment when their own fate, and that of France and of Europe, depended entirely upon them. . . . Without that resolute decision, without the courage with which the British nation repulsed the assaults of the enemy, without its determination and gigantic effort . . . what would have become of our countries and, in particular, of mine, if not to have been condemned to shame and servitude? As for me, I say in a loud voice, if I then believed myself able to bring France back from despair and afterwards little by little to reassemble her children and rally her combat forces, it was thanks to the resistance, the example and the support of England and the Commonwealth.[49]

Going even farther the next day, G admits at Carlton Gardens before the veterans of Free France that "France would have lost both the battle and the war if Great Britain had not been there."[50] Ten days later, in Ottawa, he declares,

> What was done by the one who is in your midst today, and by those who surround him, and by France, was only possible because others helped them. That which was done would not have succeeded without the British resistance, nor without the help of peoples like the Canadian people.[51]

This same man insisted, however, on the occasion of a meeting of the Council of Ministers a month later, on the "indispensable necessity for the independence of our country—which must depend on no one for the assurance of its own destiny."[52] That France must depend, or does depend, in the present or future, only upon its own resources is a notion which G relinquishes with difficulty. Thus he affirms, "I am convinced . . . that France will get back on her feet by her own efforts." And during his second retirement he remarks, "Our country may get started again tomorrow, later, or in a hundred years—but it will get started on account of us alone." And later, "We are a great country which owes nothing to anyone," claims the great chief of state.[53]

To G it seems not only heartbreaking that France cannot forego the assistance of the world, but even in some way abnormal—a France that is fully France, would she be in that condition? But it is not quite the same for relationships between de Gaulle and France. G rejects the temptation to believe that de Gaulle might be laboring for France without any cooperation from the French.

Explaining, before the war, the relations between the "Man of Character" and "Action" he hastens to declare, "this is certainly not to say that he achieves it alone. . . . Let us not forget that others participate," and even that "they are not without merit." They practice the virtues of "abnegation and obedience" and are "prodigious with their efforts to do what they are told."[54] Doubtless, it is the leader who accomplishes the great acts. Although the chief sometimes needs to be aided, G usually stresses that this is a matter of others accepting necessary assignments. Looking towards coming into power the chief of the RPF exclaims, "to prepare the pay-off, . . . French-women, Frenchmen, come to my aid!"[55] "My comrades," he declares around the same time, "Know that to help rescue the nation once again, this time" (it could have been otherwise), "I need you!"[56]

He asks particularly for their support so that he may be comforted. Since "my lot . . . is solitude" in relation to "human contacts," in order to "lift the burden"[57] G has all the more need of that powerful "lever" which is the "adherence of the people." Thanking "with all his heart" the participants in a meeting, the chief explains of himself, "in the vast and onerous task we have to accomplish together, this man needs the comfort that his fellow citizens' adherence can give him. Thank you!"[58] And after the second return to power he explains in New York,

> There are responsibilities which would be heavy at any time but which are particularly so at certain moments of life and in certain periods of world history. I will say no more, but you will all have understood what comfort you have brought me this evening![59]

3. GREAT LEADERS RESTRAIN THEMSELVES

G insisted in vain from 1933 to 1940 on the creation of an armored corps, and from 1947 to 1953 on the acquisition of legislative control by the RPF. In both cases he obstinately persisted in trying to persuade individuals and masses who refused to be persuaded. Now he seems to have become slowly resolved on insisting no more: Very well, if they won't listen to me, I'll drop the whole matter!

Recalling how he "effaced" himself at the beginning of 1946, the chief of the declining RPF explains,

It's certainly true that for the moment the leader is, indeed, on the side of the road. But must he, like others, thumb a ride in order to get into all the cars?[60]

Preparing himself to return to power, G evokes the conditions under which he left: "When I saw that . . . any real governing was impossible, I withdrew. I haven't tried to force my hand." Again, in spring of 1953, as the disintegration of the RPF becomes apparent: "Well, good! I've gone back home!" In May, 1958, he stresses that it is not he who seeks power, it is the leaders of the hour who are determined to unload it on him.[61]

If G does not like to insist, he is equally repelled by forcing, one of the barriers that he sets up in himself to counteract a brutality perhaps obscurely perceived. The ideal leader described by the young G "proves himself a good prince"; "he does not abuse his power. . . . He scarcely enjoys at all the savor of his revenge" because "he is totally absorbed in action." Perhaps it is indulgent to show complete contempt when, by putting the vanquished in a particularly difficult position he assures to himself "that eminent position which returns to the strong once they are able to resist being carried away by their power."[62]

Over and over again, G has explained his refusal to establish himself as dictator after the war. The nuances of these explanations deserve to be studied closely. We may note in passing that the emphasis is not on a simple rejection of dictatorship as a morally bad system. Recalling that "the very day we undertook our mission . . . we declared our engagement to return full and complete control over itself" to the French people. Once the country's liberation was achieved, G explains his self-abnegation: "First of all this resulted from a conviction as firm as it was reasoned." He spells out the undesirable effects of dictatorship: "It would have been to renege, that is, to cheat one's own ideals." On the other hand, by democratic conduct,

> we give . . . our action and our authority the character of legitimacy. We safeguarded for all Frenchmen a territory in which they would be able to rediscover their national unity and we put ourselves in a position to resist—intransigently and effectively—any attempt from abroad to encroach upon us.[63]

In a similar tone he remarked to Stalin,

> You know better than anyone the trouble that would result from establishing in Poland a government which opinion would not accept.[64]

If the leader cannot obtain all the power he needs, the only condition worthy of him is to have none at all. The choice for G is either to live in the Elysée palace, under a constitution conceived by him, or to live "in my own village, letting history pass me by." Calling "solitude . . . my dear friend," G asks, "How could one be satisfied with any other when one has encountered history?"[65]

This "friend" *(amie),* seems to arouse feelings of voluptuous bitterness, even when G is in power. "The leader" he declares before having become so, "gives himself up to this feeling of solitude which is, following Faguet, 'the affliction of superior men'." At the apogee of the RPF, he predicts that the movement will "continue to spread . . . until it envelopes the entire nation" with the exception of "separatists" and probably "certain melancholy and shy recluses." Perhaps he is describing here the kind of man he both wishes and fears to be.[66]

"Reserve, character, greatness," observes G before the war, "these preconditions of eminence impose upon those who wish to acquire it an effort which will discourage most people." They involve a "continual self-control," a "state of inner struggle." "Happiness" is therefore "incompatible with domination" and

there one touches on the motive for otherwise puzzling retirements. Men who are universally acclaimed and whose every plan succeeds often throw down the burden suddenly.[67]

Having met Pius XII, G remarks "the supernatural charge with which he alone in the world is invested—one senses how heavily it weighs on his spirit."[68] And is not France also a unique object in the world—and is not de Gaulle the only one to be invested with a charge as great on her behalf?

In 1959, back in power, G becomes the bearer of the good tidings which cannot fail to stem from this fact.

He is gracious to "the little people" *(les petits).* "The confidence of little people . . . exalts the man of character" who feels himself obligated by this "humble acknowledgment of his due." Since he is a "born protector," his "benevolence . . . grows accordingly."[69] Thus also, once more, he contrasts himself with those "politicians": unlike them, he will not abandon the people.[70]

On great occasions he expresses his love—sometimes for those experiencing inclinations to revolt. "I address those of you," he said after the Liberation to members of the Resistance gathered at Toulouse (the Southwest of France was then chafing under the authority of Paris), "and through you your comrades. Tell them that I greatly love them."[71] Addressing French soldiers of Algeria in the course of the January, 1960, revolt, G tells them, "I know you . . . I esteem you . . . I love you."[72]

When he goes among men, G does not always insist on all the prerogatives which would place him too visibly above them—an additional mark of benevolence. Thus he speaks of his relations with the consultative assembly in Paris (1944-1945): "Certainly, my entrance and my departure take place with a certain solemnity." But, these moments aside, "I acted in such a way as not to restrict" the Assembly "in any way . . . respecting its agenda, taking a seat on one of its benches, speaking from the same podium,"—even "chatting with them in the corridors"—impressive emblem of gracious gifts bestowed by a benevolent ruler—or a benign god.[73]

Above all, G brings the gift of his own presence: "You were clamoring for Charles de Gaulle," he says from the balcony of a prefecture in 1959; "Very well, —here he is!"[74]

NOTES

1. René Moatti, *Le Monde* (April 23, 1960).
2. *Le Figaro* (April 17, 1959).
3. *Le Rassemblement* (October 16-22, 1952).
4. Charles de Gaulle, *Vers l'armée de métier* (Paris, 1944), 34.
5. *Le Rassemblement* (August 7, 1948).
6. See "A French View of Leaders: Abandonment," chapter 6.
7. Lucien Nachin, *Charles de Gaulle* (Paris, 1944), 89-91. On the same story, see also Arthur C. Robertson, *La doctrine du général de Gaulle* (Paris, 1959), 35-37.
8. Charles de Gaulle, *L'Unité* (Paris, 1956), 515.
9. *Le Rassemblement* (January 8, 1949).
10. Ibid. (July 16, 1949)
11. Ibid. (May 9, 1948).
12. Ibid. (August 7, 1948; February 18, 1950).
13. *L'Unité*, 322.
14. Charles de Gaulle, *Le salut* (Paris, 1959), 90.
15. *Le Rassemblement* (May 6, 1950); Charles de Gaulle, *Discours et Messages, 1940-1946* (Paris, 1946), 91.
16. *Le salut*, 98.
17. Ibid., 195.
18. Ibid., 222.
19. Charles de Gaulle, *La France sera la France* (Paris, 1951), 55; *Le Rassemblement* (October 16-22, 1952).
20. Ibid. (March 14-20); *Le Monde* (August 3, 1958); Charles de Gaulle, *La France et son armée* (Paris, 1938), 111.
21. Charles de Gaulle, Collection of Documents of the Institut d'Etudes Politiques de Paris (IEP), I, 433.
22. *Le Salut*, 251; *L'Unité*, 68; *Le Salut*, 244.
23. *Le Salut*, 271; IEP, I, 49.
24. *Le Rassemblement* (May 6, 1950), press conference of November 12, 1953, text distributed by RPF.
25. *Le Rassemblement* (June 11-17, 1953).
26. J.-R. Tournoux, *Secrets d'Etat* (Paris, 1959), 225.
27. *Le Figaro* (April 20, 1959); Jean Daniel in *L'Express* (January 21, 1960).
28. Tournoux, *Secrets*, 225.
29. *Discours et messages*, 46, 231, 230.
30. Charles de Gaulle, *L'Appel* (Paris, 1954), 49; *Le Monde* (September 1, 1959).
31. *L'Appel*, 54.
32. Ibid., 1.
33. *Le Monde* (January 31-February 1, 1960); *France-Soir* (September 26, 1959).
34. *Discours et messages*, 162.

35. Ibid., 334, 327, 634.
36. *L'Appel*, 1.
37. *Le Monde* (May 10-11, 1959); *L'Unité*, 563.
38. *Le Monde* (April 4, 1960).
39. Ibid. (June 15-16, 1958).
40. Charles de Gaulle, *Le fil de l'epeé* (Paris, 1932, 1944), 159.
41. *Vers l'armée*, 198, 203.
42. IEP, I, 418.
43. Charles de Gaulle, *Trois études* (Paris, 1932, 1944), 159.
44. *L'Appel*, 658.
45. *L'Unité*, 292.
46. Ibid., 709.
47. Ibid.
48. *L'Unité*, 712.
49. *Le Monde* (April 7, 1960).
50. Ibid. (April 8, 1960).
51. Ibid. (April 20, 1960).
52. *Le Monde* (May 21, 1960).
53. *Le Rassemblement* (November 20, 1948); *Le Monde* (May 8, 1956).
54. *Le fil de l'épée*, 49.
55. IEP, II, 76.
56. *Le Rassemblement* (December 31, 1949).
57. *L'Unité*, 322.
58. *Le Rassemblement* (September 18, 1948 and July 25, 1948).
59. *Le Monde* (April 28, 1960).
60. *Le Rassemblement* (July 11-17, 1952).
61. *Le Monde* (May 20, 1958).
62. *Le fil de l'épée, 52; IEP, II, 227.*
63. *Discours et messages, 742.*
64. *Le salut, 371.*
65. *Le Rassemblement* (July 11-17, 1952); *Le salut, 288.*
66. *Le fil de l'épée, 79;* IEP, I, 248.
67. *Le fil de l'épée, 79.*
68. *L'Unité*, 233.
69. *Le fil de l'épée, 74.*
70. Leites, "A French View of Leaders, chapter 6.
71. Robert Aron, *Histoire de la libération de la France* (Paris, 1959), 606.
72. *Le Monde* (January 31-February 1, 1960).
73. *Le salut, 103.*
74. *Le Monde* (February 15-16, 1959).

Chapter 8

WINNING ALLEGIANCE IN VIETNAM

EDITOR'S NOTE: The following selection was prepared during the American participation in the Vietnamese war. In it Leites exposes the reasons why the South Vietnamese government (GVN) and army (ARVN) were losing the struggle for popular support. On almost every score he finds the Viet Cong's appeals to be more consistent with the cultural patterns of the region. They presented models of authorities who were stern, just, abstinent, and paternal–all traditional virtues. Their strategies took account of popular sensitivity to humiliation. Their apparent policy goals avoided radical expropriations, focusing on rewards of dignity and restored local autonomy.

From The Viet Cong Style of Politics *(RAND report RM-6487-1-ISA/ARPA, May 1969),* v-xxviii; *19-28. Unless otherwise noted, quoted passages are from interviews with Vietnamese soldiers and citizens conducted for the Rand Corporation.*

I. LEADERSHIP MODELS: INTERESTED VERSUS DISINTERESTED

The predilection of some insurgent leaders for either brandy or girls," suggests Sir Robert Thompson, "can provide plenty of scope for psychological warfare experts and officers. One political commissar in Malaya made . . . the . . . remark: 'The only way to liberate women is to loosen their trouser belts!' "[1] A rallier might have given the opposite advice as he disconsolately recalls how

> the VC told me that people living under the GVN regime had all become scoundrels, ruffians and gamblers. Under the Front regime, everybody had to be clean, honest and hardworking. . . . Since I was a gambler, I was forced to work for the Front.

"When times are ordinary," Paul Mus points out, "disinterestedness, conspicuous poverty, an ascetic life and a physiognomy expressive of it have low propaganda value" in Vietnam. On the contrary, he continues:

> The kind of virtue which in popular conception belongs to the cycle of fire, penitence and purification then yields to another system . . . that of abundance and normalcy. . . . In Viet-Nam the silhouette of power in a period of stability is the opposite of emaciated. The Chinese character *yuan,* meaning 'round' . . . designated things respectable, particularly the mandarins. But a contrasting virtue . . . presides over revolutions.

Ho is opposed to Bao Dai, he continues, as "the sharp angle of the flame" is opposed to "the 'roundness' and plenitude of water."[2]

"If a man had guilty relations with women, he would be punished. If we drank and sang, we would be criticized." Thus runs a characteristic report of an informant about his VC unit, an account difficult to match from the files of the government's armed forces.

Fighters, it seems, not infrequently defend their right to pleasure loudly and elaborately, and to little avail. And the cadres extend the fight against pleasure to the population at large. The question, "What were the village guerrilla's missions?" may elicit, in part, this answer: "They kept an eye on the villagers to see if they took to gambling for money or cockfighting, which had been prohibited by the Front." In short, "the guerrillas acted as if they were fathers of everybody." Infuriating, but also impressive.

Consciously the cadres do not admit that they may be seeking and imposing virtue when thwarting the senses. They rather allege, in the Bolshevik manner, the existence of a "Who [will annihilate] whom?" relation between work—for the Party—and the natural man.

The cadres seem—on good and conspicuous grounds—preoccupied with whether such a relation does not also exist between dedication to the Party and devotion to the family. The best fighter is the one who has no worries about how his family fares without him. Family will neither weigh him down with obligations nor lure him with comforts nor absorb his affection. Ho Chi Minh is a bachelor. Hence, what the Party desires, without always daring to press for it too hard, is a cadre's "clean break" with his family (which will, to be sure, ultimately benefit from his work for "the people"):

> Why do you think your brother was fully indoctrinated?

> Whenever he came home, he did not care about family problems. His thoughts were only for the work . . . of the Front.

"Being in the Communist ranks," a rallier may recall with dismay, "is almost like being a priest. . . . In the GVN people think of their families first before their country. I knew I couldn't live with the VC, because it is natural that a man must think of his family first." But doing that, and, to boot, being concerned with what one's family thinks, may entail forsaking the Party:

> Who convinced you to rally most strongly?

> My mother. . . . She argued that I had served the Front for years, and that it was now time to come back to the family.

Hence the Party's attempt to have cadres *renounce* family and its half-way effort to impede contacts between members of its armed forces and their families. In multiple and varying ways an attempt is made to find the point where the sum of damage from allowing such contacts and from obstructing them is at a minimum.

On the other hand, in the Party's ideal world the families who have members connected with it will become and remain devoted "VC families" (responding to the argument that their menfolk's welfare depends on their support to the movement):

> Were they [villagers] glad to see you [the VC] around?

> Families who had children working for the Front often helped us; they gave us things to eat, for example. Families who had no one serving the VC were indifferent.

But for all that, the children and husbands thus fondly remembered and indirectly helped should not be deflected from serving the Party alone. The cadres, I would guess, are preoccupied by the incidence of reactions such as that of the informant who, when queried, "What did you think of the local government officials?" responds, "In fact, my relatives hadn't been arrested or mistreated, so I didn't have any bad feelings toward the GVN." It is the feared prevalence of such orientations which seems to call for a "clean break" with the family.

But the worth to the Party of such a stance should not be reduced by the emergence, within the movement, of intimate ties between peers other than those fostered by the Party itself (mainly, the three-man cell). Close friendships, where they are not expected, have deleterious effects and are to be strenuously forbidden.

When a loyal subject of the Northern regime is queried, "What do you think about your Uncle Ho?" the immediate answer is that "he isn't working to foster his personal interests, but the interests of others." And when informants respectful of the VC or even unconverted hard core talk about VC motivations, be it on upper levels or their own, it is not rare to find personal motives mixed with sheer attachments to the cause.

Correspondingly, the Party, in its recruitment, selection, and training by no means avoids appeals to personal interest. The rationale for preferring persons of lower-class origin over individuals from upper strata as cadres is not only that class determines consciousness, but also that there is harmony between personal and Party interest in the former case, conflict in the latter—where personal concerns are likely to win.

These, however, are aspects of the Party's conduct which it is eager to obscure. For "everybody's ambition," affirm two authorities on traditional Vietnam, "was to merit the title of *quantu,* that is, gentleman . . . and to escape the designation of *tieu-nhan,* that of a vulgar man seeking his own advantage in all matters."[3] "In periods of crisis," Mus observes about traditional beliefs in Vietnam, "manifest signs of one's being disinterested . . . carry great divinatory power [permit ascertaining that here are the future rulers]."[4] Hence the Party endeavors in a variety of modes—by allegation, but also by conduct—to present itself as nobly disinterested, and its enemy as basely self-regarding.

It is the VC which allegedly steels itself to, or even thrives on, hardships, which are stressed as much as damage is denied, and then used to justify demands on the population. "The subject," an interviewer comments on a prisoner, "said he would never work for the VC again, and he promised to move his family to a strategic hamlet when he is released. If life would be too hard there, he would have his 18-year-old son join the ARVN to support his family." Soldiering for the government may be a means for increasing one's family's income, while fighting for the VC is more apt to reduce it; it is for the future after victory that rewards are promised. There is no pay for the fighter that could be bestowed on the family, and no privileges enjoyed by the latter on account of having a delegate in the armed forces. There are only undertakings to compensate families for intolerable losses of providers—promises often, it seems, unfulfilled—and even additional burdens. The non-combatant members of a family should add sacrifices of their own to those of its fighters (e.g., paying taxes punctually and fully), so as to enjoy the informal honor of being a "Front family."

But what about the privileges enjoyed by those above the rank-and-file in the VC? "The guerrillas," one informant remembers, "had to mount guard so that the cadres could take tea quietly." And: "You would be criticized for the least little thing if you were not a high-ranking cadre. I never saw a high-ranking cadre criticized." But statements of this sort are surprisingly rare. The majority view is that "cadres have to be the best men in their section by slaving all day to set a good example for the rest of the Front members. Only by slaving all day can they be in a position to criticize the other cell members and to force the others into working hard, just like a locomotive pulling the cars. . . . Party members . . . die before the people, and enjoy fewer privileges than the people." According to another rallier, "Party members . . . must know when to go ahead to sacrifice themselves for the good of the other men. They had to undertake all the difficult jobs before other men. Suppose a unit was engaged in a battle, the Party members had to go ahead and lead the men through the enemy's fire."

When a cadre arrogates undue privileges to himself, it is apparently far from certain that he will get away with it:

Did the fighters in your platoon respect . . . the platoon's leader?

They didn't respect him because he was greedy . . .

Please explain.

During the march he always ate more than the fighters. He always wanted the best of everything. During the march, the moment the cook finished cooking the rice, he ate it. He ate it before us, so that he could eat more than his usual ration. . . . *He was a cadre and yet he was greedy.* . . . [emphasis added]

There thus emerges an apparently widely held conception of the "interested" GVN and the "disinterested" VC, precisely what the Party has aimed at. When questioned about the conduct of GVN forces in his village, a rallier readily admits that "they were nice to the people," but adds that "most of them were very afraid of death. They said that they were just waiting to get paid each month, and that they were in no mood to fight."

Both prisoners of war and ralliers apparently feel that it will please their interrogators if they express a dislike for the hardships of life in the VC, exalt the comforts enjoyed by the government's forces, and show a preference for abundance over austerity, for safety over sacrifice.

What were the reasons for your rally?

I could no longer endure hardships. I rallied in order to find better living.

The point, again, is not that these *were* "the reasons," as one would expect them to be for a large fraction of ralliers in any situation resembling the one in South Vietnam. The point is rather that this reaction, which the VC would condemn, appears to those who display it as one which will not shock or incur the prejudice of the GVN. They thus subscribe to the VC's holier-than-thou attitude toward its opponent.

As to ralliers in particular, there thus exists an important type of uncon-verted defector who has not substantially changed his view of the VC at large in an unfavorable sense. He has merely given in to what he himself regards as a weakness with regard to "hardships"—or he has acted from rage which a specific injury or insult inflicted by a particular superior has unleashed in him.

The asymmetry between conceptions—realities?—of the VC and the GVN which I have sketched finds striking expression in current images of the respective leaderships.

> What did you think of the GVN . . . when you were with the Front?

> I thought that the GVN leaders only think of their individual privileges.

Having observed that in times of crisis manifest signs of one's being disin-terested carry great divinatory power, Paul Mus, speaking in the early fifties about Bao Dai's regime, notes that "this point works against our enterprise." For while the charge of selfishness against that establishment was widespread, "accusations of this kind have never been made against the enemy leaders." When one considers "the country's characteristic sensibility," he concludes, "the import of this remark is fearsome."[5]

II. STRATEGIES

1. THE STRUGGLE AGAINST INDULGENCE

The Communists' insistence on clean, honest, and frugal living—in contrast to the debauchery thought to be more typical of soldiers in time of war—endows membership in the Communist ranks with some of the characteristics of a priesthood. It obliges cadres and Party members to set examples by their disinterestedness, courage, abstinence from common indulgences, and indif-ference to the privileges of rank and position. In the view of a surprisingly large majority of informants, including defectors, most cadres do indeed live up to this impressive image—reminiscent of some exacting and virtuous fathers—causing men and even lower-level cadres at times to chafe under the onerous example of so much virtue. The cadres themselves carry on an unending struggle against what they consider to be their baser instincts (such as the fear of getting killed, greed, lewdness, and the pleasures of eating and drinking), and they ordain heavy penalties and public humiliation for those who yield to their impulses. They distinguish between their own kind of "revolutionary liberty," which they present as orderly and noble, and that of the GVN, which they equate with unbridled indulgence. This holier-than-thou attitude toward the opponent is reflected in the statements of many prisoners and ralliers. The belief that GVN soldiers lack not only the virtues of the VC but any aspiration toward them is evident also in the fact that many ralliers explain their defecting by "unwillingness to go on enduring hardships." (Whether true or not, they obviously expect this to be deemed a sound reason according to GVN ethics, though the VC would condemn it as unworthy.) Moreover, the high moral standards set by the VC may serve to explain the occasional unreconstructed rallier, who remains essentially pro-VC, though, in a moment of weakness, he chose to escape from the hardships of that life or turned spontaneously against a superior.

The Party protests—and by conduct tries to prove—that it is nobly disinterested, whereas the enemy is basely self-seeking. Thus, while the ARVN pays to enable its soldiers to maintain families in their absence, service with the Viet Cong is unrewarded. Non-combatants are praised for sharing in the sacrifice of their fighting relatives and are compensated only for the most intolerable losses, while material rewards must await a future beyond victory.

Despite all such denials of self-interest, however, and the suggestive exaltation of Ho Chi Minh for his selfless service of the interests of others, the Party does not hesitate to appeal to personal considerations in its recruitment, selection, and training. (The coincidence of individual and Party interests at the lower economic levels is no doubt among the reasons that those strata yield the preferred recruits.) As the statements of informants show, pure dedication to impersonal goals is far less common in the motivation of fighters than is a combination of ideals regarding the country's good with concern for the welfare of one's family and the thought of personal advantage.

Renunciation of family ties is one of the sacrifices the Party exacts from its cadres, in the apparent belief that there is a negative correlation between a man's interest in his family and his effectiveness as a fighter (best exemplified in the selflessness and dedication of bachelor Ho). The Front therefore makes every effort to keep fighters away from their families as much as possible. At the same time, it strongly discourages within its units any close personal friendships among peers that might serve to take the place of family ties. Looking on such private relationships as conducive to factionalism, it tries to cater to the need they are meant to satisfy with the institution of such "safe" associations as the three-man cell.

In addition to enhancing fighting ability and adding to the priestly image of the cadres, the separation from families and communities serves a useful political purpose: in a form of moral blackmail, the Front exalts this and other hardships assumed by its members and, by appealing to people's compassion and their sense of obligation toward the few who suffer for the sake of the many, uses them to elicit popular cooperation.

2. FOSTERING EXPECTATIONS OF VICTORY

The Vietnamese Communists, even more than the Bolsheviks, stress the inevitability of victory. They dwell more extensively on the events, portents, and forecasts pointing to such an outcome than they do on the nobility of their cause or the nature of their goals. This emphasis seems to represent a survival of the Confucian concept that the legitimate authority possesses a "mandate from heaven" and thus the assurance of virtue. With a victorious course as evidence of legitimacy and with legitimacy implying righteousness, it becomes superfluous to affirm and discuss the merits of specific aims; the propagandist need only convince the people that his side—in this case the Communist Party—is winning. The certainty of victory is indeed the dominant theme in every attempt at persuasion by the Viet Cong, including all military and political instruction. Clearly afraid of what might happen if this certainty were shaken by the people's awareness of all the hazards of the war, the leadership attempts through silence or denial to divert attention from the distressing aspects of the struggle: the likely costs and dangers as well as the defeats, casualties, and damages already suffered. Historical accounts may omit entire periods of setbacks; the dead are carried from the battlefield at great risk to avoid the morale-damaging effect of their being seen; the death of a military cadre may be concealed even from his own men. Where the admission of disconcerting facts is unavoidable, the recipients of the bad news—be it the death of a fighter or the loss of land—frequently are first conditioned for the resigned acceptance of their loss by an elaborate alternation of ominous rumor and hopeful reassurance. The well-indoctrinated military cadre is taught to avoid mention of anything that might endanger his men's morale, such as talk of families or of the enemy's weapons. At the same time as the VC tries to hide its own losses, it makes much of all damage caused to, and casualties suffered by, the GVN forces. Though the "hardships" that the Front fighters must endure are talked about, they are generally understood to be those inflicted by nature and by the men's separation from their families. Some potential threats to morale are so represented as to appear exhilarating rather than frightening; thinking about the "beauty of the jungle," for instance, is designed to make men forget its terror. Many of the Front members interviewed, loyal as well as disaffected, though aware of the deception that had been practiced on them, nevertheless accepted it as useful, some even said necessary, to the effective conduct of the war.

The heavenly mandate and the moral sanction it implies form a concept familiar to the Vietnamese, who expect it to be generally understood and accepted. Thus, some of those interviewed gave as their sole or main reason for joining the Front their conviction that it was the winning side, and others cited the reverse opinion to explain their rallying to the GVN.

3. "STUDYING" AND "ACHIEVING"

Among the virtues associated with service as a VC cadre are "peace of mind" (by which the Viet Cong understands the absence of strong negative sentiments, such as fear or dejection, that would interfere with a fighter's performance) and also such positive feelings as enthusiasm and camaraderie, provided the latter does not lead to exclusiveness. The cohesion and camaraderie of the VC unit, frequently stressed approvingly in the interviews, are strengthened by common hatred of the enemy—the "traitors and aggressors"—that the VC promotes, in doctrine and in practice, as the prerequisite to dedicated service. (In the words of an informant, who was asked to name the most important factor in VC propaganda: "They always promote hatred, because without hatred nobody would fight.") Having a legitimate target for their hatred also serves as a safety valve. VC members tend not to fight among themselves and can pursue common aims without internecine strife of the kind that plagues the GVN.

An additional outlet for hostility is the "mutual criticism session." Controlled by cadres, it drains off whatever quarrelsomeness may exist and provides Front members with a vehicle for both aggression and expiation. These sessions, moreover, serve to encourage disputation and inquiry, and in so doing further the all-important activity of "studying" as a means to attaining knowledge and certainty. The Vietnamese Communists attach the greatest importance to study and investigation. It means to them understanding doctrine, historical detail, and the decisions, documents, and directives of higher echelons; it is the way to "knowing the enemy." Their stress on the definition of attitudes, on categorization and classification, and on the utmost precision is part of the "scientific method" that informs Communist planning and action. But it is in harmony also with the Confucian tradition and thus appeals readily to the Vietnamese. The lure of obtaining inside knowledge, of learning in advance of big decisions and likely events, is one of the incentives that informants name for joining the Communist Party.

Investigation and orientation are, of course, the prerequisites for action, and the stress on "study" is paralleled by insistence on "achievement." Action—that is to say, experience—itself the result of study, then becomes the subject of further analysis for the benefit of future action.

The great premium that the VC places on maximal achievement in the era of the *cong* ("common action") is reflected in the constant, unrelieved activity expected of its followers and in demands for physical performance that often reach the limits of their endurance. A concomitant of this exaltation of action is the use of forced inaction as an effective punishment.

Action, being geared entirely to the good of the movement, is accompanied by a constant fight against waste—of ammunition, of "lives that belong to the Front," of money spent to excess on traditional ceremonies. (ARVN soldiers are self-righteously condemned for allegedly being slothful and for wasting valuable resources.)

One of the drawbacks of rigid adherence to the view that study and indoctrination must precede action is that it hampers improvisation, for any unexpected turn in a situation that calls for a change in conduct first requires a period of "reorientation."

4. COERCION VERSUS CRUELTY

There are many comments testifying to profound differences between the conduct of VC cadres and that of GVN personnel toward the population, particularly in the manner in which each side administers, and justifies, the damage, coercion, or injury that it inflicts, be it accidentally, deliberately, or unavoidably. In a significantly high consensus, the accounts, reactions, and interpretations of loyal and disaffected VC followers suggest that GVN personnel often indulge in seemingly senseless brutality and appear to take pleasure in trampling crops and gratifying personal resentments or the desire for private gain in still more painful ways. Even if resort to coercion might be explained as the unavoidable means of obtaining needed intelligence, the GVN soldiers' frequent failure to follow up on information forcibly exacted would invalidate such a claim. Some informants attributed the willful cruelty of so many of the GVN forces to their sense of frustration at the elusiveness of their enemy, which, for lack of a legitimate target, makes them strike out at the people and their property.

The VC, by contrast, stresses propriety of conduct and denies that vindictiveness and other personal feelings ever enter into the damage it inflicts. It discourages and condemns the abuse of power by its cadres for their private gain or pleasure, concerned as it is not only about the likely popular reactions to patent injustices, but also about the damage that such improper conduct might do to the spirit of righteousness from which the cadres draw much of their strength.

Because the Communist Party insists that everything happens as a result of laws and known norms, not through accident or impulse, the VC is apt to construct quasi-judicial contexts (such as the "people's tribunals") within which it seeks to justify its ruthless or violent actions, though often the disguise is transparently thin. People's indignation being governed less by the magnitude of damage suffered than by the extent to which it seems to them inappropriate, arbitrary, and incomprehensible, the VC's violent acts are more readily acceptable for seeming explicable and justified by some known, intelligible standard. (Many GVN agents by failing to demonstrate wherever possible that they are honoring and executing their government's laws, miss the opportunity to cater similarly to this human penchant.)

The conduct expected of VC cadres demands the constant exercise of self-discipline. Attested to by many informants, it is in most cadres the result of a long fight against the natural propensity toward violence. As part of their hard-won restraint, cadres are taught not to strike unless they have first stated their demands, followed by an explicit warning, and to stress clemency as well as punishment. In keeping with this precept, they dramatize and try to legitimize their more drastic punitive measures by issuing (or claiming to have issued) warning to the offenders. They may also force an intended victim publicly to make a promise, the visible violation of which thereafter will make his punishment appear as just.

Informants describe the slow and deliberate acceleration of penalties by the VC (though a few striking departures from the rule have also been reported). First offenses may go unpunished, with only a warning as a reminder, and even threatened penalties may not be carried out if the offender repents and conforms. For the more serious violation, punishments range from admonition to execution. When the VC first assumes power in a given area, it is likely quite suddenly to raise the level of its threats and punishments and execute a large number of people, intending by such a show of violence to render the population fearful and docile. Once the VC is firmly established in the locality, the penalties may lessen, or at least become more predictable and thus more easily avoidable. Conversely, where its control is weak or Front forces are few, the VC may intensify its efforts just to create the illusion of great strength and numbers. As to damage it has caused and coercion used, the VC tries to show its good conscience and pure purpose by being frank, legalistic, and self-righteous about what it has done, in contrast to the GVN's tendency to be furtive on that score.

Generally speaking, the populace, which associates vague and sinister warnings, constant suspicion, and repeated minor harassment with the style typical of the GVN, prefers what it regards as characteristic of the VC, whose cadres try to confine themselves to clear threats and spell out, for the individual's choice, the consequences of compliance and noncompliance.

Coercion, a highly refined instrument in VC hands, takes many forms. The familiar one, by which a target is given to understand that his failure to cooperate could damage his family (a persuasive argument in a culture with strong kinship ties), can be extended to comrades and peers. Those who disobey VC orders may be punished or sent to exposed positions. Or they may be subtly compromised with the GVN, which is thus prompted to administer the penalty. One of the more obvious defenses is to force a man into a loose or inadvertent association with VC–sometimes to seduce him with the promise of a personal advantage–and then to convince him that he has thereby compromised himself with the GVN past the point of no return.

Every target of coercion is carefully chosen and his background fully investigated, documented, and classified. As a result, there appear to be few accidental victims and few cases of haphazardly inflicted damage, two errors of which the GVN is said to be frequently guilty and which are seen as evidence of poor intelligence and of the government's remoteness from "the people." The VC has the advantage on both counts and is thus equipped to step in and exploit any resentments caused by the opponent's fumbling.

Cadres act on the principle that instruments of threat, persuasion, and propaganda become more powerful through repetition, and become still more effective if the manner of their application is varied. Thus, they may start with a long period of gentle pressure and low impact, and then raise these, gradually or by sudden spurts, after the moderate approach has served to dispel people's initial wariness and, in recently "liberated" areas, has accustomed them to the presence of the VC.

On balance, the author believes, the Party hurts the innocent less often than does the GVN. Where it does, or where it seems to inflict disproportionately heavy penalties (as for conduct coming under the general charge of "spying for the GVN"–which conjures up terrible retribution), it frequently gives victims the option of sparing themselves such severe punishment by paying a price for their security.

Yet the cadres' relations with villagers are profoundly affected by suspicion. It is expressed most tellingly in the allegation of "spying for the GVN" (and people's *fear* of being suspected of spying) and, more generally, in the sinister construction that the Party places on innumerable phenomena of innocent appearance. Thus, anyone who has a girl friend may be accused of the kind of illicit relationship on which the Party frowns; minor criticism of policy or practice, even an innocent slip of the tongue, may cause a man to be labeled pro-GVN/U.S.; sick Front members are accused of being malingerers, and a "malingerer" who coughs is sure to be signaling the enemy. Sickness is dismissed as being only in the mind and, if it affects performance, is thought to reflect wrong political thinking. A man's seeming misfortune (such as his losing the Party's money) is assumed to cover a deliberate crime (that of absconding with it). A person who conspicuously survives where others perish is suspected of being an agent deliberately spared; and anyone's poor performance is interpreted as the prelude to his defection. Ironically and inevitably, suspicions and accusations often provoke the innocent into the very disloyalty that the VC means to prevent. But the cadres apparently find this an acceptable loss when weighed against the deterrent effect they derive from their pervasive distrust and from people's awareness of the severe penalty they may incur through the smallest criticism or a seeming lack of enthusiasm and cooperativeness.

The relative predictability of the VC's expectations of conduct, and of the price one must pay for departing from the expected, is in contrast to the whimsicality of the GVN, whose punitive actions appear to be the more strongly resented. Many complain, in particular, about the GVN's proclivity to penalize entire hamlets (rather than only the families of suspects, as the VC tends to do) for having "relations with" the Viet Cong, which often means no more than allowing its forces to pass through. People also complain strongly that the GVN treats the flight of the fearful as an act of hostility, and they are more indignant at the GVN officials' practice of extorting bribes for private gain than they are at the VC's open blackmail for the benefit of the Front.

In instances of inadvertent injury to individuals, the VC appears to make more of an effort than the GVN to allay the bad feeling engendered by the incident. If need be, the cadres will resort to elaborate lies, designed to strip the victim of the appearance of innocence and thereby to render his fate plausible. At other times, they may take the risk of admitting mistakes and offering compensation. In cases of collateral damage, they are likely to make the repairs, whereas the GVN has been reported to penalize the victims for even requesting compensation.

In contrast to their intolerance of nonconformance within their own ranks, the cadres may yield to popular criticism or displeasure, even to the detriment of the Party, particularly where such negative reactions are expressed collectively. (People's awareness that the Front may back down in the face of flagrant collective resistance may actually provide the hope that can inspire such resistance wherever there is a strong cause.) Even individual resistance to serving the VC will occasionally succeed if the cost to the Party is slight and the plea seems reasonable. (It is likely to be prompted only by such overriding self-interest as the needs of a sick child or the demands of an otherwise neglected farm or medical practice.)

5. CLOSENESS TO THE PEOPLE

The Cadres' conduct toward the population is in keeping with the Party's insistence on constant solicitude for the people's welfare, even in the face of initial distrust and hostility. The effect of their concern for such good relations is reinforced by the fact that in social and geographic origins, in dress, in behavior, and in standard of living the people identify themselves more readily with the VC than with representatives of the GVN. Whereas GVN officials and officers often seem to treat their underlings in the willful and autocratic manner of many Vietnamese fathers, the cadres are taught to emulate their hero and leader, the gentle and modest "Uncle" Ho. Many informants testify, often approvingly and sometimes critically, to the "friendly," egalitarian ways of the cadres. Some, to be sure, talk about the easygoing, even convivial, ways of some ARVN soldiers, which they find more appealing than the self-consciously restrained and seemingly distant behavior of cadres who are conscious of their high status or afraid of not living up to the VC's rigid expectations. Yet there is little indication that the informality and friendliness of GVN troops imply solicitude for the people's interests. Nor, apparently, do they preclude such undesirable acts as petty thievery by the soldiers and the withdrawal of GVN protection.

6. COERCING TO PERSUADE

The VC's avowed policy of receiving captives with clemency and welcoming anyone ready to be converted to its side, including even still-active GVN agents, is supported by its practice of forcibly recruiting enemies and re-enlisting defectors to the GVN. (The Front may even level trumped-up charges against innocent persons to make them appear as antagonists and thereby justify their forced recruitment.) The assumption is that the conditions of life shape a man's beliefs, and that, once he has been caught in the VC net, persuasion—either in small, constant doses or in concentrated fashion—supported by an effort to win his trust, will inevitably lead to his conversion.

Education, persuasion, and indoctrination are credited with powerful feats, and both the persuader and the persuaded consider them indispensable tools. In any contest of political wills, for example, it is understood that the degree of a man's political and general education can be decisive; the man who first runs out of arguments automatically accepts defeat and must submit to the view of the other.

A major part of the pattern of education for conversion is the enforced listening to the cadres' persuasion, with the threat of disagreeable penalties ensuring attendance. In classical fashion, this indoctrination, like the criticism sessions, relies heavily on monotonous repetition, and any initial interest of the listeners is likely to give way to boredom. When boredom reaches the level of pain, compliance becomes the tempting way to end the ordeal, much as it does after prolonged interrogation. In an area newly controlled by the VC, to "volunteer" is known to be the only means of escaping protracted indoctrination, which, moreover, threatens to take place at re-education centers in the mountains—a gloomy prospect, particularly for the people of the plains, some of whom liken it to forced labor. In sections where the Front expects to exercise only temporary control, it is less likely to invest in a major effort at indoctrination. It may merely try to win friends by providing entertainment and pleasing the population in other ways.

The cadres apparently are not unduly concerned about the dangers that may arise from people's resentment at having been coerced. Their faith in repeated exposure as a means of persuasion is summed up in this statement from a VC document: "After oppression, continued indoctrination should be maintained to let the POW . . . admit our oppression was right." They are prepared, however, for re-education to take time—the more difficult the conditions, the longer—during which period the target will remain inactive.

Persuasion may be used also in conjunction with plainly coercive devices (which actually leave a person no alternative to following the VC), so as to make him think, when he formally commits himself to the movement, that he is freely yielding to persuasion rather than succumbing to force or trickery. In some, this illusion coexists with an awareness of the reality, as is evident from the accounts of informants who said that they had joined "partly because they wanted to and partly because they were forced."

Many targets of persuasion have expressed their fascination with the cadres' adeptness at what is known as "sweet talk." Some have commented on the disparity between this persuasive skill and the manner of GVN officials and ARVN forces who, with the exception of some special propaganda units, tend to have far less contact with the population and to make little attempt at persuasion. Emphasis on the art of "sweet talk" and people's susceptibility to it may help explain not only their general partiality to the VC but also the exceptional "productivity" of particular cadres.

Among the qualities that informants stress frequently as distinguishing most cadres from the typical GVN officials is the former's endeavor genuinely to communicate with the people. Rather than merely issue and enforce orders they will try to "explain" the content and rationale of actions, including the purpose of impending operations, the reasons for past setbacks, the need for burdens imposed on villagers, and even the harsh judgments meted out by the VC.

In fostering a close rapport between its agents and the population, the Front exploits the Vietnamese profound fear of isolation. Part of the strategy of playing on this desire for closeness is the threat of popular (if silent) disapproval, of withdrawal of Front support, and, worst of all, of a man's separation from his family and close friends. It is always accompanied by the explicit communication of the price of liberation from such a prospect.

7. CRITICISM VERSUS INSULT

The high sensitivity of the Vietnamese to any form of insult causes them, among other things, to be keenly concerned for the sensibilities of others. In the gently stratified society of the village, where the classes mingle readily and are hard to distinguish by dress, appearance, and style of living, "arrogance" is as great a vice as cruelty and serves to describe almost any abuse of authority. The arrogant may evoke memories of early humiliation by tyrannical fathers and older brothers. Indeed, associations with a childhood overshadowed by fear of physical and moral abuse sometimes become the overriding motive for joining a movement that forswears the humiliation of others.

So vulnerable a pride and ego may warrant drastic action, including the changing of sides in war, to undo injury to one's self-respect and restore dignity. The case of the man who burnt down his own house because in his absence his friends had abused it illustrates the extremes with which a Vietnamese is capable of reacting to a slight. The Viet Cong's injunction against fistfighting and similar expressions of impulsively hostile behavior within the ranks is most frequently violated in response to an insult. And most revealing is this remark of a rallier about the alleged rudeness of GVN officials: "I wouldn't complain if they beat us if we said something that wasn't accurate, but I wish they would refrain from cursing us."

In its education of the cadres the Party spends much effort on curbing rudeness, shouting, and the use of bad language, and stresses the importance of restraint even in the issuance of threats. A considerable part of the cadres' training is devoted to cultivating refinement of speech toward comrades as well as civilians and learning to refrain from all expressions of hostility and even from physical, albeit nonhostile, horseplay.

Many informants have described the alleged disposition of GVN agents to humiliate those at their mercy. Beating the weaker is said to be their most common habit, an extension perhaps of the tradition set by fathers and landlords. Though respondents admit that the VC, too, resorts to the practice, they appear to accept it more readily from that source, for a beating by the VC tends to be related in the victim's eyes either to a tangible offense or to an immediate and necessary objective (such as prevailing on reluctant soldiers to fight).

One aspect of the GVN agent's characteristic habit of inflicting insult, in the opinion of many respondents, is his own violent response to slight. Front members who have offended a person, it is said, are likely to tolerate a hostile reaction (if not actually to make amends) as a way to evening and easing the relationship. They may even invite his criticism, or ask him to attend a VC self-criticism session.

Being themselves opposed to the use of insult and violence in human discourse, the cadres are able successfully to exploit in their propaganda and recruitment the GVN personnel's known arrogance and lack of manners. To many, the VC's respect for others is the major reason for joining the Front, just as a single instance of a cadre's contrary behavior has been known to prompt a man to rally to the GVN.

Against the ARVN's alleged practice of punishing an offense without explaining the nature of the offender's error, the Front is scrupulous about accompanying the penalty with such a critical explanation. Indeed, "criticism" may itself become the sole punishment. Though opposed to insulting any man and thereby diminishing his entire person, the cadres skillfully concentrate on the specific offense or weakness, and their power and readiness to expose and publicize it, thereby shaming the guilty in the eyes of family, community, and comrades (even if such exposure remains confined to the self-criticism session) serves as a useful deterrent to transgression. The principle of preventing future infraction of the rules by publicizing those of the past is illustrated also by the practice of criticizing the dead; in one case the VC is reported to have expelled a man from the Party at his burial service.

III. REWARDS: WELFARE VERSUS RESPECT

The attitude of the Vietnamese toward authority, and their historical experience with past rulers, help to account for the very "Asian" character of this Communist revolution, for it would be hard to explain the outbreak of rebellion in Vietnam, rather than in other parts of Southeast Asia, simply on the premise that poverty and inequality are the main causes of every revolt. In the Confucian tradition, good or bad conduct is associated with the authorities rather than with institutions, and the quality of those in power is measured more by their ability to avert damage and abuse to the citizens than by the active benefits they are able to bestow on the population. So long as the reigning authority makes few or no demands on the people, permitting them to ignore and forget the government, they are apt to see in this virtue evidence of the "mandate of heaven" and to be relatively patient, therefore, about their social and economic betterment. (Indeed, some ask no more than that the authority refrain from abusing its subjects.) Only when the virtue, and thereby the mandate, is placed in doubt by the too-frequent intrusion of the "bad official," or the authorities' inability to protect the peasant from the oppressive landlord, will patience give way to intolerance. Once they are ready to question the legitimacy of the established power, people become susceptible to the arguments, social criticism, and promises of its challengers.

Several phenomena suggest that the leadership of the Front is not deeply concerned with establishing a new order, or indeed with socio-economic ends in general. The supreme pronouncements of the Party tend to focus on large political concepts rather than on specific programs. And denunciation of the "bad GVN official," far more than of the basic social inequities, plays a large part in the movement's informal contact with villagers. To the sympathizers, supporters, and low cadres of the Viet Cong, the opposition between that movement and the GVN is not only one between attacker and defender of a certain social order, but also that between unworthy and noxious men in power and better men aspiring to replace them. (Numerous informants adduced misconduct of GVN officials as their single reason for embracing the Viet Cong; others cited the good conduct of the cadres as the only reason.)

Although the Party seeks to play on the peasants' experience of abusive authority and to incite their indignation to the point where they are willing to join or support the rebellion, its conduct vis-à-vis the peasantry since 1945 reflects its very modest estimate of pre-existing discontent, and in this respect reveals another, crucial difference between the Vietnamese and the Soviet revolution. Although Party spokesmen in Vietnam pay lip service to the Communist doctrine of the leadership of the working class, they themselves recognize the peasantry, rather than the workers, as the "main force of the revolution." Yet, unlike the Soviets, they have not catered to the land hunger of the poor by massive, ruthless expropriations of all landowners and the distribution of land to the peasants. The Party clearly does not favor such "instant" agrarian revolution, possibly because it regards it as too advanced a concept for many peasants and too great an upheaval in their society. It attempts instead to limit agrarian reform to the confiscation of land of only very rich or politically undesirable owners, permitting the more acceptable landlords to stay on and collect rent much as before, and remains vague in its promises of an eventual agrarian revolution.

Apparently the leadership believes that the loss incurred through the wrath of dispossessed landlords—especially the many "middle farmers"—would be greater than warranted by the degree of peasant discontent. Though one encounters some more radical views and occasionally measures that seem to depart from such a moderate course, they are, for the most part, attributable to overzealous lower cadres. Not until 1965, when the enlarged American effort and signs of the opponent's superior power created the need for a scapegoat, was there an outcry against the entire class of landlords, part of the short-lived, unsuccessful "turn to the left."

The informants encountered in the Rand sample bore out the Party's seeming estimate of the popular mood. Though eager for the promised land reforms, they were not unwilling to wait for them. Nor did most of them exhibit a strong sense of inequality, for it must be noted that in many villages the pyramid extending from the haves at the apex to the have-nots at the base is relatively flat, and there is considerable social intercourse between top and bottom.

Far more obvious was the indignation with which villagers recalled the acts and personal slights of bad officials. The resented government functionary is representative of the deterioration in the relationship of the local Vietnamese community toward those governing it, a steady decline that began with the arrival of the French and continued under Diem. In earlier times, as various commentators have pointed out, the village notable spoke for the community and served as its conscience, and the village council was the community's powerful and respected executive body. Under colonial rule, the rural notables were withdrawn from public affairs, and the village councils, stripped of their original powers, were burdened instead with the execution of policies devised at the center and resented in the countryside. Authority, formerly vested in the village notables, passed to officials appointed from above and afar, poorly paid men who lacked public spirit and were not answerable to the local community. With the present challenge to the established system and its claim of a "mandate," the patient endurance of what had seemed the divine order of things has in many instances given way to the admission of pent-up anger and of a desire for change which VC cadres are able to exploit with the aid of their deliberate propriety and considerateness of conduct.

The testimony of VC prisoners and ralliers permits no doubt that people's moral and emotional needs are at least as strong a factor in their motivation to rebel as are their economic wants, and that either side in the struggle, if it is to solidify its authority over those under its control, must concern itself with their dignity as much as with their material welfare.

NOTES

1. Robert K.G. Thompson, *Defeating Communist Insurgency* (London, 1965), 94f.
2. Paul Mus, *Guerre sans Visage* (Paris, 1961), 28.
3. Pierre Huard and Maurice Durand, *Connaissance du Viet-Nam* (Paris, 1954), 85.
4. Mus, *Guerre sans Visage,* 339.
5. Ibid.

PART IV.

ATTITUDES TOWARD VIOLENCE

Chapter 9

POLITICAL DEMOCRACY AND PERSONAL DESTRUCTIVENESS

EDITOR'S NOTE: In this short article Leites shows how psychoanalytic insight joined with conventional political and historical analysis can increase understanding of conditions under which political systems are fostered. He illustrates in a democratic context how the early environment of childhood may interact with the current adult world to "trigger" destructive behavior. Noting that social psychological inquiries have focused on changing childrearing practices in order to reduce aggressive behavior, he points out that the problem is a dynamic one. What does the individual "do" with his destructive impulses? He gives examples of three different kinds of "dysfunctions of the conscience," including the moral atrophy he has discussed in other papers presented here. Each dysfunctional type may threaten democracy in a distinctive way.

From "Democracy and Destructiveness," American Behavioral Scientist *V (1961), 6-10.*

I. FACT STATEMENTS AND PREFERENCE STATEMENTS IN THEORIES OF DEMOCRACY

"Political theory," as usually practiced and understood, contains two classes of propositions which it seems relevant to distinguish for many purposes: on the one hand, certain fact-statements; on the other hand, certain preference statements. Take the affirmation that there *is* a positive relationship between the degree of equality in the distribution of income, and the chances of emergence and stability of political democracy. On the other hand take the affirmation that persons fulfilling certain biological and psychological requirements *should have* equal rights in certain kinds of political participation. If we decide to define the logical term "proof" so that we may speak of "proof" in both cases, the kinds of "proof" appropriate to the two classes of statements would be rather different.

A "political theory" preference statement in favor of "democracy" may be an *irreducible* one—that is, "democracy" may be an ultimate object of positive valuation, as "happiness" or "justice" sometimes are. Usually, of course, in Western culture, "democracy" has been, and is, an object of *reducible* positive (or negative) preference statements. That is, preferences for democracy are usually derived (or derivable) from other preferences (ultimately, irreducible ones) and from fact-statements alleging certain conditions under which they are realized. For example, one may start out with an irreducible preference for "freedom of worship"; one may then come to believe that in certain "historical conditions" freedom of worship is maximized when there is "political liberty"—and hence derive a preference for "democracy."

A preference for democracy can be—and has been—derived in various ways in the context of Western beliefs as to what is and what ought to be. Democracy may be—and has been—postulated on the basis of affirming (in a variety of languages of "theory") that the subjects of government know best (though not necessarily clearly) what's good for them. Or it may be derived from the "relativist" belief that no preference is "certain"—and hence that none should be imposed by extreme means.

A fact statement—such as the one affirming widespread insight into one's needs—may thus function as a *premise for preferring democracy*. A fact statement—such as the one affirming the pro-democratic impact of but moderate inequality in the distribution of income—may also function as indicating a *condition of practicability* of democracy. These two classes of fact statements may, in the system of any given political scientist, be identical, or entirely non-overlapping, or overlapping to various degrees.

II. DESTRUCTIVENESS IN A DEMOCRATIC CONTEXT

Suppose psychologists had defined to our satisfaction the personality trait "low destructiveness." (I do not at this moment propose to spend time on such a definition, but to rely on our common understanding of the term; various elements of what may be a convenient definition will be mentioned in the rest of this discussion.) The events designated by this term would then appear to occupy a threefold position within the theory of democracy. First, the usual definitions of "democracy" include of course limitations on overt destructiveness. Second, postulations of democracy frequently include the point that *homo* need not entertain as a major end or a major means that of being *homini lupus*. Third, considerations of overall conditions fostering the emergence or survival of democracy frequently refer implicitly or explicitly, to the strength of considerateness and benevolence in interpersonal relations. Thus "low destructiveness" is a frequent element of the definition of, and preference for, democracy, and a frequently assumed condition of its practicability.

The intensive analysis of the "destructiveness" aspect of human beings has in recent decades to a considerable extent been undertaken by human scientists whose departmental designations begin with the word-part "psych": "psychologists," "psychiatrists," "psychoanalysts." The intensive analysis of "democracy" has been largely the domain of human scientists calling themselves "political scientists." This difference of names seems irrelevant for the problem at hand.

A given human being at a given moment in time may be placed (if we had—as of course we have not—perfected our language and observations sufficiently) at a certain point within a continuum of destructiveness ranging from very low to very high. We would then speak of "low" destructiveness if a person's position falls within a certain appropriately—and "arbitrarily"— demarcated sector within the continuum I mentioned.

It is obvious that different persons—and the same person at different times—occupy different positions on this continuum. It is also probable that the average positions of the members of at least some different groups are significantly different. The question of human science is then: what are the "laws" governing the occupancy of positions on this variable?

Although this problem has of course been as yet only very partially solved, it seems already possible to predict with some confidence certain formal aspects of future solutions. One of them is as follows: the level of destructiveness of an adult depends on the whole of his career-line. More particularly, we may single out two sectors of his total experience which are apt to be of considerable weight: the *current* environment he is reacting to (e.g., words of a leader of a party not my own which manifestly present my party as a fatal danger to the Republic); and *early* environments which are apt to set up enduring—though by no means unmodifiable—tendencies to feel and act according to certain patterns (e.g., not to take certain kinds of hostile words too seriously).

"Political scientists" have been particularly interested in relating feelings and acts in *politics* to their *current* political environment. Certain kinds of "psychologists" have been particularly concerned with relating feelings and acts of adults in their *private* lives to their *early* environment. Progress in insight into the conditions of high and low destructiveness depends on a fusion of these two orientations. "Human nature" is neither benevolent nor malevolent; human beings are malevolent-benevolent in different degrees and nuances when they have had differing experiences. What are the experiences—in the past *and* in the present—reducing the incidence of malevolence?

III. PERSONAL DYNAMICS OF DESTRUCTIVENESS AND POLITICAL CONSEQUENCES

Let me just point to a few foci of work in progress bearing on this problem.

One major point of much contemporary research in this area is this: human beings are often considerably more "moral" *and* "immoral" than they feel themselves to be. Both our unconscious conscience and our unconscious impulses are apt to be more extreme than our conscious ideals and wishes. Their extremism has, prominently, the nuance of destructiveness—in the service of imagined self-preservation, power, vindictiveness, or punishment of self or others for imagined sins.

To some extent (we do not yet know which) the strength of unconscious destructive strivings is independent of variable arrangements in the individual's experience with other human beings. Thus the fact that the human organism starts life with a protracted period of helplessness has a massive impact. But there is equally no doubt that known and possible varieties of human experience make for considerable differences in the strength of destructive strivings. Certain connections in this area (such as the impact of great early harshness) are well-established, and have indeed become commonplaces. But while it may by now be easy to indicate certain arrangements to avoid, if we want to minimize unconscious destructiveness, it is still very difficult to point to what should be done. In fact, there is evidence that certain efforts oriented on the fear of inducing destructiveness in the process of socialization either do not reach their aim or attain it at high cost to other values.

Given a certain level of unconscious destructiveness, human beings have still, as it were, a "choice" among a variety of "mechanisms" for "handling " it. The mechanisms used will determine the derivatives of unconscious destructive strivings in feeling, thought, and action; they will therefore be of direct relevance to the viability of democracy. Here the decisive scientific questions are: under what conditions will a certain mechanism—say, "projection"—be used to manage destructive strivings, and what consequences will its use have for democracy? And here again I must immediately add that research is yet in its initial stage. Furthermore, here, too, certain negative points are clearer than the positive ones. For instance, one important mechanism to reduce anxiety about my destructive strivings is to assure myself that there are agencies in the external world—parents, for instance, or "leaders"— who will either stop my acting on the promptings of the "the pig-dog within me," as some Germans used to say; or who—being externalized consciences— will reduce the guilt accompanying destructive behavior which they approve. "Political liberty" may for such personalities be accompanied by the fantasy, laden with (not always conscious) guilt and anxiety, of being overwhelmed by inner badness; they will hardly be its devoted defenders.

One of the many alternative mechanisms to deal with destructiveness is to put it at the disposal of the kind of conscience which is manifestly most concerned with the failings of others. Instead of being, for example, selfishly vindictive, we may become selflessly indignant. When much destructiveness infiltrates into the conscience in this way, my sense of the absolute rightness of certain specific arrangements in society may become so intense that I feel it to be wicked to tolerate the wrong just because the majority favors it. The value of freedom will tend to rank lower in my value hierarchy than the value of certain ways of using it. This, of course, tends to disintegrate democracy, which may thus to some extent depend on limiting the infiltration of destructiveness into conscience.

But here again there are undesirable potentialities on both sides of an optimal position. Democracy is threatened today not only by a fanaticism like that of certain communists. It is less obviously, but not necessarily less potently, threatened by the opposite secular Western trend of moral uncertainty which manifests itself, for instance, in the presumable decline of the capacity for moral indignation. The trend towards moral atrophy is as obscure to our understanding as it is relatively unique in available records of cultures. The dysfunctions of the conscience may be one of the major studies of the scientists of democracy.

Chapter 10

BOLSHEVISM AND RUSSIAN VIOLENCE

EDITOR'S NOTE: In this selection from a comprehensive work on Bolshevik perspectives, Leites contrasts the official Soviet view of violence with that to be found in Russian tradition and literature. He finds the wish to yield to unrestrained, destructive passion a prominent theme in the traditional culture. Guilt at this wish was typically countered by feelings of being out of control (hence not responsible) or by efforts at total abstinence. The author finds the Bolshevik mode of coping with guilt at similar wishes is to require violence as a deliberate and calculated policy in the service of the Party. Destructive force should and can be used only in amounts necessary for that purpose. Tracing the doctrine from Lenin through Stalin, however, Leites finds the estimate of the amounts of violence necessary have been steadily escalating.

From A Study of Bolshevism *(Glencoe, Ill.: Free Press, 1953), 341-361. Reprinted by permission of the RAND Corporation.*

I. THE REQUIREMENT OF INSTRUMENTAL VIOLENCE

The Party must use violence, as any other political device, according to calculations of expediency only. In 1920, Lenin recalled the conflict between the Social Revolutionaries and the Russian Social Democrats at the beginning of the century:

> Of course, we rejected individual terror only out of considerations of expediency.[1]

Bolshevik doctrine rejects, by implication, a Russian aversion against cold violence, and a Russian enjoyment of passionate violence. It requires that violence be felt as a means to an end rather than as an end in itself; that it be applied deliberately rather than whimsically, and with the goal of a new creation. Hence violence must be directed, economically, towards precisely specified targets rather than being indiscriminate, or all-embracing, in its aim; and it must be "systematic" rather than "spasmodic." Its targets must be outside the self; that is, violence must aim neither at satisfying nor at destroying the self. However limited the target of a particular act of violence, this act must be part of the great design for transforming the world (saving, not destroying it) rather than a "petty," "personal" affair. The performance of expedient acts of violence must not be hampered by love or guilt, nor by forgiveness, empathy, or pity.

I shall now consider in more detail these required and rejected aspects of violence. As Bolshevik doctrine is not vocal about them, this will largely involve an attempt to illustrate them by Russian literature.

To return to the Bolshevik preference for cold over passionate violence, a major Russian defense against guilt about destructiveness seems to have been to feel overwhelmed by destructive passion. To a Bolshevik, this would, however, merely add intense guilt for having abandoned full "consciousness," for having permitted oneself to be carried away. In Bolshevism, guilt about destructiveness is rather mitigated by the "conscious" belief in its being required *(nuzhno)* by one's dedication.

To illustrate the older pattern, in nineteenth- and early twentieth-century Russia the death penalty was often opposed specifically because of the deliberateness of its infliction. When Tolstoy in the late fifties looked at a public guillotine execution in Paris, he wrote:

if a man were torn to pieces before my eyes, it would not be so repulsive as this dextrous and elegant machine. . . . In the first instance˙ there would be no intelligent will, but the human feeling of passion; in the other there is a refined quiet and convenience in killing. . . .[2]

According to Soloviev:

the fanatical crowd which, under the influence of a mad anger, kills a criminal on the spot, is to be blamed; but deserves indulgence. As for the Society, which kills slowly, coldly, consciously, it has no excuse.[3]

In June 1918 the following conflict between the Bolsheviks and the Left Social Revolutionaries occurred:

Since February, when the "socialist fatherland" had been proclaimed in danger, executions had been carried out by the Cheka . . . without any regular or public judicial process. Both Right SR's and Mensheviks had . . . protested against these proceedings. The Left SR's . . . were still represented in the Cheka and bore their share of responsibility for its actions. But when the revolutionary tribunal for the first time pronounced a death sentence—on a counter-revolutionary admiral . . .— the Left SR's sought to have the sentence quashed . . . and, when they failed, withdrew their representatives from the tribunal . . . the objection . . . was not founded on humanitarian considerations. The charge of being "Tolstoyans" was indignantly denied; for not only had the Left SR's participated in the work of the Cheka, but they had in the past been the prime instigators of assassination as a political weapon. Their case rested . . . mainly on opposition to the imposition of a death sentence by judicial process. The Left SR's admitted that it was some- times legitimate and necessary to kill opponents, whether by assassination or by some special process such as that of the Cheka. But they were irrevocably opposed to the revival of "the old accursed bourgeois state principle" implied in a regular process of condemnation and execution by a court.[4]

The preference for being carried away by irresistible impulses is expressed throughout Russian literature in the fascination with storms and blizzards, and with the terrifying and pleasurable possibility of being overwhelmed by them. In Nekrasov's words:

Storms—let them clash and possess me!
What if the cup overflows?[5]

The association between storms of wind and of rage is indicated in Chekhov's *Under the Road* which describes an incomprehensible and passionate battle between non-human elements, the counterpoint to the Bolshevik view of history as a comprehensible and calculated battle between human elements:

Outside a storm was raging. Something frantic and wrathful . . . seemed to be flinging itself above the tavern with the ferocity of a wild beast and trying to break in. Banging at the doors, knocking at the windows and on the roof, scratching at the walls, it alternately threatened and besought, then subsided for a brief interval, and then with a gleeful, treacherous howl burst into the chimney, but the wood flared up, and the fire, like a chained dog, flew wrathfully to meet its foe, a battle began, and after it—sobs, shrieks, howls of wrath. In all of this there was the sound of angry misery and unsatisfied hate, and the mortified impatience of something accustomed to triumph.[6]

Chekhov's *The Witch* makes more explicit that the battle in nature is one of life and death (as that between the Party and the world), but also that it is incomprehensible (while the Party is the first human agency which completely understands its own battle):

It was approaching nightfall. The sexton, Savely Gykin, was lying in his . . . bed in the hut adjoining the church. . . . He was listening . . . the solitary window [in his hut] looked out upon the open country. And out there a regular battle was going on. It was hard to say who was being wiped off the face of the earth, and for the sake of whose destruction nature was being churned up into such a ferment; but, judging from the unceasing malignant roar, someone was getting it very hot. A victorious force was in full chase over the fields, storming in the forest and on the church roof, battering spitefully with its fists upon the windows, raging and tearing, while something vanquished was howling and wailing. . . .[7]

A Bolshevik must not only prevent himself from being carried away by destructive passion, he must also avoid any enjoyment in required destructive activities, and, of course, must not perform them for the pleasure they bring. In demanding this (by implication), Bolshevik doctrine opposes a trait of a major Russian self-image, the enjoyment of destruction, and engaging in destruction for pleasure. Thus Pushkin wrote:

All things that rage, all that destroy
Bring an unspeakable strange joy.[8]

In *Dead Souls* Gogol described Nozdrev:

There are some people who have an urge to do the dirty even on their closest friends and very often without any good reason for it. . . . Nozdrev had this strange passion. The more friendly you became with him, the more certain he was to turn against you . . . without at all considering himself your enemy. On the contrary, if he were to meet you again by chance, he would display every sign of friendship. . . .[9]

According to Ivan Karamazov in Dostoevsky's *The Brothers Karamazov:*

Our historical pastime is the direct satisfaction of inflicting pain.[10]

In *Notes From Underground* the hero-narrator says:

it is sometimes very pleasant . . . to smash things.[11]

Gorky describes a bazaar in Nizhni Novgorod during his adolescence:

The whole bazaar, all its business men and shopkeepers, led . . . [a] life . . . filled with . . . vicious amusements. They would willfully misdirect passersby who asked the way; this . . . had become so habitual it no longer gave them enjoyment. Having caught a pair of rats, they would tie their tails together, and then gloat over the torments of the . . . animals as they pulled each other or turned on each other; or they would put kerosene over the rats and watch them burn. Or they would tie a tin can to a dog's tail, and laugh as the . . . animal whirled about, howling and snapping.

They had many varieties of this kind of entertainment. . . . In their relations with people, they seemed to feel only the urge to scoff at, to cause pain to, to discommode others. I found it strange that books ignored this . . . ingrained inclination of people to humiliate one another.[12]

Against such non-instrumental attitudes towards violence, Bolshevik doctrine requires an utterly instrumental one: violence is work, not a pastime. It must be performed, as everything else, as a result of proper calculations. With this requirement Bolshevik doctrine opposes, again, a trait of a Russian self-image, the tendency to commit acts of violence for what is felt as no reason whatsoever. Thus the narrator in Dostoevsky's *The Possessed* says about the hero, Stavrogin:

Suddenly, apropos of nothing, our prince was guilty of incredible outrages upon various persons and . . . these outrages were . . . utterly silly and mischievous, quite unprovoked and objectless.[13]

In *In the World* Gorky tells how he compared in adolescence violence in nineteenth-century French popular literature with the violence around him:

Above all, I observed that, as portrayed in these books, even brutes, skinflints and other villains did not display the mystifying heartlessness, the derision of man, which I . . . knew here. . . . The cruelties of these literary villains were calculated; almost always one could see why they behaved so. But the cruelties inflicted here were inflicted without purpose, were entirely irrational; no one gained anything from them.[14]

And he said about the last years before the first war:

During the time I was living in Italy my mind was very uneasy on account of Russia. . . . My uneasy mood was particularly heightened by facts which indicated beyond all doubt that in the spiritual world of the Great-Russian people there lurked something morbidly obscure. Reading the volume on agrarian risings in the Central Russian provinces, published by the Free Economic Society, I saw that those risings bore a particularly brutal and senseless character.[15]

By requiring that the aim of destruction be the creation of a new world, Bolshevik doctrine opposes a Russian fantasy of total and irreversible destruction, as it is conveyed in a statement of a seventeenth-century Raskolnik from the town of Romanov:

> I wish that all Romanov, every man, wife, and child, would come to the banks of the Volga, throw themselves into the water, and sink to the bottom so that the temptations of the world should not attract them. And what is even better: that I might set fire to and burn the entire city; what joy if it were to burn from end to end destroying all the aged and infants so that none could receive the stamp of Anti-Christ.

Milyukov continues in a paraphrase:

> Romanov and Belev would be followed by "all Russia"; and, perhaps, after Russia the "entire world" would be destroyed by fire.[16]

II. THE HIGH COST OF COMMUNISM

Once it is clear that certain violent measures are necessary to the advance towards communism, the amounts of human misery and death which are involved become, according to Bolshevik doctrine, irrelevant. One is, as it were, not responsible for the violence which follows from applying to the given goal of communism the essential principle of action which Bolsheviks call consequentialness *(posledovatelnost)*.

In 1929 Stalin said:

> the expropriation of the kulaks is an integral part of the formation and development of the collective farms. That is why it is ridiculous and fatuous to expatiate today on the expropriation of the kulaks. You do not lament the loss of the hair of one who has been beheaded.[17]

In the context of the Russian horror of death against which Bolshevism reacts, differences in the amount of violence used appear as rather irrelevant, as they do not affect the sole relevant fact: everybody will die. In the context of the Bolshevik idolatry of communism, differences in the amount of violence used also appear as irrelevant in relation to the sole relevant fact: the Party will have created communism. No price is too high to obtain this end; any price asked is justified by showing that it is the minimum price demanded by history: it just can't be done less expensively. Thus Bolshevik doctrine rejects what Dostoevsky presents as the thought of a "materialist":

> even were one to presume the possibility of that tale about man's ultimate attainment of a rational and scientific organization of life on earth—were one to

believe this tale and the future happiness of man, the thought itself that, because
of some inert laws, nature found it necessary to torture them thousands and
thousands of years before granting them that happiness—this thought itself is
unbearably repulsive.[18]

What is "unbearably repulsive" to Dostoevsky is a matter of course to
Bolshevism. It takes a view opposite to that of Ivan Karamazov when he says:

Too high a price is asked for harmony; it's beyond our means to pay so much to
enter on it.[19]

Bolshevism rather seems to agree with Pasternak when he says in *Safe
Conduct* about a "beautiful woman":

the so-called world of nature is the one place where she can be herself to the full,
because when with others it is impossible to take a step without hurting others or
herself being hurt.[20]

For the Party, however, the "so-called world of nature" is not in the present;
it is the communist future in which hurting will have become avoidable.

The moral system of the Russian intelligentsia contained both an emphatic
aversion against destructiveness and an emphatic ban on "egoism." Bolshevism
uses the absolute prohibition on egoism to turn the less absolute proscription
of destructiveness. Dedication to the Party—the proof that one is not an
egoist—requires destructive action; insufficient capacity for such action shows
a lack of attachment to the great goal, and is an expression of the self-
centeredness which makes one more concerned with feeling guilt than with
transforming the world. Bolshevism shares—with a clearer (a consciously
completely clear) conscience—the belief which Veressayev expresses in the
guise of talking about physicians:

we, the representatives of the most *humane* of the sciences, are compelled to
trample the most elementary humanity under foot.[21]

This position reproduces individual "egoism" on the level of the Party.
The egoist, as we have seen, is the boundlessly greedy person who, like a
"wild beast," is willing to inflict huge sufferings on others to gain even a tiny
pleasure for himself; and who refuses even the smallest sacrifice for even the
largest benefit to others. Correspondingly, in attempting to maximize its
power the Party is willing to inflict huge sufferings on others, (though only to
gain yet greater pleasures for all); and it refuses even the smallest sacrifice of
power for even the largest current benefit to others (though on behalf of yet
larger future benefits to them).

It had been a widespread and intensely guilt-laden belief in the Russian
intelligentsia that their relatively privileged way of life was purchased by the

sufferings of "the people." *[Further research might test the hypothesis that such beliefs were related to a family atmosphere stimulating guilty beliefs of children that they had injured their parents, particularly their mothers.]* In Chekhov's *On Official Business* a magistrate is investigating a suicide in the countryside, and has a dream in which peasants whom he has encountered appear:

> He lay down and began to drop off, and suddenly they were again walking along together and chanting: "We go on, go on, go on. . . . We take from life all that it holds of what is most bitter and burdensome, and we leave to you what is easy and joyous; and sitting at supper, you can discuss coldly and reasonably why we suffer and perish, and why we are not as healthy and contented as you."

> he felt that this suicide and the peasants' misery lay on his conscience, too; to be reconciled to the fact that these people, submitting to their fate, shouldered all that was darkest and most burdensome in life—how terrible that was! To be reconciled to this, and to wish for oneself a bright and active life among happy, contented people, and constantly to dream of such a life, that meant dreaming of new suicides of men crushed by toil and care, or of weak, forgotten men of whom people only talk sometimes at supper with vexation or sneers, but to whom no help is offered, and again:

> "We go on, go on, go on. . . ."

> As though someone were knocking with a little hammer on his temples.22

There were various ways of defending oneself against such guilt—e.g., by self-destruction, as Bunin shows when, in his autobiographic *The Well of Days,* he tells a story about a young woman:

> She came of a rich and aristocratic family, but grew up full of passionate dreams about freedom and good of the people . . . (her aspirations) from her earliest youth had caused her, as one favored, such distress over her own good fortune among all the misfortunes of the people, and such shame even for her beauty that once she tried to disfigure herself, to burn with vitriol her hands too much admired by everybody.23

Bolshevism offers a different defense: instead of feeling guilty about the sufferings which one imposes on others, indirectly and passively, by enjoying one's privileges, one attempts to feel self-righteous about directly and actively imposing sufferings on others—for the sake of the future abolition of sufferings.

While Bolshevism attempts to maximize the Party member's guilt about any tendencies to harm "the Party," it thus attempts to abolish guilt about destructive acts on behalf of "the Party."

It had not always been a Bolshevik belief that the advance towards communism involves a very large human cost. Before the seizure of power,

Lenin had predicted—as later events showed, not without sincerity—very small amounts of violence in the case of that event. In *Pravda* of May 19, 1917, he quoted from a speech by the conservative Shulgin and said:

> You will not frighten us, Mr. Shulgin. Even when we are in power, we shall not take away your "last shirt," we shall guarantee you good clothes and good food, on the one condition that you work, in a capacity for which you are fit and to which you are used![24]

In June, 1917, he expected to stop far short of the level of violence of the French Revolution:

> The "Jacobins" of the twentieth century would not guillotine the capitalist. . . . It would be sufficient to arrest from fifty to one hundred magnates and bank leaders . . . for a few weeks, in order to expose their methods. . . . Upon exposing the methods of the banking kings, we could release them. . . .[25]

In September, Lenin predicted the fate of the expropriated capitalists after the Bolshevik seizure of power:

> It will be quite sufficient for the Soviets to punish those capitalists who evade the most detailed accounting or who deceive the people, by confiscating all their property and arresting them for a short time, to break all resistance of the bourgeoisie by these bloodless means.[26]

After the seizure of power, he said on November 17, 1917:

> One reproaches us with applying terror. But we do not apply terror as the French revolutionaries did who beheaded defenseless persons, and we hope that we shall not do so. I hope that we shall not do that, for we are strong. To those we arrested we said: we will liberate you if you promise not to conduct sabotage. And we received such promises.[27]

This reflects a breakthrough of the "trustfulness" which Bolshevism combats by the requirement never to rely on promises.

In a speech on January 26, 1918, Lenin, still in the flush of easy victory, went even farther:

> And even if there are in Russia at the present time a few dozen people who fight against the Soviet power, there are very few such cranks and in a few weeks there will be none of them at all. . . .[28]

But the day before he had already said:

> If we are guilty of anything, it is of having been too humane, too benevolent, towards the representatives of the bourgeois-imperialist order. . . .[29]

In the spring and summer of 1918 it became a recurrent theme of Lenin's that the Party was using too little violence:

> There is no doubt that the Soviet power has, in many cases, not shown sufficient decisiveness in the battle against the counter-revolution. It was in these cases not steel, but jelly. . . .[30]

> our government is too soft, very often it is more like jelly than iron.[31]

In a letter of May 4, 1918, to the Central Committee Lenin wrote:

> I ask to put on the order of the day the question of the expulsion from the Party those Party members who as judges in the trial of bribe-takers (May 2, 1918)—whose bribing had been proved and admitted—limited themselves to a verdict of half a year in prison.

> To pronounce against bribe-takers, instead of the death penalty, such ludicrously weak sentences is *dishonorable* for communists and revolutionaries.[32]

About General Krasnov, who by this time had become an active enemy of the Soviet power, Lenin said:

> [after the seizure of power] the Russian workers magnanimously allowed [Krasnov] to go free in Petrograd when he came and surrendered his sword, for the prejudices of the intellectual are still strong and the intellectuals protested against capital punishment—Krasnov was allowed to go free because of the intellectual's prejudice against capital punishment.[33]

In 1921 Lenin commented on the theft of public property by officials:

> There are too few executions (I am for executions in such cases).[34]

From these developments arose the rule that the Party must guard itself against the danger of using too little violence—a graver mistake than using too much, as it exposes the Party to annihilation.

Gorky says about Lenin after the seizure of power:

> I often used to speak with Lenin about the cruelty of revolutionary tactics and life. . . .

> "What is your criterion for judging which blows are necessary and which are superfluous in a fight?" [said Lenin]. . . .[35]

That is: in doubt, destroy. In 1918 Lenin said:

> Marx and Engels . . . have viewed as one of the causes of the collapse of the Paris Commune the fact that it did not utilize its armed power energetically enough to suppress the resistance of the exploiters.[36]

In 1927 Stalin repeated:

> we do not want to repeat the errors of the Paris Communards. The Communards
> of Paris were too lenient in dealing with Versailles. . . . They had to pay for their
> leniency, and when Thiers came to Paris, tens of thousands of workers were shot
> by the Versailles forces.[37]

Thus it came to be a basic—though rarely expressed—Bolshevik belief that
the human cost of the transition from capitalism to communism is, in
absolute terms, very high. In 1919 Lenin said:

> ". . . we had to give birth to the Soviet power against patriotism. It became
> necessary to break patriotism, to conclude the Brest peace. This was the most
> frightful, fierce and bloody breaking-up. Bolshevism means to break even patriot-
> ism in a bloody manner.[38]

In general terms:

> Dictatorship—that is a cruel, hard, bloody, painful word. . . .[39]

Talking about Soviet youth, Stalin alluded in 1930 to the sufferings caused
by the regime and stressed the central moral dogma that what is necessary is
desirable. Here he gives a particularly clear expression of the conflict between
the Bolshevik orientation on total happiness in the end, and the Bolshevik
aversion against happiness now.

> not everybody has sufficient nerve, strength, character, and understanding to
> conceive the picture of the grandiose destruction of the old and of the feverish
> construction of the new as a picture of what is *necessary* and therefore as a
> picture of what is *desirable,* a picture which is rather dissimilar to the earthly
> paradise . . . of "resting" of "enjoying happiness."[40]

In the transition from a Lenin to a Stalin, and from a Stalin to a Malenkov
the ease and degree of conscious indifference to the human cost of one's
policies has probably been sharply mounting; and the intensity of the effort
to reduce that cost has much decreased. In 1919 Lenin said:

> the accusation of terrorism, to the extent to which it is correct, falls not on us but
> on the bourgeoisie. It forced terror on us. And we shall make the first step to
> limit terror to the very minimum as soon as we finish with the basic source of
> terrorism, the invasion of world imperialism. . . .[41]

In 1921 Lenin affirmed the indispensability of the Cheka, but added:

> we . . . know that the merits of a person may become his defects, and we know
> that the conditions which have developed here require imperatively that that
> institution be limited to the purely political sphere. . . .[42]

Stalin has not continued this theme.

The human cost of the transition to communism is viewed—and justified—against the background of the high human cost of the status quo. In 1901 Lenin wrote about "the Asiatically savage and cruel forms [which] the expropriation of the small producers has assumed in Russia" in terms which recall what has often been said about certain phases of Bolshevik agricultural policy:

> The masters of the . . . state are no more concerned about the vastness of the numbers of the victims of famine . . . than a locomotive is concerned about those whom it crushes in its path. The dead bodies retard the wheels; the train stops, it may (if the engine-driver is too careless) jump the rails; but after a slight interruption it will . . . continue on its way. You hear of death from starvation and of the ruins of tens and hundreds of thousands of small farmers, but at the same time you hear stories about the progress of agriculture in our country . . . you hear about . . . improved implements and the extension of cultivated meadows, etc. For the Russian masters of the land . . . the intensified ruination and starvation is nothing more than a slight and temporary hitch to which they pay almost no attention whatever, unless the famine-stricken *compel them to do so.* [43]

According to Gorky, Lenin spoke in 1907 about war in these terms:

> he said . . . as if in amazement: "No, but think of it. Why should people who are well fed force hungry ones to fight each other? Could you name a more idiotic or more revolting crime?" [44]

Thus, in informal conversation, the morally indignant refusal to accept an intensely disapproved state of affairs breaks through the crust of the Bolshevik virtue of being matter-of-fact and of taking any matters of fact as matters of course. Instead of the Bolshevik insistence that all is perfectly comprehensible (and moves towards a good solution), there appears a characteristic anguished feeling of the intellegentsia: it is all so incomprehensible, dreadful, insoluble. In 1911 Lenin wrote:

> Even in such a cultured country as Britain, which had never experienced the yoke of the Mongols nor the oppression of the bureaucrats, nor the abritrariness of the military, it was necessary to cut off the head of one crowned criminal in order to teach the kings to be "constitutional" monarchs. Hence in Russua it will be necessary to cut off the heads of at least a hundred Romanovs in order to teach their successors to stop organizing Black Hundred assassinations and pogroms against the Jews. [45]

In 1917 Lenin compared favorably the amount of violence to be used by the Party to overturn the status quo with the amount of violence used to defend it:

for the successful discharge of such a task as the systematic suppression by the exploiting minority of the exploited majority, the greatest ferocity and savagery of suppression are required, seas of blood are required. . . .

Again, during the *transition* from capitalism to Communism, suppression is *still* necessary; but it is the suppression of the minority of exploiters by the majority of exploited . . . [this] is a matter comparatively so easy, simple and natural that it will cost far less bloodshed than the suppression of the risings of slaves, serfs or wage laborers. . . .[46]

After the seizure of power Lenin implied that the two amounts of violence might be similar:

we shall crush the resistance of the propertied classes, using all those means with the help of which they crushed the proletariat. No other means have been invented.[47]

In 1918 he affirmed that the horrors of the status quo rendered "necessary" similar horrors in the process of its destruction:

do they believe, [in the camp of the bourgeoisie] that the revolution, which has been provoked by the war, by the unprecedented destruction, can proceed calmly, smoothly, in a pacific fashion, without torments, without the infliction of pain, without terror, without horror?[48]

He presented the Westernization of Russia by Peter the Great as a model, and added:

he did not hesitate to use barbarous methods in fighting against barbarism.[49]

Thus he treats as non-existent the problem whether bad means will not be self-defeating.

By 1920 Lenin had developed a major Bolshevik justification of the increasing human cost of the regime. The Party, he recalled, was killing hundreds of thousands to abolish a social order which had caused the world war, where millions had been killed for the sake of limited redistributions of wealth and power among groups of capitalists:

The popular masses . . . in Europe and America . . . ask why ten million people have been killed and twenty million crippled. To raise this question means to force the masses to come out in favor of the dictatorship of the proletariat. . . .

It is impossible to affirm that capitalist society can be transformed . . . without violence and without enormous upheavals—that society which has spent hundreds of billions of rubles for the war.[50]

Later in the same year Lenin gave a yet more explicit statement of this theme, a major base of the "calm conscience" of the Bolshevik leaders:

> There was the imperialist war; reactionary generals and officers applied terror against the proletariat; the current policy of *all* bourgeois governments *prepares already new* imperialist wars . . . and these wars result with objective inevitability from their whole policy. To lament under these conditions . . . the civil war against the exploiters and to condemn it, or to fear it, means in reality to become a reactionary. It means that one fears the victory of the workers which may cost tens of thousands of victims, and that one renders possible a new massacre of the imperialists, a massacre which cost millions of victims yesterday and will cost similar numbers tomorrow.[51]

And Stalin said to H. G. Wells in 1934:

> the substitution of one social system for another, has always been . . . a painful and cruel struggle.[52]

Thus the "mercilessness" of the Party is determined (and excused) by the fact that history possesses the same trait. Lenin said in 1917 in typical style:

> The "peaceful" petty-bourgeois hopes for a "coalition" with the bourgeoisie, for agreements with it—all this is mercilessly, cruelly, implacably destroyed by the course of the revolution."[53]

Another Bolshevik theme justifying the human cost of the Party's activity stresses that any major social change requires violence. No group in possession of contested values surrenders them without the most drastic pressure, which usually includes the massive use of violence. In 1905 Lenin wrote: "Great questions in the life of nations are settled only by force."[54] In 1917:

> It is well known that in the long run the problems of social life are decided by . . . civil war.[55]

Criticizing a non-Bolshevik Socialist shortly before the seizure of power, Lenin expressed the Bolshevik acceptance of the disorder and dirt of violence:

> He would be ready to accept the social revolution if history would lead up to it in the same peaceful, quiet, smooth, orderly way in which a German express train approaches a station. A sedate conductor opens the door of the car and calls out: "Social Revolution Station! *Alle aussteigen!*"[56]

In 1918 he repeated:

> Not a single problem of the class struggle has ever been solved in history except by violence.[57]

In 1919 he used this point against democratic "illusions":

> the devotees of "consistent democracy" ... imagine that serious political questions can be decided by voting. As a matter of fact, such questions ... are decided by *civil war.* ...[58]

If, for a political activist, a "serious" question is one significantly affecting his political results, and if he should be totally involved in politics, then he would indeed betray his faith if he were to give in on a "serious" question without using violence. That is, Bolshevism takes it for granted that no political group will attach to "formal" procedures such as "voting" a value at all approaching that which it assigns to its substantive goals.

Revolution is birth; and birth—according to a belief with a high emotional charge in the Russian intelligentsia—is very bloody. In 1919 Lenin mentioned the objections of "petty bourgeois" intellectuals to the suffering caused by the Revolution, and said:

> They had heard and admitted "in theory" that a revolution should be compared to an act of childbirth; but when it came to the point, they ... took fright. ... Take the descriptions of childbirth given in literature, when the authors aim at presenting a truthful picture of the severity, pain and horror of the act of travail. ... Human childbirth is an act which transforms the woman into an almost lifeless, bloodstained mass of flesh, tortured, tormented, and driven frantic by pain. But can the "type" that sees *only* this in love ... be regarded as a human being? Who would renounce love and procreation for *this* reason?[59]

Thus, Bolshevism opposes the person who fears action because he will dirty his hands or gloves, and who fears love-making because of its messy and destructive consequences (and, presumably, content). That is, Bolsheviks oppose in themselves tendencies to abstain from action and sexual relations so as to preserve order, cleanliness, harmlessness and innocence. In *The Memoirs of a Physician*, Veressayev, recalling his early years in medicine, expresses this rejected attitude:

> The picture of the "normal," the "physiological" process of parturition unfolded itself before me like an oppressive and feverish nightmare. ...
>
> I remember the first confinement at which I was present. ...
>
> The laboring woman had long abandoned all efforts at self-control; her moans filled the ward, while she sobbed, trembled and clasped her clenched hands; her groans could be heard in the passages and were lost far away in the great building. ...
>
> In the morning her husband ... came to the hospital, to inquire after his wife's condition. I regarded him with a feeling of odium; this was his second child; therefore he *knew* that his wife had to go through this torment, and still he remained undeterred by the knowledge. ...

And why does love exist with all its poetry and bliss? Why should there be such a thing as love if it causes so much torment? Can it be that "love" is not a cruel mockery of love, if a man has it in him to cause the woman he adores such sufferings as I had witnessed in the lying-in hospital?[60]

More neutrally Pasternak says:

Without an accoucheuse, in darkness, pushing her
Blind hands against the night, the Ural fastness, torn and
Half-dead with agony, was screaming in a blur
Of mindless pain as she was giving birth to morning.[61]

The Bolshevik attitude, without Bolshevik restraint in feeling, is conveyed by Pilniak in *The Volga Falls to the Caspian Sea:*

Did you observe . . . that all constructions are born in blood, like any other living thing for that matter? We, human beings, are born in blood, and we die because blood stops circulating. Human love begins and ends with blood. I know of no construction where there was no blood. When a house is being constructed, a worker tumbles off the rafter; once the plant is erected, the machines grind some mechanic to pieces; while a railway is being constructed, the train derails along the slope; when a canal is dug, the dam bursts through and workers are drowned . . . everything is based on blood. . . . And the red bloody standard of the revolution is a symbol of gory births.[62]

According to a further Bolshevik self-justification the violence used by the Party is the necessary reaction to its enemies' intent to annihilate it, whether this intent, at any given moment, is pursued by actual violence or merely by preparing for later violence. In an important fantasy in the Russian intelligentsia an individual would be felt to be released from any moral constraints once he believed that death is annihilation. Similarly, in an unformulated Bolshevik feeling the Party is released from moral constraints as it stands under an incessant threat of annihilation from its enemies.

In early polemics, Lenin—whose violent metaphors preceded Bolshevik violence—believed that he was mild; that his opponents were violent; and that they forced him to imitate them. Discussing in 1899 the deviation of Struve-Bulgakov, he spoke about the term "repugnant" used by Struve in a letter to Potresov about Plekhanov:

I have just re-read the rough draft of . . . my article against Bulgakov—and I see that the tone of it is conciliatory. . . . Possibly the "conciliatory" tone (I did my best to soften the tone and to polemicize as a comrade) will prove to be inappropriate and even ridiculous if such expressions as "repugnant" become current. . . .[63]

In 1919 Lenin said:

In a country in which the bourgeoisie does not put up such a fierce resistance [as it did in Russia since October], the task of the Soviet power will be lighter, it will be able to work without that violence, without that bloody path which was forced upon us by Messrs. Kerensky and the imperialists. . . . Other countries are . . . coming to the Soviet power in a . . . more humane way.[64]

Defending Bolshevik violence once more, he asked:

Is a proletarian revolution, emerging from such a war, thinkable without conspiracy and counter-revolutionary attacks on the part of tens and hundreds of thousands of officers belonging to the class of landowners and capitalists?[65]

That is, if the Party does not use violence against its enemies, it lays itself open to violence from them; the question is only, who will destroy whom. There is no third way.

In March 1919 Lenin said:

either the violence against Liebknecht and Luxemburg, the massacre of the best leaders of the workers, or a violent repression of the exploiters. Those who dream of a middle way are our most harmful and dangerous enemies.[66]

In 1921:

Either the White Guard bourgeois terror of the American, British (Ireland), Italian (the fascists), German, Hungarian and other types, or Red proletarian terror. There is no middle course, no "third" course, nor can there be.[67]

In 1927 Stalin said:

And if it is necessary that somebody be "stained with blood," we shall exert all our efforts that it be some bourgeois country rather than the USSR.[68]

However, in the crucial phases of history it is always necessary that somebody be stained with blood; hence it should be the enemy.

Finally, the human cost of the realization of communism appears as justified by the virtue and happiness it will procure. The violence expended in bringing about communism is violence designed to end violence. Gorky recalls about Lenin:

Once . . . when he was caressing some children, he said: 'these will have happier lives that we had. . . . There will not be so much cruelty in their lives. . . . And yet I don't envy them. Our generation achieved something of amazing significance for history. The cruelty, which the conditions of our life made necessary, will be understood and vindicated. Everything will be understood, everything.' He caressed the children with great care. . . .[69]

That is, Lenin is certain of the possibility of an "understanding" which Belinsky doubts and Ivan Karamazov denies. Stressing that the road to the goal is long and painful, Bolshevism, by implication, opposes a Russian fantasy of the immediate abolition of all evil, by a change of heart rather than of institutions. Thus in *The Brothers Karamazov,* Dmitri thinks about mankind:

> "Why don't they [people] hug each other and kiss? Why don't they sing songs of joy? Why are they so dark from black misery? Why don't they feed the babe?" And he felt . . . that he wanted to do something for them all, so that the babe should weep no more, so that the . . . mother should not weep, that no one should shed tears again from that moment, and he wanted to do it at once, at once, regardless of all obstacles, with all the recklessness of the Karamazovs.[70]

In *The Well of Days,* Bunin describes his childhood experience of Easter:

> in the night from Saturday to Sunday some marvelous transformation was accomplished in the world. . . . We were not taken to Midnight Mass, but we used to wake up with the sense of the beneficent transformation, so that it seemed there would be room for no more sorrow.[71]

A position intermediate between this and the Bolshevik views is indicated when Dostoevsky says about a character in *Crime and Punishment:*

> She had come to desire so *keenly* that all should live in peace and joy and should not *dare* to break the peace, that the slightest jar, the smallest disaster reduced her almost to frenzy, and she would pass in an instant from the brightest hopes and fancies to cursing her fate and raving, and knocking her head against the wall.[72]

Only Bolshevik violence, as we have seen, is calculated rather than passionate, it is not directed against the self, and does not expect to achieve the supreme goal immediately.

NOTES

1. V. I. Lenin, *Selected Works* (New York, 1943), X, 72.
2. Ernest J. Simmons, *Tolstoy* (Boston, 1946), 149.
3. John Maynard, *Russia in Flux* (New York, 1948), 284.
4. Edward H. Carr, *The Bolshevik Revolution* (London, 1950), 162-164.
5. Cecil Kisch, trans. *The Wagon of Life* (New York, 1947), 48.
6. Anton Chekhov, *The Chorus Girl and Other Stories* (New York, 1927), 202f.
7. Anton Chekhov, *The Witch and Other Stories* (New York, 1918), 3.
8. C. M. Bowra (ed.), *A Second Book of Russian Verse* (New York, 1943), 23.
9. Nicolay V. Gogol, *Dead Souls* (New York, 1921), 83.
10. Fyodor Dostoevsky, *The Brothers Karamazov* (London, 1930), 253.

11. Fyodor Dostoevsky, *The Short Novels of Dostoevsky* (New York, 1945), 152.
12. Maxim Gorky, *Autobiography* (New York, 1949), 327.
13. Fyodor Dostoevsky, *The Possessed* (London, 1946), 36f.
14. Gorky, *Autobiography,* 286.
15. Maxim Gorky, *Reminiscences* (New York, 1921), 183f.
16. Paul Milyukov, *Outlines of Russian Culture* (Philadelphia, 1948), 57.
17. Joseph Stalin, *Leninism: Selected Writings* (New York, 1942), 163.
18. Fyodor Dostoevsky, *The Diary of a Writer* (New York, 1949), 472.
19. Dostoevsky, *The Brothers Karamazov,* 258.
20. Boris Pasternak, *Selected Writings* (New York, 1949), 139.
21. Vikenty Veressayev, *The Memoirs of a Physician* (New York, 1916), 32.
22. Avrahm Yarmolinsky (ed.), *The Portable Chekhov* (New York, 1947), 459f.
23. Ivan Bunin, *The Well of Days* (New York, 1934), 286f.
24. V. I. Lenin, *Collected Works* (New York, 1921-1942) XX, Part 2, 49f.
25. Ibid., 226.
26. Ibid., XXI, Part 1, 239.
27. V. I. Lenin, *Sochineniya,* 3rd edition (Moscow, 1928-1937), XXII, 40.
28. Ibid., 240.
29. Ibid., 221.
30. Ibid., 4th edition, XXVII, 205f.
31. V. I. Lenin, *Selected Works* (Moscow, 1941-1950), VII, 339.
32. L. B. Kamenev (ed.), *Leninskii Sbornik* (Moscow, 1924-1925) XXI, 223.
33. Lenin, *Collected Works,* XXIII, 138.
34. Kamenev, *Leninskii Sbornik,* XXIII, 178.
35. Maxim Gorky, *Days with Lenin* (New York, 1932), 44.
36. Lenin, *Sochineniya,* 4th edition, XXVI, 362.
37. Joseph Stalin, *Leninism* (London, 1932-1933), 98f.
38. Lenin, *Sochineniya,* 3rd edition, XXIV, 219.
39. Ibid., 291.
40. Joseph Stalin, *Sochineniya* (Moscow, 1936-1939), XII, 174.
41. Lenin, *Sochineniya,* 3rd edition, XXIV, 567.
42. Ibid., XXVII, 140.
43. Lenin, *Collected Works,* IV, Part 2, 36f.
44. Gorky, *Days with Lenin,* 22f.
45. Lenin, *Sochineniya,* 4th edition, XVII, 300.
46. Lenin, *Collected Works,* XXI, Part 2, 220.
47. Lenin, *Selected Works,* VI, 438.
48. Lenin, *Sochineniya,* 4th edition, XXVII, 140.
49. Lenin, *Selected Works,* VII, 366.
50. Lenin, *Sochineniya,* 3rd edition, XXV, 76f.
51. Ibid., 309.
52. Joseph Stalin, *Marxism vs. Liberalism: An Interview between Joseph Stalin and H. G. Wells* (New York, 1947), 14.
53. Lenin, *Collected Works,* XXI, Part 1, 256.
54. Lenin, *Selected Works,* III, 126.
55. Lenin, *Collected Works,* XXI, Part 1, 69.
56. Ibid., Part 2, 41.
57. Lenin, *Selected Works,* VII, 269.
58. Ibid., VI, 477.
59. Lenin, *Collected Works,* XXIII, 122f.
60. Veressayev, *Memoirs,* 9-12.

61. Avrahm Yarmolinsky, *A Treasury of Russian Verse* (New York, 1949), 212.

62. Boris Pilniak, *The Volga Falls to the Caspian Sea* (New York, 1931), 15.

63. Elizabeth Hill and Doris Mudie (eds.), *The Letters of Lenin* (New York, 1937), 92.

64. Lenin, *Sochineniya,* 3rd edition, XXIV, 219.

65. Ibid., 455.

66. Ibid., 66.

67. Lenin, *Selected Works,* IX, 192.

68. Stalin, *Sochineniya,* X, 46.

69. Gorky, *Days with Lenin,* 50.

70. Dostoevsky, *The Brothers Karamazov,* 547f.

71. Bunin, *The Well of Days,* 38.

72. Fyodor Dostoevsky, *Crime and Punishment* (New York, 1948), 333f.

Chapter 11

ON VIOLENCE IN CHINA

EDITOR'S NOTE: *This selection is excerpted from a larger work on Chinese political culture in which Leites seeks, in the literature of traditional China, distinctive attitudes to aggression which may persist in the perspectives of the new Chinese elite, in spite of its conscious opposition to traditional values.*

In the traditional picture of the world this theme is prominent: "Hurting another is not far from harming oneself." Anger at another may result in self-injury. In this view, meekness and self-effacement may be the best policy, for the world is dangerously irritable and one must take care not to provoke the rage of others towards oneself.

On the other hand, Maoist teachings on destructiveness seem aimed at converting tendencies to direct rage against the self into destruction of enemies of the Party. Moreover, since the dominant communist view is that the outer world is not merely irritable, but that it is resolutely murderous, there is no need to restrain one's most vigorous action against hostile forces. But at the same time the old fear persists that aggression may provoke damaging counterattacks and that in failing to yield to superior powers "one may end by slapping one's own face." Which balance is struck between these two perspectives may well affect responses of Chinese leaders to opposition inside and outside of their country.

From "One May End by Slapping one's own Face: On Violence in China." Unpublished manuscript, 1971. Emphases in quotations are supplied by the author unless otherwise indicated.

I. TAKING ONESELF AS A TARGET

1. IT IS NOT FAR FROM HURTING ANOTHER TO HARMING ONESELF.

"Can it be said," exclaims somebody imagined by Teng T'o (one of those who covertly criticized the regime in the early sixties) "that God would seal my *resentful* lips, and forbid me to utter one or two *sighs*?"[1] "I am whelmed," observes the fifth century Pao Chao, "in *sad, resentful* thoughts."[2] The young man about to commit suicide in *A peacock flew* (third to fifth century) is drawn to it by "the *grief* that surged in his *boiling* breast," by "anger and sorrow mingled," in a poet's words.[3]

When a boy's parents, in a Shantung village and our century, beat him for wetting his bed, "he cursed himself . . . *and* hated his parents."[4]

When the father of a Chinese boy from the upper stratum of a small town becomes a political fugitive in the early years of the Republic, and his uncle then decides to put him into a monastery, that decision is celebrated by a dinner. "Don't be sad," the uncle, in the boy's recollection, tells him, "everything will be all right."

> He went on with his consoling nonsense. . . . Suddenly [he] . . . became furious. He cut off his solemn speech and began to swear. He drank . . . , *cursing* my father and the revolution. The *tears* rolled down his nose and fell on his upper lip.[5]

Beyond sensing sadness and rage together, I may be uncertain which it is that is felt: "The flute," imagines an eleventh-century poet, "made a wailing sound as though the player were filled with resentment or longing . . . were lamenting or protesting."[6]

Do I intend murder or suicide? I may not know. A farmer's son having, in the 1920s, refused the wife selected for him, "his father told him that unless he married, he would kill him, or kill himself."[7] If I can't kill you, I can still dispose of myself. "Enraged," a legal case report of the late seventeenth century observes, "Mrs. Chang . . . rushed off . . . to Chang Erh-Huan's house to get even with him." But then, "finding nobody there, because all the Changs were . . . in the fields, she, in her passion, hanged herself from a beam of the house."[8] "The elder brother," discloses another such story, "knowing that he was in the wrong and could not report the case (against his younger brother) was very angry." Then, though "Chuan saw that his brother was very angry" and—probably sensing the danger not to the target, but to the bearer of that feeling—"kowtowed and apologized"—"the brother hanged himself."[9]

All while harming myself, I may feel like hurting another. "The irate woman," observes a contemporary Westerner, "hit her head on the floor. . . ." [10] "The uncle," in another report of a legal case, "was so angry that he threw himself from a cliff"; "the aunt was angry and hanged herself." In fact, a situation envisaged by traditional jurisprudence was that "parents committed suicide because they were angered by their children." [11]

The anger which makes me kill myself may be righteous. According to another legal case report, a man had, for cash, permitted another man to sleep with his wife. When the lover became unable to pay, the husband terminated his tolerance, whereupon the other man demanded restoration of the sums previously transferred, and, when berated for this request, struck the husband. "Lin, after proclaiming . . . that Wang had not only been unwilling to give him money, but had also struck him, fell into such a state of . . . passion that he hanged himself." "It was after this," concludes another report in the same collection, "that the maid committed suicide out of indignation." [12] In *The Dream of the Red Chamber* a maid chooses a less extreme course:

> Black Jade smiled coldly and said, " . . . " Li Ma was so distressed by this remark that she slapped her own face as she said, "How cruel Lin-ku-niang can be. She can say things that cut worse than a knife. . . ." [13]

I may commit suicide feeling both righteous and humiliated. When a married woman, in another case, let herself be abducted, "the result was such shame *and* indignation on the part of her father that he killed himself." [14]

That somebody rages against himself may incite someone else to get wild against everybody but himself. "Suddenly," in *The Dream of the Red Chamber*, the central character (young Pao-yu), possessed,

> leaped three or four feet into the air and began to jabber words that no one could understand. . . . He dashed about wildly . . . apparently bent on self-destruction. . . . Soon the news spread throughout both mansions. . .

And then Phoenix, otherwise a cool, efficient woman, highly capable of making others suffer for her own purposes,

> suddenly entered, brandishing a knife and threatening everybody. . . . Chou Jui's wife, aided by some . . . maidservants, managed to disarm her . . . before any damage was done. Phoenix was carried protesting back to her own room. [15]

Not only are the destruction of another and of oneself close to each other: there is also an awareness that they are. This is expressed, for instance, in that the same idea covers both: white is the color both of mourning and of autumn, the season of punishment.

I may experience hurting myself as if it were damaging another. AhQ, the famous character imagined by Lu Hsün, having been humiliated, "raising his right hand . . . slapped his own face hard twice. . . . . After this slapping his heart felt lighter, for it seemed as if the one who had given the slap was himself, the one slapped some other self, and soon it was just as if he had beaten someone else. . . .[16]

As in this case, the way of attacking oneself may be the same as that employed against others. "Before Wang could interfere," imagines a T'ang writer, "Ku raised his sword and cut off his own head." [17] During the cultural revolution it was expected that "he put up a big character poster against himself."

That attacking oneself and assaulting others can replace each other may be perceived. "Her anger has been unable to find . . . [an outlet]," observes the gross central character of *Chin P'ing Mei* about one of his women, adding: "She feels depressed in consequence." [18] "Now," remarks an organization of "rebels" during the cultural revolution about rivals, "they have torn off the mask of 'depression' and bared their ferocious look." [19]

Even better is it known that an attack on myself may hide an assault against another. Having been censured by his mother, a son "kowtowed . . . and said, 'Mother is saying things that make a son wish he were dead.' 'it is clear that you are the one who wants me out of the way,' the matriarch said." [20]

2. I AGAINST MYSELF

Threatened with punishment from without, I will, in old China, be disposed to become my own executioner. "Suddenly, realizing that he was using the forbidden form of address in referring to Yu Erh-chieh," a servant "quickly slapped himself. . . ." "All the hapless woman could do," in another case of incorrect behavior described in the same novel, "was to slap her own face and curse herself." [21] "When he sent in the yearly report in which officials were classified according to their efficiency," Arthur Waley tells about a T'ang personage (Yang Ch'eng),

> contrary to the usual practice he included the report on himself: "The Governor devotes himself wholeheartedly to the welfare of his people, but is no good at collecting taxes. Classification: bottom of the bottom class."

Soon

> an official sent to deal with the taxation business found that the Governor was not at home and, on asking where to look for him, was told to go to the town jail: "When he heard you were coming, His Excellency was sure you intended to arrest him, and to save you trouble he has put himself in prison." [22]

Committing an act which, in my surmise, may provoke somebody else's desire to punish me, I may declare my awareness of this sequel and solicit its occurrence—or pretend to do so, as in a minister's formula illustrated by the words of Li Ssu to the future first Ch'in emperor:

> Thy servant, Ssu, has petitioned for an audience only to present his stupid counsels inside the court, and then to be chopped into inches to death outside the court.[23]

Undergoing punishment already, I may take over from the one who inflicts it on me, perhaps completing what he had in mind himself—as in the frequent case of killing oneself after having endured prolonged torment. My tormentor may prefer it that way. "An emperor," observes Chü, "has the power to force anyone to die by giving him poison or a sword. . . ." For a father "to order a son to commit suicide" was even "the most common pattern."[24]

Or the inverse sequence may be chosen, self-punishment coming first rather than last. In *The Dream of the Red Chamber* a lady is enraged against a servant:

> "Strike the wretch for lying!" she commanded. Wang-erh, one of her favorite servants, came up to carry out the command, but Phoenix stopped him, saying, "Let him strike himself. Your turn will come next."[25]

Not only may I inflict damage on myself *when coerced,* I may—one of the few aspects of the domain here treated which have been clearly noted, though little inspected—do so *to coerce.* It is in this fashion that a promoter of propriety may make others conform. Thus, in three tales intended to show that one should not altogether rely on chopping off heads:

> Miao Yung [second century—NL] . . . shut himself up in his room and castigated himself until his younger brothers and their wives repented. . . .

> Lu Kung was a magistrate who depended entirely upon moral influence. Once a chief of a canton borrowed an ox and refused to return it. . . . Lu Kung urged the man to return the ox, but he could not be persuaded to do so. Lu Kung sighed and said, "This is because education has not been in operation." He intended to resign. All his subordinates wept and asked him to stay. The borrower was ashamed of himself and returned the ox.

> As in the case of Chih Yün, a magistrate might force his prisoner [an avenger whose act he approved—NL] to escape, going so far as to threaten suicide if the latter refused.[26]

So far from adding damage inflicted upon me by myself to deprivations imposed on me by others, I may threaten an attack on myself to deter one from outside me:

> When Cassia was provoked to strike her, she would . . . threaten to commit suicide "looking for knives and scissors by day, and ropes and cords by night."[27]

Or I may actually harm myself so as to hurt another, a maneuver which, when playing on guilt or shame, has often been noted as prominent in China. When, in *The Dream of the Red Chamber*, the hero (Pao-yu), during one of his quarrels with his beloved (Black Jade) attempts to destroy a piece of jade essential for his well-being,

> Pervading Fragrance [his maid] said, "You should not destroy it, when you are quarreling with your mei-mei. She will feel that she is responsible." This touched Black Jade's heart, for it was what she herself had in mind. Pao-yu, then, was not as thoughtful as Pervading Frangrance. She cried and threw up the medicine she had taken a moment ago.... Purple Cuckoo said to her mistress, "You must take care of your health. What would Pao Erh-yeh [Pao-yu] think if he imagined that he was the cause of your illness?" This touched Pao-yu, as Pervading Frangrance's remark had touched Black Jade.[28]

But damaging another through depriving myself has not always depended on that other's moral sensibility. "When one views the adversary not as a rival, but as an enemy," observes Granet about feudal China as recorded by Ssu-ma Ch'ien,

> one sends forth, to start the engagement, brave men ... who cut their throat, with a loud cry. A soul of fury emanates from them ... which attaches itself to the enemy as a substance of ill luck.[29]

Instead of damage I inflict on myself, the weapon I may use against another is a demand that he attack me; attributing to him an intent to do so. Perhaps with solid evidence, as when Phoenix in *The Dream of the Red Chamber* has overheard her husband, while making love to a woman, envisaging the situation after her death: "Phoenix ... threw herself at Chia Lien, crying that he might as well kill her then and there, since he wanted to get rid of her." (Whereupon, unusually, "Chia Lien ... seized a sword from the wall and said he would gladly oblige if she insisted.") The reaction may not be different when the other has been less explicit, as in one of the many instances in the same novel when Black Jade has been disagreeable to Pao-yu:

> My son takes interest in playing with lances and cudgels instead of doing farm work. When his mother remonstrated with him, he paid no heed, and she became angry and died.

Hence release is prevention:

> She wanted to make him stop crying, yet feared to stem the flow of the poisonous humors of anger that, if not dissipated, might cause him to be ill.[30]

If rage unreleased is dangerous to the one who harbors it, the discharge of anger is not safe either. In *The Dream of the Red Chamber*, a mother, wanting to save the life of her son who is being beaten by his father, pleads with her husband not to endanger his own life by the exertion required to extinguish that of their child.

"To kindle a fire and burn oneself";[31] "to put on a grass raincoat when extinguishing fire, is to provoke calamity on oneself"; "when a man un-loosens his coat and takes fire into his bosom, he is provoking misfortune to fall upon him": for such truths to be worth stressing, one must sense a penchant for unwittingly harming oneself.[32]

3. FIGHTING THE DISPOSITION TO DAMAGE ONESELF

In old China damaging oneself is disapproved as an attack on one's ascendants. "When the boy does hurt himself," observes Muensterberger, "he is severely punished since he . . . might deprive his father of his male descen-dant."[33] As "his parents give birth to his person all complete," argues the *Book of Rites* about the son, "to return it to them all complete may be called filial duty." Now it is only "when no member has been mutilated, and no disgrace done to any part of the person" that "it may be called complete." Hence "a superior man does not dare to take the slightest step in forget-fulness of his filial duty." Indeed, a son "should not forget his parents in a single lifting up of his feet, nor in the utterance of a single word." Therefore "he will walk in the highway and not take a bypath, he will use a boat and not attempt to wade through a stream," and for the same reason "an evil word will not issue from his mouth," so that "an angry word will not come back to his person."[34]

While the demand just stated was stressed in old China, Communists have been much less outspoken on the issue of self-destructiveness; not, I would surmise, because their feelings on the matter are less strong. (Why this difference, I have not understood.) What Communists have conveyed, of course, is (1) that the individual should be willing to let the Party's (instead of the family's or the ruler's) enemy inflict damage on him, as the price to be paid for his hurting the enemy on the Party's behalf; (2) that he should avoid any damage to himself not profitable to the Party—the theme corresponding to the classical one stated above and, as I just noted, now muted; (3) that the (pen-)ultimate objective is not, as of old, avoidance of destruction, but rather its accomplishment with regard to the enemy; and (4) that the Party knows how to reduce the cost to itself of attaining this objective. "Local . . . guerrillas," reports Smedley about the war against the Japanese, "who had formerly fought under the slogan of 'Kill Japanese, then die,' were taught by the New Fourth Army training camp how to 'kill Japanese and live'."[35]

Communists have not only been chary of mentioning the penchant to damage oneself, but also moderate when they did take note and, of course, disapprove. Observing in the fall of 1966, in a speech to "rebels," that "there is now a mode of struggles by which people invariably sit down and stage a hunger strike," Chou En-lai explains that "they cannot be criticized, or . . . they will be more indignant than ever." They should merely "be persuaded not to adopt this way. . . ." Yet more, "we will not say whether it is good or bad, but will only say that it should not be adopted." Once more, "if they have already begun the hunger strike, it will be necessary to treat them earnestly, so as to cool their anger."[36] After all, the "rebels" themselves have been reverting to the classical stance of asking to be damaged, in standard phrases such as "we must be ready to let the masses struggle against us—even kill us."

Faced with the return of such penchants, the Maoists (a word I shall use to designate those conducting the Cultural Revolution) have tended to present the regeneration which they demand as a war waged against oneself, offering an approved avenue for the urge to turn rage inside. "We are resolved," declares a "worker-PLA group," "to lead the broad masses of teachers and students to . . . explode a revolution deep in their souls, and fiercely seize power from 'self interest' in their minds." Let us, a student proposes, "fire violently" on self-interest in one's mind.[37] "With Bethune's scalpel," declares a poem, recalling the Canadian surgeon who furnished the subject for one of Mao's three "constantly read" pieces, "the cancer of 'self' we'll incise." "Men Ho," explains an account of a Maoist hero, "looked upon combatting 'self' as he would upon a bayonet fight with an enemy on the battlefield."[38]

II. MAKING ONESELF INTO A TARGET FOR OTHERS?

1. A DANGEROUSLY IRRITABLE WORLD

In traditional China this feeling was strong: almost anything I do may provoke somebody's rage and induce him to strike at me. "I know not," Chinese have read in the Book of History, "whether I may not offend the powers above and below." Hence "I am fearful and trembling as if I should fall into an . . . abyss."[39]

Only a sage is exempt from the fault of giving offense. "Their words," says The Book of Filial Piety about "high officers," "are broadcast to the world, yet give offense to no one."[40] And only with a "heart and belly friend" can I be sure that he won't take offense at anything that may appear when I pour out my heart to him: as Ruth Bunzel has pointed out, his central quality.

Will my success, of whichever kind, not make you envious, angry, damaging? While "the average West Towner," Hsu observes about the community described by him, "wants to . . . achieve success, and show that he has something which the others do not have"; "he would . . . prefer to emphasize the fact that the merit . . . belongs to his parents and ancestors, or is occasioned by fate . . ."; for "to show that he personally has something which the others have not, would be embarrassing to the latter . . ."[41] —and hence, I would guess, dangerous to the former.

A major objective, then, in choosing conduct becomes that of minimizing the rage of others about what I will have done. A proverb warns, "don't do anything to cause men to frown at you, and there will not be a man to grind his teeth at you." Another advises how to limit the damage others will inflict on me: "if you want your dinner, don't offend the cook."[42] A couplet tells, "if one does nothing to cause the arching of eyebrows, he will have no one to spit in his face."[43]

Goodness is, also, that which, astonishingly, causes no rage: "good deeds may fill the empire without provoking anyone's dislike."[44] But—so, I would surmise, runs a suspicion, widely entertained and rarely expressed—Do such deeds, incessantly extolled though they are, really exist? Am I capable of them? And, in any case, do they not come at a high price to myself? All I am usually able to do is to avoid more anger than I arouse.

> Patience advised Chia Lien not to go in, saying "I would not go in if I were you. Lao Tai-tai . . . was very angry. . . . She has just recovered somewhat. . . ." "Since she is no longer angry, I don't think I have anything to worry about," Chia Lien said. "Lao-yeh asked me to come and will be angry with me if he finds out that I did not."[45]

The application of this calculus does not guarantee impunity, but its neglect renders loss certain. "If I had said anything," a character in *Water Margin* surmises "would it not have been like disturbing a wasp, and getting stung?"[46] I am surrounded by beings, human and others, who have the capacity of hurting me grievously; who may do so without my having in any way made them attack; but who may also be mercifully unconcerned with me as long as I leave them punctiliously alone, or ingratiate myself with them; and who will surely pounce if I displease. Thus one major belief; side by side with which there is another, to which I shall now turn.

2. A RESOLUTELY MURDEROUS WORLD

"The power," says Ou-yang Hsiu (eleventh century) in a famous passage about the season of autumn,

> by which it lays waste and scatters far and wide is the unexpended fury of the breath of heaven and earth. For autumn is the minister of punishments. . . . Its purpose is . . . execution.[47]

"The flood threatening people's lives and property," we are told in an account of a Maoist hero's life, "was like a knife in Lei Feng's heart, a whip lashing his body." "These words," we read in a contemporary story when a cadre recognizes his error through listening to the self-criticism of a colleague, "like bullets striking steel plates, made a strong impression on Kitchen Squad Leader Chiang Hao."[48] "The pain occasioned by the mourning for three years," the *Book of Rites* explains, "is like that of beheading; that arising from one year's mourning is like the stab from a sharp weapon."[49] *The Dream of the Red Chamber* employs a standard locution when, to its central character, "the news that Chin-chih had died was like a knife plunged into his heart.[50]

Not only is destructive intent thus easily felt (under the guise of metaphor) behind any painful event for which it is not affirmed; it may also be readily asserted. When another harms me, I might with notable ease not consider the possibility that he is doing it without awareness or with indifference: it is with intent. When, in *The Dream of the Red Chamber,* the maid Swallow has picked twigs, for her own pleasure, in a garden punctiliously tended by an older woman, Hsia Ma,

> it so happened that Swallow's mother came looking for her just then. . . . Hsia Ma said [to her], "Come and see for yourself what your daughter has been up to. She has no respect for anyone, not even me. Worse yet, she is even trying to ruin me."[51]

Such a certainty of belief is felt, perhaps, in China as less out of the ordinary than in the West.

When somebody attempts to help me, I might not find it difficult to discern that he endeavors to hurt. When, having received bad news, "Black Jade threw up all the medicine she had just taken and much more besides . . . coughed until it seemed that her lungs would burst," her devoted maid "Purple Cuckoo hurried to her and began to pound her back to relieve her"; but Black Jade pushed her away saying, "Go get a rope and strangle me. It will suit your purpose better." The one thus interpreted may not perceive others differently. When Black Jade, ill, does not yet know that Pao-yu is going to marry somebody else, and two of her maids, believing her to be unconscious, talk about it so that they might be overheard, "Purple Cuckoo returned and scolded them saying, 'You two should not talk here. Are you afraid that she won't die soon enough?'"[52]

In such an atmosphere, I can plausibly allege somebody else to be engaged in the covert enterprise of destroying me, in order to accomplish this very design of mine against him. A mistress in *The Dream of the Red Chamber* is driving a well-behaved maid to her death thus:

> She found fault with Lotus in everything she did, declaring that she was deliberately . . . driving her to her death. . . .[53]

It is on reactions such as these that the communist, and particularly Maoist presentations of the enemy feed. *[Of course, that public image is not fully believed by the leadership, a point which I shall try to take into account below.]*

The enemy is all hate. "With hatred carved in his bones . . . ," a "rebel" publication says in standard fashion about Peking's deposed boss, P'eng Chen, or: "the faces and eyes of these . . . bandits were burning with . . . hate against the revolutionary rebels," one such group may say about its rivals. " 'Hatred' and 'revilement' represented the common language of all the landlords, rich peasants, counterrevolutionaries, undesirable characters, and rightists . . . in China at that time," recalls *People's Daily* about 1962 in the summer of 1966. "They really harbored 'deep hatred' towards the Communist Party . . . gnashed their teeth and poured out abuses."[54]

The enemy desires to make me suffer atrociously and forever "Liu Shao-ch'i," a worker alleges to recall—in standard fashion for 1968-1970—"said, 'Don't praise socialism too much' when he came to our factory." What did he mean? "Liu Shao-ch'i wanted us working people to undergo suffering and endure hardship for the second time."[55]

Exploiting, the enemy's business, is killing—a theme which in China has not only plausibility, but also patina:

Mencius [asked] . . . , "Is there any difference between killing a man with a stick and with a sword?" The King said, "There is no difference." "Is there any difference between doing it with a sword and with the style of government?" "There is no difference," was the reply. Mencius then said, "In your kitchen there is fat meat; in your stables there are fat horses. But your people have the look of hunger, and on the wilds there are those who have died of famine."[56]

In the slightly different words of "rebels": "The landlords would never get rich without killing poor people."[57] At greater length:

The bloody facts are that the paradise of landlords, rich peasants and capitalists was built . . . on the burial ground of working people. "You can never make a fortune without murdering the poor people." This is the catchword for making a fortune among the landlords, rich peasants and capitalists. . . . The . . . Rent Collection Courtyard in the former manorhouse of Liu Wen'tsai . . . of Tayi County in Szechuan [reproducing the bitter past in sculpture—NL] is an example. . . . The Rent Collection Courtyard of Liu Wen-tsai was built on . . . [a] sea of blood and . . . [a] mountain of corpses of poor peasants.[58]

In poetry:

When in the past the haves a mill would build
Its walls were but the have-nots' flesh piled up,
Workers blood and sweat mixed into the plaster, from their
    dry bones its every girder made.

And in arithmetic for the first grade:

> There were two able-bodied persons in Master Tung's family. They sweated blood
> 365 days in the year for four years. . . .[59]

The enemy wants to kill us all: "poisonous as a snake, he harbors the intention of destruction," proclaims a rebel publication.[60] "All reactionaries try to stamp out revolution by mass murder" reports *People's Daily* in 1967,[61] which seems not too wild a statement in relation to the conduct of the Kuomintang from April 1927 on. In the course of the campaign against "Rightists" after the end of the "Hundred Flowers" in 1957 one target—a member of the Geological Institute—could be credited, presumably not absurdly, with having "repeatedly declared an intention of killing all Communist Party members" whereas according to a student, allegedly, only "ten million out of the twelve million Party members should be killed." Another opponent supposedly "clamored for what he called letting the masses see the color of the bowels of the Communist Party."[62]

The preferred target of Maoist persuasion is one capable not only of perceiving that the one whom I hitherto believed to be friend is foe, but also that my death is his central aim. A woman, according to a reportage in *Chinese Literature,* awaiting operation for an enormous intestinal cancer, talks with her male nurse:

> "I am in my thirties. . . . Who would have expected four years ago that a little
> bump on my belly would swell up to something as big as this. . . . [sic]
>
> "And who allowed that to happen?"
>
> "Why . . . [sic] the big hospitals."
>
> Li shook his head. "No, not the hospitals."
>
> "Who was it, then?"
>
> "Liu Shao-chi," Li exclaimed. . . .
>
> "It was Liu Shao-chi who harmed me?" Chiu-chu's eyes were wide with surprise.
>
> Li explained the . . . struggle between the two lines in medical and health work.
>
> Chiu-chu ground her teeth. "So he's the one. . . ."
>
> Li [said] . . . "Liu doesn't want any of us poor and lower middle peasants to
> live. . . ."[63]

The fallen leader may have mused about the "masses' " willingness to accept "slander" as did, previously, ministers with regard to rulers.

To designate acts of an enemy in which force is not used, metaphors of violence may seem the most fitting; as in the characterization of Confucius as "a hangman who killed people without shedding blood"; or in the depiction of Liu's "line" as "an invisible knife which kills without leaving a bloodstain."[64] During the Cultural Revolution it was standard to speak about "white terror" where very much less than the terror of April 12, 1927 in Shanghai, or May 21 of the same year in Changsha was meant. The "line" attributed to the Liu of the earlier sixties—"striking at the majority [of rural basic-level cadres] and protecting a small handful [the bosses of the Black Gang]" may be presented as "an attempt to kill all our rural cadres with one blow."[65] A certain "capitalist roader" responsible for the suppression of the student movement in Hunan is, according to "rebels," its "hangman," another "the executioner strangling the launching of the mass movement for the study of Chairman Mao's works."[66] While the Peking *Kuang-ming Daily* in the fall of 1966 discerns in an intellectual who had belonged to the fallen local leadership (Lin Mo-han) "a big killer in disguise," the *People's Daily* specifies that he is "an executioner who smothered many revolutionary songs."[67]

When in December 1936 Chairman Mao delivered his lectures *Problems of Strategy in China's Revolutionary War,* P'eng Te-huai, "rebels" are to claim later, "remarked *ferociously:* 'What makes Mao Tse-tung discuss this question at this time? Is this necessary?' "—just as Lin Mo-han, with regard to art "ferociously laying emphasis on raising standards, . . . said. . . ."[68]

If any disapproved act may appear to express rage, a vigorous affirmation of dissent surely will be thus perceived or presented. "When I came back from abroad last time," P'eng Te-huai reminisces when criticizing himself at the 8th Plenum of the 8th Central Committee, "Huang K'o-ch'eng told me the conditions at home, and remarked that conditions in some areas, especially Kansu, were serious. . . ." In fact, "he . . . was *somewhat enraged* and *expressed the point of view* that the People's Communes had been set up too soon."[69] Recalling that "in April 1966 the *Liberation Army Daily* published articles to refute the nonsense that 'giving prominence to politics is to be affirmed by professional affairs' " and that thereupon "China's Khrushchev's agents in the Department of Agricultural Mechanization attacked *angrily:* 'On this problem, we have a dispute. There will be a day when it can be made clear. If politics is not affirmed by professional affairs, I wish to see, by what it can be affirmed?' He said also: 'Politics must be affirmed by professional affairs. You wait and see! In the future it will still be this exclamation' "— recollecting all this, *Agricultural Machinery and Techniques* discerns "From these curses, one could almost hear the sound of his clenching teeth."[70]

Anger expressed against something small is, then, of course, perceived as rage directed towards something else and big (sensibility in China about this movement of the soul is acute). When in a cartoon of the early sixties recalled in the winter of 1967 "a smoker is smouldering with anger because he could not light his cigarette after finishing a box of matches," "this is . . . an outburst of wrath of counterrevolutionary sentiments."[71]

Any defense is an offense against the assailant. The "masses" having told the perpetrator of the "Wuhan incident" (the most flagrant attack against Peking during the Cultural Revolution) at his public trial (August 4, 1967), "You have . . . schemed the 'July 20' incident. Why do you deny it?" and Ch'en Tsai-tao having replied, "I have never schemed the incident," the "rebels" comment: "His answer was a frantic counteroffensive against us. . . ."[72]

Any retreat is an onslaught. To support the claim that "the handful of class enemies . . . [are] launching extremely frantic counterattacks," one may recall that "China's Khrushchev, for instance, made two . . . statements of repentance in succession."[73]

While the enemy here as in other respects appears as similar to oneself, it is the Communists', and especially the Maoists' desire that he seem radically different. One well-known and accented theme serving this point is to deny, in opposition to the Confucians, that a "human nature" exists: only class natures do. It is even rare to hear an affirmation one might expect to be correspondingly stressed, namely that "in communist society . . . common human nature will be formed."[74]

Less explicitly and, I would guess, more impressively, it is conveyed that the enemy is not human at all. "The time-honored custom in China," Lu Hsun noted,

> when you want to attack someone, is to give him a label or "nickname." This is the method used . . . since the Ming and Ch'ing dynasties. If for instance you want to accuse Chang or Li, they will seem too normal if you just use their names; but if you call them "six-armed demon Chang" and "Li the white-browed tiger," the magistrate need not examine the facts to be convinced they are scoundrels.[75]

"Heaven must have been blind to give you a human skin"; a locution such as this (employed, for instance, in the film script Guerrillas of the Plain) seems to express the belief that sufficient badness indicates one's being something else than human.[76] "They are a perfect pest!" exclaims a character of Ju Hsün's about "a father and a son in my place." "They are," he continues, "scarcely human."[77]

Perhaps particularly so for creatures with human appearance who damage. "Although a robber-man is a man," writes a Mohist (during the period of the warring states), "yet to love robbers is not to love men, and not to love robbers is not to love men. Likewise, to kill a robber-man is not to kill a man:"—this thinker, in the words of Fung Yu-lan who quotes him, thus "tries to prove that . . . the execution of robbers does not prevent us from universal love for men," as "the most important fact about a robber is that he is a robber, not that he is a man. . . ."[78]

Political crime may be felt as reaching not less deep than common crime; and which divergence on grave matters is not criminal? "Not to have a correct political point of view," Mao is often quoted (e.g., by an Anwhei writing group) "is like having no soul"; for is not "politics," according to another major utterance, the "soul" of all action?[79]

The bad ones are animals. Having convinced a king that the Taoist hierarchy in his realm, hitherto favored, is wicked; having received from the ruler the commission to kill its members; having done so and seeing the king, despite all, sad at the news, Monkey explains:

> Have you not seen that the first Immortal's corpse showed him to have been merely a tiger? The second has turned out to be a common deer. And if you have the bones of the third fished out of the cauldron, you will find that he was nothing but a ram. . . . [80]

In ancient thought, Granet observes, the four kinds of barbarians are related to four species of animals.[81] Considering "a man who observes no rules of propriety," the *Book of Rites* asks: "is not his heart that of a beast?"[82]

Any killer is a beast. "A high fever tossed me," Tan Shih-hua remembers about his childhood early in this century. "All the time an evil snout belonging to someone who hated and wished to kill me stared at me from under the canopy of my bed."[83]

Ferocious animals are even more dangerous when they assume human shape. "The beasts have . . . mingled with the men," observes Lu Hsün sadly; "and since they all have human faces, one cannot tell the difference."[84] A proverb warns how, exploiting your goodness—and naiveté—they will destroy you, like "the leopard that cries in the forest at night in the voice of a human being, until men go out in rescue groups, never to return."[85]

The more humans they already have thus destroyed, the greater becomes their capacity to kill. "The Social Democrats," Agnes Smedley is told around 1930 by Communists, "also cry like the leopard, but their voices are just a little thinner than those of the Nanking Kuomintang—because they have not yet eaten quite so many peasants and workers."[86]

That the enemy is a beast of course justifies killing him. *[Instead of beasts, enemies may be ghosts—a matter I shall leave to another paper, as it concerns specifically the enemy within.]* "Served her right!" exclaims after the act a character in a nineteenth-century novel. "She was not a human being; she was a wicked infamous beast! Why let such a creature survive?"[87]

There may be light dismay if the corpse turns out to be human after all. "He tore out her entrails with both hands," we learn in a classical short story.

> He carried the gory mass to the light and examined it. "I should have thought" he muttered to himself, "that such a vile woman . . . would hardly have had the entrails of a human being; I am surprised to find that she has! How then could she have concocted so poisonous a plan?"[88]

But then punishment itself may supply what was lacking. "Chinese, that is, human beings," explains Granet, "can't reside in the world's marches without losing . . . their human stature." Hence "those banished . . . assume, as soon they are expelled to those parts, the half-animal character of the beings in these desolate border areas."[89]

III. SHOULD WE PURSUE?

Is it desirable that I annihilate my enemy? Granet maintains,

> When a Chinese dynasty proclaimed its advent, . . . it took care to attribute fiefs to the offspring of the superseded dynasty. They were charged with preserving in these closed domains the regulations . . . of a . . . cycle which had ended.

Similarly

> the altars of the fallen dynasty were not destroyed, but merely walled in . . . [for] one foresaw that the type of civilization whose memory . . . and seed they preserved, would return.[90]

While Mao believes himself to be accepting Lenin's "who-whom," he in fact tends towards the classical Chinese belief: sometimes he implicitly denies the desirability, and even the feasibility, of annihilating the enemy. Affirming that "construction" and "destruction," "flowing" and "damming," "motion" and "rest" are "locked in a life and death struggle," the very choice of entities compels him to affirm not that one element of each of these pairs will or should ever supplant the other, but rather that "there is no construction without destruction, no. . . ." Having recalled Lenin's affirmation that "mutually exclusive" opposite tendencies are present in all phenomena, and having even underlined the words I put between quotation marks, Mao goes on to maintain the "interdependence" of contradictory aspects present in all things, and, finally, to approve as "dialectical" what "we Chinese often say": "Things that oppose each other also complement each other."[91]

The existence of some badness fosters the very combat of the good against it. "That erroneous things . . . exist," explains Mao, "will help people learn to struggle against them better."[92] "The world needed Khrushchev," he tells Edgar Snow a few months after the loss of this enemy. "China," he explains, "would miss him as a negative example."[93] Thus "it . . . does not matter to have rightists serve in the Cultural revolution committees of the schools, because they . . . can be regarded as teachers by negative example."[94]

Not only would the force of good sag without the stimulus of evil: without an environment which it opposes, it would perish. It becomes easier to express that point when what is opposed is not the traditional enemy himself: "If there were no contradictions *in the Party* and no . . . struggle to resolve them, the Party's life would come to an end."[95] Again, "struggle . . . [is] perpetual; otherwise there would be no world"; hence "it is impossible to have no disputes . . . to be tranquil without any ripples."[96] But the belief thus expressed has starker applications. "Without death," Mao recalls, "there would be no life."[97] Considering "the true, the good and the beautiful" and "their opposites . . . the false, the evil and the ugly," he notes that "the former would not exist without the latter." Fortunately, then, "there will always be false and ugly phenomena."[98] "The greatest of all calamities," observes the *Tao Te Ching,* "is to attack and find no enemy."[99]

Apart from the enemy's preservation being perhaps desirable, pushing one's advantage, personal or even collective, at his expense is, in the classical view—no doubt largely ineffective, but for all that not unimpressive—an expression of the cardinal vice of man, selfishness. Envisaging a case in which "his brothers have property and are to divide it," Hsün Tzu observes that "if they follow their original nature . . . they will . . . endeavor to seize the property." But, "reform them by . . . rules of proper conduct and justice, and they will be willing to yield to outsiders."[100] In contrast, for Communists to foster the interests of their side against the enemy is virtue itself. So this particular classical objection is replaced by an obligation to do precisely that about which one felt feebly squeamish.

A movement recommended by classical doctrine to the gentleman is that of declining an opportunity profferred. "The message," stipulates the *Book of Rites* about relations between courts,

> was transmitted [only] after the messenger had thrice declined to receive [the courtesies offered to him at the gate]; he entered the gate of the Ancestral Temple after thrice in the same way trying to avoid doing so; . . . thrice he yielded the precedence offered to him before he ascended the hall. . . .[101]

In contrast, Mencius points out, it is "the little ones" who "push themselves forward and grab" rather than being *ch'ien-yang,* modest and yielding. "In the matter of a cup of liquor and a dish of meat," the *Book of Rites* explains,

> one may forego his claim and receive that which is less than his due; and yet the people will try to obtain more than is due to their years. When one's mat has been spread for him in a high place, he may move and take his seat on a lower; and yet the people will try to occupy the place due to rank. From the high place due to him at court, one may in his humility move to a meaner place; and yet the people shall be intrusive even in the presence of the ruler.[102]

Here again Communists attempt to make a virtue of vulgarity: another (weak) classical obstacle transmuted into an obligation: to "grasp," a movement now extolled.

The same has of course happened to whatever modest restraint chivalry or mercy provided towards a defeated foe. When "the responsible person of the revolutionaries" of the East Wind Commune in Hangchow observed that "some comrades consider it too much to trample on enemies who have already been knocked down. . . . They show mercy to them," he hardly needs to add words of condemnation.[103]

Propriety apart and more importantly, there is the old suspicion, discussed above, that any act of mine may displease others and thus end in a net loss to me. "The carpenter," a proverb warns, "makes a cangue and wears it himself."[104] Having observed that the hexagram *chin* "denotes advancing," that movement, the *Book of Changes* predicts, "is sure to lead to being wounded"— particularly when force is used: "dogs that like to fight never have a whole skin."[105]

> He, who by Tao, purposes to help a ruler of men
> Will oppose all conquest by force of arms;
> For such things are wont to rebound,[106]

de clares the *Tao Te Ching,* expressing a special case of a belief which, though it has obviously not commanded conduct, has not altogether lacked strength. That it has not is shown, for instance by the unceasing polemic of Communist leaders (Maoists and others alike) against "some people [cadres] . . . [who are] too lenient . . . so that they can . . . have everything peaceful"; in fact, some cadres "place their fear of offending . . . culprits above everything else. . . ."[107] "Rebels" themselves speak of "cadres of the 'Three Seldom and One Peace' type":[108] they seldom speak, seldom make known their attitude, seldom offend people and live in peace. In other words, they come close to the conduct enjoined by the proverb: "Do not tell what you see, do not know what you are asked . . . if you have nothing to do, go home early."[109]

Warding off the apprehension that any forward conduct of one's own may, in the end, turn out to be disadvantageous, Communists are apt to assert such a predicament for the enemy. "The . . . result of Chamberlain's policy," Mao predicted at the outbreak of the Second World War, "will be like 'lifting a rock only to drop it on one's own toes'." Employing the same locution a few months later about "die-hards" in the Kuomintang, he pointed out that "they invariably start by doing others harm, but end by ruining themselves." "We once said," he recalls with satisfaction, "that Chamberlain was 'lifting a rock only to drop it on his own toes,' and this has now come to pass." "They," he predicts about the Kuomintang "reactionaries" once again five years later, "will be 'lifting a rock only to drop it on their own toes'"; four more years later he can repeat that

> on January 1 [1949] . . . the Kuomintang reactionaries began to lift a rock called the "peace offensive"; they intended to hurl it at the Chinese people, but now it

has dropped on their own feet.... The rock has smashed the Kuomintang to pieces.[110]

"To start with the aim of doing harm to others only to end up by ruining oneself—such is the ... law governing these people," such is the epitaph authorized (if not written) by Mao for Khrushchev.[111]

An exhilarating aspect of the enemy harming himself through trying to hurt us is that his weapons become ours. "America is our arsenal, and Chiang Kai-shek our quarter-master," said the PLA in the big war of the later forties; "they are delivering the goods to the door, and we will not issue a receipt" declared one "rebel" group about another in the small war of the later sixties.

Thus one celebrates a triumph over apprehensions which are, however, apt to persist underground: that of assuming cost exceeding the worth of the objective—"breaking the vase while trying to hit the mouse"[112] —and, especially, that of underestimating the counterblow one is inducing: being "the man who does not weep so long as he sees not the coffin";[113] who has forgotten that "before you beat the dog, be sure to learn the master's name."[114]

Communists do not express a belief which was visibly present earlier and is unlikely to have disappeared since: that human beings are tempted to attack somebody much stronger than they, so that they won't reach the objective of their enterprise (perhaps, to boot, a not very important one); disposed to undertake their assault in conditions where they are especially vulnerable, so that they will be terribly damaged; and tend to be unaware of all these glaring aspects of the situation when behaving like that—in short, to "pull a tooth from a tiger's mouth." It seems appropriate to warn that "if you chase a pig in a passage, he will turn ... and rend you."[115]

The disproportion between the strength of the attacker and that of the target may be such that the former will be destroyed by the very act of attacking: "at the first stroke of an egg against a stone, the yolk runs out"; one may "run against a stone to wound one's foot."[116]

Or I may choose to attack more weakly than I should if taking the offensive at all, enhancing the action's sinister absurdity. "I should think," one character in *The Dream of the Red Chamber* counsels another, "that Lao-yeh ought to think of how to avoid the further displeasure of Lao-Tai-tai, instead of tickling the tiger's nose with a straw."[117]

Am I not looking for disaster? The literal meaning of an expression signifying "seeking trouble" is: "The rat gnawing the cat's tail; it wants to be killed." Or do I pretend being the superior man exempt from retaliation of whom the *Book of Changes* reports that "he treads on the tail of a tiger which does not bite him."[118] Or a daredevil who prefers a small chance of victory to the dominant probability of disaster?

Chiu-tung ... [was] a maid whom Chia Sheh had given to [his son] Chia Lien. . . . Because she had been given to Chia Lien by Chia Sheh, the maid felt her position superior to that of [Chia Lien's recently acquired concubine] Erh-chieh. . . . She was not to be trampled upon by a woman who entered the house through adultery, she would say in Erh-chieh's hearing. Phoenix [Chia Lien's wife who wants to destroy the concubine] egged her on. She would take Chiu-tung aside and say to her, "You are young and reckless. You must know that she is Erh-yeh's [Chia Lien's] favorite. Even I dare not claim equality with her. It is foolhardy for you to offend her." As expected, this inflamed Chiu-tung and made her heap more abuse upon Erh-chieh. . . .[119]

Any action, in such an atmosphere, may arouse the suspicion that it will reveal itself—too late—as a "foolhardy" move of "offending": "Only fools catch flies on a tiger's head," opines a character in *The Scholars.* "Much better to say nothing and offend nobody."[120]

Even if an attack is not bound to be disastrous from its very conception and inception, it may—in a related apprehension often voiced in old China—become that when pressed; hence the advisability of *shou-ping,* to call off a battle, to end a campaign.[121] "Leave some leeway in everything," recommends Chu Po-lu (seventeenth century) in his *Aphorisms on Running a House,* like Mao in 1969 in his "instructions" on running a country; "blessed with success, do not go further."[122] For, as the *Book of Changes* observes about the sung hexagram, "if he must prosecute the contention to the . . . end, there will be evil"; "contention is not a thing to be carried on to extremity"; "when . . . advance continues without stopping, there is sure to come distress." He who attempts to seize all will lose all: "He whose greatness reaches the utmost possibility is sure to lose his dwelling. . . ."[123] It is the abstention from pressing one's advantage which maximizes benefit: "Who stops in time," declares the *Tao Te Ching,* "nothing can harm . . ."—hence, a good general "effects his purpose and then stops; he does not take further advantage of his victory. . . ."[124]

Communists, of course, continue an opposed and less vocal tradition, that of Tso Chuan who asked "Why abstain from wounding anew those whose wound is not mortal?"[125] —and, with morals added, of Mo Tzü who refutes the Confucian thus:

He says: "When the superior man is victorious, he does not pursue the fleeing enemy. When the enemy is kept at bay, he does not shoot. When the enemy retreat, he will help them pushing their carts. . . ." Suppose a sage starts out to destroy a curse on behalf of the empire. He raises an army to punish the wicked and cruel state. When he is victorious, let us suppose him to follow the Confucian way and to command his army: "Don't pursue the fleeing enemy. Don't shoot when the enemy is at bay. Help them pushing the carts when they retreat." The wicked men will thus be set free, and the curse of the world will not yet be removed. This is . . . to ruin the world.[126]

"Oppose," demands Mao, speaking about war, but enunciating a rule for any kind of action, "fighting merely to rout the enemy, and uphold fighting to annihilate the enemy"; for "injuring all of a man's ten fingers is not as effective as chopping off one, and routing ten enemy divisions is not as effective as annihilating one of them": annihilating all ten of them being, to be sure, the supreme objective.[127]

What is denied here is the dread possibility that if I, still weak, allow myself a rate of growth and/or a level of attack against my strong enemy which go beyond certain limits, I will greatly reduce the otherwise substantial chance that he will leave unused his temporary capacity to crush me. Thus, in 1926-1927, the Party leadership (in later presentation and probably also in fact, wanting to protect the young and growing movement against blows such as those inflicted on it in the "February 7 [1923] incident" by a warlord), restrained its growth and combativeness—only to make doubly sure that it would be grievously hurt, in the surprising and appalling spring of 1927. Twenty years later, looking back on the war against Japan, Mao notes the presence in the Party of "such ideas as . . . not daring to arouse and give full rein to mass struggles, not daring to expand the Liberated Areas and the People's armies in the Japanese-occupied areas. . . ."[128] Such "ideas" are all the more to be combatted, as he himself is capable of demanding that in policy on land "we must not be so hasty as to cause . . . counter-attacks by the landlords. . . ."[129]

The more I displease a (still) formidable enemy, the more unfavorable will—for those believing in a dangerously irritable world—his reaction be. During the war against the Japanese one could find in the Party, Mao notes, "the belief that the more our forces expand, the more the diehards [the Kuomintang] will tend towards capitulation, that the more concessions we make, the more they will resist Japan. . . ."[130]

In contrast, Communists—affirming the world to be resolutely murderous—strain themselves to accept a negative relationship between the levels of accommodating to the enemy and being accommodated by him. "The more . . . we expand north of the Yangtse River," Mao continues after the passage just quoted,

the more will Ku Chu-tung [a KMT Commander] be afraid to act rashly [against the Party] south of the Yangtse River. . . . Similarly, the more the Eighth Route Army and the new Fourth Army and the South China Guerrilla Column expand in northwestern, northern, central and southern China, and the more the Communist Party grows throughout the country, the greater will be the possibility of averting the danger of capitulation [by the KMT to the Japanese]. . . .[131]

The same relationship holds not only for the growth of one's force, but even for the level of its use against the enemy. "From the viewpoint of destroying the enemy's overweening arrogance," Mao explains with regard to the Japanese, "battles of annihilation . . . are one of the prerequisites of foreshortening the war and accelerating the emancipation of the Japanese soldiers and the Japanese people." For "cats make friends with cats, and nowhere in the world do cats make friends with mice."[132]

When, a historian recounts,

> Yüan [Shi-kai] . . . tried to purchase Sung Chiao-jen by giving him a checkbook for a bank in Peking and allowing him to write checks for any amount he desired, . . . Sung . . . returned the . . . checkbook to Yüan [but only after] drawing a little money to show his appreciation:[133]

he believed the enemy to be placable.

Communists try not to forget that he is implacable (soon Yüan had Sung assassinated): the enemy's intent to annihilate me is as high as it could be, fixed at that level, insensitive with regard to the amount of damage I inflict on him. "You are too irritating," Mao has friendly critics say about the Party. However, he observes, "we are talking about how to deal with domestic and foreign reactionaries," and "with regard to such reactionaries the question of irritating them or not does not arise." "irritated or not irritated, they will remain the same . . ."; that is, their intent is as destructive as that which would issue from maximum "irritation." Thus

> we must learn from Wu Sung [in *Water Margin*] on the Chingyang Ridge [where he killed a tiger with his bare hands]. As Wu Sung saw it, the tiger on Chingyang Ridge was a maneater, whether irritated or not.[134]

So far from placating my enemy when limiting the damage I inflict on him, I am merely preserving his capacity to hurt me. "Strike a serpent without killing it," teaches a proverb, "and it will turn and bite you"; "if you do not kill a man outright, he will always remain your enemy." [135] "Hitting at them," Maoists observe about the famous "handful" of enemies, "without toppling them will lead to endless disasters in the future."[136]

But, on the other hand, once I have greatly weakened my enemy, have I not also reduced his will to harm? There are, "rebels" note, "people who think that . . . dogs 'baptized' in water have repented and will not come out to bite people again."[137]

Even if this were not the case, does the very weakness of an enemy not render him harmless? "Even though there is some activity of the capitalist spontaneous force," the "capitalist roader" T'ao Chu allegedly explained in 1960, "this will at most give rise to a few 'peddler capitalists.' There is nothing dreadful about this!"[138] "A common rightist," Liu supposedly recommended in the summer of 1966,

> is not to be taken into custody. He will be allowed to carry on his living and work. He will continue to talk. Let him talk. Nobody will listen to him. It's unimportant even if some people listen to him. What are you afraid of?

"The conservative forces," "rebels" discern,

> do not ... struggle against ... [the] handful of persons [in authority and taking the capitalist road] on the pretext that they are 'dead tigers' not worth our beating.[139]

This "dead tiger" belief is all the more important for Maoists to combat as it is also, sometimes, their own. "To 'open wide,'" Mao himself explains in the late winter of 1957,

> means not being afraid of ... anything poisonous. ... [We] should [not] ... be afraid of ... poisonous weeds. ... Recently a number of ghosts and monsters have been presented on the stage. Seeing this, some comrades have become very worried. [However,] in my opinion *a little* of this does not matter much; within a few decades such ghosts and monsters will disappear from the stage altogether, and you won't be able to see them even if you want to. ... Of course I am not advocating the spread of such things, I only say "*a few* of them do not matter much."[140]

In the predominant Maoist view, however, anything short of my annihilating the enemy raises the prospect of my being annihilated by him. "At the time of Duke Li of Chin," Han Fei Tzu recalls,

> the six Nobles were very powerful. Therefore, Hsü Tong and Ch'ang Yü-ch'iao remonstrated with him saying: "When chief vassals are powerful ... the state is ... endangered." "Right," said the Duke and ... wiped out three nobles. Again, Hsü T'ong and Ch'ang Yü-chiao remonstrated with him saying: "... To punish certain and not all of the men guilty of the same crime is to make the survivors resent and watch for a chance." In response the Duke said: "In one morning I exterminated three of the six nobles. I cannot bear exterminating all of them." "Your Highness cannot bear exterminating them, but they will bear causing Your Highness harm," said Ch'ang Yü-chiao. To this the Duke would not listen. In the course of three months, the remaining nobles started a rebellion and ... killed Duke Li. ...[141]

"With power and to spare we must pursue the tottering foe," demands Mao in a poem often quoted in the later sixties, "and not ape Hsiang Yu, the conqueror seeking idle fame."[142] His poem refers to the fact that when the Ch'in dynasty broke down, Hsiang first prevailed over Liu Pang, had him in his power, spared him, of course only to be destroyed by the one whom he had thus permitted to found the Han dynasty. "The revolutionaries," Lu Hsün recalls about the overthrow of the Ch'ing dynasty, "said: '... We will not beat a dog in the water; let it crawl ashore.' This was just what the others did. They lay low until the second half of 1913 and ... then suddenly came forward to help Yuan Shih-kai kill many revolutionaries. ..."[143] "In one article," Mao recalls when delivering a eulogy about the dead writer, "he advocated hitting the dog in the water. He said that if the dog in the water were not hit, it would jump out of the water and bite you—at least it would splash you all over with mud"[144]—which is putting it with rare mildness. Rather, "if the revolution is abandoned halfway, it will mean . . . giving the Kuomintang a chance to heal its wounds, so that one day it may pounce suddenly to strangle the revolution . . ."; [145] or, twenty years later and from a provincial pen, "if the present campaign is not carried out . . . we cannot thoroughly topple the . . . enemies," which, in turn, "will lead to our downfall."[146]

"Whereas the people of the world, at their tasks," as the *Tao Te Ching* perceives, "constantly spoil things when within an ace of completing them."[147] we must act, in the "rebels' " language, "with the spirit of beating a drowning dog thoroughly . . . ," not flagging from mercy or security, but harder than during any preceding phase of the operation, just because the temptation to relax is stronger. The enemy furnishes a model: "In 1960 Li Ta lectured his students: 'You must beat Stalin as if he were a dying dog.' "[148]

There may have been a strong and little expressed belief in China that it somehow is not feasible to kill the dog. "There is . . . no departure [of evil men] so that they shall not return," observes the *Book of Changes* on the Thai hexagram.[149] When Sun Tsu recommends to "leave an outlet free" upon having surrounded an army, for "do not press a desperate foe too hard," he seems to take it for granted that I have to take into account the future damage his high irritation (to use Mao's word quoted above) might induce him to inflict on me; he appears to accept as evident that I cannot or will not kill him, so that his latter states of soul will not (supernatural paths excluded) endanger me. In contrast, the Communists focus on annihilating the enemy as a way out of fearing him; in fact, given his ferocity, as the only way out.

The older penchant toward restraint (at least in aspiration or pretense) survives, however, among the Communists in a stress on deceiving the enemy about my strength by limiting its use. Making the adversary underestimate my force, I induce him to venture into a position in which he will be more vulnerable to my delayed strike. "The exposure of their revisionist nature," explains a Maoist about the Peking leadership liquidated in the spring of 1966,

> required a certain course of time and certain "soil and weather" conditions. Even a poisonous snake comes out of its hole under certain weather conditions. The moment these poisonous snakes came out of their holes, they were captured by Chairman Mao and the Party's Central Committee. . . .[150]

"Somebody," Liu explained, according to "rebels," shortly before becoming himself a target, "thrusts his head out, just a little bit; if he is hit on the head, he immediately draws back. You have to wait until he exposes himself completely, then it will be good." "Demons," so the *People's Daily* states the law long after Liu has become their King, "can be wiped out only when they are let out of the cage, and poisonous weeds can be got rid of only when they come out of the soil."[151] Hence "we should . . . endure the situation," as Mao in March 1959 points out to a Party conference with regard to elements opposing the communes, "in order to let these people expose themselves fully."[152]

Specifically, enemies, usually protected by false appearances, should be given time and facilities to reveal their "true form." "It is not possible for . . . counterrevolutionaries to use . . . rightist slogans," Liu explains in the summer of 1966 as Maoists are soon (but only in part) going to do about him. "They use leftist slogans. . . ." Hence, "it is difficult to recognize them without allowing them to dominate for a period." Hence, he allegedly advised his listeners at the Peking College of Construction Engineering with regard to "reactionary" students, "you should let them carry out their activities until they seize leadership. Let them dominate for a period of time and put Communist Party members under rectification"; thus "they will betray themselves."[153]

So that hidden enemies disclose themselves, they may be promised immunity with regard to doing so, and then struck down after all. Thus former members of the Kuomintang who, "on the establishment of the regime . . . were ordered to register with a promise of pardon in return for spontaneous self-declaration," and of whom "large numbers . . . perished during the campaigns in 1950-1951."[154] And thus of course those to be called "Rightists" during the so-called Hundred Flowers period, 1956-1957, about which the *People's Daily* observed, once the operation was completed, that "in order to let all the bad elements betray themselves, the Central Committee . . . adopted the attitude of indulgence. . . ."[155] But then children may be, acceptably, teased by adults into expressions of feeling for which they are punished (as Lucian Pye has noted), and the "heroes" of *Water Margin* promise numerous prisoners their lives if they inform, obtain the intelligence, and then kill, without actor or author seasoning the sequence with a word of justification, not to speak of censure.[156]

Instead of luring an enemy *into the open* by a delay in striking at him which he mistakes for lack of capacity or intention to do so, one may, by deferring assault, induce him to *stay* where his vulnerability will increase with time. "You must not," instructs Mao to his immediate subordinates in late 1948, "wipe out all the enemy forces at Changchiakou, Hsinpao-an and Nankow, because that would compel the enemy east of Nankow to make a quick decision to bolt." Also, "in order not to prompt Chiang Kai-shek quickly to decide to ship his troops in the Peiping-Tientsin area south by sea we are going . . . to spare the remainder of Tu Yu-ming's armies. . . ."[157]

Reducing my level of attack on the enemy, I may make him underestimate my strength, which may in turn induce him to delay an attack which he should be conducting now while I am still weak. "We . . . exposed too early," recalls, according to "rebels," P'eng Te-huai in his self-criticism at the 8th Plenum or the 8th Central Committee about the offensive against Changsha in 1930, "the strength of the Red Army." Thus "we attracted attention [of the Kuomintang] to the Red Army from the warlords, urged [sic] them to stop fighting among themselves and made them accelerate their attacks against the Red Army." Similarly, "in 1940 . . . the 'Battle of the Hundred Regiments' . . . exposed too early our own strength, attracted the main force of the Japanese Army . . . to the advantage of the Kuomintang. . . ."[158] The calculation here recommended is close to the rejected one (described above) with which the name of Ch'en Tu-hsiu is connected; only the enemy, irritable there, has become merely deceivable here, so that we are still in correct thought.

IV. MAY WE YIELD?

"The result of my act of protest," Mao concludes the narrative of how he ran away from his beating teacher when ten, "impressed me very much. It was a successful 'strike.'" From the famous episode three years later when he threatened his father with suicide—still in the older pattern sketched above—"I learned that when I defended my rights by open rebellion, my father relented, but when I remained meek and submissive, he only cursed and beat me the more."[159] Surveying the Party's relationship with the Kuomintang during the war against the Japanese, Mao observes that "the three large-scale anti-Communist campaigns and countless other provocations were not beaten back by . . . concessions . . . by the Communist Party; they were beaten back . . . in . . . stern . . . self-defense."[160]

"He feared not," Mencius observes about a personage of whom he approves, "any of all the princes. A bad word addressed to him he always returned." "When I was young," Mao recalls, when he finds himself, for the first time after a quarter of a century, under severe attack from within the Party, "my attitude was that if others do not provoke me, I won't provoke them; if they provoke me, I will also provoke them; whoever provokes me first, I will provoke him later. I have not abandoned this principle. . . ."[161] "In 1927," he observes, recalling disaster at a moment when the Party has emerged greatly strengthened from the war against the Japanese, "our Party was still in its infancy": it "did not have . . . experience in . . . the policy of giving tit for tat." "Since the pro-British and pro-American big landlords and big bourgeoisie," he had noted years before, "are still using the stick and carrot in dealing with our Party, the policy of our Party is to 'do unto them as they do unto us,' stick for stick and carrot for carrot." In fact, "if a . . . revolutionary force is to avoid extermination by Chiang Kai-shek . . . it has no alternative but to wage a tit-for-tat struggle against [him]. . . ."[162]

Abstaining from retaliation against attack will not, as those may believe who perceive the enemy as dangerously irritable, limit damage, but enhance it—bring about what one endeavors to avert. "If we lack . . . a . . . policy for dealing firmly with these incidents," Mao explains about offensive actions of the Kuomintang against the Party during the war with the Japanese, "if we let the Kuomintang die-hards continue their 'military and political restriction of the Communist Party' and are in constant dread of the thought of the breakup of the united front," it is then that "there will be a real danger of the breakup of the united front." Those who "think that struggle [the Party retaliating against Kuomintang attacks] will split the united front" are wrong: "if unity is sought through struggle, it will live; if unity is sought through yielding, it will perish."[163]

However, my "tit" should not exceed a fair proportion to the enemy's "tat"—for reasons which are not given; as if the fear of irritating the enemy were making itself felt. "After repulsing one . . . attack," Mao requires in the situation just evoked, "we should know when to stop. . . ." [164] "It is a breach of etiquette," one group says to another during the Cultural Revolution, "not to return calls. Since you bombard our proletarian headquarters, we will smash the bourgeois headquarters."[165]

More than that, though the principle of tit-for-tat is affirmed without qualification, conduct in clear though unnamed violation of it may be publicly extolled. While "the Kuomintang newspapers and periodicals have never for a moment stopped vilifying the Communist Party," Mao recalls in Yenan's *Liberation Daily*, "for a long time we did not say a word in reply." Even when "the Kuomintang disbanded the new Fourth Army . . . wiped out over 9,000 men . . . arrested Yeh Ting, killed Hsiang Ying and imprisoned hundreds of its cadres," what did we do? "We maintained our forbearance . . . simply lodging a protest and demanding redress."[166]

After all, "that countries could . . . adopt with success . . . a foreign policy of 'giving way' (*yang*) as opposed to one of push and grab *(chin-ch'u)* is," as Arthur Waley observes, "a . . . part of Confucius' way." [167] Devoting themselves to the smashing of "Confucius' shop," Communists, one would expect, will, unawares, consume some of its goods, perhaps packaging them differently.

The principle of tit-for-tat is directed against one variant of the traditional belief in the high productivity of *yang:* my being nice to others will dispose them to repay me in kind, as in the case of the twenty-four model sons regenerating their parents by repaying cruelty with piety. "A family, known as a good neighbor," observes Martin Yang about a Northern village, "always gives way to others": "thus, all the villagers like to do business with them and . . . speak well of them. . . ."[168]

But there is yet another idea behind the classic appreciation of *yang:* a hero, in ancient thought, is, Granet writes, "a being without rigidity, no bones, all muscle," capable of "overcoming hardness by softness."[169] Thus he avoids the ruin which, Mao agrees, comes from "stubbornness." "The diehards," so the "masses" recited at the first trial of Liu Shao-Chi's wife (April 10, 1967) "are stubborn, but not firm, and eventually their stubbornness will change into dog's dung."[170]

The one capable of *yang* turns passivity into activity and thus conforms to the cyclical nature of events, knowing that "a state of fullness . . . should not be indulged in long."[171] "If heaven *falls* on you," a proverb advises, "*draw* it over you as a quilt."[172] As much as Communists are loath to believe that kindness will be repaid in kind, they may start agreeing with the traditional view of *yang* here. "Is it not," Mao asks, "self-contradictory to fight heroically first and then abandon territory? Will not our . . . fighters have shed their blood in vain?" This, he replies, "is not . . . the way questions should be posed." For "to eat and then to empty your bowels—is this not to eat in vain? To sleep and then to get up—is this not to sleep in vain?"[173]

"When the wind is strong," declares a proverb, "yield to the wind; if the rain is heavy, yield to the rain." [174] "We must never," instructs Mao—talking about guerrilla, but with a meaning which has been extended well beyond that kind of "struggle"—"fight . . . without certainty of success."[175]

Yang preserves. "In life-long concession of road and dyke," a proverb calculates, "one neither loses a hundred paces nor a single plot."[176] "As for loss of territory," Mao explains, "it often happens that only by loss can loss be avoided"; indeed, "this is the principle of 'give in order to take.' "[177] When the Party abandoned Yenan in 1947, it explained to the population, in words attributed to Mao: "Hold Yenan, lose Yenan. Surrender Yenan, keep Yenan."[178] This being an accented point in Mao's analysis of war, I need not elaborate.

Yang conquers. "If he yields it," predicts Hsün Tzu, "it will come to him"; "the superior man . . . yields to others and yet conquers." [179] "What is, of all things, most yielding," observes the *Tao Te Ching* about water, "can overwhelm that which is of all things most hard";[180] "when it attacks things . . . resistant, there is not one of them that can prevail. For they can find no way of altering it. . . . The yielding conquers the resistant." "He who knows the male, yet cleaves to what is female," explains the same work, "becomes like a ravine, receiving all things under heaven." Clearly Communists reject being "the female" which "by quiescence . . . gets underneath" and thus "conquers the male"[181] —but perhaps not quite. "Ambush by luring the enemy," Mao instructs, "occurs when our troops, so to speak, prostrate themselves and hold out both arms, enticing the enemy to penetrate deeply."[182] In less striking fashion: "the clever boxer usually gives a little ground at first. . . ."[183] If he is stubborn, as was, according to Mao, the Party leadership in 1934, all ground may be lost and the march to a new abode might be long. Here too, the point having been stressed by Mao himself, I need not insist.

To be sure, to the Communist "giving ground" is something about which he should relish only his capacity of doing the repugnant when it is useful, in contrast to the traditional cult of ceding. Having admonished to "endure provocation," to "repress wrath," to "forgive an offense," a proverb concludes with the demand to "yield a point." [184] "He seems to have difficulty in advancing," observes the *Book of Rites* about the scholar, "but retires with ease and readiness; and he has a shrinking appearance, as if wanting in power...." [185] Whereas Communists have not ceased to adopt the Westernizing stance recommended by Ch'en Tu-hsiu in the first issue of *New Youth:* "Be aggressive rather than disposed to retreat." [186]

If the enemy assimilates the retreat of Communists to the "shrinking" of scholars, this will only enhance that maneuver's usefulness. "Chiang Kai-shek and Chen Cheng," Mao notes with satisfaction when the last turning point in the civil war has been reached, "made a wrong appraisal of the ... fighting methods of the People's Liberation Army ... mistaking our retreats for cowardice and our abandonment of a number of cities for defeat...." [187]

"Only after AhQ ... had his ... pigtail pulled and his head bumped against the wall four or five times, would the idlers [who had attacked him] walk away, satisfied at having won" Lu Hsun imagines about his negative hero. "AhQ would stand there for a second, thinking to himself, 'It is as if I were beaten by my son. What is the world coming to nowadays....' [sic] Whereupon he too would walk away, satisfied at having won." Now, in contrast to the Communist's capacity to retain,

> whatever AhQ thought, he was sure to tell people later ... so after this anyone who pulled or twisted his ... pigtail would forestall him by saying: "AhQ, this is not a son beating his father, it is a man beating a beast. Let's hear you say it: a man beating a beast!" [And] then AHQ ... would say: "Beating an insect—how about that? I am an insect—now will you let me go?[188]

But a Communist, if he calculates that he has to accept demands made on him, will not go beyond them. "Chiang"—such is the conduct which even "heroes" adopt in *Water Margin*—"lying on the ground pleaded for mercy. Wu Sung replied that if he wanted to save his life he must agree to do three things. Chiang ... said that instead of three Wu Sung could make three hundred demands, and all would be agreed to." [189] But a Communist, of course, will not surrender unconditionally. It is the contrast with such traditional propensities, whether real or merely imagined, which reinforces the Communists' sense of having broken with the old yielding—while garnering all the advantage from the capacity to give ground.

NOTES

1. Quoted from *People's Daily* (May 18, 1966), *Current Background*, No. 792, 54.

2. An *Anthology of Chinese Verse,* trans. and annotated by J. D. Frodsham with the collaboration of Ch'eng Hsi (Oxford, 1967), 153.

3. Arthur Waley, *Chinese Poems* (London, 1946), 99; Lu Hsün, *Selected Works,* I (Peking, 1956), 215.

4. Martin C. Yang, *A Chinese Village* (New York, 1945), 217.

5. *A Chinese Testament: the Autobiography of Tan Shih-hua,* told to S. Tretiakov (New York, 1934), 148.

6. Su Tung-p'o, *Selections from a Sung Dynasty Poet,* trans. by Burton Watson (New York, 1965), 88.

7. Agnes Smedley, *Chinese Destinies* (New York, 1933), 6.

8. Derk Bodde and Clarence Morris (eds.), *Law in Imperial China* (Cambridge, Mass., 1967), 461.

9. T'ung-tsu Ch'u, *Law and Society in Traditional China* (Paris, 1965), 9.

10. Derk Bodde, *Peking Diary* (New York, 1950), 113.

11. T'ung-tsu *Law and Society,* 58, 49.

12. Bodde and Morris, *Law in Imperial China* 358, 378.

13. Tsao Hsueh-Chin, *The Dream of the Red Chamber,* trans. by Chi-chen Wang (New York, 1958), 85.

14. Bodde and Morris, *Law in Imperial China,* 359.

15. *Red Chamber,* 208.

16. Lu, *Selected Works,* 87.

17. E. D. Edwards, *Chinese Prose Literature of the T'ang Period* (London, 1938), II, 136.

18. *The Golden Lotus,* trans. by Clement Egerton (London, 1939), IV, 2.

19. *Current Background,* No. 861, 32.

20. *Red Chamber,* 248.

21. Ibid., 423f, 477.

22. Arthur Waley, *The Life and Times of Po Chü-i* (London, 1949), 67.

23. Quoted in Han Fei Tzu, *Complete Works,* trans. by W. K. Liao (London, 1939), I, 21.

24. T'ung-tsu, *Law and Society,* 22.

25. Red Chamber, 422f.

26. T'ung-tsu, *Law and Society,* 19, 254, 85.

27. *Red Chamber,* 511.

28. Ibid., 226.

29. Marcel Granet, *La civilisation chinoise* (Paris, 1929), 313.

30. *Red Chamber,* 285, 11, 227.

31. Wen-Shun Chi, *Readings in Chinese Communist Documents* (Berkeley, 1968), 265.

32. W. Scarborough and C. Wilfrid Allan, *A Collection of Chinese Proverbs* (New York, 1964), 373, 314.

33. Warner Muensterberger, "Orality and Dependence: Characteristics of Southern Chinese," *Psychoanalysis and the Social Sciences,* III (New York, 1951), 47.

34. Mencius, *The Book of Rites,* trans. by James Legge (Oxford, 1885), II, 229.

35. Agnes Smedley, *Battle Hymn of a China* (New York, 1943), 261.

36. *Current Background* (October 3, 1966), 57.

37. *People's Daily,* quoted in *Current Background* (May 6, 1969), 27, (May 14, 1969), 35.

38. *Chinese Literature* (June 1969), 62, (July-August 1968), 49.

39. Mencius, II, Part 4, ch. 3, 6.

40. *The Hsiao Ching,* trans. by Mary Leila Makha (New York, 1961), 9.

41. Francis L.K. Hsu, *Under the Ancestors' Shadow* (New York, 1967), 267.

42. Scarborough and Allan, *Proverbs,* 315, 93.

43. Chi-chen Wang, *Traditional Chinese Tales* (New York, 1944), 124.

44. Scarborough and Allan, *Proverbs,* 228.

45. *Red Chamber,* 311f.

46. *Water Margin,* 361.

47. Cyril Birch and Donald Keene (eds.), *Anthology of Chinese Literature* (New York, 1965), 373.

48. *Chinese Literature* (February 1967), 52, (October 1968), 77.

49. Mencius, II, 157f.

50. *Red Chamber,* 117.

51. Ibid., 378.

52. Ibid., 351f., 520.

53. Ibid., 508.

54. *Current Background,* No. 874, 16, No. 861, 25, No. 798, 51.

55. Hunan Radio quoted in *Union Research Service* (December 6, 1968), 252.

56. Mencius, 133.

57. *Current Background,* No. 836, 50.

58. *Rural Youth,* quoted in *Union Research Service,* December 1, 1967, 239.

59. *Chinese Literature* (January 1969), 67, (May 1969), 44.

60. *Joint Publication Research Service,* No. 47885, 41.

61. *Current Background,* No. 897, 27.

62. Quoted in Roderick Macfarquhar, *The Hundred Flowers Campaign and the Chinese Intellectuals* (New York, 1960), 139, 154, 225.

63. *Chinese Literature* (April 1969), 15f.

64. Ibid. (March 1969), 83.

65. Chekiang Radio in *Union Research Service* (August 25, 1967), 220.

66. *Current Background,* No. 824, 50.

67. *Union Research Service* (December 9, 1966), 301.

68. *Current Background,* No. 891, 5, No. 812, 13.

69. Ibid., 31.

70. *Union Research Service* (October 22, 25, 1968), 91f.

71. *Kuang-ming Daily* in *Union Research Service* (March 21, 1967), 353.

72. Ibid. (November 14, 1967), 178.

73. Chekiang Radio in *Union Research Service* (August 22, 1967), 212.

74. Quoted in *China in Crisis,* ed. by Ping-ti Ho and Tang Tsou (Chicago, 1968), I, 457.

75. Lu, *Selected Works,* II, 172.

76. *Chinese Literature* (June 1969), 47.

77. Lu, *Selected Works,* I, 219.

78. Fung Yu-lan, *A History of Chinese Philosophy* (Princeton, 1952-1953), I, 273f.

79. *Peking Review* (March 20, 1970), 10.

80. Wu Ch'eng-en, *Monkey,* trans. by Arthur Waley (London, 1961), 284.

81. Marcel Granet, *La pensée chinoise* (Paris, 1934), 92.

82. Mencius, I, 64.

83. *A Chinese Testament,* 84.

84. *China in Crisis,* II, 197.

85. Quoted by Agnes Smedley, *China's Red Army Marches* (London, 1936).

86. Ibid., 278.

87. Wen Kang, *Die Schwarze Reiterin* (Zurich, 1954), 250.

88. *The Inconstancy of Madame Chuang and other Stories,* trans. by E. B. Howell (New York, n.d.), 159.

89. Granet, *Pensée chinoise,* 92.

90. Ibid., 99f.

91. Mao Tse-tung, *Selected Works* (Peking, 1961), II, 369, I, 316, 343.

92. Mao Tse-tung, "Speech at the Chinese Communist Party's National Conference on Propaganda Work," (Peking, 1966), 26.

93. *The New Republic* (February 27, 1965), 21.

94. *Current Background,* No. 891, 61.

95. Mao, *Selected Works,* I, 317.

96. "In Camera Statements of Mao Tse-tung," *Chinese Law and Government,* I, No. 4, 51.

97. Mao, *Selected Works,* I, 338.

98. Mao, "Propaganda Work," 99.

99. *The Way and Its Power,* trans. by Arthur Waley (New York, 1958), LXIX.

100. Hsün Tzu, *Works* (London, 1928), 306.

101. Mencius, II, 458.

102. Ibid., 286f.

103. Chekiang Radio in *Union Research Service* (August 25, 1967), 219.

104. Scarborough and Allan, *Proverbs,* 372.

105. *Book of Changes,* trans. by James Legge (Oxford, 1899), 436.

106. *The Way and its Power,* LXIX.

107. Quoted by John Gittings in *Far Eastern Economic Review* (May 22, 1969), 451.

108. *Current Background,* No. 861, 4.

109. Scarborough and Allan, *Proverbs,* 94.

110. Mao, *Selected Works,* II, 264, 413, III, 291, IV, 341.

111. "Why Khrushchev Fell," *Red Flag,* Nos. 21-22 (1964).

112. *Dream of the Red Chamber,* 402.

113. Scarborough and Allan, *Proverbs,* 27.

114. Quoted by Dennis Bloodworth, *The Chinese Looking Glass* (New York, 1967), 135.

115. Scarborough and Allan, *Proverbs,* 315.

116. Ibid., 313, 316.

117. *Dream of the Red Chamber,* 299.

118. Scarborough and Allan, *Proverbs,* 311; *Book of Changes,* 222.

119. *Dream of the Red Chamber,* 429.

120. Wu Ching-tzu, *The Scholars* (Peking, 1959), 116.

121. Chi, *Chinese Documents,* 183.

122. *One Hundred and One Chinese Poems,* trans. by Shih Shun Liu (Hong Kong, 1967), No. 99.

123. *Book of Changes,* 69, 437, 438.

124. *The Way and its Power,* XLIV, XXX.

125. Granet, *La civilization chinoise,* 334.

126. *The Ethical and Political Works of Motse* (London, 1929), 204.

127. Mao, *Selected Works,* I, 199, 248.

128. Ibid., IV, 171.

129. Ibid., II, 449.

130. Ibid., 434.

131. Ibid.

132. Ibid., 177.

133. Li Chien nung, *The Political History of China, 1840-1928* (New York, 1956), 288.

134. Mao, *Selected Works,* IV, 415f.

135. Scarborough and Allan, *Proverbs,* 169, 188.

136. Shanghai Radio in *Union Research Service* (February 16, 1968), 178.

137. *Current Background,* No. 848, 1.

138. *People's Daily* in *Current Background* No. 840, 18.

139. *Union Research Service* (April 30 and 26, 1968), 103.

140. Mao, *Selected Works,* I, 25f.

141. Han Fei Tzu, *Works,* II, 6f.

142. *Ten More Poems of Mao Tse-tung* (Hong Kong, 1967), 2.

143. Lu, *Selected Works,* II, 211.

144. *Current Background,* No. 891, 7.

145. Mao, *Selected Works,* IV, 302.

146. Kiangsi Daily in *Union Research Service* (August 30, 1968), 238.

147. *The Way and its Power,* ch. 64.

148. *Union Research Service* (May 14, 1968), 165, 154.

149. *Book of Changes,* 81.

150. *Red Flag,* quoted by Philip Bridgham in *China Quarterly,* No. 29, 22.

151. Speech reported in *Union Research Service* (April 26-30, 1968), 105; *Current Background,* No. 885, 31.

152. Mao, "In Camera Statements," 23f.

153. *Union Research Service* (April 26-30), 113f.

154. *China News Analysis* (November 26, 1954), 5.

155. Macfarquhar, *Hundred Flowers,* 144.

156. Lucian Pye, *The Spirit of Chinese Politics: A Psychocultural Study of Authority in Crisis in Political Development* (Cambridge, Mass., 1968).

157. Mao, *Selected Works,* IV, 291.

158. *Union Research Service* (February 27, 1968), 210, 212.

159. Edgar Snow, *Red Star Over China* (New York, 1961), 125f.

160. Mao, *Selected Works,* IV, 44.

161. Mencius, 186; Mao, "In Camera Statements," 33.

162. Mao, *Selected Works,* IV, 19, II, 464f.

163. Ibid., II, 385, 422.

164. Ibid., 426.

165. *Current Background,* No. 821, 2.

166. Mao, *Selected Works,* III, 142.

167. Arthur Waley, *The Analects of Confucius* (London, 1938), 65.

168. Yang, *Chinese Village,* 52.

169. Granet, *Pensée chinoise,* 87.

170. *Current Background,* No. 848, 4.

171. *Book of Changes,* 267.

172. Scarborough and Allan, *Proverbs,* 214.

173. Mao, *Selected Works,* II, 182.

174. Scarborough and Allan, *Proverbs,* 95.

175. Mao, *Selected Works,* II, 426.

176. Scarborough and Allan, *Proverbs,* 239.

177. Mao, *Selected Works,* I, 221.

178. Jan Myrdal, *Report from a Chinese Village* (London, 1967), 340.

179. Hsün Tzu, *Works,* 100f.

180. *The Way and its Power,* ch. 43.

181. Ibid., ch. 78, 28, 61.

182. Mao Tse-tung, *Basic Tactics* (New York, 1966), 102.

183. Mao, *Selected Works,* I, 211.

184. Scarborough and Allan, *Proverbs,* 238.

185. Mencius, II, 403.

186. Quoted by Enrica Collotti Pischel, *Le origini ideologiche della rivoluzione cinese* (Turin, 1958), 151.

187. Mao, *Selected Works*, IV, 137.

188. Lu, *Selected Works*, I, 84f.

189. *Water Margin*, 409.

Chapter 12

VIOLENCE AS STRATEGY IN
REBELLION SITUATIONS

(with Charles Wolf Jr.)

EDITOR'S NOTE: The following discussion, part of a chapter in a book written jointly with Charles Wolf, Jr., is concerned with conditions under which, in a struggle between rebels (R) and those seeking to maintain their authority (A) violence will be effectively used to win victory. However, violence need not be chosen for strategic reasons. Uncalculated violence— casually employed or expressing passion—is discussed by Leites in the part of the chapter not presented here. The selection which follows weighs the effectiveness of various forms of planned coercion in securing compliance of populations in insurrections. Although it takes examples ranging from Jesse James' gang to the Spanish army in the Napoleonic wars, it was written at a time of high involvement of the United States in the Vietnamese war. It is apparent from Leites' analysis that he believes that the conditions under which violence could be effectively used in that war (e.g., superior intelligence gathering, publicity for draconian measures) gave overwhelming advantage to the side supporting the rebellion.

From Rebellion and Authority, *(Chicago: Markham, 1970), 90-131.*

I. INFLICTING DAMAGE TO DETER OPPOSITION

How can one, in the formulation of the Chinese proverb, "kill just one and frighten ten thousand others?" One mode is to cow by a combination of ferocity and capriciousness. The intention may be to evoke this reaction on the part of the population: while one will never be completely safe with *that* power, the least unsafe thing to do is to stay on the safe side with regard to its demands. (The capriciousness is intended to reinforce the impression of power, but it must not be *so* massive as to make compliance with demands seem as unsafe as non-compliance.)

Another, and probably more effective, mode for R is to take seriously the cliche that "force is the only language they understand," and to make its force a language—that is, a set of events (signs) related, with not too much variance, to another such set (referents). R may then combine severity and regularity—may be draconian.

> [When popular discontent was on the increase in Athens around 620 B.C., Dracon, while not proceeding to a reform of the laws] met . . . the demands for publication of the laws, in writing, so that men might know . . . what penalties a magistrate or court had the right to impose.[1]

As one observer notes:

> The FLN with one killing, would set an example strong enough to scare a large crowd into acquiescence and, once successful, would stop.[2]

What contributes to such an effect will be discussed below.

To be sure, when infliction of damage is justified by its coercive effect, the claim may be wrong and also a cloak for other motives. If during the Algerian war "the forces of order kill prisoners . . . ostensibly . . . because they hope to impede recruitment to the rebels,"[3] one wonders whether this obvious gain was thoughtfully compared with a plausible cost: impeding defection. The covert joke may become a flagrant one, as observed by another eyewitness in the same conflict:

> As we approach, two men flee from a hut. One of them . . . is wounded in the stomach. He is dying. The captain orders that he be left alone: "He should suffer before he croaks, that will teach him to flee."[4]

What contrast to a serious draconian stance, as it is described by a French officer talking about his opponents in Indochina (and probably making them a few—perhaps only a very few—feet taller than they actually were):

> The Viets spill rivers of blood ... but always according to a precise line. The various penalties ... are inflicted ... with a definite aim in mind, and after an analysis of the situation.... The peasant ... comes to believe that the Party is ... omniscient.... The man who has a "correct" attitude ... has nothing to fear.... The system of the Viets excludes all surprise. *Every peasant knows what is going to happen to him, he knows in advance the consequences of his attitude, whether he behaves "badly" or "well."* It is this forecast solidly implanted in the brains which is the greatest force of Ho Chi Minh's camp.[5]

The point is to be as implacable (in the case of disobedience) as one is restrained (in that of compliance), having rendered oneself, in the first place, well-informed about who has behaved how. "Above all it is important," explains a French officer analyzing the conduct of his Viet Minh counterpart (a woman), "to administer constantly the proof that there is no violation ... without heads rolling." Thus:

> once she had ordered a village to cut a road. To be sure, when night fell hundreds of peasants got busy.... But around daybreak [they] began to think of the trouble with the Foreign Legion ... they were getting into. So they began filling up the ditch they had dug a few hours before. [A bit later], dozens of heads rolled. Since then, the Viet Minh securely enjoys the preference of the villagers, who zealously finish off wounded French soldiers.[6]

If both opponents follow similar lines in this regard, what will determine the outcome? It is an obviously crucial question on which extant knowledge or even reflection is meager. Sets of factors conveyed by such words as *resources, appeals,* and *stamina* will presumably then come into their own, in addition to severity and the accuracy of targeting.

The conditions of impunity offered by a draconian system must be such that they impose only a reasonable cost. If the cost of compliance is unreasonably high, even though lower than the extreme penalty threatened for disobedience, the targets' reactions, in feelings and longer-run conduct, are apt to be different from those of the reasonable-cost case. This is "extortion."

A side choosing coercion may genuinely want to convince its targets that it knows how to pick out all the guilty ones and only them, even when they are in close collocation with innocents. Recalling how the few obstinate collaborators with the French in the Casbah were liquidated, the head of the FLN's organization for violence in Algiers (Saadi Yacef) describes the end of one such cafe owner by the action of a famous specialist (Ali Lapointe):

Ali intervened at the head of a small commando. Medjebri and two of his acolytes were the sole targets. At the moment when Ali entered that Muslim cafe, many customers were already present. . . . Ali directed his fire . . . so that only the three condemned men were hit; there was no innocent victim whatsoever.[7]

A draconian side will stress that its policy, in the expression of the Viet Cong, has "two faces": clemency and punishment. It may tend toward indicating that every target, even the worst enemy, always has it within his power, until the very moment of being sanctioned, to limit damage to himself by some known, feasible, and not too costly conduct. The enemy deterred may then also be the enemy changing sides.

A side oriented toward coercion may wish to choose its examples among targets that are liked as little (disliked as much) as possible by the public that is to be influenced. If an unpopular district chief is publicly disemboweled by the Viet Cong, and his family's arms and legs broken, the message to the farmer may not be less impressive, and may perhaps be less revolting, than if the victims were taken from among his own group. And the chance of denunciation (informing) by the population will be reduced by the unpopularity of the target. On the other hand, a side may want to show—probably nearer to the successful completion of its campaign (that is, in the later stages of R)—that nothing will save even the otherwise most popular violator from his due punishment, thus adopting a stance which, the side hopes, is both morally impressive and conducive to prudence.

One step beyond the pure coercion just described, a side may hold targets responsible for the commission or prevention of acts that are neither definitely within, nor clearly outside, their control to perform or to impede. According to a German military order in the occupied Soviet Union:

In case of sabotage of telephone lines, railway lines, etc., sentries will be posted, selected from the civilian population. In case of repetition, the sentry in whose area the sabotage was committed, will be shot.[8]

The effect may be to keep people on their toes to prevent their heads from being lost. Again, during the German occupation of the Soviet Union:

In the villages of Byelorussia, it was only rarely that peasants attacked the Germans or German installations at night, and tilled the soil by day. . . . The inhibiting factor was that after such activity had become known in the village and thereby to the Germans, the whole village would probably be wiped out by the Germans. . . . Informers came forward to save the village by surrendering one person.[9]

But there are limits to be kept; perhaps less effective than the severity of the punishment threatened is the feasibility of avoiding it—particularly when the rule in question is an explicit one. According to an observer, a colonel of the South Vietnamese army acting as province chief introduced his own land reform campaign. In Vinh Long, families with sons or husbands known to be fighting with the Viet Cong, or to have gone north in 1954 with the Viet Minh, were given three months to get them back. "I take half their land and say to them that if after three months they have not got their men back, I will take their homes and property," he told me. . . . "At the end of that time I give them another three months. If their men are not back then, they go to a concentration camp and lose their property, which we divide up among those who are for us." "How on earth do you expect them to get their relations back from North Vietnam?" I asked. "That's their business," replied the Colonel. "In this province the men who are willing to fight for us [and] their families . . . are those who will do well."[10]

But when the feasibility of compliance—crucial for the impact of such conduct, though the colonel does not quite seem to perceive that—appears to be low, as perhaps in this case, does not the demand itself become a mockery, a pretext for damaging which merely adds insult to injury? Still, the effect may also be one of cowing: if they punish me for even what is beyond me, I had at least better do all I can. Or there may be a mixture of both reactions, depending on the magnitudes of various factors: How free does the victim feel to condemn, oppose, or flee the side in question? How does he evaluate the cost and prospects of counteraction?

One further step beyond coercion-by-regularity consists in adding, to a full application of known and practicable norms, a striking but limited unit of damage that is grossly arbitrary. Having robbed their first bank in Liberty, Missouri, with a parsimony of violence, Jesse James' whole band galloped out of town.

At this moment George Wymore (or Wynmore), a 19-year-old student at the college, was hastening to his class. When the horsemen came thundering down the street towards him, he ran to get into a house. One of the riders wheeled his horse, drew a revolver and fired four times. When he was picked up later, quite dead, it was found that every one of the four shots had taken effect, and any one of them would have been fatal. . . . Jesse . . . wanted to establish . . . . a *precedent of deadliness,* so that future towns, when he raided them, would know that he and his gang would kill on the slightest excuse or without excuse.[11]

Here compliance (or noninvolvement) ceases to guarantee impunity, but disobedience still spells punishment. The victim of torture-for-intelligence cannot be sure that the pain will subside if he talks; but he may be rather certain that it will not unless he does. Threatened with some damage from which there is no protection in any case, the target may be expected to develop a reaction already noted: better avoid all that I can predictably escape! Will he be less or more motivated in this sense than when compliance guarantees impunity? Again, there will be forces working in either direction: one may be stricken by terror in the face of such ferocity, or one may be impelled by rage as well as discouraged by the possible futility of compliance.

Coercion at large, as well as that variant of it called deterrence, requires unceasing effort to produce and maintain a favorable environment.

The serious coercer will strive for ever higher levels of intelligence, aiming at a situation in which inflictions are consonant with norms (whether declared or inferable from conduct)—in which he damages most of the guilty and very few innocents. When it comes to choosing between substantial losses to the latter and a notably incomplete reaction to the former, the aversion against making a mistake will, in a person genuinely oriented toward coercion, be as strong as that against letting a violator enjoy impunity. The coercer disapproves of such practices as the following, from an allegation about Americans fighting Philippine rebels:

> John T. McCutchen, a conservative reporter, told of what usually happened when the body of a mutilated American was found: ". . . a scouting party goes out to the scene of the killing . . . and they proceed to burn the village and kill every native *who looks as if* he had a bolo or a rifle."[12]

To enable itself to act on less uncertain evidence, the A—initially, probably much less well-informed about the rebels than the rebels are about A—must allocate a substantial fraction of its resources to intelligence. This effort, however, may be thought doomed to failure (how does one distinguish the innocent from the guilty in a faceless mass?) or be unnecessary (are the population and the rebels not close to each other?). The situation then arising is described by a French officer in Indochina:

> We whites are, after all, lost in the yellow mass as in a fog. We see badly, we divine badly, we are groping. [Hence] the Viets are beating us in the war of atrocities.[13]

Thus R may have the basis of intelligence for correct targeting for massive infliction of extreme damage, while A, lacking that basis, may be incapable of coercion even if it aspired to such practices.

Not only must the coercer arrange to *be informed* about what the coercees do, he must also arrange to *inform them* about what they can expect from him, by warning and setting examples. Here again, effort is required to ensure that the target population be clear as to what precise lesson is to be learned from damage presented in support of a rule. Hence, damage-inflicters may spread the knowledge of their acts in overt ways, difficult to hide—as when the FLN cut off the noses and ears of people who had, say, smoked despite the prohibitions, and now were impressed into service as walking examples. During the Napoleonic war in Spain

> the Spaniard who had helped the Frenchman has his right ear cut off, and bears on his forehead, branded by a red-hot iron, these words: "Long Live Mina" [a guerrilla leader].[14]

Intending both to render their new laws familiar and to prove how correct and complete their intelligence is (how omniscient, hence how powerful, hence how destined to victory, hence how worthy of support on all grounds they are), rebels often leave with fresh corpses a summary of detailed charges. In the Irish revolution, which was notable for the rarity of informers,

> many dead bodies, often of Irishmen who had served in the British Army, were found by the roadside, shot by the IRA with a label attached to them bearing the words: "Convicted as a spy. Spies and traitors beware."[15]

To be sure, nothing prevents A from imitating its enemy. When "Tiger" Tam, Minister of the Interior, wins "the Battle of Saigon" in 1950:

> one finds numerous corpses abandoned in the streets . . . with numerous wounds inflicted by a knife. Attached to them is a paper with the reasons for their condemnation. This is in the usual Viet Minh manner for the execution of "traitors"; but the grounds indicated are quite out of the ordinary. . . . "so-and-so is a communist assassin who has been executed for his crimes."[16]

Being outspoken about extreme damage inflicted may convey disregard for the decent opinions of local mankind, and thus may cow, if it does not do the opposite—but at least an intermediate reaction is less probable. In the case of an organization with a penchant for self-righteousness which it is capable of communicating, proclaimed ferocity may encourage the population to believe that here is the next legitimate authority, quasi-judicial, quite judicious, and very fearsome.

Nontotalitarian authorities, on the other hand, who under the stress of conflict, resort to procedures greatly at variance with their usual standards may be too ashamed and afraid of world opinion to admit what they have done. Instead, they may trust that the population's, if not R's own, media (such as the "Arab Telephone") will bring the news to those to be deterred (which indeed happened, for instance, after the French repression in Setif, in the spring of 1945). Or they may simply prefer to risk wasting the coercion than to have its use publicized and possibly exaggerated.

It is often affirmed that being severe toward the population, or, worse, inflicting considerable amounts of damage on it, does not pay: one is more apt to arouse than intimidate. However that may be, certain characteristics of damaging behavior by either side—apart from the level and sum of damage inflicted—are apt to affect popular reactions.

II. CONDITIONS OF COMPLIANCE

1. *Compliance may vary directly with the degree to which the severity of the sanctions inflicted by one side is understandable*—that is, is seen to exist

for reasons other than cowing. The population may be out of sympathy with R, but may also appreciate that, given its business, informing merits death. The population may even understand that the rebels, lacking facilities for locking people up and fearful of escapees turning informers, may have to punish severely or not at all. On the other hand, if, say, a minor lack of respect provokes one side to an extreme sanction, this is more likely to be resented in a way that in the long run reduces compliance—unless that side maintains so overwhelming a threat towards its targets that awareness of misdeeds is obliterated from consciousness.

2. *The less complete the enforcement of a rule, by incapacity or discrimination, the lower the compliance*—not only because of the chance of impunity thus provided, but also, again, because of the impression of weakness and injustice thereby generated. To this extent, more damage, suitably allocated, might be better received than less damage randomly imposed.

3. *The less a side*—while insisting, with severe threats, on a certain kind of conduct—*is capable of protecting the compliant population from the other side's making good on its perhaps even severer threats, the more resentment, and in the long run the more resistance, that side is likely to provoke.* When "the peasant has his choice," proposes a participant-observer of As fighting Rs in less developed countries,

> the government must be ruthless. . . . When, however, an area is outside government control . . . the government has no right to be ruthless. [Yet] there was a tendency in Vietnam to get this the wrong way round.17

"In the past," recalls an eyewitness-actor about the treatment of the Huks before Magsaysay, "the farmer who gave food to the Huk, however unwillingly, had been treated as . . . [a] supporter of the enemy." With the new policy under which the rebellion was defeated, "the assumption was that if he was . . . in need because of taxes levied on him by the Huk, he was a person entitled to help from his government."18 (However, to what extent would the gain from such a policy be offset by increased compliance with the other side's demands?)

4. *A side* (usually a nontotalitarian A) *may arouse unfavorable reactions among its targets,* reactions well beyond what they might have been *had a given amount of damage been administered in draconian fashion,* if it appears to be not only harsh but unintelligible and unpredictable as well. Its rationale, if such can be fathomed at all, may change erratically. Sharp deviations from the patterns of strong coercion are apt to create in the population a belief in A's incompetence and destructiveness. On the first count, A may appear doomed, contemptible, and hateful (in its weakness, causing misery); on the second, again, hateful and doomed.

"As for myself," a Eurasian officer—lord of a semiautonomous domain in the Mekong Delta during the first war there—explains:

I destroy the villages which must be destroyed. I kill those who have to be killed. But the French destroy and kill at random because they don't have the necessary information.... Of me the farmers say that I am just. But they fear the Expeditionary Corps because its conduct is unforeseeable.[19]

"It is not only their uselessness," says a French officer in Vietnam about the "unjust atrocities" that according to him were common in his army, "which is shocking, but above all the revelation, through them, of lack of discernment." The latter "causes both hate and contempt"—and rage, though it may be inhibited by fear, about being put into a situation where, with the best of will, one is unable to limit damage to oneself to reasonable levels. "The peasants," this officer explains,

simply can't divine what the Expeditionary Corps is going to do when it appears in a village; it may just as well set everything on fire as distribute medicine.[20]

An officer recalling the conflict in Algeria notes:

Two or three times in a row we visited the same village, distributing candies ... pamphlets ... food and medicine. Then, for weeks, we abandoned the village to its fate. Or, the day after, we arrived as warriors ... candies changed into grenades, pamphlets into lists of suspects, good words into threats. Now, acting on intelligence or caprice, we were going to perform population control.... Somebody looking suspect was just out of luck. A passerby, arousing suspicion, appearing at the wrong time or place ... was apt to become ... one "killed while escaping."[21]

While such conduct may cow its targets, it is more likely to work against compliance, even apart from the bad feelings it arouses. If those who obey often are penalized while, in other cases, those who disobey avoid punishment, the case for damage-limitation is weakened. So it may also be if the combination of much arbitrariness with high overall damage makes one suspect a campaign aimed at mere annihilation—in the face of which chances of survival may seem enhanced through resistance.

III. SOME STRATEGIES OF VIOLENCE

1. REPRISAL

A side may inflict reprisals against damage done to it, both for punishment and deterrence—the latter frequently a pretext for the former, which in turn may cloak vengeance, which, on its part, may justify pleasure in hurting and wrecking.

While in one major type of reprisal the victims are presumably members of the other side, in another situation—for instance, when As are impressed with

R's dependence on support by the population—a contiguous (usually in space, but possibly in time) sector of the population may itself become the target. After all, it is easily at hand, in contrast to the infuriatingly elusive rebels, and suspect by opportunity as well as by a (not always fully conscious) equation in A's mind between R and the population.

Hence, "from the moment at which the French army has suffered heavy losses" in an encounter with the Algerian rebels, explains one of them, "the nearest village . . . should be considered as no longer in existence."[22] And in another Algerian episode:

> We pursue them all day from one village to another, in helicopters, in jeeps and on foot, without stopping, for they never stop. As we go along, we set fire to all the [houses] where we find traces of them, and to a few others.[23]

No case is, or can be, made for the assertion that "traces" indicated the continued presence of the notoriously mobile enemy, or for the implicit contention that, had he been present, he had enjoyed complicity from the population whom he was otherwise supposed to "terrorize."

If survivors connected with such reprisals feel a sense of collective responsibility for the initial deed, perhaps because it happened close to them or was committed by members of a group of which they feel a part, and if the reprisal itself is not felt to be disproportionate, such conduct may seem acceptable to the population. But if the first condition is not met, and if it is not clear how the victims could have prevented the initial act at all—or, at any rate, at reasonable cost to themselves—there is little coercion: hardly a lesson to be learned for future conduct. If *any* member of the population may have to pay for *any* participant in an R whose cause has some measure of appeal (in contrast to that of a gang), the R may indeed come to seem to represent the population: one of its cardinal tenets is validated.

In addition, reprisals at random may hit persons whom a side may want to spare, in view of their contributions to its cause, or the shock produced by damage befalling them.

Still, if large enough numbers are killed in this way, random reprisals may be expedient for some time (here again it is the middle road that is apt to be inexpedient), partly because they inhibit the rebels themselves. In 1945 the French, with rebellion in Algeria at a low level, reacted to the death of about 100 Europeans by killing about 15,000 Muslims in Setif; it may have worked. In 1955, with rebellion much higher, the French responded to similar damage by killing perhaps 5,000 in Philippeville; it didn't work. Would 50,000 have done it? The figure of 500,000—mentioned at the time on the mainland in oral and popular recommendations—would probably have produced a striking effect for a far from negligible time. But, apart from certain totalitarian regimes during certain periods, the regard for the public on which A depends, as well as its own conscience, may make it choose a middle level of violence, offering even less prospect of effectiveness than the low or high extreme. (Repugnance to the high level of violence on moral grounds is so strong that the mention of its possible effectiveness is largely avoided in public print. Our violation of this taboo makes us liable to being misinterpreted as advocating, retrospectively, the largest number of deaths mentioned in the above example concerning Algeria. We do not. If we were to advise an A having such an option, we should on moral grounds rule out even considering it. That does not change the shape of reality of which we spoke.)

2. PROVOCATION

One may inflict damage for the purpose of provoking one's opponent to raise his level of counteraction: he will believe it will do him good, but I foresee that it will harm him. (I may be mistaken, and fatally induce him to abandon the ineffectual middle ranges of violence to which he was accustomed for its devastating higher reaches.) In the first half of the sixties, violent actions by rebels in Latin America against civilian governments or against Americans (such as the kidnapping of a U.S. officer in Venezuela) were often suspected of aiming at a local *golpe,* or intervention, by the United States.

When the relations between my opponent and the population are not bad enough, for my taste, I may desire to make my enemy nastier by wounding him harder. Presumably, this was a motive behind the preference of communist elements, in the resistance against the German occupiers during World War II, for killed isolated German soldiers and then disappearing—confidently expecting that reprisals not only would seem disproportionately large in the population's judgment, but would also make victims far beyond the Party's immediate sphere. In the occupied Soviet Union

> the Germans had issued warnings that any damage to German installations or personnel would be punished by reprisals on the population living in the vicinity of the crime. The partisans would simply kill a German soldier in some safe place, and . . . leave his body in a village street. The Germans almost always . . . retaliated by burning down the village and killing its inhabitants, [though] often it was obvious that the body had been moved, because there was no blood on the ground.[24]

"Along the route of retreat of the paratroops," an observer reports about an episode of the first war in Vietnam,

> "the Viets had planted on bamboo spikes the heads of the soldiers they had killed, like so many milestones. Some of the men went berserk from it, others cried hysterically when they recognized the head of somebody they had known; others just swore softly that they'd kill every Vietnamese they'd find as soon as

they got to a Vietnamese village. . . ." They *did* burn down the first Vietnamese village they found.[25]

At the time of the conflict between the Zionists and the British in Palestine, "children in communal settlements were taught a 'spitting drill' to be used against British soldiers with the objective, sometimes achieved, of goading them into incidents."[26]

It may be particularly useful to induce an opponent to kill his own supporters. As the famous Eurasian officer who was operating on the French side in Indochina explains to an observer:

> The French are blind. They fall into all the traps laid by the enemy. Once they discovered the body of one of their men, frightfully tortured, at the entrance to a village. They set fire to the village, having no inkling of the fact that it was pro-French. The Viets had deposited the mutilated corpse there, warning the inhabitants not to touch it.[27]

Apart from modifying preferences, successful provocations may change the outcome of calculations (on limiting damage or maximizing advantages) in a sense welcome to the provoker. For instance, life in the forces of one or the other side may be refused by a villager so long as his normal environment endures, but may be accepted when it is destroyed.

What I want to provoke may not be enhanced pressure by my opponent against my potential allies, but enhanced intervention by a third party against him. One way of doing this is to cause my opponent to inflict such damage on me as will trigger the third party's intervention on my behalf—a calculation sometimes attributed, in another context, to nuclear-minded Frenchmen (interested in reducing the probability of being abandoned by Washington in case of a forward move by Moscow).

Or, I may myself damage what is of value to the third party whose intervention I want to bring about, finding an excuse to do so in the course of fighting my opponent. When the Cuban rebels of 1897 seemed to adopt a policy of burning cane fields owned by Americans, there arose "suspicion that these tactics were designed to coax us into extracting Cuban chestnuts from the Spanish fire."[28]

Should R start off with a bang—which has obvious advantages for its growth—or begin inconspicuously in order to delay A's reaction? Fearing a countervalue response by its opponent, a side (usually R) may abstain from inflicting counterforce damage that would otherwise be indicated—a reaction, as we noted above, contributing to the usefulness to A of *high* reprisal. For example, an American officer who had commanded U.S. Philippine guerrilla forces in central and southern Luzon admitted that

> the Japanese, through brutality to the Philippine people, forced us to abandon harassment. We tried various means of keeping them from retaliating against the . . . civilians, but none worked.[29]

Similarly, an observer of the Southern Sudanese rebels in the mid-sixties noted:

> From time to time the Anya-Nya carry out ... raids on administrative centers; but these have now diminished because the army's policy of massive retaliation has had some success. The rebels have decided that the consequences for the civilian population of the towns are too tragic to make such raids worthwhile.[30]

A similarly prudent behavior may be adopted if a side believes it is better off not to unleash a counterforce *exchange*. "To Jimmy's way of thinking," explains an observer about a Mau Mau general staying put in the jungle,

> he had but to bide his time and build up his food stocks ... balancing his nuisance value against the effort it would take the Army to move him. The important thing was not to exceed the limit. He had an instinct for correctly interpreting his intelligence, which was good. . . .[31]

The student rebellions of the sixties in the West occurred in conditions in which provocation assumed a major role for both A and R, in view of the following circumstances:

1. The counterforce capability of R with regard to the establishment at large was low.

2. That of A, in relation to R, was high.

3. As long as violations of established rules and inflictions of damage by R were below a certain level (rising as the decade proceeded), they did not appear to justify the crushing counteraction which (2) rendered possible. The evolving pattern came to include intruding upon, molesting and insulting members of A chosen for "confrontation"; inspecting, throwing into disarray and even damaging objects in their offices; "occupying" premises.

4. But making itself suspected of having induced a coronary in a member of A (fatal to the President of Swarthmore, mild to the Dean of Harvard) was already too much for R, and might expediently be followed by cessation or reduction of attack: punishing itself, rather than suffering a retribution it had rendered acceptable, and thus wiping the slate clean with a view to resuming the offensive. Paving stones were an accepted weapon against the forces of order for a month in the Paris of 1968—on condition that they not kill. A single death clearly due to the rebels would have had a significant impact adverse to them.

5. Similarly, had even one rebel then been killed clearly by the defenders of the status quo, they would have incurred a notable disadvantage.

6. Not only was there a high sensitivity to the damage inflicted by A and R, the preoccupation with the human costs of the battle tended to prevail—with the exception of the upper levels of R and A—over interest in its outcome—in contrast, say, to a contest between landowners and peasant rebels aiming at their extinction, where the mutual infliction of extreme damage is apt to be taken for granted. When students confront academic authorities, demands concerning, say, student power or R.O.T.C. are soon likely to take second place to the insistence on, say, amnesty or the enforcement of discipline.

7. In such conditions, it is of major worth for R to provoke A into an inexpediently (for it) high level of "repression." University administrators or "pigs" may act on the sentiments aroused in them when hit by dirty words or substances; autonomously or uncontrollably (not that an *attempt* is always made on higher levels to restrain them) they may counterattack to a measure which splits A itself, and causes its desertion by needed elements of R. This is what happened when the forces of order reacted sharply (though their casualties may not have been below those of their opponents) in the "Battle of the *rue Gay-Lussac*" in Paris, during the night of May 10-11, 1968, inducing the government's capitulation to the rebels a day later.

8. A, in its turn, is equally interested in having R go beyond those levels or amounts of violating rules and inflicting damage which have come to be accepted as bordering on the permissible. Thus it was noted in Paris, during the spring just recalled, that the police, recurrently, did not use its capability for preventing, at low cost, the assemblage in the streets of large number of its opponents or the construction of barricades by them. It may have preferred—once having incurred the cost mentioned under (5)—offering television audiences repeated spectacles of masses surging through the city and barricades having to be overcome by bulldozers. One month after the first big battle, ordinary folk were still descending from many parts of the city upon the latest battleground to collar the rebels and ask them to stop.

3. HITTING THE WORST—AND THE BEST

A side (usually R) may inflict damage for the purpose of arousing positive reactions toward it on the part of those unsympathetic to its victims. The Robin Hoods prefigure their future reign of justice by punishing oppressors and exploiters, employing some of the rituals customary in the established order for the corresponding acts. Helping underprivileged elements in the population to improve their lot in various ways, R may require strength which it can turn against its beneficiaries, now obtaining compliance inspired by the desire to limit damage. That is, first the rebels assist the population's effort to limit damage to itself from A; then, having grown by that campaign, they in turn threaten damage to the population, *unless.* . . . The rebels may then begin to deplete the stock, not of the "bad," but of the "good" agents of A: those who are efficient without being obnoxious, and those who achieve unusually good relations with the population. As an observer noted about South Vietnam:

as early as 1957, the cream of village officialdom had been murdered by the Communists, who had correctly identified this group as a key element in the struggle. [32]

And in Algeria a participant-observer remarked about the rebels:

If they have to choose between liquidating a police officer who everyone knows is a monster and liquidating [an officer] who is trying to make contact [with the population], they will pick [the latter] without a moment's hesitation. [33]

Both kinds of targeting will spare agents of A who are neither here nor there. In 1960 in South Vietnam, there was

a period of ... terror directed at ... officials in the countryside who were either unjust administrators or who, by their good example, served the government well ... the mediocre, those who saw and heard no evil [in the Viet Cong], survived.[34]

Indeed, they were encouraged in the trait that protected them: "the assassination pattern ... stimulated mediocrity among civil servants"—an effect which the rebels went so far as to foster by explicit, though discreet, suggestions:

Especially to low-ranking civil servants, the National Liberation Front would convey the idea that it would not harm a Government of Vietnam representative providing he arranged that the programs for which he was responsible were not implemented in any effective way.... A civil servant would imagine he could enjoy the best of both worlds: he could perform well enough not to arouse the suspicions of his superior, but not so well as to earn the hostility of the NLF. He might even be in contact with the NLF so as to be certain they understood his position.[35]

4. BEING GENEROUS

Just as an R may seek to please by making itself the secular arm of natural law against a perverted order, it may desire to impress by unexpected generosity—to abstain from inflicting *expected* damage on enemies so as to foster their disaffection from A, or even their conversion to itself. This device is likely, however, to be productive only to the extent that A does not inflict extreme damage on any agent whose loyalty is open to even marginal doubt. If it does not, it may, for instance, be to the rebels' advantage to be nice to prisoners. In 1947, a participant-observer's colleague

visited a camp in central China where the Nationalists kept five thousand Communist prisoners. "Where were they caught?" he asked the Nationalist general in charge of the camp. "Between you and me, we have no more than ten real Communist soldiers among these prisoners." "Who are the others, then?" "Nationalist soldiers caught and released by the Communists. We don't want them to contaminate our army."[36]

On the other hand, here are the musings of a French officer who has captured an Algerian rebel:

If I set him free ... either he mends his ways and will have his throat cut by his brothers ... or he doesn't, and then, in order to prove that we have not contaminated him, his first gesture will be to cut a throat.[37]

The other side's ferocity may thus counter the device of being humane.

5. INSULTING

Whatever its motive, an act of inflicting injury may also insult the victim, making compliance (if that be desired) less likely. This is especially apt to happen to a side (usually A) associated with ethnic or class strata that hold in contempt the groups with which the other side (ordinarily R) appears to be connected.

The latter's insulting behavior is often a leaning-over-backward against an obscure temptation to accept their superior's sentiments about them. When lower orders maltreat their betters, they unwittingly acknowledge, through their very rage, the formidable stature of their victims—who may sense this and then find their treatment more bearable.

But the insults heaped upon the injuries administered by masters to their inferiors are likely to express a more serene conviction that the latter are low in all senses of the word; such insults are harder to take "lying down." For instance, in Algiers:

> One day, a sergeant got a bit high and then scoured the neighborhood in a truck, picking up all the Arabs he came across wearing good European clothes—without even bothering to ask for their papers. He came back with his truck completely full. After assembling his captives in the muddy courtyard, he first made them do a few squats and pushups. Then, because he saw they were trying not to get their clothes dirty, he continued with more and more strenuous exercises. "Stand up! Lie down! On your back! On your stomach! Move your legs, your arms, your head . . ." When one would collapse, completely out of breath, a good jab with a bayonet brought him to order again. We were at the windows, laughing, jostling to get a better view.
>
> Since then, it has become an unwritten rule to make a particular search for well-dressed Arabs. Heaven help the suspect caught with a necktie on and with his shoes shined. [38]

Insult may be harder to take than injury: its presence interferes with the determination of conduct by calculations of limiting damage or enhancing gain. The very fact of continuing to calculate in the presence of insult may somehow be associated with the particular loss to be avoided: by taking it lying down (as my tormentor is confident I will), I prove the correctness of his assertions about me. In sharp opposition to this reaction, as noted above, one of the major motives of an R connected with lower groups is precisely to demonstrate the falsity of one's masters' unfavorable conceptions about oneself, just because these conceptions have an obscure and powerful hold on one.

Combining *little* injury with *much* insult is the least expedient combination, where rage is least impeded by pain and fear. It is also one to which nontotalitarian As, as shown by some of the incidents already noted, are particularly drawn.

6. ASSIMILATING THE POPULATION TO THE ENEMY

If R is associated in A's eyes with inferior ethnic or class groupings, A may, as noted, find it impracticable to distinguish between the guilty and the innocent in the faceless mass (or not useful to do so, if one wants to produce impressive body-counts), and regard it as sound practice to presume that any member of the appropriate sector of the population is a rebel. According to a historian reconstructing the mood of Napoleon's soldiers in Spain:

> The prevalent opinion in the Army is this: the more Spaniards who perish, the fewer enemies we will have.[39]

"Most of my buddies," a conscript reports about Algeria,

> were convinced that all their troubles were the fault of the *bougnoules*. They wanted to kill as many as they could as soon as feasible, so as to go home as quickly as possible.[40]

IV. THE POPULATION UNDER CROSS-FIRE

1. THE DOMINANCE OF DAMAGE-LIMITING

As noted earlier, the effort to limit damage may prevail over aspirations to better one's condition or act according to one's ideals; the more so, the fiercer and longer the conflict. "The villagers," guesses a French officer in Algeria

> aren't going to vote for those who build schools for them nor for those who promise independence; they are going to vote for the one who can hold the threat of death over them.[41]

The target's life may be manipulated in a complicated fashion so as to raise the level of threat to him from one's opponent. Having asked villagers whether they receive visits from the other side and having got an (untruthful) "no" for an answer, a side may arrange an ambush near the village which will damage the other side, or at least be noted by them. Thereupon the first side may re-enter the village and say to the villagers (as in the campaign against the Huks):

> You people have been . . . foolish. . . . Our soldiers came here to see if you needed any help. You lied to them. You said there were no Huk here. They knew you

lied, and so they waited for the Huk to come. They killed some, and captured some, but others got away. You know what those Huk are thinking now—the ones who got away? They are thinking that somebody here betrayed them.[42]

The villagers, agreeing with this estimate, change sides. "I don't need to kill Viet cadres," the boss of Hue during much of the first war in Vietnam confides to an observer:

When I suspect somebody . . . I put him into prison on whatever charge, [and] then I release him without apparent reason. Suspected by the Party, he is eager to clear himself by the excellence of his work. I pass false information to him which he transmits to the Viets, who will liquidate him when they find out. If he is valuable, I call him and demonstrate to him that he is irremediably "burned" with his side. I save him by recruiting him. It is thus that I have acquired my best officials.[43]

What may be mistaken by a side for an expression of the population's antipathy toward it may simply be fear of the damage foreseen to result from the other side's reacting to the first side's approach (for example, by recruitment in a village). And, as noted earlier, a side may be prepared to recruit persons for rather high levels of participation under duress.

As an analyst observed about the occupied Soviet Union during World War II:

Even though the peasant knew who was going to win the war, in many cases where the Germans had . . . adequate forces . . . [he] might decide that it was safer to submit to the Germans and be hostile to the Partisans. [Although] he jeopardized his future by working with the Germans, he could not afford the luxury of making long-range estimates. . . . He tried to survive in the immediate future.[44]

That is, calculations of damage that may befall one during the conflict may dwarf estimates of injury derived from the combination of a particular war record with a particular war outcome.

Members of the population may desire to stay with one side as long, and only as long, as it is profitable or prudent to do so, veering toward its opponent when assessments against these criteria begin to point in the opposite direction—that is, when a change of rule impends, or day is about to break (night to fall). Or the population may—a frequently noted maneuver—attempt to satisfy both contenders at the same time.

If one can plead with a side that one's compliance with its opponent's demands was due to duress, perhaps the sanction will be lightened or lifted. Hence, if a side does not insist strongly enough on compliance, one should wait until it does (and probably make it do so by an initial refusal). "One of the first steps," a French officer recalls about his civic action programs in Algeria was to open a first-aid station. . . . When the population failed to respond to an invitation to use the station, for fear of being seen making contact with the enemy, it was necessary to resort to forced treatment. Twice a week the battalion doctor would make a tour. . . . Another . . . step was to open, or reopen, schools. Again, parents and children did not respond to the first request for attendance; but on being told that, as of a given date, they would be fined for their childrens' truancy, the parents decide to cooperate.[45]

2. HOW DOES A SIDE MAKE ITSELF STRONGER TOWARD THOSE IN THE MIDDLE?

One limits damage by veering toward (1) the more predictable side, (2) the side imposing a lesser cost on impunity, (3) the more severe side. Preferences with regard to these three "goods"—or to the latter two adjusted for expectations—vary. There are, for instance, those individuals who are little tempted to transgress and are hence mostly interested in a low cost of impunity; those who are much tempted to transgress and are hence interested in a side's severity (mildness); and those who especially dislike uncertainty and are hence interested in a side's predictability.

"Severity" refers, of course, both to the level of threats and enforcement, including the chances of concealment and escape. To be stronger with regard to the population may thus also mean, as we already noted, to be harsher toward it. As recounted by a French paratroopers' chaplain:

An old Muslim, arrested for having sawed off telegraph poles, explains to a captain who expresses surprise about his deed: "Sir, the French come and tell me: you musn't saw off poles; if you do, you go to prison. I say to myself: I don't want to go to prison, I won't do it. The French leave. At night, the rebel comes and says: saw off the poles from here to there. I answer: no, the French would put me into prison. The rebel tells me: You cut the poles or I cut your throat. I calculate: If I don't cut the poles, he'll surely cut my throat; he has done it to others, in the next village. I prefer going to prison. So, Sir, I cut the poles; you caught me; put me in prison!"[46]

A population beset by both rebels and forces of order may feel there is much to choose, where observers accustomed to less uncomfortable situations fail to perceive the difference. One may strongly prefer a high probability of death to its certainty, if that appears to be one's alternative. We shall surely kill you unless you kill so-and-so, R may say to a person approached. The other side, to be sure, may kill you for doing it. But also, they may not find out, or not find you; even if they do, their legality may enable you to survive.

Or one may choose the side threatening a merciful death against the side promising a painful one. "At the time of the last elections," recalls a French officer serving in Algeria

Muslims came to me and said: We are coming to see you, but we shall not vote. If we did, we would have our throats cut. You can kill us with your gun; it's more agreeable to die that way than by the knife.[47]

3. REACTIONS TO UNINTENDED DAMAGE

So far we have dealt with damage to the population which is intended by a side. But what about the flies who get crushed when elephants fight? On what factors does a population's reaction to collateral damage from the conflict between A and R depend?

Sometimes the population will be hostile to a side in the measure in which that side's fire, though directed at the opponent, makes it suffer. Thus, hostile reactions by moderate student groups against university authorities occurred frequently in the late nineteen sixties (at Harvard, Columbia, and Berkeley), when those authorities called upon the police to oust militant students who had occupied university property, and the police in energetic pursuit of their mission struck against bystanders, as well as occupiers.

But, clearly, rage—and in particular rage against the directly inflicting side—is not the only possible response, as the reaction of occupied Europeans showed during World War II. (Also, if the population's major reaction does conform to the hypothesis previously mentioned, the cost of this to the inflicting side, directly and indirectly, may or may not be higher than the immediate tactical gain from the strikes in question.) In some cases, elements of the population may be sufficiently hostile to the side against which the attacks were intended to nourish their aversion with this very suffering (as, to some extent, in the situations during World War II previously referred to). Or they may at least be willing to pay a certain—possibly a substantial—price for a preferred outcome of the war. And their reaction is apt to be influenced not only by the amounts of injury produced, but also by their estimate of each side's eagerness and skill in avoiding "unnecessary" damage to the population, directly and indirectly. Once again, ruthlessness, negligence, and clumsiness may be attributed either to the inflicting side or to its opponent who provoked such reactions or gave it no choice; the attributions are, as in the campus disorders noted above, likely to be based on matters of fact, as well as of rumor and sentiment. Finally, the entire dimension of the legitimacy of damage may be dwarfed by the search for, and the execution of, maneuvers to limit it.

If a side imposes a certain conduct of the population for which the other side then punishes it, the population's reaction will depend on a variety of factors: its assessment of the utility of the conduct for the side that imposed it (being much harmed for little is galling); the degree to which that side promised protection from its opponent and yet did not deliver it; the degree to which it assumes some responsibility for the misery it has provoked. These considerations would seem hard to overlook. That they *are* overlooked is suggested by an incident related by an observer of the first war in Vietnam:

Luong-Ha is a Catholic village . . . to the southeast of the Plain of Reeds, at about 20 kilometers from RC-16 [a highway]. It was obeying the Viet Minh peacefully.

Then, in Saigon, a program for extending pacification was prepared. And so a column [of the Expeditionary Corps] went to Luong-Ha. The priest and his peasants were drawn in, a militia constituted ... a post and towers built for defense. Then the column left again, leaving behind it a platoon commanded by a French captain. As a result the village was massacred at night.... The Viets immobilized the soldiers by mortar and machine gun fire. They passed between the post and the towers, and killed a good part of the population.

When the French returned shortly afterwards, the vicar reported:

Nobody is working in the fields anymore, nobody is reconstructing his house. The Viet Minh cadre has told us ... that this was just a warning: next time all the men will be shot. We ask of the French to leave important forces in the village, to send us rice and medicine.

The observer in question (Lucien Bodard) concludes his account of the incident as told to him by the French officer in charge:

But he raised his arms to heaven and remarked to me, "These people are insatiable. I'm not God, after all. I can't put troops everywhere. And I've no budget for rice."

Yet the officer attempted compensation for these incapacities: before leaving the village, he distributed a substantial number of military decorations.[48]

NOTES

1. A. R. Burn, *The Lyric Age of Greece* (London, 1960), 287.

2. David Galula in *Counterinsurgency: A Symposium,* Rand Corporation, R-412-ARPA (1963), 27.

3. Robert Bonnaud, *Itinéraire* (Paris, 1962), 45. Author's translation.

4. Benoist Rey, *Les Egorgeurs* (Paris, 1961), 57. Author's translation.

5. Lucien Bodard, *La Guerre d'Indochine, I, L'Enlisement* (Paris, 1963), 445f. Emphasis added, author's translation.

6. Ibid., 252f.

7. Saadi Yacef, *Souvenirs de la Bataille d'Alger* (Paris, 1962), 83. Author's translation.

8. Quoted by Aubrey Dixon and Otto Heilbrunn, *Communist Guerrilla Warfare* (London, 1954), 142.

9. Herbert Dinerstein, unpublished manuscript, 34.

10. Denis Warner, *The Last Confucian* (Baltimore, 1964), 31.

11. Paul I. Wellman, *A Dynasty of Western Outlaws* (Garden City, 1961), 71, 73. Emphasis added.

12. Leon Wolff, *Little Brown Brother* (Garden City, 1961), 318. Emphasis added.

13. Bodard, *L'Enlisement,* 452.

14. J. Lucas-Dubreton, *Napoleon devant l'Espagne* (Paris, 1945), 346.

15. Edgar Holt, *Protest in Arms* (New York, 1960), 205.

16. Lucien Bodard, *La Guerre d'Indochine, II, L'Humiliation* (Paris, 1964), 269. Author's translation.

17. Robert E. K. Thompson, *Defeating Communist Insurgency: Experiences from Malaya and Vietnam* (London, 1966), 146f.

18. N.D. Valeriano and C. T. R. Bohannan, *Counter-Guerilla Operations: The Philippine Experience* (New York, 1962), 209.

19. Bodard, *L'Enlisement,* 287.

20. Ibid., 444, 446.

21. Philippe Héduy, *Au Lieutenant des Taglaits* (Paris, 1960), 133. Author's translation.

22. Quoted by Robert Davezies, *Le front (Paris, 1959), 155.*

23. Pierre Leulliette, *Saint Michael and the Dragon* (New York, 1964), 153.

24. Dinerstein, ms. cited, 39.

25. Bernard Fall, *Street without Joy,* 3d edition (Harrisburg, Pa., 1963), 268.

26. Christopher Sykes, *Crossroads to Israel* (Cleveland, 1965), 285.

27. Bodard, *L'Enlisement,* 287.

28. Wolff, *Little Brown Brother,* 39.

29. B. L. Anderson, in A. H. Peterson, G. C. Reinhardt, and E. E. Conger (eds.), *Symposium on the Role of Airpower in Counterinsurgency and Unconventional Warfare: Allied Resistance to the Japanese on Luzon, World War II,* Rand Corporation, RM-3655-PR (1963), 27.

30. *The Economist* (April 23, 1966), 348.

31. Dennis Holman, *Bwana Drum* (London, 1964), 108.

32. Bernard Fall, *The Two Vietnams* (New York, 1966), 281.

33. Jean-Jacques Servan-Schreiber, *Lieutenant in Algeria* (New York, 1957), 70.

34. Warner, *The Last Confucian,* 160f.

35. Douglas Pike, *Viet Cong: The Organization and Techniques of the National Liberation Front of South Vietnam* (Cambridge, Mass., 1966), 248, 257f.

36. Galula, *Counterinsurgency,* 52.

37. Quoted by Héduy, *Au Lieutenant,* 293.

38. Leulliette, *Saint Michael,* 288f.

39. Lucas-Dubreton, *Napoleon,* 364.

40. Jacques Tissier, *Le Gâchis* (Paris, 1960), 73.

41. Héduy, *Au Lieutenant,* 267.

42. Valeriano and Bohannon, 171.

43. Bodard, *L'Humiliation,* 365.

44. Dinerstein, ms. cited, 39.

45. Galula, *Counterinsurgency,* 77.

46. Louis Delarue, *Avec les Paras du 1er R. E. P. et du 2e R. P./Ma.* (Paris, 1961), 24f. Author's translation.

47. Quoted by Claude Dufresnoy, *Des officiers parlent* (Paris, 1961), 124. Author's translation.

48. Bodard, *L'Enlisement,* 302-306.

PART V

THE PSYCHOLOGY OF POLITICAL ATTITUDES

Chapter 13

GERMAN ATTITUDES
AND NAZI LEADERSHIP

(with Paul Kecskemeti)

EDITOR'S NOTE: During and soon after World War II a number of works appeared seeking to explain the psychological basis for German acceptance of Nazi authoritarianism. Leites' and Kecskemeti's, one of the earliest of these, differs from comparable studies in several ways. First, it focuses on German reception of a particular German dictatorship–that is, it seeks to identify, in the language of politics under the Nazi regime, distinctive traits echoed in widely selected samples of German cultural products. The approach incidentally helps one to see why it was a German sociologist. Max Weber, who first used the term "charisma" in a political sense. Second, the study offers hypotheses concerning the origins of these distinctive cultural traits in the dynamic terms of psychoanalysis, stressing the ambivalent nature of German political and social attitudes. It gives attention to evidence of a temptation to "surrender to weakness" as well as to more familiar traits of the "compulsive character" such as "rigidity." Thus, it better accounts for behavior such as the unprecedented cruelty of some Nazi officials than does the more static approach linking character types to social structures. A third feature is the work's distinctive policy orientation. Prepared during the war for the United States Office of War Information, it is directly related to answering such questions as these: Under what conditions is anti-Nazi propaganda likely to be effective with Germans? Why are German assassination plots against Hitler repeatedly aborted? What themes would be most effectively stressed in allied attempts to "reform" the German public under military occupation?

The monograph, "Some Psychological Hypotheses on Nazi Germany," first published in mimeo as Document No. 60, Experimental Division for the Study of Wartime Communications, Office of War Information (Washington, D.C., 1945), appeared in The Journal of Social Psychology 26 (1947), 141-183; 27 (1948), 91-117, 241-270; and 28 (1948), 141-164. This selection is from 26, 158-165; and 27, 91-107, 253-270.

I. REVOLT AND SUBMISSION

Conformist attitudes towards authority were, on the surface, prevalent in German culture. They were, however, to a considerable extent defenses against anxiety-charged non-conformist tendencies. This corresponds to the typical ambivalence of the compulsive character towards authority.

The German scene was replete with indicators of this state of affairs; we shall mention a few of them.

(a) In German communications, references to "loyalty" and "betrayal" took a large place. Loyalty or "Treue" (which, as K. Lewin states, is typically equated with "obedience"[1]), was one of the key value symbols in German culture; the nuances of preoccupation with "Treue," however, often indicated "interfered with" tendencies towards "Untreue." One may recall that in many adolescents "ideals of . . . undying loyalty are . . . a reflection of the disquietude of the ego when it perceives the evanescence of . . . its . . . object-relations." Compulsive neurotics who in general are meticulous in keeping oaths and promises, at certain moments "try to do away with (aufzuräumen) this whole compulsion."[2]

"Treue" was frequently claimed to be a characteristically German quality: "deutsche Treue," "treudeutsch," "Nibelungentreue." In many references to "Treue," however, a certain *demonstrative* note betrayed preoccupation with "Untreue": cf. such privative adjectives as "bedingungslos," "unbedingt," "unwandelbar," "unabänderlich," "unverbrüchlich." It is a widespread German belief that "the Germans seem less firm and stable than other people."[3]

"Treue" was often praised in stereotyped formulas. "Die Treue ist das Mark der Ehre," was a widely quoted dictum of von Hindenburg. The SS chose a similar formula as its motto: "Meine Ehre heisst Treue." On the other hand, antonyms of "treu," such as "Treubruch," "Wortbruch," and even attenuated shades of meaning such as "Wankelmut," had an extraordinary emotional impact. Similar inferences may be drawn from presentations of disloyalty as "impossible" rather than undesirable. Thus Gauleiter Bohle stated (German home radio, April 20, 1944): "The German cannot and must not choose whether he wants to be a German or not—he has been placed in this world by Providence as a German."

In all these contexts "Treue" is largely understood not as fidelity to a partner, but as loyalty to an authority. This preoccupation indicates that the subject wants to be sure that nothing will interfere with his unconditional loyalty. The SS motto "Meine Ehre heisst Treue" carries this sentiment to ominous length: no act, however immoral, can dishonor me as long as I am loyal to my superiors. In this case, moral nihilism is consciously embraced, partially as an antidote against any guilt and urge to resist authority.

(b) One often encountered in German culture anxiety-charged preoccupations—often consciously or unconsciously fostered by authority itself—with the question whether one had fully satisfied authority demands. Correspondingly, the subject strongly preferred that authority demands be formulated in a complete specific and precise way (preferably in writing), so as to exclude doubt as to whether an act was justifiable ("verantwortet werden konnte") or arbitrary ("eigenmächtig"). A characteristic blame formula, used by superior talking to an inferior, is "Was fällt Ihnen eigentlich ein?"

Acts conforming to authority demands were apt to be tense.

The subject sometimes tended to do too much; this over-zealousness may in some instances have disguised anti-authority attitudes (cf. below). On the other hand, there was also a tendency to do nothing that was not expressly approved: "was nicht erlaubt ist, ist verboten."

(c) Another indicator of interfered with anti-authority tendencies was the violent rejection of critical attitudes towards authority. Whatever was communicated by the "massgebend" authorities was often accepted, and acted upon, in an unquestioning way, "stur," as the German expression has it. (In the Second World War, fanatical Nazis in the Army were sometimes called "sture Panzer" by their fellow-soldiers.)

In German political philosophy there were on the one hand frequent rejections of the idea of stable situations. A state of flux or "dynamism" was often preferred to "static" order. On the other hand, there was a widespread yearning for the *perfect* State in which all flux and criticism would finally come to rest. In this instance too, nothing short of the allegedly altogether exceptional suffices to banish doubt: the perfect State has divine attributes.

Many Germans found it painful to be loyal to a state which was held to fall short of "perfection." Hence the tendency either to accept claims of such perfection (as in the images of the Frederician, Bismarckian, Hitlerian state) or to disinterest oneself in politics. The admission of much criticism (stimulating doubt and indecisiveness) by the state itself—as in the Weimar Regime— was widely regarded as a confession of imperfection. It may be noted that many Germans were against the image of a Frederick, or Bismarck, or the reality and image of a Hitler, not primarily because these leaders are authoritarian, but because their State, although it claims to be the perfect State, in fact is not the perfect one.

Guilt about tendencies towards doubt and criticism led not only to their repression, but also to a high value status of "faith." "Gläube, glaubig" were key value terms of the Nazis who capitalized on the fact that many Germans have a strong (largely reaction-formative) tendency to keep their "faith" (if they have one) intact in face of the strongest temptations to disbelieve ("Anfechtungen"). "Faith" as the supreme value is, of course, part of the Lutheran tradition according to which "to have faith" is "to be saved." It is in line with this tradition if a contemporary German dreads "losing his faith" as the greatest disaster which could befall him (cf. on the other hand the beatific expression often accompanying the statement "ich glaube," "ich glaube an Deutschland," etc.).

We are here in the domain of a polarization typical of the compulsive character. For "criticism," which in the Nazi sphere was a counter-value term (often deprecated as "negative Kritik" or "zersetzende jüdische Kritik"), corresponds to various compulsive traits that of being "rechthaberisch" and "eigensinnig," and the inclination towards doubts. There was a time in German culture when "Kritik" had a high value status; from the time of Kant to the first World War, "Kritische Philosophie" was mostly regarded as the higher form of philosophy. Such "criticism," however, often was to a large extent disguised conformism.

In recent German culture, temptations to be critical of authority were combated in many ways. Where the ultimate argument of "faith" was not used, the subject often resorted to the thesis that the perspective (or the intelligence) of a mere private individual is too limited to judge the ways of authority properly. One may recall in this connection the well-known formula used by German prisoners of war "ich bin ja nur ein kleiner Landser. . . ." Many German prisoners refused to discuss political questions, declaring that they were not "trained" ("geschult") in things political.

Such statements, of course, may have had diverse motivations, such as the fear to offend—either the Nazis or the Allied interrogators. But in many cases another fear is important: that of damaging one's faith by giving full rein to one's criticism. The sentence "Politik sollen die machen die dazu berufen sind" is especially revealing, because "berufen" is originally a religious term ("chosen" or "called"): politics is nothing for the "laity." The underlying idea is not so much that political activity requires specialized skill (Nazism was rather unfavorable to an emphasis on differential skills), as that it is a matter of a special quasi-religious qualification ("charisma"). This is in part why the proper relationship to one's political leadership was so frequently "faith." Once this faith is won, nothing must be allowed to interfere with it; and the person consents to the deprivation of diminishing himself ("wir sind ja nur kleine Klecker"), rather than to risk losing his faith. Of course, such adoration is close to cursing. In another aspect of the same attitude the private individual washes his hands of the whole mess: the "kleiner Klecker" may take his revenge by denying any affiliation with authority-in-trouble.

When some event occurred which would reflect upon the government rather unfavorably, beginning doubt was often waived aside by the remark that while the whole thing is "incomprehensible" to the private individual, it is probably under the full control of authority: "es wird schon seinen Grund haben." Unfathomable constellations ("undurchschaubare Zusammenhänge") may conceal a "stroke of genius" ("genialer Schachzug") of the government, and thus be a token of the legitimacy of its authority.

Together with criticism, the initiation of positive proposals concerning future policy may be thoroughly interfered with. Many Second World War anti-Nazi prisoners of war abstained from putting forward any post-war plans for Germany; they appeared willing to leave decisions about post-war Germany to the Allied occupants. Such attitudes tend to be accompanied by intense reluctance against pressing demands on authority—unless authority has explicitly committed itself (e.g., by a legal norm) to their realization.

In certain cases, discussion of decisions of authority was not evaded but rather settled by some stereotyped formula to the effect that the very fact that an order emanates from the legitimate authority is sufficient to justify its fulfillment; thus any scrutiny as to the possible "human" aims it may serve, and as to the wisdom of the means chosen is excluded. Such formulae are, e.g.: "Befehl ist Befehl," "man tut seine Pflicht," "my highest God is my duty" (Frederick the Great). In not infrequent cases, the superego becomes highly heteronomous, the authority taking the place of the "conscience" of the subject; even decisions about "what one has to believe" are left to authority.

During protracted enterprises of uncertain outcome (especially war), this tendency often served to silence the demand to be given specific assurances about ultimate success before engaging oneself fully. When success seemed unlikely, "blind" obedience was of course particularly invoked by authority. (It is true that this blind obedience, dignified as "Treue"—was also usually presented as somehow ensuring ultimate success, while disobedience or "Untreue" was said to bring about ultimate doom in retribution.)

"Blind" obedience is, on the one hand, a defense against anti-authority tendencies; its ultimate effect, however, can be a strengthening of these tendencies. Erikson has noted that the intensity of anti-paternal tendencies in German culture was fostered by the low "integration of cultural ideal and educational method" in a widespread type of father-son relationship; since the father demands compliance with orders which are but little related to accepted ethical principles, there is relatively little "sense of obligation in command" and a low "sense of dignity in obedience."[4] In addition, the pattern of "blind" obedience may be invaded by the very anti-authority tendencies which it is warding off: if any order of one's "legitimate" authority appears as valid, any order of *any* authority occupying its place may be submissively reacted to. The behavior of isolated Second World War prisoners towards their captors frequently exemplified this tendency, which often appeared to the captors as "lack of personal conviction."

(d) As a further example of a defense mechanism against anti-authority tendencies in German culture, one may mention the high anxiety about possible "blasphemies" against authority, and reaction-formative deference rituals. One may recall that tendencies towards coprolalia are a "common finding in the compulsion neurosis"; "there is hardly a single compulsion neurosis without 'religious' symptoms—e.g., obsessive conflicts between faith and impulses to blaspheme.[5] Nazi word rituals presumably furnish characteristic illustrations of this conflict.

We may turn to some of the psychological factors making for much interference with anti-authority tendencies in German culture, and the resulting predominance, in consciousness, of submissive attitudes of devotion and respect: "Ehr furcht," "Hingabe," "Aufgehen in—," etc.

First of all, political authorities—as distinguished from the country as such, "Heimat," "Muttererde," which presumably have partially maternal significance—probably had largely paternal unconscious significances. Anti-paternal tendencies, however, were presumably typically profoundly stimulated as well as interfered with early in the life of very many German children; these interferences tended later to be transferred to authorities with paternal significance.

Second, the impact of acts of adult authorities on their subjects showed significant similarities to the impact of acts of fathers upon their children. This presumably called forth tendencies to establish anew corresponding interferences (with certain differences of course).

For both situations one may mention two factors resulting in profound interference with tendencies directed against (early familial and adult extra-familial) authorities, and making for ostensibly spontaneous positive reactions towards them.

(a) Strong anxiety-charged beliefs that any overt act directed against authority would fail (that the authority is unassailable).

(b) Strong anxiety charged beliefs that authority will react intensely to overt acts directed against it with grave deprivational consequences for the aggressor.

In recent history the (esoteric) political theorem seems to have been widely and consciously held by German elites (with the partial exception of the Weimar regime) that the foremost method of preventing hostile acts of the governed, and winning their "spontaneous" love reactions, consisted precisely in maintaining the two beliefs mentioned. Hence representatives of authority were usually taught never to lose their aplomb ("unerschütterliche Sicherheit des Auftretens") and to react to hostile acts from below with trenchant severity ("mit unnachsichtlicher Schärfe").

The higher in such a situation the estimate of the power of authority, the stronger the belief that aggression would fail and bring retribution, the more complete the interference with anti-authority tendencies. This is one reason why in such a culture ostensible "love" reactions towards authority depend to a high extent on beliefs in its high power, while beliefs in its weakness sharply releases hostile reactions.[6] Further, the greater the deprivations which authority has already inflicted on the subject (which may appear as indicators of power) the more the latter will be convinced that aggression would fail and bring retribution. Hence ostensible "love" reactions to authority tend in such a culture to covary to a high degree with its severity and hostile reactions with its gentleness. Such reaction trends are of course by no means uncommon in other cultures. What is being put forward as a hypothesis here is that they were highly conspicuous in German culture. Correspondingly, Germans not infrequently seemed to perceive the instability of their attitudes towards authority in response to changing power-situations. Second World War prisoners sometimes declared "I am no longer a Nazi at the moment."

These reactions, which were to some extent conscious, were accompanied by various beliefs, such as the belief that power is an indicator of "Recht," and powerlessness of "Unrecht." Or power was glorified as a value in itself ("das imponiert mir"). In recent history, it repeatedly occurred that the popularity of a statement or of a regime sharply increased with increasing power and ruthlessness behind it, and sharply decreased with a loosening grip. The Weimar regime was greatly hampered by the fact that it was associated not only with "defeat" but also with "powerlessness"; when it showed what appeared as "weakness," its popularity sharply declined. Second World War German prisoners of war often indicated that they would withdraw allegiance from the Nazi regime in case of defeat.

One factor stabilizing the subject's allegiance to authority was, however, the subject's tendency to exaggerate the power of authority. Frequently, high power apparently continued (more or less consciously) to be attributed to authority as long as its accustomed organizational forms were preserved. Thus German Second World War prisoners' morale depended to a considerable extent upon whether semblances of the organization of the Wehrmacht could be preserved in captivity or not. Germans also frequently exaggerated the steepness of power and deference pyramids in cultures outside Germany, projecting the German pyramid shape onto them. During the Second World War, the belief was widespread in Germany (and, of course, was deliberately fostered by Nazi propaganda) that critics of the government in the U.S. and Britain were shot without any ado.

It is noteworthy in this connection that omniscience—including a complete knowledge of the acts and feelings of the subject by virtue of an "all-seeing eye"—was frequently more or less consciously attributed to authority. A naval officer said in a broadcast on Hitler's birthday in 1944, describing an interview with the Führer: "Ich hatte das Gefühl: dem kannst du nichts vormachen. Er sieht durch dich sozusagen hindurch." This feeling betrays fear of being "found out" in case of the slightest deviation from conformism, even without any overt act of hostility. Germans critical of Nazism often attempted to silence guilt feelings about their passivity by saying "ich kann ja nichts dagegen machen" "man muss ja mit den Wöfen heulen," etc. (with, of course, a very considerable reality basis for such judgments). Complete conformism, accordingly, appeared frequently as the most desirable condition, first, because it seemed to diminish the danger inherent in anti-authority slips arising from "mental reservations"; and second, because it facilitated acquiescence in ("making the best of") a situation which seemed unalterable anyhow.

Allegiance to authority was further stabilized by the projection of the subject's own interfered-with aggressive tendencies against authority to the authority itself, thus increasing the estimate of the severity of retribution in case of non-conformism.

II. HARDNESS AND SOFTNESS

A widespread valuation in German culture extolled "hardness" (as a symptom of "strength") and repudiated "softness" (as a symptom of "weakness").

By "hardness" is meant a readiness to accept extreme deprivations in order to avoid being subdued by an enemy, or in order to satisfy authority demands. These two attitudes are closely related to each other: to "give in" is contrary to the norm sponsored by authority. The deprivations accepted for the sake of continued resistance may have been greater than those which the enemy was expected to impose after surrender; the idea of surrender aroused intense anxiety, not only because the victorious enemy would impose deprivations on the self, but because admitting defeat, i.e., accepting the rôle of the weaker party, appeared intolerable in itself. Hardness in accepting deprivations, whether as a concomitant of fighting an enemy or of obeying other authority injunctions, was on the other hand a source of heightened self-esteem as well as diminished anxiety and guilt. In addition, it was often taken to be a guarantee of future indulgences (of which one has shown oneself "worthy"). Softness was a source of lowered self-esteem, heightened anxiety and guilt, and fraught with threats of being punished by extreme deprivations.

As to hardness in resistance, it was during Germany's recent history comparatively easy—as is well known—to induce many Germans to live up to this demand. As the deprivations imposed by the Second War grew in intensity, and pessimism about its outcome deepened, Nazi propaganda increased its efforts to capitalize on the tendencies towards "hardness" described above. The consequences of a "moment of weakness" were presented in the direct light. The sacrifices imposed by the war were typically presented as "tests" ("Nervenproben" or "Belastungsproben"). The individual was given a choice between what we might call a "positive performance" ("saving" himself and his group, etc.) and a "negative performance" (in which case he would "give himself up" and also his group). A frequent implication—related to omnipotence phantasies—was that Germans can be beaten only "by themselves," i.e., by an act of "treason" against themselves. Should they commit this "crime," they would "deserve" defeat with all its dire consequences (cf. Hitler's November 8, 1943 speech). This way of presenting things was presumably designed to strengthen already close association between "strength" and "morality" on the one hand, and "weakness" and "immorality" on the other.

Typical symbols about the "negative" and the "positive" performance reveal intense fears of performing negatively and the largely reaction-formative nature of the "positive performance" in idea and act. For instance, the positive performance was often presented as the negation of the negative performance. Similar inferences may be drawn from frequent protestations that one will "never" surrender (affirmations which are presumably also intended to undo past negative performances). Sometimes, fears of surrender were consciously expressed and focused upon a "weak" sector in the German people or character. Thus the Rheinisch-Westfälische Zeitung on September 11, 1944, denounced in typical vein "the usual German tendency towards self-surrender out of . . . weakness." The same paper on August 20, 1944, wrote: "Frequently and not without justification have we been described as a people without strength of character. But this time we will not give in." (This idea is, of course, merely a variant of the "Germans can be beaten only by Germans" theme: all the Germans need to win any war is "strength of character"; whenever they lost in the past, it was because they were lacking in this.)

It is consistent with this "narcissistic" tendency that in the standard elaborations of the hardness-softness variable in German culture very little attention was focused on the enemy; the spotlight was on the reactions of Germans.

The major epithets characterizing the positive and negative performances were, as already implied, "hard" and "soft," "strong" and "weak." On the one hand, there is "stark sein," "innere Stärke," "Charakterstärke," "Charakterfestigkeit"; on the other hand, "schwach werden," "Schwächlichkeit," "Charakterschwäche." Both pairs of opposites (also "straff" and "schlapp") were frequently used in classifying all kinds of things; acts of aggression, of course, appeared as "hard," while love and benevolence tendencies, and objects associated with them, were presented as "soft." Thus "Kultur" was often associated with "softness." Heavy metals were favorite incarnations of "hardness": "eiserne Nerven haben," "das eiserne Herz" (a Goebbels formula). Hitler asked the Hitler youth to be, among other things, "hart wie Kruppstahl." (The anti-Nazi organization sponsored by the Social Democrats in the last period of the Weimar regime called itself "Eiserne Front.") A closely related pair of opposites was "Nachgiebigkeit–Unnachgiebigkeit," with the positive value accent on the latter.

The positive performance was pictured as one which maintains *intact* the person or group by resisting enemy forces bent upon destroying its structure. The negative performance was perceived correspondingly as resulting in the person's or the group's disintegration. Characteristic expressions referring to the positive performance were: Bestehen, beharren, standhalten, durchhalten, ungebrochen sein. On the other hand, expressions characterizing a disposition towards the negative performance stressed the aspect of disintegration: zersetzt, zermürbt. To give in to pressure was spoken of as "sich breitschlagen lassen." The critical test itself was sometimes referred to as a "Zerreissprobe."

A prominent group of expressions stressed *firmness* against onrushing hostile forces: Festigkeit, Festbleiben; fest wie ein Fels im Meer; this contrasts with "ins Wanken geraten," as the beginning of the negative performance. A closely related group of much used metaphors referred to *erectness* of position in warding off enemy forces seeking to hurl one to the ground: in allen Stürmen aufrecht, such nicht klein kriegen (unterkriegen) lassen, sich nicht niederzwingen lassen, ungebeught, unbeugsam. Predisposition for the negative performance, on the other hand, is "Rückgratlosigkeit." On the point of yielding, one may "sich aufraffen." The accomplished negative performance is described as "zusammenklappen."

As for the *subjective* side of the positive and negative performance, the typical stereotype was that in the positive performance, the subject retains control over the strong dysphoric affects accompanying deprivation (selbstbeherrschung), while in the negative performance, the subject is overwhelmed by affect or gradually loses its power over it (nur noch ein Nervenbündel sein, Nervenaufzehrung, Ruin des Nervensystems, Verlust der Nerven Kraft).

There was a characteristic tendency to regard *all* psychic factors as tending towards the negative performance: thus "menschlich" was closely associated with "Schwache" and "Starke" with "Keine Nerven haben." ("Nerven" sometimes referred to physiological elements as in the phrases mentioned before; and sometimes—as in the phrase just cited—to subjective components of anxiety.) Control of affect is referred to as "unerschütterliche Ruhe wahren," "grosse innere Ruhe," "Kaltblütigkeit," "Gelassenheit," "souveräne Uberlegenheit." There was a tendency to deny anxiety in the vein of "wir Deutsche fürchten Gott und sonst nichts auf der Welt." On the other hand, there is "seelisch aufgelöst sein," "seelisch zugrunde gehen."

In the positive performance, the *expression* of pain is greatly interfered with: "nicht mit der Wimper zucken," "die Zähne zusammenbeissen." On the other hand, the negative performance is characterized by full expression of distress. Thus uninhibited tearfulness characterized the reactions of many

World War II German soldiers after they themselves (or their units or superiors) had surrendered. But extreme protesting complaints about deprivations imposed by the enemy were included in the image of the positive performance. (Cf. the larmoyant complaints about the Versailles treaty or Goebbels' lamentations over the persecutions the Nazis were allegedly subjected to under the Weimar regime.) Thus, the rule was: deprivations imposed by one's own authority must be borne with minimum, deprivations imposed by an "enemy" must be reacted to with a maximum of protesting and complaining. As Robert Ley said in Vienna in November, 1944, "if we have to sacrifice and renounce things, we may do so in the full knowledge of the reasons and in the hope of a wonderful future to which we thereby acquire a right; what we cannot bear is that such sacrifices and deprivations should be imposed arbitrarily by an enemy, as a punishment." And the same Ley wrote in the Angriff of September 3, 1944, that "we Germans do not complain that our destiny is hard and that it imposes cruel tests and inhuman trials on us; we National Socialists are accustomed to being treated ruthlessly and do not want it otherwise."

As for *overt action* in the "positive performance," it is characterized by extreme perseverance, regardless of the magnitude of the risks (Unentwegtheit, Beharrlichkeit; und wenn die Welt voll Teufel wär, es muss uns doch gelingen; trotz allem, Todesverachtung, Todesmut). Courage (Mut) is the central term summarizing all these desiderata. That "Mut" was to a considerable extent reaction-formative against spontaneous "weakness" tendencies is well illustrated by the "motto" given out at a Nazi party meeting in August of 1944 at Gelsenkirchen by the Deputy Gauleiter Schaller: "Herrgott, lass uns nicht feige werden" (i.e., do not allow us to commit the crime of surrender but maintain us on the road of our duty, that of being "courageous").

In describing the proper attitude in a crisis, Goebbels (in Front und Heimat, quoted by *DNB* on June 5, 1944) mentioned the following four desirable traits: Mut, Entschlossenheit, Kaltblütigkeit, and Verantwortungsfreudigkeit. According to the preceding discussion, it may be assumed that in reality these traits were often lacking and at least just as often reaction-formative when they were not lacking.

We may now discuss some of the presumable major unconscious significances of the positive and negative performance in a crisis. (These considerations are also largely applicable to the closely associated positive and negative performances in "dishing it out" rather than "taking it," as well as to positive and negative performances in inflicting deprivations upon the self, i.e., "Härte gegen sich selbst" and self-indulgence.)

1. The positive performance is presumably frequently unconsciously an act of father-identification (a "masculine" act), while the negative performance tends to have the significance of a mother-identification (a "feminine"

act). If we confront the images of the "positive" and the "negative" performance (as given above) with the child's images of paternal and maternal
behavior and demands in the patriarchal family, it will be evident that the
"positive" performance shows an affinity with the father and the "negative"
perfo mance with the mother. The position acts and values of the father are
"strong" and "hard," those of the mother "soft" and "weak." (Apparently,
the following family situation was not infrequent in German culture: the
father proposes to chastise the male child; the mother is against it, but is too
weak and subdued to interfere; hence she absents herself with signs of distress
from the scene of the punishment.)

What is the rôle of father and mother identifications in the character type
here considered? (a) The typical solution of the oedipal situation presumably
involves a superego modelled on the father opposing other aspects of the
personality modelled on the mother. (b) The anal-sadistic regression of the
compulsive character involves the coexistence of intense active "masculine,"
"sadistic" tendencies on the one hand and intense passive ("feminine")
tendencies on the other.

2. The negative performance is presumably unconsciously associated with
libidinal oedipal tendencies of the male child towards his mother; thus the
intense anxiety connected with these tendencies, and the strong interference
against them following the liquidation of the oedipus situation, tend to color
the negative performance correspondingly.

3. The negative performance is presumably unconsciously associated with
passive homosexual tendencies towards the father which are also related to
identification with the mother. The anxiety and interference directed towards
these tendencies then tend to extend to the negative performance.

Many male Germans seem on all three counts thus far mentioned to be
anxiously and guiltily aware of strong "feminine" tendencies in themselves to
which they oppose a largely reaction-formative "masculinity."

Therefore, "masculinity" often has "duty" character: it has to be striven
for, strenuously conquered and defended, rather than simply being given or
absent. At first, masculine behavior patterns are inculcated by the father who
combats maternal influences which would tend to keep the boy "attached to
his mother's apron strings" and make a pampered "Muttersohnchen" of him.
Later, the school and the army take over the task of "making men" out of
boys with feminine tendencies. In all these situations, "masculine" behavior is
at a premium.

The male German's attitude towards women has often been marked by
conscious and unconscious fear, aggression and contempt; the same is true of
objects having a "feminine" significance, e.g., the arts[7] (the Nazi characteristically describes the "Prussian aristocracy" as "something masculine and at
the same time artistic and cultivated"). These attitudes partly take over the
father's "superiority" vis-à-vis the mother, and partly represent reaction-

formations against positive tendencies towards the mother. In heterosexual relations, the male partner's attitude has presumably been often characterized by a polarization between sentimentality and brutality.

4. The positive performance is presumably unconsciously an act of obedience to, and desexualized love for, the father. The negative performance, on the other hand, connotes disobedience to, and aggression against, the father. (It may be noted here that in the compulsive character obedience in accepting deprivations sometimes has an unconsciously aggressive significance against authority, e.g., by being obedient "regardless of the consequences," the subject may, with unconscious reproachful demonstrativeness, let things reach the point of complete or partial self-destruction.)

The more severe the deprivational "test" is, the greater will be the temptation of behaving negatively. That a test is a "hard" one means that in many phases of the conflict the enemy turns out to be superior, and forces the self, and the authorities recognized by the self, to bow to his will (e.g., to abandon an important position). In the measure, however, as the (paternal) authority turns out to be weak, the self's unfavorable tendencies towards it will be strengthened; by the same token, favorable tendencies towards the enemy will become stronger. This is implied in the close association of "strength" with "morality" which is typical in the character type involved. The German domestic situation after Hitler's coming to power in January of 1933 illustrates this point. The more ruthlessly the Nazis dealt with the political organizations of democratic Germany, the more they procured at least the benevolent neutrality of large numbers of their rank-and-file who turned away from their former allegiances—which now appeared "wrong," because they were weak. This well known example shows how superior strength of a formerly "hostile" power may result in at least partial transfers of allegiance. The behavior of many German soldiers in World War II also displayed this characteristic. In general, their attitude towards their major enemies tended to grow more or less favorable in direct relation to their estimate of these enemies' power. Forecasts of enemy victory were often accompanied by expressions of readiness to transfer allegiance totally, e.g., by emigration. "One should start learning English." The mechanisms involved were often partially conscious, i.e., the enemy's strength or weakness was expressly acknowledged as a major datum determining the favorableness or unfavorableness of one's attitude towards him. Enemy victories were frequently followed by mellowed feelings. "They can't be as bad as that" (implicitly: "God is with the stronger battalions").

As long as these tendencies towards renegadism are not consummated, they provoke strongly reaction-formative counter-tendencies; at the height of the crisis, both antagonistic tendencies reach maximum strength. The counter-tendencies may assume various forms of which the intensely asserted obligation of loyalty to an authority in distress *("nun erst recht")* is one.

Such loyalty, however, was seldom invoked as the exclusive motive for continued resistance; it was usually coupled with the assertion of the ultimate recovery of superior strength. The prevalent tendency in German culture was to back the winner and to shun lost causes. Those who fought for lost causes largely did so by mistake.

5. The positive performance may have the unconscious significance of a licit act of anal retention; the negative performance may stand for an illicit act of anal expulsion. One may recall the drinking ceremonies of students' corporations (Verbindungen): a test situation was created in which the positive performance is retention. Certain characteristic terms referring to the positive performance, such as those of the "Selbstbeherrschung" group, may have had a partially anal-retentive significance.

6. The positive performance may be accompanied by phantasies of omnipotence. One may recall that certain types of compulsive characters are "indulging in ascetic performances in order . . . to show themselves that they can do it."[8]

7. The positive performance may be accompanied by self-admiration and by conscious or unconscious intent to induce admiration by others. Its "restraint" aspect ("lerne leiden ohne Klagen") presumably often has a conscious or unconscious demonstrative character; the person "zeigt, dass er im Stillen leidet"; he shows "auffallig verborgenes Leiden."[9]

(a) *Beliefs about conditions and consequences of the reaction types.* The images of the "positive" and "negative" performance in a test situation were accompanied by characteristic beliefs about the conditions and the consequences of these performances.

One such belief was that the chances of proper performance in a crisis vary directly with the amount of previous training ("Schulung," "harte Schule") in accepting deprivations. "Hardening" ("Abhärtung," "Ertüchtigung," "Austreibung der Weichheit") was regarded as a major condition of the positive performance; this is related to the emphasis on early discipline making "men" out of boys. There was the stereotype of the hero achieving greatness "under the blows of fate," and conversely, that of the person straying from the right path ("auf die schiefe Ebene geraten") due to unchecked earlier indulgence ("Verwöhnung").

As to the consequences of the two types of performance, the major belief was that the hedonic balance will ultimately correspond to the value of the performance in the critical test situation. In other words, a positive performance, no matter how great deprivations it involves, will ultimately be rewarded by indulgences more than compensating for the deprivations; a negative performance—regardless of the momentary relief it may bring—will ultimately result in maximal deprivations, i.e., lastly, total annihilation (in the Nazi phrase: "schwach werden bedeutet Untergang"). These relationships were frequently taken for granted, without detailed explanation. Such beliefs are presumably related to omnipotence phantasies on the one hand and to the unconscious parental significance of the external agencies determining the hedonic balance on the other: the parents will cease meting out punishment only if the child obeys parental injunctions.

A closely related belief was that the acceptance—in the vein of a price paid—of a certain amount of deprivations is a necessary (or: sufficient) condition for the attainment of a proportionate amount of indulgences (cf. the stereotypes "Preussen hat sich grossgehungert"; "es wird einem nichts geschenkt").

(b) *The Manipulation of "Zusammenbruch."* Guilt and anxiety concerning a "collapse" (e.g., military surrender) frequently lead to the use of a number of devices which are analogous to those utilized to combat guilt about acts of aggression. Thus, one encounters denials, displacements of responsibility, and justifications. The following devices used in connection with military desertion and surrender may be mentioned here:

In many cases in the Second World War, German soldiers who deserted and surrendered to the enemy arranged circumstances so that it could appear to others as well as to themselves as if they had been captured against their own will. Even when there was successful self-deception, awareness of what had really happened presumably remained on deeper levels. In cases where the nature of the act committed was not concealed in consciousness, euphemistic terms were usually preferred to blunt ones (such as "Uberlaufen"), which were tensely avoided.

Where surrender as such was not denied, guilt and anxiety were frequently reduced by the use of "regular" forms for this irregular content. Thus collective and "organized" surrender was vastly preferred to individual acts. The individual's responsibility was thus diminished.

Surrender was often excused as legitimate according to accepted military standards, e.g., the enemy was "overwhelmingly superior"; but such standard behavior often showed characteristic nuances. Thus the enemy was sometimes asked to stage a token battle (or a demonstration of his forces) "proving" that further resistance would indeed be useless.

A typical excuse was that the "load" of the situation had become "unbearable," i.e., that the subject was prevented by physiological factors, or something akin to them, from continuing to resist. "Nervous breakdown" (Versagen der Nerven, die Nerven verlieren, uebermässige Nervenbelastung, etc.) and "complete exhaustion" were the typical physiological reasons given for one's "collapse," for which one is not responsible as they are forces majeures. (The excuse was less strong than that of hopeless military inferiority; it was not "honorable" to yield to a "Nervenzusammenbruch," but just barely excusable. A "hero" would not succumb to it. Hitler once said in this sense: "Der deutsche Soldat hat keine Nerven." German medical officers in general were reluctant to recognize "battle fatigue" and similar conditions as legitimate diseases, but they more easily accepted as bona fide maladies those cases in which psychogenic symptoms had a prominent somatic facade. Transfer of allegiance from one authority to another was also often justified by the generally "unbearable" character of the situation. Typical expressions used in this context were: "Es kann so nicht mehr weitergehen," "es muss anders werden." These stock phrases accompanied the decline and fall of the Weimar republic—and of the Nazi regime.

III. DESTRUCTIVENESS AND CORRECTNESS

The behavior of the compulsive character is "pervaded by manifestations of . . . sadism or of reaction-formations against sadism." "Overt or concealed tendencies to cruelty, or reaction-formations against them, are . . . findings in all compulsion neuroses." Psychoanalytic observers have called attention to many related traits in compulsive characters: their "meanness," "angry outbursts" and "sullen fractiousness." Freud found them "garrulous," "defiant," and "quaelerisch"; Abraham described them as "malicious." They are "difficult to live with." All this indicates a high propensity to unprovoked aggressiveness, manifested either directly or by hostile attitudes such as "Schadenfreude." Besides such "gratuitous" aggressiveness, one also finds a high degree of vindictiveness, which was noted by Freud. "The desire for revenge . . . is . . . in many people of this type . . . developed to an extraordinary extent."

Aggressive behavior in compulsive characters is related to a variety of factors, of which the following may be mentioned:

1. Fixations on, and regressions to, early tendencies to destroy objects by anal expulsion.

2. Intense urges toward domination.

3. Reaction-formations against "passive," "feminine" (homosexual) tendencies in males. Aggressiveness may in such contexts have the significance of counteracting fears of being "yellow." One of the major types of highly destructive Nazi activist was the "elegant pansy."

4. Aggressive tendencies may aim at executing, reinforcing, and demonstrating identification with the patriarchal father. The high intensity of this identification may in turn be a defense against a high intensity of positive oedipal tendencies directed towards the mother. Another major type of destructive Nazi activist was the "baby face" type.

This variety, as well as the preceding one, is accompanied by the conception that aggression is desirable as "manly" and "strong," as against "weak" and "feminine" non-aggressiveness. In this context, aggressiveness may achieve the status of norm-fulfilment.

5. Intense aggressive tendencies tend to result from high balances of deprivations over indulgences in early life.

6. Aggressive tendencies may aim at counteracting the person's feeling of not being "real."

7. Aggressive tendencies may aim at undoing past failures of aggressive moves. Undoing, it may be recalled, is a characteristic mechanism in the compulsive personality.

8. Aggressive tendencies may operate to alleviate anxiety and guilt accompanying doubts as to whether one has performed correctly.

9. Aggressive tendencies accompany complusive "orderliness" and " "purity" strivings in the face of targets presented as affected by disorder and dirt. According to the general hypothesis proposed in this study, aggressive tendencies associated with the compulsive character were frequent in German culture (though doubtlessly to considerably differing degrees among different groups), while at the same time their completion against a large number of objects was severely interfered with by the norm-system on which life was oriented. The aggression pent up under the impact of the restraining norms was, however, released in their "interstices."

Open aggression was mostly found in three types of situations. First, in characteristic outbreaks of rage (Jachzorn) Diesel speaks of a German "nervous excitability."[10] Second, where aggression could be construed as counter-aggression, e.g., when a person usually protected by restraining norms had committed an offense. Third, against individuals and groups not protected by restraining norms, i.e., "enemies."

The first type of aggression is not calculated by the aggressor; the fit of rage seizes him more or less "against his own will," breaking down his usual control. In the second type one often has the impression that the individual has been more or less consciously waiting for an opportunity to commit aggression. Certain characteristic German expressions have an undertone of long pent up expectation: "Na, dem werd ich's aber zeigen! Den werden wir uns mal vornehmen!"

The third type of aggression was not merely "excusable," as a fit of rage was, and not merely "justified" as counter-aggression against an offending member of the in-group was. It was not only institutionalized as elsewhere in Western culture, but also endowed with much prestige of norm-fulfilment, as is well known. Particularly in this type of aggression, but also in the first two types mentioned, the psychic emphasis was on the act of aggression rather than on its target which was widely interchangeable.

German language showed an important rôle of aggression terms, such as "jemandem auf die Füsse treten," "einen Fusstritt geben," "in die Fresse hauen," "vor den Kopf stossen," "auf Biegen und Brechen," "über den Haufen werfen," "auf die Knie zwingen," "rücksichtslos durchgreifen," and, in general, the prominent use of the verb "schlagen" (or "hauen") in expressions such as "auf den Kopf schlagen," "sich verhauen," and in compounds such as the Nazi term "schlagartig." Certain other widely used expressions characterized the "electrically charged" social atmosphere, such as "Krach," "Mord und Totschlag."

Images of the enemy (within and outside of the culture), especially the images proposed by the Nazis, contained a large number of terms denoting an aggression extreme in its methods and effects. Various kinds of political language were full of expressions such as "Vernichtungswille," "Zerstör-ungswut," "Mordbrenner," "Bartholomäusnacht," "in Grund und Boden vernichten." (Such extreme charges, against enemies, of course, were often projections of aggressive tendencies of the self.)

When speaking of himself, the individual often admitted or alleged "uncontrollable" rage ("rasende Wut"); one may recall the use of the verb "rasen" (instead of "laufen") in the Hitler Youth. But it is decisive to note that such an individual may be subject to "uncontrollable" rage when dealing with an inferior (or equal) in status; when the offender is a superior, he will rather spontaneously "control" himself. This selection of targets of com-pleted aggression is characteristic of the personality structure here described. It can be in part understood if we remember that, in early stages of the life history of individuals of this character type, intense aggressive tendencies against powerful father objects have been severely interfered with. As a result, aggression tendencies in later life will be restrained or completed according to whether the power imputed to the prospective object of aggression is high or low. (Aggression out of "manliness" aspirations also often requires the certainty of success, i.e., a weak adversary, although not without qualifica-tions.) Thus the consciousness of power of a subject of this type may come to depend on the range and effect of his completed acts of aggression, and on the anxiety levels of others concerning his future aggressions.

Although it is impossible at present to give an exact survey of acts of aggression in German culture, whereby the proportion of completed acts of aggression against relatively powerless and relatively powerful targets could be ascertained, it seems to be safe to assume, on the basis of the available "impressionistic" evidence, the completed acts of aggression against relatively powerless objects were far more frequent. The behavior of Nazis, at any rate, showed this characteristic to an extraordinary degree: they were always careful to attack only their enemies after having isolated them, and, in general, to attack only without deliberately taking chances. SS practices apparently included violence against unduly exhausted members, and a major Nazi type of junior officer, the "Pimpf" or "Bubi" type, as he was designated by his victims in the Wehrmacht, closely approximated the "bully-coward" stereotype. It may be assumed that this pattern of distribution of aggressive acts was also highly diffused in pre-Nazi German culture, although not carried to such lengths as under Nazism.

Among the implications of this pattern is the "insatiability" of aggression: as each successful aggression diminishes the power of the target, it increases the probability of subsequent acts of aggression against it. Another implication is the absence, or out-and-out rejection, of "fair play" ideologies, to the extent that the aggression pattern in question enters consciousness. Those ideologies tend to be replaced by maxims of the "Wer fällt, den soll man auch noch stossen" type. Many German soldiers of the Second World War showed a conscious preference for wars against weak opponents and justified Nazi war policy—or sometimes even German atrocities committed in the East—by the initially plausible under-estimation of enemy power. (This type of justification co-existed with the more usual one according to which Germany was "forced" to go to war.) On the other hand, Nazi propaganda often pretended to criticize Germans for their excessive adherence to fair play; the Nazi front newspaper Die Südfront, January 18, 1944, complained about the German "Nationalübel, grundsätzlich für den Schwächeren Partei zu ergreifen." Such grossly false assertions were probably made in the conscious or unconscious intention to alleviate guilt about aggressiveness.

The character type which displays this pattern of aggression also tends to show a similar distribution of positive and negative emotional and value attitudes towards objects, that is to say, objects which are deemed powerful tend to be loved, and positively valued, while objects deemed powerless tend to be hated and negatively valued. (Correspondingly, a gain of power will be accompanied by strengthened love impulses; a loss of power will elicit, or intensify, hate impulses.) It is especially characteristic of this type that moral valuations follow the same pattern: the powerful object is morally good, the weak one, morally bad.

A paradoxical situation may arise if a subject of this type suffers severe deprivations at the hands of a powerful enemy, so that he is led to acknowledge his own weakness and enemy's strength. In view of the above pattern, the subject may then show a tendency to love the enemy and hate himself. German morale, and loyalty to Nazism, in the Second War was threatened by this type of situation.

By virtue of the same pattern, the character type in question will tend to interpret any concession made by an adversary and his reliance on non-violent techniques (e.g., negotiation) as signs of weakness, and hence react to them with increased aggressiveness. This point has often been made in connection with certain ill-fated attempts at "appeasement."

The compulsive character tends to project on to others the relationship between power and aggression specific to himself; hence he often under-estimates the magnitude of the counter-aggression he will arouse against himself. Since he might not stand up against someone whom he deems decisively more powerful than himself, and also tends to take manifestations of violence as indicators of power, he tends to exaggerate the effects of threats and acts of violence on certain other character types. This type of mistake has repeatedly proved the undoing of policies of Germany's rulers.

Certain techniques of intimidation which were successful in German culture often boomeranged when applied elsewhere.

IV. ORDER AND DISORDER

"Orderliness" has, of course, often been noted as a dominant trait in German culture. "Ordnung" was a high value term, and "Ordnung muss sein" an imperative which generally carried conviction and overrode many other postulates. If something is "in Ordnung," or a problem "bereinigt," it is all right; ·revolutionary intentions were often expressed by a determination "gründlich Ordnung zu machen" or "aufzuräumen." Order and cleanliness expressions thus stood prominently for desired states of affairs; conversely, disorder—dirt expressions stood for undesired situations: "Unordnung," "Chaos," "Verwirrung," "Konfusion," "heilloses Durcheinander," "Schweinerei" were terms which played a high and highly anxiety-charged rôle. Characteristically, "Ordnung" usually carried the connotation of something "artificially" imposed rather than spontaneously emerging.

Germans themselves often declared love of order to be a distinctive trait in which they differed from other nations. In describing the German soldier's "nostalgia for the homeland," Goebbels wrote (Das Reich, April 30, 1944):

> Sie vermissten ausserhalb unseres Reiches die gewohnte öffentliche Ruhe und Ordnung, die Präzision des Verkehrslebens, die Sauberkeit des Strassenbildes, die solide und zuverlässige Haltung ... der Menschen, die Stetigkeit der nationalen Führung. ..."

Speaking about the same time, a Gauleiter (K. Gerland, of Kassel) named "order" and "cleanliness" (besides "loyalty" and "honesty") as the "foundations" of life.

A high cathexis of orderliness-cleanliness may foster a high rôle of propriety judgments as against ethical judgments. (This may be related to the frequently "absolute" parental prohibitions on certain infantile phallic activities and destructive tendencies as distinguished from the necessarily more accommodating regulation of anal processes.) [11] In the everday life (as against the more reaction-formative ideologies) of German culture propriety evaluations seem to have played a high role as against ethical evaluations. One may recall the rôle of terms like "Anstand" ("anständig" shows the approach to ethics from a propriety basis), "Sitte," "ungebührlich," "das gehört sich (nicht)," "Unfug," "Skandal."

It is well known that desires for a complete and specific norm system were widespread in German culture. E. Diesel quotes an official statement to the effect that "the length of time a piece of carbon paper may be expected to last is dependent on the quality of the individual product so that it is impossible to lay down any definite rule which shall be universally applicable," and adds: "this last clause gives expression to the German's most deeply cherished desire."[12] On the other hand fascination with extreme deviations from norms was indicated, e.g., by typical images of the "Genie" above the law.

The desired orderliness may even go beyond the conformity of reality to a complex system of norms and include its conformity to factual allegations which have psychologically become independent of their empirical basis: "higher . . . officials have been known to complain to the inhabitants of a particular place that there is something not in order . . . because it (the place) does not quite agree with the description in the guide book."[13]

On the other hand the tendencies combated by reaction-formative orderliness found various incomplete expressions. To mention a minor one, the "peculiar significance we (Germans) attach to mountain climbing" may have been related to the fact that "the higher parts of the Alps" are the "only regions into which Germans can still escape from the cramping orderliness of civilization."[14]

Manifest violations of conformity to norms were usually reacted to with great intensity; the maintenance of "order" was frequently, with probably significant explicitness and emphasis, considered to be the chief function of the state and of the organs of law. The calculable character of law (Rechtssicherheit) was often quite consciously considered as more important than the intrinsic "rightness" of a legal system. Extremely "unjust" laws were widely accepted under the Nazi regime since the mode of their promulgation was considered "Ordnungsmässig"; but criticism of the few instances of "disorderly" Nazi "activism" was widespread and spontaneous.

As to the demand for regularity of events through time, Germans were in many situations highly intolerant of irregularities in the time-sequence of acts of others affecting them. This could, for example, be observed in the case of supply difficulties of German Second World War soldiers.

"Orderliness" of action was widely regarded as a major indicator of Power. Hence the incessant emphasis of Nazi propaganda in the defeat phases of World War II on orderliness-in-retreat. (A German home radio report on the Western front said August 29, 1944: "The majority of our formations left the pocket in so orderly fashion that it defied imagination.") Conversely, a high degree of orderliness of enemy action was an intensely demoralizing factor.

As to the striving for totality, there was the significant rôle of prefixes like "All-," "Gesamt-," "Ganz-," "Voll-," "Total-." This was accompanied by much anxiety lest something should have been omitted ("entschlüpft," "versäumt") and by apprehensions about an alleged German tendency to do too many things at once as well as to do them by halves. The phantasy image of the perfect "Organisation" was one that is as "allumfassend" as it is "engmaschig" in its "Einbegiehung" of its objects.

The high emphasis on classifying activities in German culture is well known.

V. DOUBT AND CERTAINTY

A great number of phenomena in German culture could be cited to illustrate tendencies towards doubt on the one hand, and the "will to believe" on the other.

One of them is the frequent polarization between "dogmatism" and "criticism" in philosophical discourse. The procedure of generalized doubt was regularly applied, but usually not in the Cartesian fashion. By the method of generalized doubt, Descartes intended to separate out those judgments which are entirely "rational" and consequently "evident" to every "reasonable" being. In many German philosophic systems, however, what remains after the application of generalized doubt is most frequently some inspirational or voluntaristic element, something attainable to the exceptional individual by a supreme effort, rather than a *locus communis* in which all reasonable individuals can share. This is true of the Kantian "idea" as well as of Nietzsche's conception of the "super-man." Either ecstatic inspiration or a supreme effort of the will is needed to overcome doubt.

There is polarization also as to the precision, specificity, and completeness of symbols. This, again, is characteristic of compulsive characters. On the one hand they show an "inclination towards vagueness." But vagueness tends to be utilized by doubts for objections and for forbidden interpretations. Correspondingly, German culture shows both high vagueness and precision tendencies. As to the latter, there is the accent on "Wissenschaftlichkeit." There is also a vein of circumstantially cumbrous explicitness in German communications ("da möchte ich denn doch nochmals ganz unzweideutig feststellen. . . .") There is a significant revulsion vis-à-vis "talmudistische Spitzfindigkeiten"; this may indicate a fear of the use of precision tendencies for doubt purposes, corresponding to compulsive "hair-splitting" propensities. On the other hand there is the "metaphysical" vein in German discourse. E. Diesel comments on the protracted German discussion of the "significance" of the "Stämme" as against the "Reich": "As so often with Germans, one is left in doubt as to *what* it is that is significant or insignificant."

The relationship between pro-authoritarian and anti-doubt preferences in German culture is well known. One frequent comparison the Nazis made between the free regimes and their own was: "Some say one thing and others another; therefore it's best to put your trust in *Der Führer;* otherwise a person won't know *what* he ought to believe."

Even beyond the preference for the authoritarian variety of "regimenta-
tion" there is a widespread striving for finding oneself in a highly "defined"
situation (preferably with rules "schwarz auf weiss") and very negative
reactions to badly defined environments: "am Ende weiss man gar nicht wo
man hingehört," "man kennt sich gar nicht mehr aus." Thus there is a
tendency towards the adoption of easily ascertainable indicators of subjective
nuances (cf. the rôle of "Du" and "Sie").

The rejection of doubt-indecision as such and the cultivation and dogmatic
certainty and decisiveness were, of course, driven to extremes in the Third
Reich. As Hitler said (in a confidential address to senior German officers on
October 16, 1943): "The greatest poison is doubt" ("Das grösste Gift ist der
Zweifel"). General Kabisch formulated the following maxim in an article
published April 6, 1944: "Sei nicht ungläubig, sondern gläubig." Strenuous
exertions in combating one's doubts and indecisions were a major value,
already, in pre-Hitler Germany.

The constant fight against doubts which was characteristics of Nazi propaganda indicated, of course, a strong tendency towards doubt. The kind of
"faith" which Nazi Leaders demanded ran counter to established habits of
thought; it required a violently hostile attitude towards a great variety of
previously accepted objects. Nazism involved a dramatization of existence
which was characteristically polarized as to doubt and certainty. On the one
hand, it asserted certain dogmas in rigid fashion. But it demanded, on the
other hand, that the individual should always be ready to face extremely
precarious situations, involving utter uncertainty of existence. Thus, Nazism
illustrated in extreme fashion the ambivalence towards certainty and uncertainty.

NOTES

1. Kurt Lewin, "The Special Case of Germany," *Public Opinion Quarterly* VII
(1943), 562.

2. Theodor Reik, *Aus Leiden Freuden* (London, 1940), 185.

3. Eugen Diesel, *Germany and the Germans* (New York, 1931).

4. Erik H. Erikson, "Hitler's Imagery and German Youth," *Psychiatry* V (1942),
478-479.

5. Otto Fenichel, *Psychoanalyse der Neurosen* (Vienna, 1930), 192.

6. Erich Fromm, "Sozialpsychologischer Teil," in M. Herkheimer (ed.), *Studien
über Autorität und Familie* (Paris, 1936).

7. Diesel, *Germany*, 101.

8. Ernest Jones, *Papers on Psychoanalysis* (London, 1941), 541.

9. Reik, *Aus Leiden Freuden*, 89.

10. Diesel, *Germany*, 151.

11. Geoffrey Gorer, "Themes in Japanese Culture," *Transactions* of the New York Academy of Sciences V (1943), 106-124.

12. Diesel, *Germany*, 115.

13. Ibid.

14. Ibid.

Chapter 14

PSYCHOLOGICAL HYPOTHESES ABOUT RUSSIAN POLITICAL CULTURE

(with Elsa Bernaut)

EDITOR'S NOTE: Here are placed in sequence two short selections from widely separated parts of a book analyzing the symbolism of the Moscow trials in terms of the political culture of Russian Bolshevism.

In the first part Leites hypothesizes about a widespread characteristic of Russian family members to be preoccupied with damaging one another. Especially prominent are fantasies of the destruction of women—wives or mothers—by men.

The second part shows a tendency, in Bolshevik reasoning, to attribute this kind of guilty thought to others.

From Ritual of Liquidation: The Case of the Moscow Trials *(Glencoe, Ill.: Free Press, 1954), 73-77, 337-342.*

I. HYPOTHESES ABOUT A TYPE OF RUSSIAN FAMILY

I should like to describe briefly a few aspects of what might have been one characteristic type of family relations among the pre-Bolshevik Russian intelligentsia, and indicate some of the possible unconscious connections with the attitudes ascribed to the defendants in this chapter (and in chapters to follow). In view of the lack of evidence on both points, the statements made here should be regarded merely as a set of quite speculative hypotheses. The passages from Russian literature are merely illustrative and deal partly with human relations outside the family, which, presumably, are modeled on family relations. For the sake of brevity, I shall only allude (e.g., in speaking about "intense" emotions) to frequencies and degrees of certain feelings and acts which would have to be more specifically indicated for purposes of validation. I shall not attempt to specify in each case the degree of consciousness of the subjective states mentioned.

(1) A family member feels intense anxiety and guilt for having inflicted damage, wittingly or unwittingly, on the other members of his family, or for being about to do so.

> In Turgenev's *On the Eve,* there is no indication that the heroine in any way damaged her husband, who has died. Nevertheless she feels afterwards, consciously and spontaneously: "who knows, perhaps I killed him. . . ."[1]

Compare the Party member's (the son's?) apprehension as to his impact on the Party (the mother?).

(2) A family member is intensely apprehensive that outside forces (human or otherwise) will inflict damage on another member of his family.

> In Dostoevsky's *The Insulted and Injured,* a young man says to the young woman he loves:
>
> "We quarreled once; I don't remember what about. . . . We wouldn't speak to one another. I didn't want to be the first to beg pardon and I was awfully miserable. I wandered all over the town, lounged about everywhere, went to see my friends, and my heart was so heavy, so heavy. . . . [sic] And then the thought came into my mind, what if you fell ill, for instance, and died? And when I imagined that, I suddenly felt such despair as though I had really lost you forever. My thoughts grew more and more oppressive and terrible. And little by little I began to imagine going to your tomb, falling upon it in despair, embracing it, and swooning with

anguish. I imagined how I would kiss that tomb, and call you out of it, if only for a moment, and pray God for a miracle that for one moment you might rise up before me; I imagined how I would rush to embrace you, press you to me, kiss you, and die, it seemed, with bliss at being able once more for one instant to hold you in my arms as before."[2]

Compare the apprehensions of the Party member about the internal and external dangers to the Party.

(3) A family member is intensely apprehensive that another member will inflict damage on himself.

In *The Brothers Karamazov,* Dostoevsky describes the attitude of a mother towards her fourteen-year-old son:

"Though she had loved him passionately those fourteen years, he had caused her far more suffering than happiness. She had been trembling and fainting with terror almost every day, afraid he would fall ill, would catch cold, do something naughty, climb on a chair and fall off it, and so on and so on."[3]

Compare Bolshevik (parental?) apprehensions about the self-destructive "spontaneity" of the "masses" (the children?).

(4) A family member may be accused by the others of harming them. Compare the charges and countercharges within the Party.

(5) A family member may be accused of being unaware of the damage he (or some other factor) inflicts upon the family. Compare the charges and countercharges within the Party.

(6) A family member tries very hard not to damage other members of the family.

In Chekhov's *The Duel* two friends converse:

" 'Answer one question for me, Alexander Daviditch,' Laevsky began. . . . 'Suppose you had loved a woman and had been living with her for two or three years, and then left off caring for her, as one does, and began to feel that you had nothing in common with her. How would you behave in that case?' "

" 'Of course, it is difficult to live with a woman if you don't love her,' said Samoylenko. . . . 'But one must look at the thing humanely, Vanya. If it were my case, I should never show a sign that I did not love her, and I should go on living with her till I died.' "[4]

In *Reminiscences of Anton Chekhov,* Kuprin writes about Chekhov: "his jokes never left any bitterness any more than he consciously ever caused the slightest pain to any living thing."[5]

In *The Memoirs of A Physician,* Veresayev recalls that in his early years as a physician he was obsessed by the fear of unintentionally harming his patients:

"My aspirations did not seem to rise above the one desire—not to do the patient who sought my aid any harm."

He comments on this "rule": "its systematic application would condemn me to complete inactivity. . . ."6

Compare the Bolshevik requirement that the Party member conduct himself protectively (avoid destructive behavior) towards the Party, and destructively towards the rest of the world.

(7) To protect the members of one's family it is necessary to maintain a state of anxious vigilance and supervision.

In Solugub's *Light and Shadows* the following characteristic passage occurs:

"Volodya's mother began to look at him with careful and anxious eyes. Every trifle now agitated her."7

This parallels the Party's attitude toward the masses, and the Party leader's attitude towards the Party.

(8) To protect one's family it is necessary to do things for them instead of letting them take their own actions (e.g., on the part of the mother towards her son). This parallels Bolshevik attitudes as indicated in (7).

(9) Whenever a family member is harmed, reparative action should be taken with a maximum of energy.

In Tolstoy's *Kreutzer Sonata*, the hero says:

"Our whole life with the children, for my wife and consequently for me, was not a joy but a torment. . . . She tortured herself incessantly. Sometimes when we had just made peace after some scene of jealousy, or simply after a quarrel, and thought we should be able to live, to read, and to think a little, we had no sooner settled down to some occupation than the news came that Vasya was being sick, or Masha showed symptoms of dysentery, or Andrusha had a rash, and there was an end to peace, it was not life any more. Where was one to drive to? For what doctor? How isolate the child? And then it's a case of enemas, temperatures, medicines, and doctors. Hardly is that over before something else begins. We had no regular settled family life but only, as I have already said, continual escapes from imaginary and real dangers. It is like that in most families nowadays you know, but in my family it was especially acute. My wife was a child-loving and a credulous woman."8

(10) The resentment engendered by the burdens which parents feel are created by the existence of their children may be expressed as an aversion to having or loving children.

The hero in Tolstoy's *Kreutzer Sonata* says:

"Ask most mothers of our propertied classes and they will tell you that they do not want to have children for fear of their falling ill and dying. They don't want to nurse them if they do have them, for fear of becoming too much attached to them and having to suffer. The pleasure a baby gives them by its loveliness, its little hands and feet, and its whole body, is not as great as the suffering caused by the very fear of its possibly falling ill and dying, not to speak of its actual illness or death. After weighing the advantages and disadvantages it seems disadvantageous, and therefore undesirable, to have children. . . .

"Even now, when I do but remember my wife's life and the condition she was in during the . . . years when we had three or four children and she was absorbed in them, I am seized with horror! We led no life at all, but were in a state of constant danger, of escape from it, recurring danger, again followed by a desperate struggle and another escape—always as if we were on a sinking ship."9

(11) The solicitude of one member of a family for the others is often felt as damaging, regardless of whether it fails or succeeds in being protective. Compare Bolshevik beliefs that acts which are "subjectively" revolutionary frequently turn out to be "objectively" counter-revolutionary.

(12) A family member's solicitude for the others in his family makes him suffer, and may even make him die (e.g., parents toward children).

(13) In this context a child may develop the following beliefs, inducing guilt and resentment: My parents kill themselves for me out of love for me; I kill them out of hate for them (cf. below). The same may be conveyed to him by the parents.

(14) One member of a family may be so intensely affected by the bad conduct of another member that he may be severely damaged, or die. He may attempt to interfere with the bad conduct by stressing this.

The hero-narrator in Chekhov's *My Life* recalls his father and sister:

"from boyhood I have had a habit of considering them, so strongly rooted that I shall probably never get rid of it; whether I am right or wrong I am always afraid of hurting them, and go in terror lest my father's thin neck should go red with anger and he should have an apoplectic fit."10

Compare the Bolshevik belief that any opposition will have destructive effects on the Party. (This applies also to the points following.)

(15) The witting or unwitting demonstration that one family member does not fully love another is felt to be intensely damaging; it is also a cause of great guilt for the unloving one. The unloved member attempts to induce the other to reform by exhibiting his suffering and declaring its cause.

(16) Lack of love in one family member for another makes the latter suffer because it will to the former's disobedience.

(17) In particular, a family member who lacks love for others of his family will follow his own (selfish) pleasure aims. He will thereby incur danger to himself, and thus make the others suffer through anxiety or mourning. The others attempt to inhibit his spontaneity by stressing this.

In Dostoevsky's *Poor People,* the hero writes to the heroine:

"You *must* avoid all risks lest you plunge your friends into desolation and despair."[11]

In Sologub's *Light and Shadows,* a mother says to her son about whom she worries: "if you go mad, or die, I shall suffer horribly."[12]

(18) A family member may damage other members of his family by neglecting to allay their apprehension that ill has befallen him outside (e.g., by failing to announce that he will return home late, he arouses apprehensions that he has met with an accident).

(19) A family member may damage another by refusing to be contrite after he has sinned against the other; he may add more damage by "raising his hand" against the other.

(20) A family member may damage another by deserting him, or by giving him reason to think that he will desert him in the future (e.g., children leaving home on becoming adults). There are attempts to interfere with desertion by stressing the damaging results.

In Dostoevsky's *Poor People,* an older man loves, almost entirely by correspondence, a young woman living in his neighborhood, who at one point wants to take a job in another city. The man writes:

"What would become of me? Perhaps you never thought of that . . .—perhaps you never said to yourself, 'How could *he* get on without me?' . . . What else would it end in if you were to go away?' Why, in my hieing me to the Neva's bank and doing away with myself. Ah, Barbara, darling, I can see that you want me to be taken away to the Volkovo Cemetery in a broken-down old hearse, with some poor outcast of the streets to accompany my coffin as chief mourner, and the grave-diggers to heap my body with clay, and depart and leave me there. How wrong of you, how wrong of you, my beloved! Yes, by heavens, how wrong of you!"[13]

(21) The suffering of a family member who is unloved by another is enhanced by the awareness of his own full love for the other.

In *The Well of Days,* Bunin says about his mother during his childhood:

"What was her grief? And why did she grieve all her life long . . . ? Because her soul was full of love for everything and everybody, and especially for us, her own kind, and . . . because the world was a place of . . . unutterable, or unuttered and unshared feelings. . . ."[14]

(22) In such a case a family member will reproach the other with the difference of feeling between them.

In *The Brothers Karamazov,* Dostoevsky describes the attitude of a mother towards her fourteen-year-old child:

"She was always fancying that Kolya was 'unfeeling' to her, and at times, dissolving into . . . tears, she used to reproach him with his coldness."[15]

II. THE TENDENCY TOWARDS PROJECTION

Further research would have to establish the role of the mechanism of projection in pre-Bolshevik Russian culture. A passage which might be used to illustrate the hypothesis of its prominence occurs in Sologub's *The Little Demon.* The hero, Peredonov, a provincial teacher, predicts that his advancement, which he believes to be impending, will give rise to slander against him. He decides to visit without delay some locally important persons, to pretend that such slanders are already being circulated and to request that no credence be given to them. This is his conversation with the District Attorney:

" 'Whom do you suspect?'

"Peredonov fell into thought. Quite by chance [his acquaintance] Grushina came into his mind, he recalled confusedly the recent conversation with her, during which he interrupted her by a threat of informing against her. The fact that it was he who had threatened to inform against Grushina became in his mind a vague idea of informing in general. Whether he was to inform against someone or whether they were to inform against him was not clear, and Peredonov had no desire to exert himself to recall the matter precisely—one thing was clear, that Grushina was an enemy."[16]

The history of Bolshevism shows what seems to be a high incidence of more or less sincere imputations to enemies of acts or intents of one's own, coupled with denials of such acts and intents in one's own case. (In the case of high sincerity we shall speak of "projection"; in the case of low sincerity of "pseudo-projection.") To give but a few examples, in 1926 Stalin affirmed that Zinoviev equated "the dictatorship of the proletariat" and the "dictatorship of the party":

this means . . . to bring the bureaucratization of the Party to the highest degree, to transform the Party into an infallible force, to install in the Party a "Nechaev regime," an "Arakcheev regime."

—in fact, what Stalin had begun doing. Stalin added that if Zinoviev were right:

the Party would have to replace the method of suasion by commands and threats in relation to the proletariat. . . .[17]

In 1933 Stalin (who never mentioned the *bezprizornye*) said about the crisis in capitalist countries:

> the number of homeless workers and destitute children is growing enormously, particularly in the United States.[18]

In its letter of May 4, 1948, the Moscow Party leadership wrote to the Belgrade leadership in terms applicable to the Soviet Party:

> As can be seen, the Politburo of the Central Committee of the Communist Party of Yugoslavia does not consider the Party as an . . . entity, with the right to its own opinion, but as a partisan detachment, whose members have no right to discuss any questions but are obliged to fulfill all the desires of the "chief" without comment. We call this cultivating militarism in the Party. . . .[19]

The communique of the Cominform of June 28, 1948, said:

> It is a completely intolerable state of affairs when the most elementary rights of members in the Yugoslav Communist Party are suppressed, when the slightest criticism of incorrect measures in the Party is brutally repressed. . . .
>
> such a disgraceful, purely Turkish, terrorist regime cannot be tolerated in the Communist Party.[20]

In a note to the Yugoslav Government on July 25, 1949, the Soviet government affirmed that numerous Soviet citizens in Yugoslavia were being arrested and said, in terms applicable to the MGB:

> Numerous arrests of Soviet citizens are taking place and those arrested are being kept in . . . prisons for many months without charges and . . . without any grounds, without trial or investigation.
>
> The Yugoslav authorities have established a prison regime for those arrested which is completely intolerable and agonizing, subjecting the prisoners to grossly arbitrary rule, beatings and every possible kind of outrage, dooming them to hunger and illness. The prison administration has illegally deprived the imprisoned Soviet citizens of food parcels, not even excepting those who are ill, endangering their life and health. The outrages and arbitrary rule of the Yugoslav authorities have led to many of the arrested becoming emaciated and seriously ill. No protests from the prisoners to the prison administration against such an inhuman regime produce results. . . .

The Soviet note added, in terms relevant to the "prophylactic" practices of the Soviet police:

> This shows that the real reason for the repressive actions to which the Yugoslav authorities are subjecting Soviet citizens is not the commission by them of any

crimes but only that the Yugoslav authorities see in them supporters of friendly relations between the peoples of Yugoslavia and the Soviet Union.[21]

In a note to the Yugoslav Government on August 18, 1949, the Soviet Government spoke again about the maltreatment of Soviet citizens in Yugoslavia by the Yugoslav police, describing some major practices of the MGB:

> During the cross-examination ... Dodonov was forced to stand motionless for twenty hours and was deprived of sleep, food and water for two days. When a complaint against the tortures which his son had undergone ... was addressed by Dodonov's father to Vukadinovitch, Assistant Public Prosecutor of Serbia, Vukadinovitch ... declared ... that "this is our auxiliary investigation mechanism and they know what they are doing. ..."

> The Soviet citizen Strelkach, thrown into a Belgrade prison in March 1949, was summoned nightly for cross-examination for 22 nights. ... Strelkach ... was six times placed in a cell where there was only room to stand.

> Can a regime which practices such outrages and such inhuman treatment of people be called a people's democratic regime? Would it not be more true to say that a regime allowing such mockery of human beings was a fascist-Gestapo regime?[22]

In the same note, the Soviet Government discussed the contention of the Yugoslav Government, according to which certain Soviet citizens in Yugoslavia had been arrested because, sympathizing with the Cominform resolution of June 28, 1948, they conducted "propaganda for the overthrow by violence of the state system in Yugoslavia." The Soviet note affirmed that this resolution, addressing itself to the then impending congress of the Yugoslav Communist Party, merely asked that congress either to induce the leadership of the Party to change its line, or to change the leadership. The Soviet note then proceeded to criticize the Yugoslav Party with reference to standards of intra-Party democracy hardly practiced in the Soviet Party:

> Is this path in accordance with the constitution of the Party and entirely legal? Unquestionably yes. ...

> In 1907, at a Congress of the Russian Social-Democratic Party in London, the old administration of the Party (a predominance of Mensheviks) was ... replaced by a new administration (a predominance of Bolsheviks). But not a single person in the world would have considered this act as overthrow by violence of the existing Party system.

> In 1921, at the Tenth Congress of the Communist Party, when Lenin did not have a firm majority in the Central Committee, the congress elected a new Central Committee with an assured majority of Leninists. But not a single person in the world would have regarded this act as overthrow by violence of the state system of the Soviet Union.

And this is understandable. In Marxist parties congresses meet not to extol the leaders, but to examine critically the activity of the existing administration and, if need be, to renew it or replace it. In all Marxist parties where there exists internal party democracy, such a means of altering the leadership is natural and absolutely normal. One cannot but ask: why does the Yugoslav government regard as abnormal, illegal and criminal for the Yugoslav Communist Party what is normal and legal for Marxist parties? Is it not because the Yugoslav leaders have broken with the principles of Marxism-Leninism?[23]

The answer:

"... the Yugoslav Communist Party has been transformed into a department of the political police subordinated to the Chief of Police, Rankovich."

According to the words of the prosecutor in the trial of Rajk and accomplices, Tito's attempted colonial treatment of Hungary resembled the actual treatment of Eastern European areas by the Soviet Politburo:

Tito, Rankovich and their associates wanted also to use Yugoslav military units, in the course of the execution of the putsch on Hungarian territory, because they did not trust even those Hungarian troops, which were to have been organized by Palffy and Korondy [the military specialists of the conspiracy] and, as Rajk explained, they wanted to "stiffen and supervise" the Hungarian units with Yugoslav units.

Tito's high command in the Hungarian Army, Yugoslav officers over the Hungarian officers, Yugoslav supremacy over the Hungarian state, this is the meaning of Laszlo Rajk's term, "to stiffen and supervise."[24]

In rare instances the use of pseudo-projection by the Party could be admitted. Stalin said in 1924:

the revolution tries to make every ... step of its offensive look like a defensive measure. The refusal to evacuate the army [from Petrograd in October 1917] was undoubtedly a serious offensive step ... yet this offensive was effected under the slogan of the defense of Leningrad against a possible attack by the foreign enemy. Undoubtedly the formation of the Military Revolutionary Committee was an even more grave offensive step, directed against the Provisional Government, yet it was carried out under the slogan of organizing Soviet control over the activities of the district military headquarters. Undoubtedly the open passing over of the garrison to the side of the Military-Revolutionary Committee and the organization of a network of Soviet commissars betokened the beginning of an uprising, yet these steps were carried out by the revolution under the slogan of the defense of the Leningrad Soviet against any possible action by the counter-revolution. The revolution seemed to camouflage its offensive steps with a smoke-screen of defense, in order to draw the ... vacillating elements the more easily within its orbit. This may explain the outwardly defensive character of the speeches, articles and slogans of this period, which none the less are of a profoundly aggressive nature as regards their inner content.[25]

While using projection or pseudo-projection heavily, Bolsheviks are quite aware of their use by enemies; or allege such use in a *Tu quoque* fashion.

In an analysis of Narodnik economics, in 1897, Lenin noted about one Narodnik:

> he takes the reference to the petty bourgeois character of *narodnichestvo* to be a mere wish to "offend" Messrs. the Narodniks. . . . We unwittingly remember the well-known words: "For mercy's sake, Kit Kitych, who is offending you? You yourself offend everybody!" [a quotation from Ostrovsky] [26]

That is, it is pointed out to Kit Kitych that he is using projection. In 1902 Lenin quoted Turgenev's *Prose Poems,* in which a character establishes the rule, which he attributes to "an old fox": "To abuse as loudly as possible those vices with which one is affected oneself." [27] Speaking before the Party Council on January 17, 1904, Lenin said, in connection with the charges being leveled between the Mensheviks and Bolsheviks about their utilization of "angels":

> in his letters to the Central Committee Martov even used in quotation marks the words "money-bags" and charged us with the use of this expression. In fact this expression was used not by us, but by Martov. . . .[28]

In 1907 he wrote:

> the liberal bourgeoisie unloads its "being in a state of terror" as a consequence of the revolution onto the "state of terror of the popular masses. . . ."[29]

Discussing in 1908 the Menshevik theoretician of agriculture, P. Maslov, Lenin affirmed that Maslov had changed his views without admitting it; while Lenin, he said, had admitted a change in his views on the immediate demands which the Social-Democratic Party should raise in agricultural matters:

> Maslov acts according to the recipe of the old fox described by Turgenev: blame as noisily as possible what you want to hide from others in your own conduct! Others have changed their views and have themselves pointed to this change. You should shout noisily against this change in order to veil the change of your own views![30]

In 1920 Lenin discussed Trotsky's position in the so-called trade-union discussion:

> when . . . Comrade Trotsky, in pointing to "ideological confusion," speaks of the crisis especially and particularly in the trade unions, there is something in this that is . . . wrong. . . . It is Trotsky who is suffering from "ideological confusion. . . ." he lost sight of . . . the fact that here [in the "dictatorship of the proletariat"] we have a complicated system of cogwheels. . . . This alone is . . . sufficient to give rise to ideological confusion. Trostky groundlessly accuses others of this.[31]

Referring in 1921 to a certain charge made against him by Trotsky, Lenin said:

> This charge turns entirely against Trotsky: precisely it is he who throws things from a sick head onto a healthy one.[32]

In 1917 Stalin discussed the alleged intent of the government to ally itself with the Germans against the Bolsheviks:

> the provocateur howls of the bourgeois press about the "treachery" of the . . . Bolsheviks were *merely camouflage* for the purpose of concealing the actual treachery of the generals and the "public men" of the Kadet Party.
>
> Let them [the workers and soldiers] know that whenever the bourgeois press raises a howl about the "treachery" of the soldiers it is a sure sign that those who inspire this press have already prepared the ground for treachery and are trying to throw the blame upon the soldiers. . . .
>
> They are counting on "opening the front to the enemy" and on an "agreement with the Germans. . . ."[33]

In 1927 Stalin said:

> The facts . . . say that Zinoviev slanders the Comintern, transferring things from a sick head to a healthy one. This is habitual with Zinoviev, that is nothing new from him.[34]

And in 1943:

> the Germans would wish to obtain peace with Britain and the U.S.A. on the condition that the latter two draw away from the Soviet Union, or . . . they would wish to obtain peace with the Soviet Union under the condition that it draw away from Britain and the U.S.A. Themselves treacherous to the marrow, the German imperialists have the nerve to apply their own yardstick to the Allies. . . .

In a note of June 22, 1949, the Yugoslav Government protested to the Soviet Government against the Council of Foreign Ministers having, without consultation with the Yugoslav Government, taken decisions on the Austrian treaty which implied a rejection of certain Yugoslav demands on Austria. In a note of July 19, 1949, to the Yugoslav Government, the Soviet Government rejected this protest, affirming that

> in 1947, long before the Paris session of the Council of Foreign Ministers, the Yugoslav Government attempted to reach an agreement behind the back of the Soviet Union with the western powers on the question of Yugoslavia's territorial

and economic claims on Austria. . . . During these negotiations, the Yugoslav Government so radically changed its position as in effect to renounce its previous territorial demands on Austria.

The Soviet note continued:

> The assertions . . . [in the note of the Yugoslav Government, June 22, 1949], to the effect that the Council of Foreign Ministers took decisions . . . without consultation with representatives of the Yugoslav government, concerning the Austrian treaty which . . . reject legitimate Yugoslav demands on Austria, do not accord with reality. . . . Such assertions by the Yugoslav government are obviously intended to conceal from the Yugoslav peoples the failure of the secret negotiations with British representatives which the Yugoslav government held behind the back of the Soviet government on the question of the Austrian treaty.

Hence:

> In view of the above, the [Soviet] Embassy [in Belgrade], on instructions from the Soviet government, rejects the protest contained in the [Yugoslav Foreign] Ministry's Note, which is none other than a vain attempt on the part of the Yugoslav government to justify to the Yugoslav peoples its behind-the-scenes machinations.[36]

Further research might attempt to answer such questions as the following: Which conditions have, in various phases of Bolshevik history, fostered or impeded the use of projection and of pseudo-projection? When is the use of projection itself apt to be projected and that of pseudo-projection, pseudo-projected?

Also, which are the conscious beliefs accompanying and requiring the use of pseudo-projection? For instance, when Politburo members express indignation about distinctive MGB practices as attributed to an enemy police, what are the accompanying feelings and thoughts about the MGB; and why does the construction of a replica of it in the outer world seem useful?

NOTES

1. Ivan Turgenev, *On the Eve* (London, 1950), 228.
2. Fyodor Dostoevsky, *The Insulted and Injured* (New York, 1950), 185.
3. Fyodor Dostoevsky, *The Brothers Karamazov* (London, 1940), 553.
4. Anton Chekhov, *The Tales of Chekhov* (New York, 1916), II, 4f.
5. Anton Chekhov, *Reminiscences* (New York, 1921), 61.
6. Vikenty Veresayev, *Memoirs of a Physician* (New York, 1916), 121.
7. F. Sologub, *The Old House and other Tales* (London, 1915).
8. Leo Tolstoy, *The Devil and Cognate Tales* (London, 1934), 160.
9. Ibid., 157f.

10. Anton Chekhov, *The House with the Mezzanine and other Stories* (New York, 1917), 118.

11. Fyodor Dostoevsky, *Poor People* (New York, 1917), 37.

12. Sologub, *The Old House,* 176.

13. Dostoevsky, *Poor People,* 130f.

14. I. Bunin, *The Well of Days* (New York, 1934), 39f.

15. Dostoevsky, *Brothers Karamazov,* 554.

16. F. Sologub, *The Little Demon* (New York, 1916), 102.

17. Joseph Stalin, *Sochineniya* (Moscow, 1936-1941) IX, 79f.

18. Joseph Stalin, *Leninism: Selected Writings* (New York, 1942), 262.

19. Royal Institute of International Affairs, *The Soviet-Yugoslav Dispute* (London, 1948), 47.

20. Ibid., 65.

21. *The Current Digest of the Soviet Press* I, No. 30 (1949), 39.

22. Ibid., No. 34, 22f.

23. Ibid., 21f.

24. Rajk Trial, *Laszlo Rajk and his Accomplices before the People's Court* (Budapest, 1949), 262.

25. Joseph Stalin, *The October Revolution* (New York, 1934), 82f.

26. V. I. Lenin, *Sochineniya,* 4th edition (Moscow, 1941-1950), II, 204.

27. Ibid., 3rd edition (Moscow, 1928-37) V, 155.

28. Ibid., 4th edition, VII, 163.

29. Ibid., XII, 192.

30. Ibid., 3rd edition, XII, 322.

31. Lenin, *Selected Works* (New York, 1935-1938), IX, 5f.

32. Lenin, *Sochineniya,* 3rd edition, XXVI, 234.

33. Stalin, *Sochineniya,* III, 263f.

34. Ibid., X, 5.

35. Joseph Stalin, *The Great Patriotic War of the Soviet Union* (New York, 1945), 85.

36. *Current Digest of the Soviet Press* I, No. 30 (1949), 38.

Chapter 15

PSYCHODYNAMICS AND POLITICAL CHOICE: PANIC AND DEFENSES AGAINST PANIC IN BOLSHEVIK DOCTRINE

EDITOR'S NOTE: In this essay Leites explicitly links the way policy choices are viewed by a political elite to the psychic function performed by the various alternatives. In earlier selections on Bolshevism he identified certain fantasies of destroying and being destroyed as characteristic of Russian culture; he surmised they originated in typical patterns of Russian family relationships. He noted how this preoccupation with overwhelming, destructive passion was transformed into the Bolshevik "who-whom" doctrine— which postulates that the only alternative to annihilation by one's enemies is to annihilate them first. In A Study of Bolshevism *he traced this doctrine as its users called for an ever-mounting scale of violence.*

Here Leites analyzes the imagery used to elaborate the "who-whom" mandate. He finds in the doctrine a defense against latent homosexual wishes. However, he also notes that Bolshevik concern about threats from outside the self varies from moderate estimates to extreme ones. Given a moderate appraisal, considerable intercourse with the enemy may be tolerated without great danger; fearing a more formidable attack, the tiniest penetration threatens the self with engulfment and annihilation. After he examines the psychic dynamics which, in Stalin's regime, underlay a spiralling reliance on the extreme view, he considers the possibly important policy consequences that might come if and when the Russian leaders took a less agitated view of outside dangers.

From "Panic and Defenses against Panic in the Bolshevik View of Politics," Psychoanalysis and the Social Sciences *V (1955), 135-144. [Citations were omitted in the original version—Ed.]*

*I*n the fall of 1920, at the end of the period of civil war and intervention which had ravaged Russia, the Bolshevik leaders, and Lenin in particular, saw the necessity of rapid and drastic action to reduce somewhat the incidence of hunger, cold and disease. It was decided that foreign entrepreneurs should be invited to lease, for a limited number of years, certain limited resources of raw material on Soviet soil; that is, to offer what were called "concessions" to them. When such an offer was made by the Soviet government, many Bolsheviks predicted that the capitalist concessionaires would form the spearhead of another and more dangerous intervention, that the penetration of the domain of the Party would be the beginning of the end. When at a meeting of Party officials of the Moscow area, one of them, Stepanov, spoke in this vein about the enormous danger of permitting Bruce Lockhart, the prominent British agent of 1917-1918, to return, Lenin answered:

When he says that we must not give concessions to England because Lockhart will come here, I cannot agree. We coped with him at a time when the Cheka was only a growing institution, and not as substantial as it is now. And if after three years of war we are unable to catch spies, then all that can be said is that we are not the people to undertake to run the state. To say that the foreigners who will be attached to concessions are dangerous to us, or that we shall not be able to keep watch over them, is ridiculous. Why, then, have we undertaken to run the state? The task here is purely one of organization, and it is not worth dwelling long on it.

Thus Lenin conveyed the idea that the penetration of the enemy into one's interior is apt to be fatal only if it occurs to a large extent and without one's knowing about it in detail. Lenin's opponent in effect affirmed that even a tiny penetration would produce a catastrophic avalanche against which there is only one defense: prevent the beginnings, *principiis obsta*. But this is what Lenin clearly denied.

It was, however, precisely this idea which seems to have played an important role in the terrible years 1937-1938, the years which Russians call the *Yezhovshchina,* the period during most of which Yezhov was the chief of the political police and presided over the "liquidation," by execution or incarceration in prisons and camps, of a few hundred thousand senior officials in all branches of the Soviet administration, including—particularly—the political police and, at the end, himself. At one of the three trials which were the spectacular façade of this rather silent process, the defendant Karl Radek, collaborating with the prosecution, spoke on January 24, 1937, about the great danger to the regime of the remnants of long vanished oppositions in the Party:

> When a sea shell gets under a steel hammer, that is not so dangerous. But when a sea shell gets into a screw, a propeller, there may be a catastrophe.

That is, even the tiniest bad object must be utterly exterminated if it managed to penetrate into the vital interior. Stalin made the same point, when, at the famous plenary session of the Central Committee of the Party, on March 3, 1937, he gave the directive to liquidate, in effect, a majority of Bolsheviks who had occupied positions of importance before the consolidation of his own power, that is, before 1929. He said:

> In order to win an engagement in time of war, it is necessary to have *several corps* of Red Army men. But in order to pluck this victory at the front, a few spies somewhere on the Army [Corps] staff, or even divisional staff, capable of stealing the operational plan and giving it to the opponent, is all that is necessary. In order to construct a great railroad bridge, *thousands* of men are needed. But in order to blow it up, *a few* people are sufficient. Tens and hundreds of such examples could be given. [My italics]

Stalin's realistic military examples clearly express—as did the actions for which he adduced them—the general fantasy which Radek had expressed in the passage cited: even a tiny bad object has almost unlimited destructive power once it has become an internal object, once it has penetrated into the insides of the self.

The contrast between Lenin's feeling of relative safety in 1920 and Stalin's feeling of a total lack of safety in 1937 is striking. It is all the more interesting as in any objective assessment of the dangers threatening the Bolshevik leadership at these two junctures, it would be very difficult to say that the real threat of 1937 was greater than it had been in 1920; one might, indeed, say the contrary. Space, however, does not permit me at this point to undertake such an analysis of reality as a background for my inquiry into fantasy. What is important for this inquiry is, however, this: the unadmitted and unresolved Bolshevik conflict, about how dangerous penetration of one's insides from the outside is, finds its counterpart in many other unadmitted and unresolved conflicts about how dangerous or how manageable things are. To mention only a few, according to one trend in Bolshevik feeling and thinking, mistakes are inevitable and, within bounds, harmless or even useful, if one "utilizes" them for learning from them. But in a contradicting view every mistake is very dangerous; it raises the risk of catastrophe. According to one Bolshevik view—an older one—deviations are apt to be self-correcting, or, at least, one rolls down an inclined plane not after the first, but only after the second false step. The more recent opinion, however, seems to have been that the ultimate complete "passing over into the camp of the enemy" is already contained in the first "incorrect" position taken. The Leninist theory of democratic centralism held that if divergences are more or less freely expressed in "discussions" within the Party, the necessary unity behind the decision finally taken need not be compromised; the Stalinist theory of the "monolithic" character of the Party affirms that there is no stable intermediate position between the outlawing of the public expression of differences within the Party and the dissolution of the Party—in fact, if not in form—into a "heterogeneous conglomerate" of "sovereign fractions." In one Bolshevik view, adequate control in a situation is secured when the Party occupies its "commanding heights" (e.g., the state and industry under the New Economic Policy which gave some leeway to individual peasants and small business; or the ministries of the interior and of defense, plus the trade unions and the nationalized sector of industry in the Eastern European countries from 1944 to 1946-1947). But in another and apparently now more operative view the only safely controlled enemy is the dead (at least politically dead) enemy: as long as any remnant of enemy strength subsists, there is the danger of the small discontinuously growing back to its former bigness—hence the danger of one's annihilation. It is in fact in the context of the Bolshevik fear of annihilation that the unresolved Bolshevik conflicts I mentioned should be viewed.

In Bolshevik doctrine one cannot ask whether the career of the Party may end not in world-wide victory, as the explicit dogma has it, but in a catastrophe for itself and for society at large. I should guess (mainly on general grounds but also because of bits of available indirect evidence) that Bolshevik leaders have entertained, and do entertain, severe doubts about the ultimate outcome, certainly unconsciously and probably preconsciously. In any case, it is a central point of conscious Bolshevik feeling and thought that almost any moment before final victory is replete with visible and invisible dangers of an extreme kind.

There are enemies—those outside the boundaries of the Party's domain and hostile elements inside it—whose constant aim is not merely to contain or restrict, but rather to annihilate the Party. They know—as does the Party—that all intermediary positions between total victory and total defeat are unstable in the short or in the long run, that the question is the relations between the Party and the rest of the world.

There are also the inimical factors within one's own camp: the "spontaneity" of the "masses" inside and outside the Party, as well as the natural inclinations of one's own soul. If one lets oneself go to do what comes naturally—to which the masses tend and to which even the most "hardened" leadership may feel tempted—catastrophe is apt to ensue. Internal defects are so extremely dangerous because the external enemy is always looking out for any weakening of the Party to heighten the intensity of his attack.

This catastrophe, fully developed, is annihilation. Penultimately, it is loss of control, that is, being controlled by an alien force. Thus there is another form of "who-whom?" which Bolshevism perceives behind almost any relation in politics: who will control whom? Or, who will "use" whom? Apart from the danger of an overt attack with an annihilatory aim, there is thus the even more frightening possibility of being controlled by an alien force without knowing it. An outer enemy may succeed in "provocation"; the inner enemy—one's feelings—may distort what one then wrongly believes to be a correct evaluation of reality, and thus is "carried away" into a wrong path.

What accounts for the great strength of the Bolshevik belief that there are enemies with annihilatory designs? Both the limitation of time and data does not permit me to treat this crucial question fully, but I should like to say a few words on what is probably a major factor behind this central Bolshevik attitude, namely, the classical paranoid defense against latent homosexuality.

If enemies attempt to annihilate the Party, the Party must strive for the annihilation of its enemies as a defensive maneuver, quite apart from the fact that the transformation of the world which is the Party's aim also involves that annihilation. Until communism is established, love between men is impossible. Under communism men cease to be annihilators or targets of annihilatory attacks, but their new good relations are mainly indicated in negative ways; there will be an absence of power of violence (the "withering away of the state") and also of selfishness ("to each according to his need").

The Bolshevik emphasis on annihilatory relationships between men, and the shying away from an elaboration of their future harmony, is accompanied by a pervasive struggle against the disposition to be less than annihilatory toward the enemy, and to impute something better than annihilatory intents to him. Bolshevik doctrine insists on exposing the illusion that the world has, or could conceivably have, any good feelings toward the Party. It emphasizes that if one entertains such an illusion one will perish. It maintains—"who-whom?"—that if one does not annihilate, one will be annihilated.

Hence, this position excludes a fantasy which was of importance in the older Russian intelligentsia: the fantasy that by some miraculous change of heart men may begin to love each other, and that the world will be transformed thereby this very moment. In Dostoevski's *An Unpleasant Predicament* a character says:

> Take a syllogism. I am human, consequently I am loved. I am loved, so confidence is felt in me. . . . If [people] . . . trust me, they will believe in the reforms [I propose], they . . . will, so to speak, embrace each other in a moral sense, and will settle the whole business in a friendly way. . . .

In contrast to this, the fantasy of men embracing each other is repulsive and frightening to Bolsheviks. To paraphrase Dostoevski, Bolshevism seems to prefer the following construction:

I am human, consequently I am hated. I am hated, so no confidence is felt in me. If people do not trust me, they will not believe in the reforms I attempt to introduce; they will kill each other rather than embracing each other (and me) in a moral or even in a physical sense; the whole business will be settled in a hostile way.

In the pre-Bolshevik fantasy I spoke about, evoking good feelings from an enemy may be the beginning of the transformation of the world. In the Bolshevik view, the enemy shows good feelings toward the Party either as a device of deception, or as a reward or betrayal, or as a gratified reaction to an incorrect line of the Party—that is, one which threatens annihilation.

In these cases—particularly in the most important one which I mentioned last—the good feelings shown by the enemy were until late Stalinism recurrently indicated by the image of a physical approach of the enemy: he embraces and kisses the Bolshevik. (In late Stalinism the image of espionage relations replaced, in public statements, that of illicit kissing.) I have the distinct impression that this image played a higher role in the public imagery of Bolshevism—and may still play a higher role in the esoteric imagery of the leadership—than, say, the image of the "Judas kiss," the "kiss of death," in various Western cultures. In Bolshevik parlance A may be "impudently blowing kisses" to B; A may send "amorous glances" to B; B, unable to stand "fully erect," may have been "driven into the arms" of A, "into an embrace so tight that even a split cannot undo it."

One might thus surmise that the Bolshevik insistence on, in effect, killing enemies (that is, all groups not controlled by the Party and their "agents" within the Party) and on being killed by them is in part an effort to ward off fear-laden and guilty wishes to embrace men and to be embraced by them.

This classical psychoanalytic hypothesis is consistent with some major pervasive trends of the Bolshevik psyche, to which I have alluded above: the fear of passivity, the fear of being controlled and used, the fear of wanting to submit to an attack.

Once one denies one's wish to kiss by affirming one's wish to kill, this is—in the classical psychoanalytic connection next in order—apt to reinforce one's belief in the enemy's wish to kill by virtue of the mechanism of projection. It certainly seems as if projection is rather a mechanism of choice in the Bolshevik mind. This could be rather heavily documented if time permitted. I could then also attempt to indicate certain nuances of projection which seem rather characteristic of Bolshevism—e.g., projecting the mechanism of projection itself, or engaging in pseudo-projection, that is attributing to another a property which, at or near the moment of attribution, one is quite aware of possessing oneself. In any case, I have the impression that the following thoughts of a character of Maxim Gorky's expresses a fantasy of importance to Bolsheviks. This character thinks:

A man was walking along the road. I struck him—and—no more man. . . . If it's like that, why, then, it might happen to me too any day: I might get a blow—and it's all up with me! . . . I can cause the death of any man at any moment, and any man can kill me at any moment he wants to! I can go to sleep, and someone can draw a knife across my throat or bring down a brick or a log on my head. Or any heavy weight. There are so many ways of doing it! I looked at people and thought: . . . Uncertain is your life, and you have no protection against me just as I have none against you!

Still, the warded-off disposition to have good feelings toward enemies breaks through in some ways. The strong enemy—the "bourgeoisie" as distinct from the "petty bourgeoisie"—appears as very largely sharing the traits the Bolshevik strives for and approves in himself (only that the enemy puts these traits into the service of a bad soul). But Bolsheviks are sufficiently attached to these traits—of insight, energy, skill—to admire the "bourgeois" enemy quite consciously (and seek admiration from him) when they believe him, as they in part do, to be superior to the Party; and to feel at one with him in contempt for the "petty bourgeoisie" and the "masses" on which the Bolshevik projects his weaknesses. The combat for the world between the Kremlin and Wall Street is, in the Kremlin's feelings, a fight in which the protagonists are both separated by a quite unbridgeable abyss and very close to each other. And, as I have suggested before, behind the affirmation that the fight will end with Wall Street's corpse being thrown on the refuse heap of history (or rather completely destroyed so that it won't pollute the world with the odor and bacteria it secretes)—behind this affirmation lies the apprehension that the end will be a hate death with both corpses locked in a fighting embrace.

I have now sketched the setting of the conflict between various Bolshevik protections against the danger of annihilation. Let me return to that conflict itself.

A large area of Bolshevik feelings and thoughts about protective devices against annihilation does not seem to be significantly invaded by conflict. Thus, for instance, there is little doubt in Bolshevism that there must be, within each individual and within the Party, a ruthless and incessant fight which *aims* at the utter eradication in the soul of all the manifestations of "spontaneity" and their replacement by their opposites, the various aspects of "consciousness." Thus, instead of a romantic, sentimental, moralizing adoration of Revolution, there must be a maximization of power by any means; instead of vagueness and wordiness, precision and realism; instead of being overwhelmed by feelings or by distress about the lack of them, there must be restraint of soul and muscles; instead of procrastination or precipitation, incessant but well-prepared action; instead of vacillation or doctrinaire rigidity, persistence and flexibility; instead of taking the line of least resistance, one must go to the limit of one's strength and skill; instead of dispersion of effort, there must be concentration; avoiding the danger of fragmentation, the Party must be monolithic; eschewing the danger of fuzzy boundaries, it must be clearly demarcated from the world outside; and it must not put reliance on any outside groups.

But there are, as I have already shown in the beginning of this paper, two variants within this context. In what we may call the extreme variant every—even a tiny—degree of imperfection is regarded as highly dangerous; every mistake may be fatal. According to what we might term the moderate variant, mistakes are felt to be inevitable, harmless and even productive, as long as they are within certain bounds of magnitude and duration. (When I talk about two variants, I do not mean to imply that Bolsheviks are clearly aware of this duality; they are not. The term "variant" does not refer to a group, organized or otherwise, within the Bolshevik leadership.)

In the extreme variant the Party must at all times go as far as at all feasible in excluding any contacts with enemies which are viewed as enemy penetrations of the Party's domain; and it must also at any moment exhaust all possibilities for actually destroying enemy elements. Permitting an avoidable penetration on the part of the enemy, and permitting enemies to survive temporarily though one has the means for destroying them, raises, in the extreme variant, an acute danger of annihilation which outweighs whatever advantages these moderate policies seem to possess. It is precisely this which is denied by the moderate variant, as Lenin's words of 1920, which I quoted above, show. What I call the moderate variant of course agrees that the basic question is always "who-whom?" And what I call the extreme variant agrees that the Party must always allow for the existing strength of outside enemies which renders impossible their immediate liquidation and makes that liquidation a very long drawn-out process. But while both variants thus admit "coexistence" with enemies, and its temporary character, the moderate variant envisages certain contacts with enemies and a certain non-utilization of one's destructive power which the extreme variant rejects. That is, in the moderate variant the Moscow Politburo might have envisaged the possibility of accepting Marshall aid for its domain and of granting more areas in Eastern Europe a regime resembling Finland's.

Two questions emerge here: what are the typical unconscious meanings of the positions I have sketched and what are the factors governing their relative weight? The lack of appropriate data and the incompleteness of my inquiry do not permit me at this moment to give more than a perhaps suggestive description of what is involved.

In the extreme variant small bad objects appear omnipotent in a destructive sense; that is, the self (the Party) appears as almost helpless both in relation to dangers outside and inside the soul. Hence the Bolshevik must be perfect in order to protect himself against his frailties and to be able to deny them; if he cannot destroy an enemy (particularly, his most dangerous remnants), he must avoid him.

In contrast, in the moderate variant, the Bolshevik tells himself that small bad things—be they some small degree of uncontrolled affect, or some small amount of unliquidated enemy remnants, or some small extent of enemy penetration into one's domain—are after all really small.

In 1930 Stalin imputed an exaggerated apprehensiveness about small unfavorable events to the leaders of the Right opposition, and said:

> when the lightest cloud makes its appearance on the horizon . . . they already fall into a panic lest something may happen. A cockroach stirs somewhere, without having time even to crawl out of its hole, and they are already starting back in terror, and beginning to shout about a catastrophe. . . . We try to convince them . . . that it is only a cockroach, and there is no need to be afraid. But all in vain. They continue to shout as before: "What cockroach? That's no cockroach, it's a thousand wild beasts! It's not a cockroach but . . . the ruin of the Soviet government!"

Stalin's description of the two variants of Bolshevik feeling about danger—one of the few explicit Bolshevik statements on the matter—suggests a variety of unconscious factors which may be involved; and a variety of connections with the conflict about homosexuality which I discussed above. There are, on the one hand, the devouring—and, we may add, from the knowledge of other uses of this image, self-destructive—"wild beasts," a major term of parental reproach against the impulse-gratifying child. There is, on the other hand, the cockroach, in the case of which the wild has been transformed into the dirty, the big into the small, the frightening into the contemptible, the devouring into a crawling thing to be crushed. Perhaps, then we have here the metamorphosis of an object with predominant oral and genital significance into one with a predominant anal meaning in connection with which Bolshevism mobilizes a set of "compulsive" defenses—I have named some of them above—against the danger of annihilation (e.g., the Bolshevik must be precise and factual in his calculations, complete his actions and not disperse effort). Not only is the sense of danger then reduced, but one's own destructiveness facilitated: in destroying the enemy one does not act as a "wild beast," one merely "dirties one's hands" in eliminating a low piece of life; and Bolshevism is emphatic in claiming that one must never be afraid of dirtying one's hands. But, as I said, the lack both of data and of time prevents my speculating further on the unconscious meanings of the two variants of feeling I have attempted to distinguish.

Nor can I take up at this point a crucial question which emerges here. As I have implied throughout this paper, with the passage of time the extreme variant of Bolshevik feeling about danger seems to have gained strength in relation to the moderate one. As the power of the Politburo inside the regime increased, and the power of the Soviet Union arose, the apprehensiveness of the Politburo seems to have mounted, too. The prominence of the extreme variant of Bolshevik feelings about politics is a crucial fact in the present situation; it renders, among other things, internationally controlled disarmament more improbable than it would otherwise be. How can we explain the increase in the level of the Politburo's apprehensiveness as its power increased? Our present insight in this matter is very slight; one might hope that a real effort to apply a psychoanalytic orientation to this problem would increase considerably our understanding of a point in the present situation which is now as mysterious as it is central.

Chapter 16

PSYCHOLOGY AND POLICY IN FRANCE: DON'T FENCE ME IN

EDITOR'S NOTE: This selection, from a longer work on French politics, gives insight into a characteristic French political style. A stress in French culture on preserving freedom of action, on not being restricted by commitments nor confined by labels, seems to have its origins in the French child's early experience of his parents as both capricious and controlling. However, another effect of these childhood constraints may be persistent, distinctive regularities of conduct on the national political scene.

From The Rules of the Game in Paris, *translated by Derek Coltman (Chicago: University of Chicago Press, 1969), 9-24.*

I. ENJOYING OPEN OPTIONS

The child is always in danger of finding itself fenced in by grown-ups—literally shut up in a room, perhaps even in the "junk room," when it has managed to "get on their nerves" too much, or until it has "calmed down." These are measures in which the desire the adults feel to protect themselves from the child and the desire to inflict punishment upon it are mingled—or are thought to be active—in varying degrees. Grown-ups may also deprive the child of outings, thereby constraining it to remain in a proximity to them that cuts across the isolation with which the reprobate is being punished.

Since *enfermer* (to shut up) is also used, according to Paul Robert's *Dictionary*, "to express limitation," the child would appear to be fenced in to some extent in every sense: it is not allowed to choose for itself, or, at least, the number of possibilities it is free to reject or retain is narrowly circumscribed.

Having attained adulthood, the child may experience a strong inner tendency to shut itself up inside situational frames that will restrict its possible paths of action. We often prefer—or behave as though we prefer—everything we do in a given sphere to be governed by rules that are not at all easy to obey. The fact that they may appear arbitrary or even absurd—thus resembling many of the laws imposed upon the child—produces scarcely any diminution in our attachment to them, an attachment whose deep hold on us is often masked by surface movements of lively but feeble opposition. On the one hand, we insist that "where there is constraint there can be no pleasure"; on the other, we claim with Montesquieu that "restraint is good for us; it is like a wound up spring."[1]

Valéry reminds us, for example, that "in eras of high civilization . . . the poet was kept in chains. He was burdened with curious embargoes and shackled with inexplicable prohibitions."[2]

This perpetuation of one aspect of childhood is not limited to the poetic use of language, for "our syntax . . . equals our classical prosody in the rigor of its conventions. It is remarkable that a people generally considered to be excessively free in its thought . . . should have restricted itself in its speech with constraints that are in many cases inexplicable."[3]

There are other pleasures that can be experienced only by shutting oneself up. The junk room may be succeeded by the dreamer's loft, by the cellar night club, or by the speleologist's unfathomable abyss.

My childhood once past, on the other hand, I enjoy refusing to allow myself to be circumscribed. Or rather it pleases me to believe that I do. (In fact, my very insistence upon this attitude may give rise to suspicions that I am only too willing to accept a quite converse reality.) This means that I have a horror of feeling myself ensnared in any way, of being like Ronsard's lover (quoted in Robert's *Dictionary* under *empêrter*, to ensnare): "The lover is an animal, an animal ensnared/In the toils of love. . . ." The idea that I may become *embourbé*, bogged down—"I am caught in a bog, there is no way out of it" (Robert under *embourbé*)—is an anxiety-producing prospect, whereas that of casting off bonds brings relief and sets me at peace with myself.

"I wanted to remain free for all the possibilities hovering over me," as Montherlant puts it.[4] "To retain one's liberty of action"—"to remain free to act, to have freedom of action,"—"to keep oneself unattached" (available), "to tie oneself up" (commit oneself) as little as possible: this is a strong aspiration, or at any rate a vigorous myth we entertain about both ourselves and others. Paul Valéry notes that "power and money have the glamor of the infinite; it is not such and such a thing, nor such and such a faculty of action that we desire to possess specifically. No man feels an insane yearning for a reasonable power, or for the exercise of government as a simple and everyday profession, or for money as the value of precisely determined objects.

No, it is the vagueness of power that is the source of the vast desire, because I never know what I may come to desire."[5]

During the phony war, a certain writer discovered that one of his colleagues had succumbed to a passion for warlike matters, but that his fascination was exclusively with naval operations:

> "Maulnier," I said to him, "war is also fought on land." "This time that's not so certain," he replied. "And besides, I know nothing about that side of it. The fascinating thing about ships is that you can move them about so easily in any direction you like. You can plan everything, imagine everything, set no limits on yourself. . . ."[6]

The best moment is therefore that which precedes the act. "I have already said," Valéry reminds his readers, referring to the works of man, "that the starting point of our works is various freedoms: freedom of material . . . of form . . . of duration." These are all "things apparently forbidden to the mollusc—a creature confined by its one simple lesson." But they are also things that are lost, in man, in the transition to the act. While the orchestra is tuning up before the concert we experience an "emotional stirring" that "has something more universal about it than any possible symphony," a "disturbance" that "contains all such symphonies mingled in it . . . that suggests them all." It is "a simultaneous presence of all futures." In such a context "the mind" is "pure expectation" in which

I am still distinct from all thought; equally aloof from all the words, from all the forms that are inside me. . . . O my presence without a face, what a gaze, that gaze of yours without person or object, what a power that undefinable power of yours. . . .[7]

When the number of possible paths before me is reduced, what may shock me most is not the loss of specific advantages from a particular act henceforth excluded—an act that I could be sure of not wishing to perform as long as there was nothing to prevent my doing so—but simply the fact itself of my liberty's having been curtailed. On his way to a post in the Sahara, a lieutenant of Montherlant's invention is obsessed by the fear that he will be unable to find a woman there to make love to. But having located one, this is what he feels:

The obsession had existed in his brain long before it had existed in his flesh, if it ever had existed in his flesh. What had been angering and disturbing him was not so much the idea of continence as the sensation of a material impossibility. And now that he was certain of possessing, his peace of mind was almost as great as if he had already possessed.[8]

Once obstacles have occurred in the path of any given action, an inclination to perform it is likely to arise. At the time when French political circles first began to pay some attention to the Euratom treaty, in the summer of 1956, the ambition for France to produce her own nuclear weapons was, in those circles, very weak. But the formal agreement proposed at that time seemed to be creating obstacles in this respect, so that the interest now being taken in the treaty suddenly strengthened many politicians' conviction that their country ought not to be without the new weapon.

Though we may perceive that there are several "solutions" to any given problem, in the sphere of politics or any other, we may also observe, regretfully, that "there are not *that* many. In order to combat this notion, we may say with Marshal Juin (speaking of what would happen if the C.E.D. were rejected), "There are substitute solutions available in plenty. . . . I have mine just as everyone else has his."[9]

There are those who openly say: "Let us not deceive ourselves for an instant: we are not free to choose from a large number of hypotheses" (on the subject of Algeria's future), and those who say, of a still pending solution to a major problem, that

it is tomorrow's secret, but that secret is nevertheless enclosed within certain limits. Juridical subtlety will certainly be able to think up many formulas within those limits. But it is impossible, all the same, to think of any that cannot be contained within one of the three following categories . . .

(on the extent to which West Germany should be rearmed).[10] But such people, in political circles, are often held to be jackasses—or else cunning devils who are trying to promote their own formula by deceitfully obscuring the number of "substitute solutions."

Any attempt to "hedge me in with false alternatives," or to "spreadeagle me between false options" will excite a reaction of lively distrust mingled with indignation. Refusing to "allow myself to be hedged in by false dilemmas," I shall assert that "it is not impossible to find a solution . . . on the sole condition that the full extent of my liberty shall be preserved" (on the conflict between the Sultan and the Glaoui).[11]

Since experience has shown that "everything can happen in France," that even the most unexpected combinations are eventually realized with the passage of time, the future—when it is not dominated by a belief in the inevitable and/or desirable continuance of the *status quo*—is often impregnated with the belief that "everything is possible," that "no hypothesis can be excluded," that "you never can tell," that "the whole question may suddenly be reopened" (though even this belief, when strongly held, can also in fact help on occasion to perpetuate the established state of things).

Before and during an important debate or parliamentary crisis, for example, those who claim to know all about the particular question often do their utmost to predict as many possible outcomes to it as they can.

II. REFUSING COMMITMENT

Though I may tend to take pleasure in limiting the possibilities open to others, or in considering them as being limited, when it comes to myself I am only too anxious to deny that the fact of my having ventured into a specific present has in any way reduced the future paths still open to me. What? People think that by doing this or that I have restricted my own freedom of movement? They will soon see how wrong they are!

According to Bernard's angel in *Les faux-monnayeurs,* "we are the dependents of a past . . . that past puts us under an obligation. Our entire future has been blue-printed by it."[12] But there is a likelihood that the man to whom such a remark is addressed will reply, again with André Gide,

> I do not wish to be a slave . . . to my past, a slave to my future projects, a slave to my faith, to my doubt, to my hate or my love.

> Though I may agree to serve . . . I want the terms upon which I lease out my life to be both freely consented to and renewable at any given moment.[13]

The idea that the stakes may all be down on the table from the very start often inspires a revulsion whose violence is proportionate to our secret conviction that such is in fact the case.

In opposition to the attraction of the rut there is my refusal to accept the continual "renewal" of my past as an inevitability. According to Montaigne, "the quality most objectionable to a proper man is ... the obligation to a fixed, particular fashion." In *Le Rouge et le Noir,* "the most *fin de siècle* of men" exclaims: "Why am I expected to be of the same opinion today as I was six weeks ago? That would mean I was the slave of my opinions."[14] In other words, becoming aware of having predetermined my future—by having ventured into some present obligation—may arouse a wish to reestablish the liberty thus compromised.

This may be specifically observed in the case of resolutions taken by persons or assemblies with regard to their own future conduct. Grown-ups insist that children shall think consistently; but adults may see the fact that they themselves are acting against their own expressed intentions as a precious sign of their privileged status.

"If I knew what I must do tomorrow, I should immediately try to find something else," Jules Renard confesses.[15] Parliamentary assemblies under both the Third and Fourth Republics—according to a widespread belief in political circles that was doubtless also a reality—were very fond of jettisoning official schedules established either by themselves or their competent organs in order to follow, without warning, the unpredictable desire excited by unpredicted events. Similarly, to take one example, a parliamentary group—in this case the Socialists—faced with the task of resolving some internal problem may "decide not to apply its own ruling in this instance." And in the case of a law already formally passed it often appears desirable to be able to apply it "without ... allowing ourselves to be trapped by its dispositions as though in a prison."[16]

In order to make myself capable of obeying a particular resolution, I sometimes do my utmost to close my eyes to the fact that I have made that resolution, as with the soldier at the front who never stops protesting: "heroism, what crap!"—until the day he dies a hero.

People may claim that some particular and precipitate act on my part must perforce entail the performance of such and such another, upon which I have not yet decided; but is this a truth or a trap? Might I not maintain, ultimately, that nothing obliges us to anything? Thus, under the Fourth Republic, to be a minister in a government could still be viewed as compatible with all sorts of actions expressing a really rather imperfect solidarity with one's colleagues. To approve, as a member of the National Assembly, of a general policy statement by the government did not apparently oblige me to support the specific measure with which the group in power eventually executed the declared policy (if the wording used in the particular case was sufficiently precise to permit such a formulation); in fact, under the Fourth Republic, the "contract of investiture," so punctiliously drawn up and analyzed at the time of a government's formation, had always long fallen into oblivion by the time of its demise.

If, at the moment of envisaging a given path of action, we see ourselves threatened by some trammeling obligation, is it not possible for us to avoid it by altering the course of that path slightly, so that we are still able to perform the desired action while also reducing its dangers? As, for example, when the members of a political group (the Socialist Republicans), at a time when Félix Gaillard was forming a government, "authorized M. Chaban-Delmas to accept the Ministry of Defence . . . [he] will nevertheless hand in his resignation as chairman of the Socialist Republican party. Thus the latter will not be committed by his presence in the government." When the transition from one government to another (from Guy Mollet's to that led by Maurice Bourgès-Manoury) eliminated a party (the Socialists) from the Hôtel Matignon while allowing it to retain certain key posts, the advantage that the party in question expected to reap from the "operation" was explained as follows: "a government that includes Socialists will enable the [Socialist party] and its secretary to keep a tight hand upon French politics . . . without taking any direct responsibility for them, thus retaining its freedom of critical opposition."[17]

Why should I not commit myself to a course of action I intend later to abandon? It is often seen as both legitimate and profitable to advance far in the direction of an apparent goal only to do an about-face at the last moment; one is always free to "go into reverse"; it's the other fellow who gets "his fingers burned"! Changing one's mind about what one is apparently in the very process of performing—that's freedom!

For example, when a parliament is required to pronounce upon the principle or even the details of a projected law or treaty while it is still being drawn up, many members are tempted to take up specific positions with the feeling that they will nevertheless still be free, when the moment of final decision arrives, to adopt the opposite point of view; even though there is likely to be some difficulty in justifying such a reversal of opinion by claiming that the case has altered in the meantime.

When the French parliament came to make its decision on the extent to which West Germany should be rearmed, this tendency played a major role. In the autumn of 1954, the government presented the Assembly with the *Acte de Londres,* which was a detailed prefiguration of the U.E.O. treaty shortly to be drawn up. This act was put through by the Assembly "as though it were mailing a letter"; but this was because "once more, while giving their approval in principle, many will make mental reservations as to the future and see to it that they are still able to reverse this initial approval."[18] And, indeed, when the moment of decision arrived (several months later), the treaty in question did experience the greatest difficulties. This is why, on a comparable occasion (before a vote on a motion in favor of the then embryonic Euratom treaty), a prime minister (Guy Mollet) insisted: "A vote in favor of this motion will also signify that we are committed in advance to approving, in several months' time, the treaty that will by then have been drawn up, if it is in conformity with the decisions we make at this point."[19] But this is how a deputy (Valéry Giscard d'Estaing) described the attitude of certain of his colleagues as they prepared to vote in favor of the treaty instituting the Common Market, despite their belief that it could well cause havoc in the economy: " 'That doesn't matter. Let's ratify the treaty for the moment, there's always a chance we may leave the Market.'" The speaker then judged it expedient to refute this line of thought: "If we leave the Common Market, we shall leave it humiliated, diminished, discredited. We cannot entertain such a hypothesis."[20]

On the other hand, those obsessed with a concern to collect sufficient votes to get them over the next bridge are tempted to encourage rather than to destroy this belief that one can always "take back one's vote." I may take the same attitude toward myself—for example, when attempting to reconcile myself to some line of action that I consider repugnant but also inevitable. By persuading myself that such and such a first step is easily reversible, I end up by getting myself irretrievably enmeshed in a mechanism of which I refuse to let myself become aware until it is too late.

A member of the opposition (Camille Titeux) once said to a party leader (Edgar Faure) in the Assembly: "there is no member of this Assembly more adept than yourself . . . at entering into commitments that do not commit you."[21] But is this not precisely the principle of a branch of wisdom whose practitioners are often extremely respectable men? "His philosophy," said Valéry of his predecessor in the Académie (Anatole France) "safeguarded him against excessively rigid resolutions. . . . He did not pledge *(engager)* his future."[22] Under "pledge the future" *(engager l'avenir)* Paul Robert refers us to the figurative sense of "mortgage," for which he quotes "mortgage one's present chances," and also Chateaubriand's lament when selling his memoirs: "No one can ever know what I have suffered from being obliged to mortgage my own tomb." In order to illustrate "to bind someone" *(engager quelqu'un),* Robert first of all gives "this signature or contract binds you," but follows it with: "Words bind no one. That doesn't bind me in any way. He avoids anything that might bind him." For *engager* also signifies, in a literal sense, "to cause to enter or penetrate into something that fastens onto, that does not leave free," and, in the corresponding figurative sense, "to cause someone to enter into an opinion, a feeling, an affair, an undertaking, etc. that will hold him fast, that will not leave him free"; which is to say, in colloquial and vulgar terms, "to drag into, to draw into, to con into." That the first illustration Robert gives of this meaning of *engager*—"he succeeded in drawing him into this business"—may already be assumed to conjure up an undesirable situation is perhaps indicated by those that follow: "He has drawn him into a nasty business, into hot water. A dictator who commits his country to a military venture." Similarly, for the reflexive form *s'engager,* "to engage oneself in an enterprise," is followed by: "To engage oneself in a tricky affair.... He went into it head down, without thinking.... He committed himself too far." Then come all the other verbs immediately brought to mind by this sense of *engager:* "venture, commit, expose, risk, compromise." And in the case of *s'engager;* "venture oneself, embark upon, undertake, throw oneself into, hurl oneself into, place oneself in the van...." Here again, words evoking danger seem to predominate.

As an illustration of *engagement,* Robert gives: "He is bound, hampered, prevented from acting, by a previous engagement." How frightful! What a good deed it must be then "to free, to set loose, to disentangle someone from an engagement." And corresponding to this meaning we also find an example of the figurative use of *dépêtrer,* to extricate: "to extricate someone ... from a thoughtless engagement."

That I may engage or commit myself with pleasure, that my happiness may depend upon it does, it is true, seem possible; but it would also appear to be the act of a most extraordinary man: "This work, this choice, this decision ... engages his whole being." This exalting and exalted sense of *s'engager* is, as we know, a neologism created by "intellectuals": "To participate actively, in accordance with one's deepest convictions, in the life of the human community, while willingly engaging (committing) one's conscience, one's reputation, one's goods ... to such a project." But before presenting us with the cliché: "A committed writer," the dictionary takes just one more backward glance at the more ordinary human emotions: "To be afraid of committing oneself."

III. DISENGAGING

Corresponding to the perils incurred by those who commit themselves, or allow themselves to be committed, we find—as I have already remarked—the relief experienced by the person who is freed, or who frees himself, from an engagement or commitment. (The former risks desertion; the latter inflicts it.) *Dégager* (to disengage) is "to withdraw what has been given in pledge *(gage).* It is also "to free, to deliver, to extricate from a critical or embarrassing position." Or again, "to free from that which restrains ... from that which conceals ... , to free a mixture of its impurities ... , to untie bonds, to loose shackles." Applied to clothing, *dégager* means "to make looser, freer, to restore ease of movement," to medicine: "to free an organ from that which is incommoding it." To be *dégagé* means to possess freedom and ease of manner. There is work *dégagé* from all ambition, from all material considerations," and also the "soul *degagée* from all terrestrial bonds." It is against this background of good things that we should consider the meaning of particular interest to use here. *Dégager* is:

> To free from an obligation.... See enfranchise, liberate. To release someone from his word, his promise; to give him back his word, his promise. To release someone from a sin he has committed. See absolve. To release someone from a burden, a debt.... See unload, disencumber, dispense, exonerate....

And similarly with the reflexive form *se dégager,* which Paul Robert illustrates as follows: "To free oneself from all responsibility.... To free oneself from a promise, an undertaking.... To free oneself from one's bonds. To detach oneself from a crowd.... To rid oneself of a habit, a routine, a prejudice."

We sometimes hear of politicians unwise enough to have spoken in rather too precise a way about their own future actions—announcing some specific goal, letting fly with a "never" or an "always" on some specific subject—only to find themselves constrained, shortly afterward either to give themselves the lie, which is embarrassing or to abstain from some useful line of action. Although the politician is unlikely to neglect the advantages to be gained from a nicely calculated false promise, he also experiences the feeling described by Montaigne with regard to "undertakings wholly mine own and free":

> if I tell the goal, I feel that I am obliging myself to it, and that committing it to another's knowledge is to bind oneself to it in advance; I feel that I am promising it when I tell it. So I air my intentions very little.[23]

"Let us not hedge in the future with excessively strict formulas!" the veteran politician cries to those of his colleagues who are in danger of letting themselves be carried away by the present situation.[24]

One should never go into anything, or any place, without making sure that one has some convenient means of egress. Which is to say, both easily accessible and inconspicuous—after the model of Costals entering marriage: "I am going into this business as I went into the war, and perhaps as I go into everything: concerning myself at my moment of entry with the means I may need to get out of it again." Or after that of M. d'Auligny drawing up a contract: "Whenever M. d'Auligny had successfully inserted some phrase into a contract that constituted, in his mind, an open door that would enable him to evade his commitments, then he was in his seventh heaven." "The artist," Montherlant says finally, this time referring to himself, "ought never to commit himself to a state that is either irreparable or too difficult to modify," a maxim that appears to be equally valid for the politician, indeed, for any man.[25] "Everything you do that takes the form of an irremediable, unrecapturable act—is another step toward old age. Oh cling to the reversible."[26]

Thus, ambiguity, so often decried, here appears an indispensable tool in the hands of the man struggling to retain his freedom. By using vague words we keep the future open and inconclusive—as a mother may when negotiating her daughter's marriage:

> Two years earlier, Solange had refused a young civil service engineer. But Madame Dandillot, succumbing to the attractions of inconclusiveness . . . had made it quite clear when passing Solange's refusal on to him that "the future was not closed. . . ." Once a year, for two years, the tenacious engineer continued to call upon Madame Dandillot; the same inconclusiveness still reigned, and the door was still left ajar.[27]

Cardinal de Retz, when recommending a certain "decision" to Monsieur, notes that "he is not decisive, he leaves or always appears to leave his Royal Highness with a freedom of choice, and consequently with the power to select whatever may suit him from the 'chapter of accidents',"[28] It is in this same spirit that we find Camille Chautemps, in Bordeaux during June of 1940, suggesting that the government should continue its flight as far as Perpignan. Once there, it would have greater freedom to choose: "either to remain in France, or to board a cruiser at Port-Vendres." [29] When faced with opposing arguments that we are unable to decide between, we like to adopt a course of action that does not apparently exclude the subsequent application of either.

IV. ABSTAINING FROM ACTION

The surest method of safeguarding my freedom of action is still that of abstaining from action altogether. During the Algerian war, a general officer (Paris de la Bollardière) refused a decoration as a token of protest against certain methods employed in the prosecution of that war. But an individual who subscribed to the point of view being discussed here, if pressed by his friends to imitate this gesture, would have exclaimed: "You can't be serious! If I sent my ribbon back, I should no longer be in a position to send it back!" Or, in abstract language,

> The accomplishment of the exterior action does not radically deprive us of the ability to think that it is still to be performed. . . . How often one catches oneself reliving the state of oscillation and equipoised possibilities in which one existed before having acted, as though it were some Other who had subscribed to the act, and as though it were impossible for the Self, under pain of no longer being the Self, to accept that *the deed counted?* It is as though our Self felt a repugnance at becoming that Other who has committed himself to the irreversible. . . . We recognize ourselves solely in the provisional and the pure possibility: that is what is really us.[30]

The passage of time—if I am to give credit to a feeling closely associated with that just described—gradually curtails the number of possibilities open to me, until that moment when the last of all disappears with my death: "I was born *several* . . . and I die *only one.* The child on the way is a numberless host that life quickly narrows down to a single individual; the one that actually manifests itself then dies. A quantity of Socrates was born with me, from which, little by little, the Socrates due to appear before the judge and drink the hemlock emerged." Similarly: "We are made *(faits)* of something that happens *(se fait)*: something that happens at the expense of the possible," since "life's sequence eats up our initial reserves . . . of possibilities." "I do not know what to think of M. Paul Valéry considered as a determined object," the same author wrote in his old age; "even though at my age one is of course bound to end up as one." [31] The young André Gide expressed the same feeling:

> I sense a thousand possible beings within me; but I cannot resign myself to wishing to be only one of them. And I am terrified, at every instant, at every word I write, at every gesture I make, to think that each of those things is one more ineradicable stroke added to the image of me that is gradually becoming fixed. [32]

Is this death in life unavoidable? Perhaps not, Valéry suggests:

> We believe that if we start again from our childhood we could become another person, have a different history. . . . This possibility of grouping the same elements in various ways persists. . . .
>
> There is no time *lost,* no time really past, as long as those other personae are still possible.

Is refusing to let oneself be trapped not the same as escaping old age— escaping death? "Life is the preservation of the possible." [33]

V. AVOIDING PREDICTABILITY

By dint of impositions of all sorts, grown-ups try to make that disturbing creature, the child, into a predictable being. Once an adult himself, this creature imagines himself capable of caprices, if not actually capricious. The use that grown-ups make of their time must not appear too predictable, especially when such predictability is, less consciously, very much desired, and when the grown-up is in reality rather rarely given to leaving his rut. "To do no more than is required," Montherlant asserts, "is one of the great secrets in the service, in art, in love—in life." [34]

If the child lies, we tend to classify it "a liar"; if it gets itself dirty, a label saying "dirty" may even be attached to it physically; if it steals, it may have to copy out "I am a thief" a hundred times. A single act conjures up the idea of a permanent essence. In school, a child psychiatrist tells us, "when setbacks occur . . . the resulting failure situation immediately appears almost impossible to break out of. . . . The child is held to be a poor student." There is a strong tendency to "establish rigid student types: the good student, the student with an academic bent, the dunce, the trouble-maker. Once the label has been applied it often becomes definitive, and the child has to drag it around like a ball and chain."[35]

This is yet another aspect of childhood that the adult is attempting to slough off by preferring to be considered unpredictable. Since grown-ups often are in fact unpredictable in their dealings with children, thereby causing them suffering, the children will later transmute the distress inflicted upon them into delight in inflicting it. To the degree in which their parents sometimes spoil them, sometimes yell at them, sometimes take no interest in them at all, passing from kisses to slaps, from praise to insult, children are likely to be impatient for the moment when the privilege of being unpredictable devolves upon them in their turn.

"This man was so crammed with inner riches that his replies were difficult to predict, and he himself did not know what he would come up with . . . what feelings would prevail in him, what desires would spring up, what ripostes, what illuminations!"[36]—a precious quality indeed in that Monsieur Teste! According to "a friend," Colette "proclaims that the true charm of life consists in not knowing exactly, at any given moment, what one will be doing an hour later."[37] "I don't know what I shall do," says Valéry, "but I *shall give myself a surprise;* if I doubted that, I should be nothing."[38]

To claim that I am unpredictable, and to require that others should not destroy that belief, may be all the more important to me if the converse is in fact true: "When dining out, Maurice always eats boiled beef followed by cheese, and the glum waiter asks him before every meal: 'What would Monsieur like today?' "[39]

What may prove particularly attractive is a mixture of the expected and the unforeseen, such as that provided by knowing an end result without knowing how it will be achieved. Montherlant, observing the beginning of a love affair, writes: "It is exquisite to watch her coming and going, knowing now that she will be mine, whereas an hour ago nothing was certain. . . . This moment, when one has the certainty that the thing will take place, without knowing exactly how it will take place, is perhaps the most exquisite in the whole of any affair. . . . To say to oneself: 'She is mine,' without her being so, and yet her being so, all the same."[40] Or the mixture may be provided by a mutable interplay of elements within a fixed framework, as in the case of Herbart's brothel: "At the Big Ape, Madame Jeanne controlled the frolics of her inmates with the severity of a ballet mistress. . . . Whatever random chance presided over the composition of the clientele, the same play was played out every night, full of the unexpected, yet subject to rigorous rules."[41] Under the Third and Fourth Republics, those who moved in political circles often employed the same image when referring to "the play being performed"—and enjoying such a long run—in the Assembly.

Reminding us that we "sometimes do things that 'are not at all like us,' " Valéry adds: "It is good to do such things with deliberate intent, in order . . . to render ourselves . . . less easily predictable both to ourselves and to others,"[42] "Sleep must be caught," Proust advises us, "at the very moment when we thought we were doing anything but going to sleep."[43] "I like not being where people think I am," Gide tells us.[44]

We can make ourselves less predictable by means of frequent and abrupt changes in behavior, such as those that characterized the life of the French parliament under the Third and Fourth Republics. Those who took part in it sensed, with a feeling of unease that marked their pleasure, that "the unpredictable is king"; the "volte-face, normal."[45]

Whenever a difficult problem presented itself, a cascade of contradictory votes—particularly in committee—was by no means unusual. For instance, in a committee of the *"chambre de réflexion"*: "An amendment of major importance proposed by M. Maroger, accepted at 4 p.m. by 14 votes to 8, then rejected at 11 p.m. by 13 votes to 12, was finally adopted at 4 in the morning."[46]

According to one great parliamentary journalist, "the Assembly . . . totally disrupts its work schedule every three days."[47] A few years later, a deputy generally considered by his colleagues to be a very serious politician (Jean Minjoz), when commenting upon the improvement that had taken place in this respect, recalled a quite recent period when "our labors were paralyzed almost daily by continual disruptions of the agenda." But several months later, one of the most respected members of that parliament (Charles Barangé) was still able "to invite" the National Assembly "to undertake discussions that shall at least be inspired by a purposeful order." It was in order to restrain this tendency that the Fifth Republic introduced so many "safeguards," in a spirit that led the chairman of its first Assembly (Jacques Chaban-Delmas) to say: "After the division, I shall give the Assembly precise indications as to its daily agenda for this week and the week following, so that each of you, my dear colleagues, will know what to expect (applause)."[48]

Although someone else's unpredictability may appear distressing or dangerous, it can also appear fascinating, or even, and quite often, as the necessary condition of a strong attraction. Costals says of his mistress: "I am incapable of predicting what her reaction will be in any specific case. When dealing with her, I have the impression of being engaged in subtle diplomatic maneuvers; I do everything by groping in the dark and the grace of God."[49] A journalist once said of a great politician: "The secret of fascination is surprise. George Bidault can be excellent or execrable. We flock in crowds to find out 'what he'll be like today.'"[50]

The other ceases to appear unpredictable as soon as he or she is no longer the object of an intense attachment. Having observed at Balbec that "every time we see them, young girls are so little like what they were the time before," Proust adds:

> I am not saying that a day will not come when, even to these . . . young girls, we shall assign extremely rigid characters, but that is because they will have ceased to interest us, because their every appearance will no longer be an apparition for the heart quite different from what it was expecting, leaving it overwhelmed each time by a fresh incarnation. Their rigidity will be the product of our indifference.[51]

NOTES

1. Montesquieu, *Mes pensées*, in *Oeuvres complètes* (Paris, 1949), 1307.

2. Paul Valéry, *Pieces sur l'art* (Paris, 1934), 8; *Variété* in *Oeuvres* (Paris, 1957), I, 741.

3. Paul Valéry, *Regards sur le monde actuel* (Paris, 1945), 183.

4. Henry de Montherlant, *Service inutile* (Paris, 1935), 23.

5. Paul Valéry, *Tel quel* (Paris, 1943), 39f.

6. Lucien Rebatet, *Les décombres* (Paris, 1942), 214.

7. Valéry, *Variété*, 900, 721, *Tel quel*, 127f.

8. Henry de Montherlant, *L'Histoire d'amour de la Rose de Sable* (Paris, 1954), 8.

9. Speech reported in *Combat* (April 5, 1954).

10. Maurice Violette, Assemblée Nationale (AN) (October 11, 1955), *Journal Officiel (JO)*, 5018; Antoine Pinay, AN (August 31, 1954), *JO*, 4484.

11. Pierre-Albin Martel in *Le Monde* (April 13, 1953).

12. André Gide, *Les faux-monnayeurs* (Paris, 1925), 440.

13. André Gide, *Journal, 1889-1939* (Paris, 1948), 670.

14. Montaigne, *Essais*, Book III, ch. 13; Stendhal, *Le Rouge et le Noir*, Part II, ch. 4.

15. Jules Renard, *Journal* (Paris, 1935), 110.

16. Raymond Barrillon in *Le Monde* (January 14, 1955); Roger de Saivre, AN (October 13, 1955), *JO*, 5089.

17. Jacques Fauvet in *Le Monde* (November 6, 1957); (June 9-10, 1957).

18. Adolphe Aumeran, AN (October 7, 1954), *JO*, 4581.

19. AN (July 11, 1956), *JO*, 3385.

20. AN (July 24, 1957), *JO*, 3252.

21. AN (February 23, 1955), *JO*, 885.

22. Valéry, *Variété*, 726.

23. Montaigne, *Essais*, III, 9.

24. Reported in *Paris-Presse* (September 13, 1958).

25. Henry de Montherlant, *Le démon du bien* (Paris, 1937), 56; *Les Auligny* (Paris, 1956), 29; *Carnets, 1930-1944* (Paris, 1937), 390.

26. Paul Valéry, *Lettres à quelques-uns* (Paris, 1952), 120.

27. Montherlant, *Le démon du bien*, 181.

28. Cardinal de Retz, *Memoires* (Paris, 1949), 622.

29. Jacques Benoist-Mechin, *Soixante jours qui enbranlèrent l'Occident* (Paris, 1956), II, 378.

30. Paul Valéry, *Regards sur le monde actuel* (Paris, 1945), 55.

31. Paul Valéry, *Eupalinos* (Paris, 1944), 71f.; *Variété*, 722; *Mélange* in *Oeuvres*, I, 326; *Lettres*, 246.

32. Gide, *Journal*, 28.

33. Valéry, *Tel quel*, II, 263; *Mélange*, 288.

34. Henry de Montherlant, *Le solstice de juin* (Paris, 1941), 245.

35. M. H. Revault-d'Allonnes in *L'Ecole des parents* (December 1953), 27; Didier Anziou, *L'Ecole des parents* (May 1954), 35.

36. Paul Valéry, *Monsieur Teste* (Paris, 1946), 69f.

37. Sylvain Bonmariage, *Willy, Colette et moi* (Paris, 1954), 144.

38. Valéry, *Variété*, 483.

39. Renard, *Journal*, 273.

40. Montherlant, *Carnets*, 252.

41. Pierre Herbart, *L'Age d'or* (Paris, 1953), 52.

42. Valéry, *Tel quel*, II, 186.

43. Marcel Proust, *Sodome et Gomorrhe, A la recherche du temps perdu* (Paris, 1954), II, 982.

44. André Gide, *Si le grain ne meurt* (Paris, 1928), 250.

45. André Stibio, *Carrefour* (November 7, 1951).

46. *Année politique*, 1948, 227.

47. Jacques Fauvet in *Le Monde* (November 28, 1952).

48. AN (July 21, 1955); *JO*, 4001; (November 23, 1955), *JO*, 5954; (January 21, 1959), *JO*, 151.

49. Henry de Montherlant, *Les jeunes filles* (Paris, 1936), 221.

50. Jean Ferniot in *La Nef* (January 1958), 31.

51. Marcel Proust, *La prisonnière, A la recherche*, III, 66.

PART VI

CHANGES IN POLICY AND BELIEFS

Chapter 17

LANGUAGE AND POLICY:
COMINTERN TREATMENT
OF CHANGES IN LINE

EDITOR'S NOTE: The following selection illustrates the dynamic interaction between symbols and policy. It analyzes how leaders of the Communist International treated their party's policy changes in the period 1919 through 1941. From the changing frequencies and forms of denials and admissions of change of line, Leites hypothesizes trends in the beliefs and attitudes of those at the center and those at the periphery of Comintern leadership.

In the version of the article presented here, much of Leites' original documentation has been omitted in order to focus on his perceptions of the link between policy perspectives and semantic patterns. The period considered is one in which Stalin increasingly dominated the Soviet party and through it the Communist International movement. Comintern language was marked by an increasing denial or ignoring of variation in line at the center. This change probably reflected, Leites believes, a decreasing realism of the Comintern elite, accompanied by decreasing allegiance to its own exoteric ideology.

Since Stalin's death some tendencies Leites perceives here have persisted and some have been reversed. His analytical approach may be used to interpret such recent changes of line in the center as those described in the concluding essay of this volume and such changes at the periphery (and the center's reaction to them) as have recently appeared in the French and Italian party leadership.

Adapted from "Interaction: The Third International on its Changes of Policy," in Harold D. Lasswell and Nathan Leites (eds.), The Language of Politics *(New York, 1949), for which the author is indebted to Ithiel Pool for a number of suggestions and criticisms. That version was revised from Document 25, Experimental Division for the Study of Wartime Communications, Library of Congress, May 1, 1942.*

I. INTRODUCTION

The present study sets itself the task of analyzing those symbols of the Communist International which are dealing with its own symbol-practice variations through time. *[Customary abbreviations used here will be "CI" or "Comintern" for the Communist International, "ECCI" for its Executive Committee, and "CP" for Communist Party.]* To use the terminology of certain recent epistemological trends: It is proposed to investigate the "meta-language" of the Comintern about the changes of its own "object-language." The ulterior aims of this research are twofold. First, it is intended to be a contribution to the study of the symbolic aspects of revolutionary techniques since World War I. Second, the analysis to follow may be relevant for the construction of a more general theory concerned with the dynamics of dogmas, political and other.

For the study of these dynamics in contemporary politics, the Comintern seems to present perhaps the most important single case. This may be asserted for a number of reasons, among which the following are conspicuous: (1) the political dogma of the Comintern possesses a higher degree of elaborateness than that of any other major political movement of our time; (2) this dogma has been subjected to variations through time which in frequency and amplitude excelled those of its competitors; (3) these variations found a degree of acceptance on the part of affiliates of the Comintern which probably also excelled that shown in comparable situations in rival movements. In this connection, the present study can be envisaged as a consideration of *some* of the "techniques" used by the élite of the Comintern to produce assent to "changes of line."

The sources used were, for 1919-1935, the verbatim reports of the extant seven world congresses of the CI held annually until 1922 and thereafter in 1924, 1928, and 1935. For the period since 1935, I have used the *International Press Correspondence (Inprecorr)*—since 1938 renamed *World News and Views*—a weekly publication of the CI. For the shift in policy accompanying the outbreak of the Russo-German war in 1941, the *New York Daily Worker* was also taken into account. As to the dissolution of the Comintern in 1943, the May 15 resolution of the Presidium of its Executive Committee was taken as the text.[1]

The following major policy changes of the CI were investigated:[2]

[338]

1. *The turn to the right of 1921.* This was a turn, from a policy oriented on the immediacy of revolution and exhibiting extreme forms of aggression against other labor organizations, to a policy related to the diagnosis of an "ebb" in the revolutionary process; maintaining relative legality; and offering, as well as practicing, collaboration with other labor organizations in a "united front from above," as well as "from below," and in "workers' governments."

2. *The turn to the left of 1924.* This was a turn toward a refusal of collaboration with other labor organizations under the symbol of the "united front from below" and to the reinstatement of the "dictatorship of the proletariat" as an ostensibly immediate goal.

3. *The turn to the left of 1927-1928.* After the intervening period of 1925-1927, with its relaxation of aggression against other labor organizations—expressed most sharply in the Anglo-Russian trade-union alliance and the "Farmer Labor Party" policy of the Communist Party of the USA—this was again a turn toward a refusal of collaboration with "social fascists," toward "dual unionism" and insurrectionary gestures.

4. *The turn to the right of 1934-1935.* This was a turn toward a "proletarian united front from above," "organic unity of the workers' parties" and a "people's front."

5. *The turn to the left after August 23, 1939,* coincided with the codification of a change in relationships between the Soviet Union and Germany.

6. *The turn to the right after June 22, 1941,* coincided with the outbreak of the Soviet-German war.

This study will deal with typical symbolic structures of admissions and denials of these changes of line, as exhibited in the sources mentioned. It should be added, however, that there is plainly a third method of "referring" to such changes, which is silence.

G. B. Shaw asserted that Stalin "has acted in every military crisis as if the German army and its present owner did not exist."[3] One may perhaps with more justification claim that the Stalinist Comintern increasingly tended to treat policy change as so entirely nonexistent as not even to bother to deny their occurrence. More and more the Comintern came to "live in the moment." If a policy change occurred, most attention was concentrated on proving why the new policy was correct, and not on whether, and if so why, it was new. The factors influencing the incidence of *denials* of policy changes (which will be dealt with below) were presumably also operative here.

II. DENIALS OF CHANGE

Denials of change may be classified according to certain *formal* characteristics. Thus, it is possible—and for some analytic purposes presumably significant—to distinguish *negations* of change from *affirmations* of constancy.

Such affirmations are to be found in all the cases studied. This, however, does not imply that the magnitude of the rôle of this theme as against other simultaneously occurring, and often contradictory, themes remained constant. Affirmations of this kind were typically, for obvious reasons, made by that nucleus of the dominant faction of the Comintern which had been responsible for the old policy, and which remained in power under the new dispensation.

The frequency and prominence of the use of this device seems to have shown an ascending trend during Comintern history. This could be related to a number of factors, among which we may mention: the trend toward elimination of internal dissent; the presumably decreasing trend of intensity of allegiance to their exoteric ideology on the part of the Comintern élite; the presumably decreasing "realism" of that élite.

One way of discrediting allegations of policy change is to impute negatively preferred motives to their authors. Another way consists in "turning the tables" against them. One motto here is: "Not we, but you, are changing." (In such cases we may or may not find ourselves in the presence of "projection," in the strict psychological sense of the term.) Thus, Sinoviev states at the Fifth Congress: "I think I can assert and prove that it is not we who propose to revise the resolutions of the Third and Fourth Congresses, but precisely Radek and the other Rights."[4] In a similar fashion, an article in the *Daily Worker*, after the outbreak of the Russo-German war, stated:

> Many of those who have been shouting about a war against Hitlerism to forward the game of Empire are now hard pressed to explain their inconsistency when a real war against Hitlerite aggression is being waged by the Soviet Union. . . . To hide such inconsistencies . . . these people turn around and try to twit the Communists for their "inconsistency."[5]

Among the factors making for a high level of denials of policy change throughout Comintern history, the most obvious, and probably also the most important one, is this: the degree of "*subjective* elasticity" of Comintern affiliates in the various levels of the hierarchy probably fell far short of the very high measure of "*symbolic* elasticity" provided by the structure of the ideology of the CI. That is, the nuclear symbols of Comintern ideology were such as to permit of the derivation of a large range of policy changes, but at the same time actualizations of this symbolic flexibility, *if recognized as such*, were apt to call forth negative subjective reactions of adherents, ranging from slight bewilderment to outright shock. (We have no reason to assume that the Comintern in this respect furnished an exception from a very widely diffused pattern of social behavior, but the particularly high ideological elaboration of Comintern strategy and tactics tended to enhance the degree of subjective [as distinguished from symbolic] rigidity of its adherents. This was often taken for granted by those groups within the Comintern who defended a denial of a policy change [which had actually taken place] against others who pro-claimed its occurrence).

Evidently, the degree of subjective rigidity to be found differed between various strata of adherents at any given time, and varied through time. The extreme scarcity of evidence on these matters does not permit us to go beyond plausible guesses.

One would expect, at a given moment in time, an inverse relationship between the altitude of the position of persons within the Comintern hier-archy and the degree of their subjective rigidity in the sense alluded to above. (However, one might want to qualify this, insofar as the lowest levels of the hierarchy, i.e., the more or less inactive sector of the simple party members, were involved: their only slight degree of politization would seem to make for a rather low subjective rigidity in relation to policy changes.) Furthermore, for any given policy change one would expect an inverse relationship between the degree of subjective rigidity and the time which had already elapsed since the moment the policy change "broke." This would be one of the main factors making for the typical concentration of denials of policy change immediately after such a change became apparent. Thus, to mention only one instance, in the first days after August 23, 1939, denials predominated; as the days passed, admissions increased.

Through time, we may surmise a declining trend of the phenomenon discussed. A number of factors probably played a rôle in bringing this about. In this connection, one could cite: the accumulating impact of the lengthen-ing series of ever more violent policy changes; the declining depth of beliefs and of interest in beliefs (at least in regard to "substantive" tenets, as against the "formal" dogma that the directing organs of the movement are always right); and, in the upper and middle levels of the hierarchy, a selection of personnel with the maximization of subjective flexibility as one of the major goals in view. This decline of subjective rigidity tended to diminish the *incentives* for denying policy changes. But counteracting factors were present. On the one hand, the increasing amplitude of policy fluctuations tended to increase these incentives; on the other hand, the trend toward disappearance of intraparty criticism on major points of policy, and toward the consolida-tion of an unwritten infallibility-dogma in favor of the Comintern leadership, tended to *facilitate* denial operations. *[It is possible also to observe, through time, an increasing rôle of "flat" as against "derived" denials in Comintern symbolism, and also a decreasing trend in the elaborateness of derivations, so far as they were used. The difference, in both these respects, between 1924 (the Fifth Congress) and 1935 (the Seventh Congress) is striking. It goes without saying that these trends are sensitive indicators of the "totalitariani-zation" process which the Comintern was undergoing.]*

If one investigates the *differences* in the relative rôle of denials of policy changes in the various instances at hand, the most important relationship to come into sight is that between the *direction* of the change and its denial: at least up to 1939 turns toward the right were more intensely denied than turns toward the left. Although it is not proposed to go all the way to quantification in this report, it seems safe to say that denials played the smallest rôle in the Sixth Congress (which codified the sharpest turn toward the left) and the largest rôle in the Seventh Congress (enacting the biggest turn toward the right). The explanation for this is not far to seek: while the predispositions toward the term "left"—and toward the types of behavior to which it ambiguously alludes—were on the whole positive within the Comintern up to 1934-1935, the contrary was true for "right." Thus, the incentive to deny was stronger in the case of right, than in that of left, turns. After the protracted impact of the unprecedently right policy initiated in 1934, this situation was probably reversed. Presumably, the predispositions toward rightness and leftness changed and, as a consequence, the turn to the left in 1939 was much more denied than the 1941 turn in the opposite direction.

III. ADMISSIONS OF CHANGE AT THE CENTER

Admissions of change may refer to the center or to the "sections" of the Comintern. Admissions of change at the center may be investigated with a view to ascertaining, in the first place, the factors which are advanced to justify it. The following discussion will, for the sake of convenience, be organized around the Comintern's treatment of its admitted *symbol* changes; it will be seen that, *mutatis mutandis,* the same considerations can be made with reference to the *practice* changes involved.

1. SYMBOLIC ASSIMILATION

The admittedly new symbols may be asserted either to coincide in their meaning with the old symbols or to diverge from them. In the first case, one is dealing with a situation bordering on a denial of change: it is only a difference in "formulations," not in "purport," which is admitted. The symbolic device which is typically used in this connection is one which may be designated as "the technique of *symbolic assimilation* between the old and the new." That is: the old and/or the new symbols and practices involved are falsely presented in such a fashion as to minimize the differences between 'them.

But if the new symbols were conceded to be incompatible with some of the old ones, the elaboration of the admission usually did not stop with the allegation of mitigating characteristics. To them were almost always joined allegations about changing context factors implicitly or explicitly justifying the admitted symbol change.

These factors can plainly be of two kinds: either changes of "the situation"—i.e., of certain features of the environment and/or of the self—or changes of one's insight into the situation.

2. "CONDITIONS HAVE CHANGED"

The justification of an admitted symbol change by reference to changes in "the situation" was the vastly more popular one of the two symbolic patterns just mentioned—so much so that Radek, in a late and daring exercise of his buffoon function could jest:

> Even if Comrade Sinoviev were to sign a thousand times the undertaking never to enter into a bloc with the social democrats, he is going to do so the day it becomes necessary; he will only declare that the situation has changed.[6]

The theme here involved occupied, within the sphere of admissions, an important place at the sharpest turn toward the left (1928), as well as at the sharpest veering toward the right (1935), and also at the occasion of the 1913 dissolution. On the former occasion, Bucharin explicity rejected the justification of the policy change by insight augmentation ("why have we modified our estimate of the general situation? Not because we are cleverer than we were, but because the situation has changed"); and he emphatically declared in his report that "the change in the objective situation is the only important cause which determines our tactics."[7] Bucharin's intensity of emphasis was presumably polemically directed against those who regarded the turn to the left as a partial incorporation of the political line of the 1927 opposition in the USSR. Bucharin—despite the almost absolute ban of silence on "Trotskyism" in the central reports delivered to the Sixth Congress—could not refrain from mentioning that "certain comrades establish a correlation between the change of our line and certain secondary factors. . . . It would be childish to think that we try to 'radicalize' ourselves because of the reproaches of the opposition. These arguments do not even merit an answer."[8]

Dimitrov also affirmed that the new policy inaugurated was caused by the "new . . . questions which life itself and the development of the class struggle present us."[9] The theme we are treating was, for obvious reasons, the one adopted almost to the exclusion of all others after June 22, 1941. An editorial of the *Daily Worker* states, with reference to the manifesto issued June 29 by the National Committee of the CPUSA, and formulating the new line: "The manifesto begins: 'The people of our country face a new world situation.' From this it derives all the necessary conclusions for the people's guidance." As W. Z. Foster put it, in his speech to the National Committee: "Hitler's attack upon the Soviet Union changes the character of the war, and thereby makes necessary changes in our Party's attitude towards that war."[10]

Sometimes the universal proposition affirming the dependence of the "correct line" on the context was expressed by affirming the dependence on the context of meanings of the terms used in formulating a given line: a way of expression which is plainly related to the uncritical Comintern attitude toward language. A probable instance of this was the following remark in Molotov's speech to the Supreme Council of the Soviet Union on October 31, 1939:

> In connection with these important changes in the international situation (sc.: since August 23, 1939) certain old formulas, formulas which we employed but recently, . . . are now obviously out of date and inapplicable. We know, for example, that in the past few months such concepts as "aggression" and "aggressor" *have acquired a new concrete connotation, a new meaning.*[11]

If, thus, in many cases, the new aspects of the situation were characterized in relation to the old line, they were in other cases related to other elements of the total system of symbol and practice. The other elements were previous predictions—"we have at the time of the old line foreseen the change in the situation which requires its abandonment"—or statements about the positive or negative relevance of the new aspects for the realization of the movement's major goals. Two major themes appear here: according to one, the alleged changes in the situation constitute advances; according to the other, they portend threats which can be combated (by a change of policy). It is the first of these themes which appeared much more frequently and emphatically than the latter.

It was plainly the dominant symbol pattern, in the case of turns to the *left,* which was justified by references to a change in the situation; for such a change was then almost always one or another form of the "intensification of the crisis of capitalism." In cases of a turn to the *right,* this symbol pattern was found to be less frequent and prominent, but still playing a very important rôle.

Favorable changes in the situation which were taken to justify policy innovations were not only asserted to be changes of the environment rather than of the self; they were also often affirmed to have been *demanded* by the self from the environment for some time past. Thus the environment was presented as at last "coming around" to a higher degree of conformity with demands which had for a longer or shorter time been made by the self. The classical instance of this is furnished by the assertions concerning the socialist parties when turns were toward the right. Thus, at the Seventh Congress it was asserted: (1) that the Comintern had long since desired more positive relations with the socialists who had, however, up till recently refused, and (2) that finally the socialist parties seemed to show a greater willingness for cooperation under the "pressure of the masses."[12]

The characterization of relevant situational changes not as advances, but as threats—huge but not overwhelming—was no less prominent at the Seventh Congress. The twin threats of "fascism" and war were referred to as grounds for the new line.

IV. ADMISSIONS OF CHANGE OUTSIDE THE CENTER

After having discussed the center's admission of its own changes in symbol and practice, we now proceed to deal with the center's admissions of variations occurring in other parts of the movement.

Here we encounter the following typical theme: the admitted symbol-practice changes outside the center were presented as rectifications of previous (intentional or unintentional) "deviations" from the invariant center line. That is, the existence of deviations *at* the center was denied, that of past deviations *from* the center affirmed.

The denial of deviations at the center was an invariant element of the more ceremonial parts of the symbolism of every one of the congresses. One of its typical forms was the assertion that the permanent organs of the Comintern, particularly the Executive Committee, have "correctly executed the line" laid down by the preceding congress. There are exceptions to the pattern, but these exceptions are unvaryingly of a rather harmless sort, and their frequency and importance declined steadily.

The pendants to the denials of change at the center in the cases studied were the admissions of change for parts of the movements outside it. Such admissions in their turn entail two allegations: that of the past existence of "deviations"—without the collusion of the center, on the one hand, and that of their present rectification, typically presented as occurring by influences from the center, on the other hand. In the case of a turn toward the left, there will thus be allegations of right deviations and a concentration of "fire" against them as the "main danger," and at the occasion of a turn toward the right, there will be affirmations about the existence of "ultra-leftism," and a direction of "struggle" against them as "the biggest hindrance to the carrying out of a really bolshevist policy." In such cases, certain subsidiary themes were frequently introduced to elucidate the genesis of such deviations. One set of such themes which was predominant at the Fifth Congress revolved around the alleged "mimicry" behavior of the deviationists. It was said that they slyly presented their early symbolic deviations as differences of style rather than of content and thus were able for a time to deceive the good-natured and unsuspecting center, the vices of which are here, as elsewhere, but the excesses of its virtues. Thus, Sinoviev is able to plead guilty merely to a rather attractive fault: too great conciliatoriness in matters of form. Needless to say, here again the assertions of the historian would be of a rather different tenor, for those behaviors outside the center which are presented as deviations from the old line have, in fact, quite frequently been applications of it, undertaken with the consent and even at the behest of the center.

The high frequency with which a given behavior was presented at one moment as conforming to the "line," and as deviating from it at a later moment, has certain implications for the technical terminology of the Comintern.

For a number of types of political actions the Comintern has evolved sets of three standardized terms or term compounds (for each of which there may be synonyms). One refers to the "correct" ("bolshevik," "marxist-leninist-stalinist") action, whereas the two others designate opposite kinds of deviations. Each of these may or may not be distinctively ultra-left ("sectarian," "doctrinaire," "formalist") or right ("opportunist," "liquidationist," "reformist"). Thus, the "correct" behavior of the Party towards the "masses" is flanked by the "divorcement from the real life of the masses" (the "unwillingness to learn from them" and "to make it easier for them to come over to the positions of Communism"), on the one hand, and it is threatened by the "reliance on the spontaneity of the masses" and the "lack of a sufficiently distinct Communist line," on the other hand. That is, besides the "correct" line there is a certain manifestation of "sectarianism" on the one hand, and of "chvostism" ("tail-end-ism") on the other. Or, so far as the mixture of propaganda content between manifestly revolutionary symbols and others is concerned, the correct position is to be distinguished, on the one hand, from a neglect of, and, on the other hand, from an overemphasis on, "partial demands." Or, with reference to the relationship of action to "principles," the correct behavior again lies between an "opportunist lack of principles" and "sectarian simplified methods of solving the most complex problems on the basis of stereotyped schemes." If it is a right deviation to "give communism a Western haircut" (as Ruth Fischer said at the Fifth Congress), it is a "left deviation" to "lose the specific features of the specific conditions in each individual country out of account." (Cf. Dimitrov, as stated at the Seventh Congress.) In these cases, the "correct" action can be represented as occupying a *middle* position on a continuum between hypo-quantities and hyper-quantities. In other cases, the "correct" action is located at the *extreme* of a continuum, and there are two standardized terms or term compounds present, one referring to the correct extreme, the other to the rest of the continuum. Thus, there can not be too much of a "taking advantage of the difficulties of the class enemy."

What happens, then, in the situation described above, is that at one moment one term out of a set of two or three is applied to a given behavior, and that the other term, or one of the two other terms, is applied to the same behavior at a later moment. This is, in its turn, made possible by the absence of precise definitional delimitations of the terms involved against each other—

a linguistic situation which is significantly implied in a commonplace 1925 remark of Stalin, quoted by Dimitrov at the Seventh Congress: "It is necessary that the Party be able to combine in its work the greatest adhesion to principle (not to be confused with sectarianism) with a maximum of contacts and connections with the masses (not to be confused with tailism)."[13]

If, thus, the symbolic devices adopted imply high ambiguity of the terms referring to correct and incorrect shapes of various kinds of political actions—an ambiguity which is, in its turn, enhanced by the use of such terms in the fashion depicted—they have plainly the same implications for the terms of which those sentences are composed which state "the line" itself. As we have surveyed a number of them in our previous discussions further corroborations seem at this point hardly necessary. *[We may note that to the resources implicit in the ambiguity of the formulations of the "line" of the moment could be added those created by the distinction between overt and covert violations of this line. Thus, at the Seventh Congress, Dimitrov asserted that, in the latter years, "sectarianism" manifested itself no longer "in primitive, open forms as in the first years of the existence of the Communist International," but rather "under cover of a formal recognition of the Bolshevist theses. . . ."[14] There has been an ascending trend of such allegations in Comintern history: a trend which contributed to the flexibility of the center.]*

We may add here that the degree of ambiguity to be adopted for the formulation of a "line" was apt to become an object of contention between the center—interested in the maximization of that ambiguity as a factor facilitating the employment of the symbolic devices just discussed—and oppositionist groups outside of the center who regarded higher precision as safeguards against "arbitrary" actions of the center against them; actions which could and did present them with a trap of the "If-it's-not-one-thing-it's-another" variety. Thus, at the Fifth Congress, the right Clara Zetkin deplored that "sufficient clarity has not yet been achieved as to this question: How shall the various sections . . . execute the united front policy? . . . The resolutions of the world congresses must be able to be directive for us without explanations, without commentaries." In the same vein, the "ultra-left" Bordiga states: "We demand . . . a clear and precise fixation of the tactics of the Comintern. Even if its contents will be other than those which we demand, . . . they ought to be clear. We want to know where we are going."[15]

But in the case of the right, as well as the left, the demand for more precision (the presumable motive for the demand which we alluded to above) was not overtly stated. Whereas that motive was one of delimiting the power position of the center, the oppositionists claimed—with real or feigned naivete—that their motive ran exactly in the contrary direction. Bordiga's colleague Rossi explained:

It is ... necessary ... to say in which form these tactics (sc.: the united front) ought to be applied; otherwise, it will not be possible to condemn a party which on its own initiative ... has found an application of the united front which it deems correct.[16]

As if Rossi did not know, or could not have known, that it had just then proved "possible," "despite" the vagueness of the Comintern formulations, to condemn the Brandler-Radek leadership of the German Communist Party for a certain "application of the United front" tactics which it had not even developed "on its own initiative," but rather on the behest of the center!

In the same ostensibly naïve fashion, Clara Zetkin pointed out:

If we give the president of the Executive Committee the right to elucidate what a resolution of the world congress really means ... then we give the same right of interpretation to any other member. The monolithism of our discipline and action will thereby be broken.[17]

Certainly the Fifth Congress was the last at which these words could have been spoken!

NOTES

1. In quotations from these reports, the congress involved will be referred to by its Roman numeral. For the first five congresses the reports in German—published by Carl Hoym, Nachfolger Louis Cahnbley, Hamburg 1921 (I, II, III), 1923 (IV), without year (V)—were used (and translated by the author) unless otherwise indicated. For the last two congresses the reports published in English were adduced from the edition of the "International Press Correspondence," with the exception of Bucharin's Sixth Congress report on behalf of the Executive Committee, for which the French edition of the *Inprecorr* was consulted and translated. The page references concerning the Sixth Congress all refer to the 1928 volume of the *Inprecorr,* and those concerning the Seventh Congress refer to the 1935 volume unless the 1936 volume is indicated.

2. Cf., for the context: Harold D. Lasswell and Dorothy Blumenstock Jones, *World Revolutionary Propaganda* (New York, 1939); Franz Borkenau, *The Communist International* (London, 1939); Arthur Rosenberg, *A History of Bolshevism* (London, 1934).

3. George Bernard Shaw, letter to the *New Statesman and Nation* (May 31, 1941).

4. V, 467.

5. Louis Budenz in *The Daily Worker* (June 26, 1941).

6. V, 189.

7. VI, 865.

8. VI, 16.

9. VII, 1650.

10. *Daily Worker* (July 1, 1941), 6.

11. Molotov, speech to the Supreme Council of the Soviet Union, *World News and Views* (November 4, 1939), 6f. Emphasis added.

12. Dimitrov, VII, 960; Pieck, VII, 912; 855.

13. VII, 976.

14. VII, 975.

15. V, 335f., 402.

16. V, 156.

17. V, 336.

Chapter 18

ON AMERICAN POLICY IN VIETNAM

EDITOR'S NOTE: By 1967 Leites had reached the conclusion that the American position in Vietnam was both morally untenable and militarily doomed to failure. Some of the bases for this belief are described in analytical terms in the selections on Vietnam and on violence in rebellions which appear earlier in this volume. In this short paper from a journal of opinion he turns to policy advocacy. In the form of a response to a book of Edwin Reischauer,[1] *he shows why he believes American hopes of influencing North Vietnamese leadership to capitulate are based on illusions. He also explains his belief that the terms of United States commitment to the government of South Vietnam make withdrawal of American forces from that country morally justifiable and politically advisable.*

"Further Comments on Reischauer and the Choice on the War," from Bulletin of the Atomic Scientists *(June, 1968), 40-43.*

*W*hile Edwin Reischauer begins his remarkable analysis by indicating that "this is not a book about Vietnam," it is only on that country that I shall follow him here, and only on points or formulations with which I disagree. To them (designated by "R") I shall present alternatives ("A"), without being able to show in these pages why evidence seems to me, on balance, to support the latter. Like Reischauer, "I put forward these ... views ... with some diffidence, because I am not an expert either on Vietnam or on military matters" (pages 18-19).

R: It "seems highly probable" to Reischauer that a Vietnam in which the Communist Party had consolidated the control it had won in the summer of 1945 (rather than, first, losing much of it) would have developed a "relation to China not unlike that of Tito's Yugoslavia toward the Soviet Union"; also because "Ho, like Tito, had had cordial relations, with us" (page 30).

A: Mr. Reischauer's alternative history seems highly probable to me, too. But the particular factor quoted here—whatever "cordial" here means— appears to me unrelated both to the conjectured course of events in Asia and to the actual development in Europe.

R: A Vietnam under Communist control from 1945 on would have been "paying lip service" to China (page 31).

A: Even that is not too probable. There is no traditional dogma in Asian communism affirming the Chinese Party's superiority; and the Vietnamese Party probably feels its record—including a seizure of power in its entire country at a moment when the Chinese still seemed far from that level of success—to be at least as impressive as that of its Northern neighbor against whom no foreigner has intervened since 1945.

R: In 1945 Ho "apparently" expected our continued "friendship" (page 30).

A: He does not seriously conceive of "friendship" with the leading state of the non "socialist" world. No evidence is available which would allow us to guess what Ho at the end of World War II expected the course of his relations with Washington to be. He had more to "hope" for in economic aid from us than from China (ibid). Our capacity for aid was larger, but what about our intention, actual or predicted by Ho?

R: "The United States ... gave no indication at Geneva [in 1954] that it would oppose the elections [scheduled for 1956 to decide on the unification of Vietnam]" (page 24).

A: It was hard to believe, and was little believed, that the United States would do anything but "oppose" them if a date were ever set: the majority of the voters (in the North) would have been under totalitarian control. That such elections "would throw the South into the hands of the Vietminh" was not an "assumption" (page 25), but a certainty. To say that "our greatest and most obvious blunder" was not to "support the Geneva agreements" in this regard (page 31) is to assert it to be a grave mistake not to vindicate the totalitarian practice of elections by American "support."

R: The leadership of the Vietnamese Communist Party, ruling the North from the summer of 1954 on, was "outraged" by the "flouting" of the Geneva agreements with regard to elections (page 26).

A: The moment any such leader sensed in himself any attachment to *pacta sunt servanda,* or any depth of outrage about anything an enemy does, he would feel shattered about his own "degeneration." The leaders in question did not expect Diem, or anybody else attempting to rule from Saigon, to aspire to ceremonial suicide by pressing for elections, about which they themselves were, to borrow Mr. Reischauer's words about these years, "curiously passive" (pages 26-27).

R: A consequence of our "underwriting ... [Diem's] refusal to go through with the unification of Vietnam" was that the Party's (I shall use this word to designate the Vietnamese Communist Party) "*animosity* towards us increased" (page 31, my emphasis).

A: Our support of Diem's refusal to transfer the South to the Party's domain by the election mentioned in the Geneva agreements increased the Party's *expectation of a conflict* with us.

R: One component of the Southern rebellion in the later fifties was "organized" activity by "Southern Vietminh" (page 27).

A: The dominant contribution to the insurgents' organization was and is furnished by the Party, which maintains much centralization despite the country's division, and whose leadership is "Northern" mainly in the sense that national headquarters are in the North where the Party rules. Much of the "organized" activity by "Southern Vietminh" in the later fifties is likely to have been in conformity with policy set by the Central Committee of the all-national Party.

R: The return to the South of Southern Vietminh who had gone North after the Geneva agreements began after the announcement, in late 1960, that a "National Liberation Front" had been founded in the South (page 27).

A: It began before.

THE TWO REGIMES

R: After the Party's conquest of power in the North its policies produced "agrarian unrest" (page 27).

A: At that time the Party destroyed—fully, in an economic sense, and to a considerable extent, in a physical sense—the well-to-do farmers, with a severity at least equaling, say, the "liquidation of the Kulaks as a class" in the Soviet Union of the late twenties.

R: In May 1963 a "serious" Buddhist "uprising" broke out in the South, and in the spring of 1966 a "large scale" "uprising" (pages 27-28).

A: These were less than what is ordinarily meant by an uprising.

R: Diem's suppression of Vietminh remnant and of "all open opponents" was "ruthless"; it made "something of a police state" of the South (page 26).

A: If these (proper) words be chosen to describe Diem's conduct, other terms should perhaps be selected to designate the higher level of threats raised and damage inflicted by the Party, before and after conquest of power; and I have missed in Mr. Reischauer's account a sentence which would be a full counterpart to the one quoted. When he speaks of the Party's "dictatorial, oppressive" rule in the North (page 29), the reader little informed about Vietnam may gain the impression that in the author's view North and South are coercing their citizens to about the same degree. Indeed, Mr. Reischauer follows his conjecture that a Vietnam under the Party's control since 1945 "would probably not have been something we would have approved of" with the reminder that "we have not found much we could approve of" in the South either (page 29).

VIETNAMESE BALANCE OF POWER

R: "People usually discuss what Hanoi or Washington might be willing to concede, and what pressures Peking and Moscow may bring." However, "the problem lies with the two ... protagonists in the war: the supporters of Saigon and ... the National Liberation Front"; on the one side the Vietcong, and on the other "the South Vietnamese military establishment and a congeries of quarreling religious bodies and political factions," which are, however, "held together ... by a determination not to fall under Communist rule" (page 8).

A: On the one side there is the Party, in power in the North; in the South, presenting itself and operating largely through its front, the Front.

In the congeries on the other side, the resolve to fight each other seems to surpass whatever "determination" there is to contribute to the prevention of the Party's conquest of power in the South. Vietnam is the only country in the world which remained non-Communist after 1945 solely to the extent to which the threatened or actual presence of foreign soldiers sufficed for this purpose. As Reischauer himself puts it in another context, "all along ... probably the only ... alternative to what has happened ... was to allow Ho ... to take over the whole of Vietnam" (page 28).

TERMINATION THROUGH NEGOTIATION?

R: The bombing of the North "may so build up" the "hatred and distrust" of "the North Vietnamese" toward the United States that it "increases their determination to go on fighting," reduces their "willingness to negotiate" (page 6).

A: The particular North Vietnamese who, under whatever influence from the people at large, make the decision to negotiate or not, are the leaders of the Party. They are apt to view it as a grievous mistake—as many other less austere politicians also do—not to entertain extreme distrust of enemies at all times, and as a sacred obligation to transform hatred of the enemy into conduct which will reduce as much as feasible losses at his hand, enhance as much as possible advance at his expense. Of course, they do not always succeed in disciplining emotions, but the record shows that they are apt to be as brutal toward their own souls as against enemies.

R: One policy is to "go on fighting on somewhat the present terms, in the hope that in time we could bring about a deescalation . . . and . . . persuade the Vietcong and Hanoi to seek a settlement . . ." (page 9).

A: While it is possible to indicate conditions in which the leadership of the Party might decide to deescalate, it is harder to imagine situations in which they would prefer explicit self-limitation to temporary reduction in activity— unless they came to believe that the former would decisively weaken Saigon (in which case it might not be acceptable to us) or furnish a pretext for an American withdrawal. But the acquisition of such insight by the Party's leaders is obstructed by their horror of yielding beyond present necessity, as well as by their certainty that only pressure works.

R: "I wonder if any sort of agreement will ever be reached until one side or the other recognizes that it faces eventual defeat" (page 8).

A: Particularly then each side may prefer unadmitted (where feasible) or properly embellished withdrawal to formal renunciation, or (for us) the appearance of "peace with honor" soon to be followed by utter failure.

R: After the American elections of 1968, the Party may be "more inclined" toward a negotiated peace if it is given, in the South, a "tolerable" alternative to an "apparently endless" war (page 18).

A: With dedication, courage, and skill, the Party has been fighting for more than 20 years; there were interruptions, to be sure, but while they lasted, the Party looked toward the resumption of the struggle. Though the trend has been in its favor, there have been lengthy phases of stagnation and regression; the leaders expect them to recur, and have not ceased molding themselves and the cadres to be tenacious in stalemate and adversity.

At least until the early seventies, therefore, the Party is more apt to decide in favor of lying low in the South—as it did from the middle to the later fifties—than to reconvert itself so as to operate in an alien legality, supposing Saigon were to offer it a genuine chance of that kind.

ESCALATION

R: Attacking on the ground in the North "would probably only mean . . . that we would have two guerrilla wars on our hands . . ." (page 10).

A: Worse. Even if we succeeded, with a much enlarged investment cost, in depleting our opponent's armed forces in both parts of the country, induced him to disperse into small units and to avoid encounters with us—if we were as successful as the French in Algeria, 1959-61—the maintenance cost of this result would probably include a protracted continuation of our massive military presence. This kind of forecast made de Gaulle, in late 1960, decide upon "disengagement" from Algeria.

WITHDRAWAL

R: The "counterstrategy" of building a "more tenable defense" (against the expansion of the zone where Communists rule in Asia) in "sounder terrain," such as Thailand, would mean "the further spread of American military power into areas where the Vietnam war had just shown that our type of military power was . . . ineffective" (page 13).

A: The withdrawal would have been caused not by what Vietnam and, say, Thailand have in common—being in Southeast Asia—but rather by what has made a difference between them for more than three decades: the Vietnamese Party's performance—the level of political and military energy generated by it per capita of cadres and country—is among the highest in the world; that of the Thai Party, insignificant. On the other hand, those opposed to the Party in Bangkok have been less feeble, and less prone to consume their forces in struggles among themselves than has been the case in Saigon.

R: Withdrawing from Vietnam would be "welching" on a commitment.

A: Yes, as to the texts of assurances given. No, with regard to a rarely stressed, but hardly hidden, condition never clearly renounced by Washington: the enterprise of preventing the Party's conquest of power by arms in a country should be a genuinely common enterprise of its anticommunists and their foreign allies. That the internal resistance against the Party might be and might remain feeble was hardly envisaged in the American mainstream until recently. That is the case of Vietnam, familiar today, but unexpected by those who initiated and enlarged American intervention between the mid-fifties and the mid-sixties. Imagine a weird world: a temporarily cohesive, impressively large, reasonably dedicated, and moderately efficient Freedom Front capital Hué utilizing much of its human and material resources in its civil war—and insisting on our doing the rest, urging us to destroy what must be, as, to a noticeable extent, the occupied Europeans did a quarter of a century ago—that is the "doctrine" of "containment" applied to Vietnam. At no point has it been resolved, at any level in the United States, that we assume henceforth the obligation to endeavor, by our own force, stopping the Communist Party in a country where the balance of the will and skill to believe and persuade, to coerce and suffer, to kill and die, is decisively in its favor.

NOTE

1. Edwin Reischauer, *Beyond Vietnam: The United States and Asia* (New York, 1967).

Chapter 19

THE NEW SOFT LINE:
A CHANGE IN SOVIET STYLE

EDITOR'S NOTE: The selection which follows is taken from a longer article about increased trade between America and Russia and the expectations and reactions generated thereby. American hopes are that through increased contact with the West, Soviet society would become more like our own, providing a better basis for political cooperation. As Leites describes them, Soviet explanations of the "new economic togetherness" follow the "change of line" defense patterns which he has described in an earlier selection in this section.

Here, however, Leites discerns an important change in the "operational code" of the Kremlin leaders. Their new approach in dealing with Europe and America is marked by a greater realism about how to increase Soviet influence on Western opinion. Leites examines conditions that may have contributed to this revision of strategy. He considers what psychological mechanisms may be at work, especially those which allow Russian leaders to control anxieties about being penetrated by their enemies—anxieties discussed in early papers in this volume.

From "The New Economic Togetherness: American and Soviet Reactions," Studies in Comparative Communism *VII (1974), 246-285, originally part of a report prepared under the auspices of the RAND Corporation for the Defense Advanced Research Projects Agency (R-1369-ARPA, December 1973). The author is most grateful to Charles Wolf, Jr., and Robert E. Klitgaard, who contributed greatly to the original by numerous and important queries, rectifications, and amplifications, and to Frank Hoeber and A. Ross Johnson for additional comments. He is also indebted to Lilita Dzirkals for expertly selecting pertinent documents.*

I. JOIN THEM AND YOU MAY YET BEAT THEM

Being, for all its efforts to obscure or deny, very much on the asking end, the Politburo, even in earlier dispositions, would not want to be unpleasant. But this powerful reason for avoiding offensiveness happens to operate at an advanced stage in the Soviet rulers' long march toward the difficult insight that, contrary to their primitive conviction, a premium on rudeness is not always awarded by history. It is perhaps because of this nearing insight that the Politburo has resorted more thoroughly than ever to a soft style—which has, to be sure, several well-known antecedents, but whose quantity, in the cliché of dialectics, this time makes for several novel qualities. In doing so, it seemed until the late summer of 1973 that the Soviet rulers might increase not only the chance of obtaining the economic benefits they are after, but also the probability of making the sharp political gains that eluded them in their earlier pursuit.

Since the time when the pages to follow were written, in mid-1973, the chain of reactions initiated by enhanced repression (noted below as a component of the new Soviet stance) and intensified dissent in the Soviet Union has reduced the effectiveness of the Politburo's soft style in foreign relations, though it has at the time at which I add these remarks (mid-October 1973) not impaired the Soviet rulers' obstinate resolve to persevere in their "24th Congress" line, presumably expecting that their lack of response to Western "provocations" (now, as I shall note, called that more in private than in public) will permit their policy to outlast what they may predict to be a flurry of Western orneriness, as well as contribute to its cessation.

Rather than attempting at this point to take account in full of the changes that have occurred since mid-1973, I shall—while not eschewing references to them—analyze the situation of around the time of Brezhnev's visit to this country. This is not mere history. The attitudes then prevailing, while momentarily overlaid by the sensational irruption of returns to older reactions, have not become negligible; in fact, they may become dominant once more in a not remote future.

To bring out how much Soviet style has changed within a few years, one might recall an incident forgotten, I would surmise, by most of those who were not professionally concerned with it. In March 1969 the Warsaw Pact issued another call for a conference on European security. "The Budapest appeal," Harlan Cleveland, then U.S. Ambassador to NATO, recalls, "was better dressed than at its earlier début, wrapped in the chilliest of Cold War accusations against the West, at a Bucharest meeting in 1966." In the month following the Soviet move, the North Atlantic Council was to celebrate in Washington the twentieth anniversary of the Alliance. Some of the foreign ministers assembling for this occasion were, Cleveland remembers, "sorely tempted" to respond favorably to the Pact's appeal: an important move of the Politburo seemed to be about to make significant progress. Had nothing more happened on the Soviet side, the same participant-observer conjectures, "The Ministers . . . would probably have . . . [mentioned favorably] the Budapest appeal in their final communiqué." But then

> as a prelude to the . . . meeting in Washington, which had been publicly scheduled for months, the Soviet Navy conducted in the Atlantic . . . the largest naval exercise they had ever put on there . . . [and] nearly all of these ships after the maneuvers passed through the Straits of Gibraltar to bring the Soviet Mediterranean Squadron up to . . . [its] greatest strength. Then . . . the day before the NATO session . . . a . . . statement [was] . . . issued by the government of the Soviet Union—berating the Alliance . . . in language reminiscent of the early 50s.

The Ambassador remembers:

> The Soviet statement fell like a great stone into the Ministerial meeting. The . . . text first became available . . . from Agence France Presse . . . I watched the AFP ticker item hit the . . . delegations, passed from Minister to Minister with whispers of shock and disbelief. I could almost feel the temperature drop. . . . Why, I asked myself, do the Soviets so often slap the West across the face with a dead fish just when . . .?[1]

Some members of the Soviet ruling group may have asked that old question (no doubt not even novel to them), this time more insistently, of themselves and their colleagues; and the ensuing resolve to reform may have been more genuine, effective, and enduring even in the face of "provocations" such as those offered by the West in the summer and autumn of 1973.

One reason, I would surmise, was the sharp change in the military balance in the Politburo's favor during the preceding years. Among the several beliefs that made up the traditional Bolshevik faith in the efficacy of rudeness, the most ingrained, I would conjecture, was their conviction that when one apprehends that an enemy endowed with military superiority may attack, defeat, even annihilate one, an intensely hostile tone toward him is an indispensable element of one's arsenal for dissuading him from using his superior potential. As that potential disappeared, the other beliefs favoring a stance of hostility—e.g., its alleged usefulness for making advances—could perhaps be examined in the light of accumulating and hardly supporting experience.

In any case, Politburo behavior from 1971 on leaves little doubt on this point. A majority in the Politburo has greatly increased its awareness that there are many situations where one most fully "utilizes" another's weakness not by pressing against him, but rather by giving him a semblance of support; many circumstances where one maximizes the probability of a desired change, again, not by pressing for it, but rather by appearing to find the status quo livable, while suggesting that there might be something better in the direction in which one had been vainly straining. Thus the Politburo has seemingly discovered that, for a while at least, the most effective way to work for our removal from Western Europe is *not* to work for it.

From its origins until a recent date, the Politburo had taken it for granted that the optimal moment to counterattack is the earliest one, and the mode in which to do so, in kind—only more strongly. It now knows better. For instance, influential Americans have, as we have seen earlier, accompanied their acceptance of our new economic closeness to the Soviet Union with public forecasts of "political gains" therefrom, forecasts both, no doubt, expected by members of the Politburo and repugnant, even frightening, to them. In cruder times, Moscow would have responded with blasts to hope. This response, however, would have reduced our enthusiasm, and perhaps moderated our offers.

Now they do it differently. They have resolved, I would surmise, to start with the stance that their major countermeasure against our real or imaginary penetrations should be a latter-day application of Lenin's dictum at the introduction of the NEP in the late winter of 1921: we can allow a strengthening of bourgeois and petty-bourgeois elements in city and countryside on condition of putting the Mensheviks in prison. (This saying, I feel confident, has been frequently heard in office conversations among Moscow influentials, 1972-1973.) The advice was acted on in 1921, and it has been acted on again, well before the matter became prominent in the summer of 1973. As to the changes in Soviet economic organization called for by Americans, the Politburo has proved capable of not budging (while hardly rebuffing), or not permitting itself to be victimized by the high visibility that both its previous "relaxation" (minute though it was) and its recent "tightening" (limited though that was, too) afforded to the few dissenters who had been incautiously permitted to accumulate merit abroad. According to a Western analyst writing in the spring of 1973, the latest plans for industrial reorganization then developed in Moscow took a hard line on the monopoly of foreign trade, and there has been a shift on the issue of the ruble's convertibility with Western currencies from "vague and occasionally accommodative formulations" to "outright rejection."[2] At the same time—this is my point—rebuttals to numerous declarations that a main U.S. objective in intensifying economic relations with the Soviet Union is to accomplish what the Politburo no doubt calls, within its walls, the "restoration of capitalism" there—such rebuttals have been infrequent and sober. Without this sort of response, the atmosphere in the United States would not have developed so favorably toward the Soviet Union as it did until recently—a condition that, it may seem to us, was easy to fulfill, but that, I submit, came hard to the Soviet Union.

It is rare to see the traditional standard virulence in verbal counterattack perpetuated, as when we read that

a significant section of the U.S. *bourgeois* press ... *cynically* referring to the agreements reached in May 1972 ... are *essentially* demanding for themselves a "free hand" for ideological *diversions* and *provocations under the guise* of "extending contacts," the "free exchange of ideas" and so forth.[3]

In the more restrained style now in the ascendant, taking a view more broad and more serene, it will be recalled that

the history of the Soviet Union's economic relations with other countries shows examples illustrating the attempts of imperialist circles ... to launch *unfounded* attacks on the foreign trade monopoly ... , [even] to use trading channels for purposes *hostile to socialism*.[4]

Going even farther, these circles "spare no effort to circumvent ... [the foreign trade] monopoly ... to establish direct trade contacts between capitalist firms and individual Soviet enterprises."[5] But such alleged penetrations are merely met by recalling that "the importance of maintaining ... the foreign trade monopoly was repeatedly emphasized ... by the Party's leading bodies,"[6] that it "is *of course absolutely unrealistic* to make the development of economic cooperation between the USSR and the capitalist world dependent on a change in the ... foreign trade mechanism of our country." Indeed, the foreign trade monopoly arises "from the socialist ownership of the means of production and the planned nature of the socialist economy."[7] This monopoly is required even more (in Bolshevik sensibility, something already totally commanded can always become even more so) when the Politburo's economic policy bears some resemblance to the NEP. One is reminded of the ancient resolution (by the 13th Party Congress of early 1924) that demanded the maintenance and strengthening of the foreign trade monopoly "particularly in conditions of the ... NEP ... [also] as an instrument to protect the country's wealth from being plundered by ... foreign capital."[8] Such is the new moderation in counterattack, a moderation strikingly exhibited in the late summer and early fall of 1973 by the tone of restraint with which Soviet leaders and media (no doubt following a directive from the top) responded to the highly unexpected and offensive (in both senses of the word) Western moves against them which then emerged and developed.

Counterattack may even be—an unheard of thing in the past—withheld altogether when it plainly appears to be harmful, as in the case of Sakharov's attack against the regime. The latter proved capable of switching over to silence when the mounting intensity of the dissenter's onslaught evoked a rising response abroad. Or counterattack may be renounced from the start and replaced by more than silence, the transmutation of real enemy into pretended friend. Take a minor but significant case, the Soviet treatment of the American pronouncement that perhaps went farthest in envisaging the new economic era as an instrument of political penetration. A forecast was made by John Hardt and George Holliday that in the new epoch, to cite the close paraphrase of *The New York Times,* "the Soviet Union . . . [might] allow foreign companies to have more [sic] influence on its decision-making" (June 10, 1973).[9] Now, apart from this frosting on the cake, much in the report—though it assesses the potential for economic gains for the United States as small—favors recently projected developments on grounds acceptable to the Politburo. What that body—through the formal or informal directives issuing from it—has now added to its already respectable arsenal is the capacity not to react at all to (merely verbal) hostility, but rather to use all the congenial elements that compose that hostility in a compound that now can be thoroughly decomposed:

> The report gives an all-round appraisal of . . . the authors of the report note . . . the report admits . . . the authors of the report point out . . . the report refutes . . . the authors of the report point to . . . the report stresses. . . .

—all verbs devoid of badness and hence reserved in Soviet language to introduce affirmations that share that property.

As to the black aspect of the piece, it is being whitened by a procedure already observed in operation above, the use of words that cover the bad with the good: "The authors of the report believe that . . . trade would bring . . . *political* advantages too."[10]

From its beginnings until a recent date any given stance of the Politburo was apt to be dominated by the combat it was conducting against its enemies of the time. It has now become capable of, and is in fact, doing otherwise. For the Politburo (by which, in such a context, is always meant, of course, a majority of its members) may have sensed that the very prevalence of high hostility *(never mind against which targets)* in its public posture rendered more plausible its enemies' allegation that, despite its protracted protestations and prolonged inactions, it was still bent upon political-military aggression. On the other hand, pervasive *mildness* in public stance might undercut such suspicions; it might even dominate, in Western perceptions, a simultaneous raising of military posture, which, if accompanied by the earlier disagreeable tone of voice, might have turned out to be starkly impressive. As it is, few in the West outside the limited circles of military specialists and last cold warriors have been impressed by the recent changes in the military balance favorable to Moscow.

For example, instead of conveying, if not declaring, that one expects enmity, one now avows the contrary. "I've seen your picture in the paper," declares Brezhnev when meeting Senator Church, "and I always thought, from your face, that I'd like you." According to the journalist who reports this, the Senator is "delighted."[11] Stating what is already obvious and still surprising, an observer (John Newhouse) notes that "the Soviets ... are challenging neither NATO nor the ... European Community," after a quarter of a century of making only limited progress with an unremitting stance of hostility. Instead of continuing their traditional presentation of these entities as dangerously evil, the Soviet rulers are now content with suggesting—more in sorrow than in anger, more in regret than in sorrow, more in hope of progress than in regret—that without these organizations things would be (even) better than they are. For the Politburo has finally understood that such mellowness is more damaging than their traditional pushing and pulling. "In accepting the Common Market," Newhouse discerns—a maneuver that may seem routine to us but that comes hard to them—"Moscow hopes to blunt any incentives ... to develop comparable political and defense institutions."[12]

Enemies may still be presented in the older vein. Thus, according to *Kommunist* in the spring of 1973, "the opposition to detente ... still has substantial reserves," so that "it is indispensable to exercise unceasing vigilance"—a dread word still connected with the liquidation of Party cadres by Stalin—"and to be ready to repel any schemes of the aggressive ... circles of imperialism."[13] To be sure, in the late summer and early fall of 1973 this presentation of the West increased, as already noted, but only in moderate response to what was no doubt to the Politburo an unexpected Western counteroffensive instigated by Western top levels. But prior to this what was in the ascendant, particularly in the domain under discussion, was a more harmless enemy: Jackson-Javits-Meany, whose wickedness then appeared to be dwarfed by the futility of their endeavors. In earlier times, any enemy of the Politburo, however limited his power, was apt to be judged as a potentially grave danger to be countered fiercely. The regime's present difficulty with a few famous dissenters may show what happens if every effort is not made to stop the rot at the start. "As influential and active as the anti-Soviet forces in contemporary America may be," remarks a Soviet journalist in non-standard and contrasting fashion, "it becomes ever more difficult for them to oppose the wish of Americans to ..."[14]

Yet further reducing its initial ascription of enmity to most sectors of the world not controlled by it, the Politburo has accelerated the process of *entering into* innumerable activities from which its members had earlier held themselves aloof—a stance that had magnified the impression of hostility they conveyed. Just as the Party used to proclaim itself of "a special kind," so did the Soviets at large. Now, while they maintain, though in less shrill fashion, an assertion of unique excellence, they have taken further strides in transmuting their appearance from that of forbidding and menacing loners into that of omnipresent and at least tolerable joiners. To use the vocabulary of Trotskyites (discoursing on whether to remain by themselves or to go where others are, so as in the end to dominate a larger sphere), the Politburo has considerably enhanced its degree of "entrism." "Ties" with the West, rather than mere "relations," have in the Party's public stance become one of those strived-for goods, such as the "ties" of the Party with the people. Such ties, their multiplication and tightening, are now no longer commonly presented as directed against a specific person, nor even as in the service of a particular objective; they rather appear (in another striking departure from the previous disposition to view the present as merely a means to a transfigured future) as ends in themselves. That there have been, according to Newhouse, "more contacts between the two halves of Europe in the past three years [1970-1972] than in all the preceding years since World War II"[15] may indeed be something which the Politburo in private receives in unmodified Bolshevik fashion—as a means to more power, and a gloriously economic one—but which it publicly welcomes for its own sake (an obvious condition for the new conduct being productive). The new relations between the United States and the Soviet Union, Brezhnev exults on American television, "are all becoming part of the daily lives of the [two] peoples."[16] At the same time, his minister of foreign trade makes a joke—innocent, yet perhaps also revealing that means have not really become ends in the Kremlin: "I am a devout supporter," the old Bolshevik Patolichev quips in Blair House, "of more contacts, contacts, contacts which would bring more contracts, contracts, contracts."[17]

The Politburo has learned to cater to the American belief in a direct relationship between the number of "constructive" agreements we are signing with a country and some desirable quality of our relationship with it. That the trend away from confrontation is in the process of becoming "an established pattern" is, to the Under Secretary of State for Economic Affairs (William J. Casey) indicated by "the impressive *number*" of agreements signed in Peking and Moscow in 1972 as well as by the prospects of *additional* ones." [18] Brezhnev points out to Americans that these new agreements, when signed, together with those concluded during the past year, will "make up *an impressive file* of documents in cooperation in some widely ranging field."[19] Such emphasis discourages conjectures on the amount and direction of that file's impact.

And then there are institutions. Completing their entry into the preexisting ones and becoming charter members of numerous new ones in which the present higher level of cooperation is embodied, the Politburo undoes what it probably regards as two of the great Stalin's mistakes, the refusal to enter into the "Marshall Plan" organizations and the absence from the central bodies of the United Nations at the time when the war in Korea broke out.

On the occasion of the 22nd Washington State International Trade Fair held in Seattle during the summer of 1972, the Seattle-King County Economic Development Council, one of its members reports, arranged numerous activities for the 80-member Soviet delegation "so they could become better acquainted with our area and its business leaders"—a cocktail reception, a formal dinner, to be sure, but also "individual visits to American homes by the Soviets." Another effort by Americans to multiply contacts? Not quite, because all this was done "at the request of the Russians."[20] While it is not certain that we have converted Soviet officials to our taste, it seems plausible that these higher authorities in Moscow who presumably requested their emissaries to request lots of personal contacts with Americans have become aware of our proclivities, or, rather, have finally understood the importance of "utilizing" them. "To live at peace," Brezhnev tells Americans on television, expressing a belief that is more surely theirs than his, "we must trust each other; and to trust each other, we must know each other better."[21] Whatever the Politburo's scepticism, or worse, as to whether this is true, it appears to have yielded to the awareness that these are beliefs of ours which are not neglected without cost.

All of which may have seemed to the Soviet rulers, until a very recent date, noticeably cost-effective. For one thing, the Politburo was not challenged, until the mid-summer of 1973, on its accustomed degree of control within its domain. For another, it maintains, or improves, its military posture—a matter on which it has not yet been seriously queried. Furthermore, it enhances the importance of those in the West whose economic stakes in transactions with the Soviet Union may make them averse, say, to economic sanctions against a politically or militarily forward Politburo. The latter is probably coming to appreciate more fully the impact of *short-run* interests of *particular* sectors within the "capitalist class" on the policies of a capitalist state that Bolsheviks used to idealize as the guardian of the *long-run* and *general* interests of that class. "It is not unreasonable," Ambassador Green remarks about what may be a similar situation, "for Chinese leaders to believe that U.S. businessmen who benefit from U.S.-PRC trade might influence American . . . opinion in ways that may be *mutually* beneficial."[22] Would it not be even more reasonable for Chinese leaders to foresee that such influence would be *unilaterally* beneficial to them, for they would worry less about the possibility that Shanghai businessmen interested in U.S.-PRC trade would arouse Chinese opinion on behalf of their special concerns?

Finally, the Politburo's stance, again until a very recent date, contributed to making any aversion toward the regime of the Soviet Union a familiar archaism comparable to a maintained reluctance to buy a Volkswagen, reducing the perspective that Moscow may come to dominate Western Europe to the fear that Bonn may become preponderant in its Western part. As *Pravda* recalls in the late spring of 1973, "the bankruptcy of frantic anti-Communism is a symptomatic event of our days."[23] No wonder *Kommunist* rejects "the frequent proposals of those who want to castrate the political meaning of the peaceful coexistence between countries with different social systems, replacing it by 'purely' economic, scientific, cultural information and tourist aspects." [24] The essence is the weakening of anti-Communism. "Stable economic ties," thus runs a standard theme expressed by the Soviet top level itself, "are exceedingly important . . . from the point of view of creating favorable conditions for the solution of . . . international problems." [25] Decoded: "the recent extension in commercial and economic ties between socialist and capitalist countries in Europe has acted like a torpedo on 'Cold War' policies" [26] the latter term, of course, being Moscow's designation for all policies noticeably deviating from those proposed by itself.

During what may be privately viewed as a second NEP, it is appropriate (I have already given examples) to quote from the first. "What is at the bottom of our improved international position," the People's Commissar of Foreign Affairs said in early 1924, "is . . . especially our improved economic ties with all countries." [27]

While we may see behind the Politburo's changed stance "the Administration's patient efforts to bring . . . the Soviet Union . . . into closer contact with the . . . world," [28] the Politburo may have a lower estimate of the influence that we exert on it. Indeed, it may, with whatever degree of lucidity, be aware of having progressed in insight and proficiency on the matter of how to handle *us*.

II. WE ARE JUST ANOTHER EUROPEAN COUNTRY

Talking to Germans about economic relations between the Soviet Union and the FRG, Moscow Radio may observe, recalling the bad fifties and the still unsatisfactory sixties, that "the trade volume between *the two most important European industrial states* could not be compared with. . . ." [29] *International Affairs* reports the signing of contracts under which "France is to participate in building *Europe's biggest automobile works* at Naberezhniye Chelny. . . ." [30] *"The great European powers,* be they socialist or capitalist . . . ," says a prominent intellectual. [31] Of course, "the consultations . . . in Helsinki [are] between *32 European states*, the United States and Canada." [32]

It is in such passing fashion, when speaking in some detail about, for instance, economic connections between the Soviet Union and Western Europe that the Politburo attempts to have the idea sink in that the Soviet Union is as European as Belgium. Having started as "one-sixth of the world" related to Communists everywhere in the other five, the Soviet Union has come home to *"our continent,"* which, agreeably, "accounts for one-fifth of the world's population, 47 percent of national income . . . 55 percent of the industrial output on our planet . . . [and] almost half of the world's scientists and researchers." What I have illustrated is a more effective way of rejoining Europe than emphatic assurances that the socialist states have "the interest of all European nations at heart,"[33] or the call for "a new Europe—a Europe of trust and cooperation."[34] Of course, here as elsewhere, the theme as such is far from new; but the modes of conveying it, together with the changes in actual relations, seemed—at least until the summer of 1973—to give an old approach greater impact.

Demand for the "economic integration of East and West Europe"[35] are now elaborated with a specificity that used to be reserved for East Europe alone. There are "at the present time," a Soviet analyst explains, "in the West as well as in the East of Europe some national industrial complexes which comprise, if not all, then a considerable fraction of the branches of con-temporary industry." This has "evident negative consequences" such as "the presence of many . . . duplicating and relatively small-scale productions and enterprises in the various countries," a "structure" which in its turn is "a consequence of enduring political tension," and hence is now obsolete. In contrast, "Europe's economy might have a considerably more unified char-acter"; it could in fact be "based on the complementary structure of the economies of her various states." Specifically, "socialist and capitalist coun-tries might develop particular branches and productions," which would be "calculated to satisy each others' needs during a long period."

The complement to pan-European specialization is "all-European pro-jects," which Moscow has been proposing for some time: "The creation of a single energy system," "the construction of a European network of pipe-lines," "the development of various forms of communication,"[36] "the orga-nization of transcontinental freight carriage," "the . . . utilization of sea and ocean resources"[37]—standard points. It is in comparison with pan-Europe that the separateness of Western Europe is presented as disadvantageous. It would not be optimal to isolate that "subregion"[38] from Eastern Europe, nor to "reinforce the economic dissociation between socialist and capitalist coun-tries" in Europe—which is, however, what "the policy of the Common Market is objectively[39] directed toward. [Now the mildest reproach.]

Only rarely and lightly, in keeping with the stance of having almost no enemies, will it be noted that "pan-European cooperation . . . would permit, among other things, to liquidate the retardation [sic] of Western Europe with regard to the United States of America."[40] And I have seen no recent call for the reduction of our influence in pan-Europe: the less pressed, the better achieved.

III. FURTHER COMMENTS ON THE WESTERNIZATION OF BOLSHEVIKS

Throughout my discussion of the Politburo's responses to the new eco-nomic togetherness, I have suggested how its current stance is related to changes in beliefs about the world and about ways to get ahead (as well as to protect oneself) in it. My emphasis has fallen on how much better operators the men in the Kremlin have become, at least with regard to the West—seeing us more as we really are, at the expense of previous beliefs. These beliefs, while not always explicitly stressed components of Marxist-Leninist doctrine, were always obscurely and strongly connected with it. So the increase in realism of the Politburo is likely to be one aspect of a process, of which another is a reduction in faith—hence, in drive. Which will be the larger, the increase in productivity or the decrease in energy—in 1973, 1978 . . .? The considerable unused potential for productivity in the Politburo, say as of 1958, will, I would surmise, soon have been fully put to use; while the reduction in energy from the underlying loss of faith may have proceeded slowly and may continue to do so for a long time. Were all this the case, the Politburo may be more redoubtable in 1978 than in 1988, while I would judge it to be a stronger adversary (keeping resources constant) now than it was in 1968.

Much in Soviet views and style, of course, remains unchanged: from the insistence that the West, so far as it is disposed to extend its economic-technological relations with the East, is "forced" to do so by its own difficulties and failures, to the inability to yield pride of place. What "people will long remember" is "the labor exploits of the *Soviet and Egyptian* workers who built. . . ."; "Aswan is . . . [a] victory of two people—*The Soviet and the Egyptian.*"[41]

But there is an enhanced capacity to refer to an unfavorable past without stressing the West's responsibility for it. West Berlin thus becomes just one of those "problems that have several times been the source of dangerous crises and conflicts." There is also an increased disposition to proclaim limited aims—e.g., mere "limitations on the arms race."[42] When "the cause of disarmament" is put forward, it is at least preceded by "the cause of limiting the arms race,"[43] thus giving high dignity to a circumscribed objective.

Where "class interests" once reigned alone, several aspects of soul and mind may now also be considered. Some of "the causes arousing tension in Soviet-American relations" now appear as "not at all of objective character." For "a significant influence on international relations is exercised by the forces of prejudice, lack of culture and understanding."[44] To be sure, these forces are located entirely in the United States; yet it is novel that they are recognized as non-negligible aspects of life.

One may go farther and acknowledge in oneself, as in the rest of mankind, the operation of an identical factor. For one Soviet intellectual this may still be the distinctive defect of the other, as when one discerns that "the desire [of foreign businessmen] to insist on control [of enterprises in the Soviet Union] as the only way to ensure . . . profits looks . . . like an *inertia* of thinking [as the Soviet government is willing to guarantee profits while refusing control]."[45] But, for a colleague of his, the traditional Russian theme of "inertia" is not limited to foreigners: "not always," he discovers, "can we [men given to thinking] . . . fully appreciate . . . the importance [of this or another event] —*our human nature, the power of inertia* . . . account for that."[46]

Apart from interests, the means created to serve them may become powerful in their own right: "the arms race itself," rather than conflicts of interest within "imperialism" and between it and socialism, "has become one of the most dangerous . . . threats of war." So far from "classes" always being masters of their instruments, the latter may escape from the hands of their users. "Even if they [states] do not deliberately want a world thermonuclear war," their "conflicts . . . may get out of control and make a war unavoidable."[47] More generally, "the difficulties in Soviet-American relations . . . derive . . . in part from factors which are far from always controlled by the policies of both governments."[48]

Rather than the state being the "executive committee of the exploiting class," numerous influences now are perceived as impinging on it. "Lenin," it is discovered, "urged a careful study of the arrangement of forces in the U.S. domestic political arena," "a differential assessment of the various political groupings." He, in fact, "stressed the need to reckon with the different shades in the approach by . . . U.S. public circles to . . . Soviet-American relations."[49]

If such a "shade" does not express itself in U.S. government decisions immediately, it may still do so later. When soon after the coming into existence of Soviet power "sober-minded politicians, business and public figures" began advocating "cooperation with Soviet Russia," it is true that "at the time these voices did not carry very far," that they "did not yet have enough sway crucially to influence . . . U.S. foreign policy." But for all that "it would be wrong"—perhaps a mistake committed by the Politburo in the past—"to discount their impact on U.S. public opinion."[50]

While groups whose impact formerly might have been underestimated, because they were not counted among the "ruling class," are now taken more seriously, it is henceforth also recognized that membership in that "class" does not guarantee instant influence. When the U.S. government at the end of 1971 changed "certain elements" of its economic policies toward the Soviet Union, "the discussion of these questions in the press and at conferences . . . once more demonstrated how considerable was the rift . . . between the moods of business circles [presumably desiring farther-reaching changes] and the country's . . . trade policy." At this point, perhaps afraid of his audacity, the author assumes the cost of a non sequitur for the benefit of ending with orthodoxy: ". . . [this] showed the pressure which business circles can nowadays bring to bear on the government."[51]

The asserted conflict between capitalism and socialism ceases to dominate each and every aspect of the world. "The difficulty of the problems dividing the two sides," it may now be said about the Soviet Union and the United States, "even apart from ideological differences. . . ." That this manner of reference is a singular advance is indicated by a rapid withdrawal: "The difficulty of Soviet-American relations is to a considerable degree explained by the fact that they represent two opposed social systems."[52] But the retreat is only partial: "to a considerable degree" is considerably less than the orthodox adverbial "totally," which was so taken for granted in the past that it would typically not be uttered, but rather contained, in such a sentence, in the word "explained."

The Bolshevik restriction upon the word "revolution" as referring only to the socio-political domain is abolished: Brezhnev and Kosygin render mandatory the locution "the contemporary scientific and technological revolution." That word "revolution" may even become the only current one: "by combining the advantages of *socialism* with the achievements of *the scientific and technical revolution.*"[53]

"Forces of production"—depending on science—gain in weight over "class relations." As to promises to provide the American people with guns and butter simultaneously, "even such a *rich country* as the U.S.A. has proved unable to accomplish this task."[54] When it is pointed out that "only 7 percent" of American gross national product is absorbed by military expenditures, "account should be taken of the fact that *the fraction of the national product remaining after expenditures of absolute necessity*—and hence available for improvements, reforms, social needs—is not that large."[55] "Of course," one may now begin, "technical questions are not of decisive significance," and then continue: "but much is often determined by them."[56]

Questions regarding all of mankind—where, earlier, capitalism would have been affirmed to be contrary to the interests of humanity and socialism to be consonant with them—may now make for possibly harmonious cooperation between the two social systems. Thus, the conclusion of the Soviet-American agreement on the protection of the environment is, according to one Soviet analyst, "the first step on the path of combining the resources of various countries for the solution of a problem concerning all mankind."[57] So the profit motive no longer seems to pollute by an order of magnitude more than the humanistic motives of socialism. (Imagine what would have been said about the radical differences between "capitalism" and "socialism," had ecology been prominent in 1948.)

Wanting to be nice when meeting with representatives of the "other social system," Soviet representatives have begun to use their interlocutors' word "market economy" instead of their own, "capitalism"[58]—a concession requiring the violation of one's own sacred (or what used to be that) vocabulary. For Marxists learn in Party grade school that there are two kinds of market economies: the "simple production of commodities," where producers own their means of production, and "capitalism," where they do not. Calling capitalism a "market economy" would thus, until the present, have been an act of hiding its obnoxious essence.

For Marxists, whose panacea is the abolition of private *property* in the means of production so as to abolish *profit,* the two are indissoluble. In this respect foreign concessions in the twenties were easy, granting both.[59] As of the present, Moscow is sticky on foreign property while forthcoming on profits, and now its spokesmen seem to feel no difficulty in separating what Marx had joined. True enough, one may begin, "setting up . . . enclaves of foreign property within the socialist economy is not allowed." But so what? "What is the . . . goal for an American businessman, *ownership or profits?* The latter, I suppose." Now, if profits "(at an . . . agreed rate) could be . . . *guaranteed* to him . . . to reinvest or to transfer abroad, what would be his reasons to be interested in . . . control?"[60]

Enumerating Brezhnev's foreign trips in 1971, one may begin with Yugoslavia, proceed to two people's democracies (Hungary, Bulgaria), continue with a capitalist country (France), then mention another people's democracy (the German Democratic Republic). For Kosygin, one may start with a "progressive" country (Algeria), continue with one that is not (Morocco), then follow with a capitalist one (Canada), a socialist one (Cuba), and two more capitalist areas (Denmark, Norway). But then "the strengthening of the unity . . . of the socialist countries" has become merely "an important section" of "our international activities." And the entire Soviet Union may be seen as one big firm in a competitive market comprising the world: "The [24th Party] Congress pointed out the need . . . to raise the effectiveness of the USSR's participation in the international division of labor . . . so as to react quickly to the requirements and possibilities of the world market."[61]

One may now admit (or discover) similarities between the "two social systems" which could not be avowed or recognized before. "The diversity of . . . [countries'] attitudes within the same system [capitalist or socialist]," a prominent Soviet intellectual observes, "is sometimes very marked." He even goes on to mention names: "In the East as well as in the West of Europe there are countries which, while developing close political and economic relations with states possessing a similar *[Shocking—one would have expected "the same." There are only two.]* socio-political structure, nevertheless do not adhere to the military alliances to which their partners belong." To wit: "among the socialist states this is the case for Yugoslavia; among the capitalist countries, one may cite Sweden, Switzerland, Finland and Austria."[62] Why is it worthwhile, the reader may ask, to cite this Soviet mention of the evident? Because, I submit, Soviet spokesmen, dedicated in the past to the sense and the proclamation of a total difference between *them* and *us,* avoided wherever feasible (and it would have been easy here) any explicit acknowledgement of similarities. That the limits to the present permissiveness are not too wide becomes evident when the same Soviet analyst turns to the matter of "national security interests"—again accepting Western (American) lingo. Brezhnev informs American newsmen that his government refuses emigration to people connected with "what *today* is called national security"—and points out that such interests frequently lead to "important divergences" between states on "questions of reducing armed forces, limiting and prohibiting certain types of armament." But apparently this is the case *only* "among certain states of Western Europe."[63]

When *similarities between* systems become speakable or visible, the same may happen to *differences within* each of them. Expressing a view on a crucial matter which has not already been stated in quite the same form by higher levels, a Soviet intellectual in contact with the West may now pretend (à la Victor Louis) or disclose—I would still presume the former—that he is "speaking . . . in a personal capacity and [sic] with a personal opinion."[64] (Both the flimsiness of the pretense and the magnitude of the change require repetition.)

Finally, one may even begin admitting disagreements within one's own domain. When a journalist of *Der Spiegel* asks Dzhermen Gvishiani, the most prominent and best connected young intellectual specializing in contacts with the West, whether "there are not people [in the Soviet establishment] who fear that if the Soviet Union participates in the international division of labor, it will become dependent on the world abroad," the reply is a proper one: "There is nobody among us who sees it this way." But, propriety satisfied, the new realism breaks through, though in Western high-brow language, where one talks about intellectual processes rather than about what these might allow one to observe: "A few perhaps approach this problem on different levels. . . ." Worse, such disagreements may have economic bases, making the homogeneity of socialism disappear: "on different levels, perhaps for some economic reasons." Having ventured so far, the innovator annuls what he has done by noting that the events to which he has admitted have no impact: "But there are no political obstacles in this domain in our country!"[65]

POSTSCRIPT: WHAT THEY MIGHT THINK OF WHAT WE SAY: IMAGINED VIEWS OF A SOVIET DISCUSSANT

As students of bureaucratic decisionmaking have impressed upon us for the past decade, governments are not unitary decisionmakers. If my hypothetical Soviet discussant, "representing" the ruling group in Moscow, and his opposite number in the West were taken literally in the paragraphs that follow, we would have passed beyond conjecture into myth (perhaps more with regard to the United States than to the Soviet Union). My excuse is, of course, first approximation. I fancy that a majority in the Politburo might be found for a majority of the reactions I imagine. (Thus in the imaginary monologue which follows the pronoun referents are "we, our, us" for the Soviet Union, "you, your" for the United States.)

Sometimes we agree with a point you make, but not with the consequence you draw from it.

- As our stakes in politically vulnerable economic transactions increase, we have an added incentive to avoid unpleasantness among us. But if and when important opportunities for advancement open up for us, we shall continue to prevent ourselves from degenerating—with the help of your constantly telling us that we are bound to—and shall therefore be prepared to assume the costs and risks of another bout of forward policy. All the more, as by then the Second NEP on which we are now starting may have run much of its course. (You—with respect to whom we have performed so many left and right turns—don't really believe our policies to be eternal, or to last for 40 years, just because we've said, or even contracted, so. Or do you?) Furthermore, your aid will have enlarged our resource base.

- We are like each other in many ways. Sure, we have always striven to emulate your efficiency; Stalin proclaimed it to be one of the two basic components of our style in 1924. The other component is "revolutionary sweep," which we are pleased you are so certain we have lost. So it doesn't follow that things between ourselves should be cozy in the long run just because in the style of day-to-day dealings we have more in common than with, say, older types in British and French ruling circles (the newer ones imitate you, in any case).

  Also, we don't see why you should be so pleased about our having *efficiency* in common. Although it may then be more fun to deal with each other, we are sufficiently oriented on outcomes to be gratified when we find you unlike ourselves, less efficient (for all your pride in efficiency), blind—as in not perceiving the limits of our likeness. While the pleasure of the game is perhaps then reduced (not necessarily—there is joy in deception too), our chances of winning it are increased. Despite what we are both increasingly proclaiming, we at least are old-fashioned enough to continue believing that our game remains largely—what do you call it?—zero sum. *[This may indeed be old-fashioned in a world with not only nuclear weapons but also multipolarity.]*

There are things you strive for (or say you do) which we take for granted, and from which, once again, you expect effects that we would not predict.

- You advocate contacts for the sake of mutual respect. But that already exists— and it goes perfectly well with our belief that it will ultimately be you or ourselves.

- We foresee much less clearly than some of you that either you or we will "lose control" in a crisis; should this happen, we do not believe that enlarging our non-critical relations at that point would have much effect.

Some means that you envision using for objectives we might not share would, in any case, be too weak to attain them.

- You imagine dampening conflict by enlarging on concurrent non-conflict—as if proper statesmen would allow themselves to be influenced by a spillover of feelings (what we call spontaneity), as if they were not capable of pursuing both high conflict and high collaboration at the same time.

There are means that you propose ostensibly for an end acceptable to us, but that we would suspect—because of your insistence on their benign employment—of serving a hostile purpose.

- Such as when you advocate enlarging upon non-conflict relations in a crisis, so as to convince us of your lack of aggressive designs—or perhaps to blind us to them?

Some among you announce that you are attempting to do things to us which we refuse and shall prevent from being imposed on us. These things we don't attempt to do to you, either because we don't want to or because we know we can't.

- Some among you want to come close to us so as to make us like you.
- And thus to make us resemble you.
- As well as to convert us.

There are other things announced by you in the same vein which we shall also prevent you from doing to us. These we would love to do to *you*, but we don't presume to be able to. They include:

- Making the other side more predisposed through personal contacts to keep and amplify contracts.
- Achieving wide and deep penetrations without explicit agreement by the other side.

According to you, certain symmetries are best for both of us. In our belief, certain asymmetries are feasible, being useful for us and harming to you; these we strive to obtain and maintain.

- While according to you it is best for both of us to understand each other fully, we consider it most useful for us—as it has already proved (say, in 1942-1946)—that you be blind (with our help) about aspects in which we are unlike you. Hence, your statements about "the same human qualities" are just fine.
- The same goes for our liking each other (of course, we and you are only talking about feelings that inflect conduct). We, however, have learned to provoke and sustain your liking us, without losing our ability to reciprocate (in the service of our ultimate goal).

You talk much about what you are little capable of doing to us—penetrating us—while we say little about what we can and do achieve to a greater extent—overtly entering into all kinds of sectors and structures within you. Your capacity is mildly degraded by your garrulity (our countermeasures would operate even if you talked less); our is substantially enhanced by our silence (reducing your awareness of our strategy).

You continue to enunciate certain objectives without even deigning to mention that we refuse them:

- Such as when you propose changes in the organization for our foreign economic relations, while we have consistently declared our structures in this regard to be unchangeable.

You are in the habit of announcing that you are going to produce certain impacts on us which you should know to be unacceptable to us in content and in form (we don't like being influenced and, to boot, being told that we are going to be)—as if you were the masters of overwhelming forces about which we can do nothing. While we would in any case do much, the public nature of your stance reminds us (and for this we are obliged to you) to go to the limit in counteracting your designs:

- Your plan to make us increase, beyond our own intent, the fraction of GNP allotted to consumer goods.
- Your objective of rendering us attached in soul, rather than merely expediently conforming in conduct, to existing rules of international economic relations.
- Your device of having the structure of our economy converge with that of yours through the effects of a greater orientation of ours on exports as well as through the acceleration of growth, which we intend to achieve by utilizing you.
- Your intention of making us lose faith in our economic order through the importance to us of your economic aid.
- And of achieving the same effect through more education accompanying more growth, again owing to you.
- As well as through higher consumption levels.
- And through reduction in the material differences between life with you and with us.

However, we continue to believe that Bolsheviks can utilize whatever they choose, even Pepsi, without becoming the appendage of its source.

NOTES

1. Harlan Cleveland, *NATO: The Transatlantic Bargain* (New York, 1970), 155-159.

2. Henry Schaefer, Radio Free Europe (report of May 24, 1973), 26.

3. Y. Nikolayev, *Mezhdunarodnaia zhizn'* No. 5 (1973); FBIS (May 24, 1973), G9, emphasis added.

4. I. Kovan, *Foreign Trade* No. 4 (1973), 2; emphasis added.

5. Ibid., 8.

6. Ibid., 3.

7. Ibid., 8, emphasis added.

8. Ibid., 3.

9. John P. Hardt and George D. Holliday, *U.S.-Soviet Commercial Relations: The Interplay of Economics, Technology, Transfer, and Diplomacy.* Prepared for the Subcommittee on National Security Policy and Scientific Developments of the Committee on Foreign Affairs, House of Representatives, June 10, 1973 (Washington, D.C., 1973), 74.

10. Radio Moscow in English (June 10, 1973); FBIS (June 11, 1973), G7, emphasis added.

11. R. W. Apple Jr., *The New York Times* (June 20, 1973).

12. *Foreign Affairs* (January 1973), 356-359.

13. V. Gantman, *Kommunist* No. 7 (1973), 40.

14. M. Fedorov, *Novoe vremia* No. 21 (1973), 19.

15. *Foreign Affairs* (January 1973), 353.

16. *The New York Times* (June 2, 1973).

17. Ibid. (June 23, 1973).

18. Department of State Bulletin (May 21, 1973), emphasis added.

19. On American television; *The New York Times* (June 25, 1973), emphasis added.

20. Merle D. Adlum, *The American Review of East-West Trade* (November 1972), 33.

21. *The New York Times* (June 25, 1973).

22. "U.S. Trade Prospects with the PRC," Department of State (December 1972), emphasis added.

23. Y. Glukhov and P. Demchenko, *Pravda* (June 7, 1973).

24. Gantman, *Kommunist* No. 7, 40.

25. Kosygin to the Supreme Soviet, FBIS (November 26, 1971), 14.

26. A. Vetrov and V. Kazakevich, *Foreign Trade* (November 1972), 10.

27. Quoted by I. Kovan, *Foreign Trade* No. 4 (1973), 3.

28. James Reston in *The New York Times* (June 22, 1973).

29. Moscow Radio, FBIS (May 21, 1973), F24, emphasis added.

30. L. Pronyakova and V. Yermakov, *International Affairs* (December 1972), 110, emphasis added.

31. N. Inozemtsev, *Europe, 1980* (Leiden and Geneva, 1972), 123, emphasis added.

32. Y. Nikolayev, *Mezhdunarodnaia zhizn'* No. 5 (1973); FBIS (May 24, 1973), C6, emphasis added.

33. Pronyakova and Yermakov, *International Affairs* (December 1972), 110, emphasis added.

34. N. Shmelev, *Mirovaia ekonomika i mezhdunarodnye otnosheniia* No. 1 (January, 1973), 15.

35. Inozemstsev, *Europe, 1980,* 136.

36. Schmelev, *Mirovaia ekonomika,* 14.

37. B. Pichugin, *International Affairs* (February 1972), 14.

38. Inozemtsev, *Europe, 1980,* 126-128.

39. Schmelev, *Mirovaia ekonomika,* 15.

40. Ibid., 130.

41. *Foreign Trade* (January 1972), 5, emphasis added.

42. G. A. Arbatov, *S. Sh. A.; The Current Digest of the Soviet Press* (January 18, 1972), 2.

43. Ibid., 3.

44. G. A. Arbatov, *S. Sh. A.* (February 1972), 29.

45. I. Ivanov at the conference sponsored by Stanford Research Institute and the Institute of World Economy and International Relations (April 1973), 15.

46. Inozemtsev, *Europe, 1980,* 2, emphasis added.

47. G. A. Arbatov, *S. Sh. A.; The Current Digest of the Soviet Press* (January 18, 1972), 2.

48. Arbatov, *S. Sh. A.* (February 1972), 29.

49. B. Svetlov, *International Affairs* (February 1972), 16.

50. Ibid.

51. S. Shvernev, *S. Sh. A.,* FBIS (May 3, 1972), G7.

52. Arbatov, *S. Sh. A.* (February 1972), 27.

53. N. A. Berdinnikov, *S. Sh. A.* (November 1972); JPRS 57659, 5, emphasis added.

54. Arbatov, *S. Sh. A.; Current Digest of the Soviet Press* (January 18, 1972), 3, emphasis added.

55. Arbatov, *S. Sh. A.* (February 1972), 28, emphasis added.

56. Shvernev, *S. Sh. A.,* G11.

57. N. Shmelev, *Mirovaia ekonomika i mezhdunarodnye otnosheniia* No. 1 (1973), 15.

58. E.g., Ivanov, at the SRI/WEIR Conference, 4.

59. For the Politburo's inclination to resume that arrangement, see statements made by Deputy Foreign Trade Minister V. S. Alkhimov, according to Victor Zorza, *Chicago Sun Times* (April 5, 1973) and G. Bazhenov, *Mezhdunarodaia zhizn'* No. 3 (1973), 94f.

60. Ivanov, SRI/WEIR Conference, 14.

61. *Foreign Trade* (January 1972).

62. Inozemtsev, *Europe, 1980,* 123f.

63. *The New York Times* (June 15, 1973).

64. Ivanov, dissociating property and profit at the SRI/WEIR Conference, 14.

65. *Der Spiegel,* No. 19, 73.

SELECTED BIBLIOGRAPHY OF NATHAN LEITES

"Some Psychological Hypotheses on Nazi Germany" (with Paul Kecskemeti), *Journal of Social Psychology,* XXVI (1947), 141-183; XXVII (1948), 91-117; 241-270; XXVIII (1948), 141-164.

"Trends in Twentieth Century Propaganda" (with Ernst Kris), *Psychoanalysis and the Social Sciences,* I (New York, International Universities Press, 1947), 393-409.

"Trends in Affectlessness", *The American Imago,* IV (1947), 89-112.

"Trends in Moral Temper", *The American Imago,* V (1948), 3-37.

"Psycho-cultural Hypotheses about Political Acts", *World Politics,* I (1948), 102-119.

"Interaction: the Third International on its Changes of Policy," in Harold D. Lasswell and Nathan Leites, eds., *The Language of Politics* (New York, Stewart, 1949).

Movies, a Psychological Study (with Martha Wolfenstein), (Glencoe, The Free Press, 1950).

The Operational Code of the Politburo, (New York, McGraw Hill, 1951).

"Politburo Images of Stalin," (with Elsa Bernaut and R. L. Garthoff), *World Politics,* III (1951), 317-339.

"The Politburo through Western Eyes," *World Politics,* IV (1952), 159-185.

"Stalin as an Intellectual," *World Politics,* VI (1953), 45-66.

A Study of Bolshevism, (Glencoe: The Free Press, 1953).

Ritual of Liquidation (with Elsa Bernaut), (Glencoe, The Free Press, 1954).

"Panic and Defenses against Panic in the Bolshevik View of Politics," *Psychoanalysis and the Social Sciences,* V (1955), 135-144.

The House without Windows: France selects a President (with Constantin Melnik), (Evanston, Row and Peterson, 1958).

Du malaise politique en France (Paris, Plon, 1958); revised as *On the Game of Politics in France,* (Stanford, Stanford University Press, 1959).

"Democracy and Destructiveness," *American Behavioral Scientist,* V (1961), 6-10.

"Images of Power in French Politics," Rand report RM-2954-RC (Rand Corporation, Santa Monica, 1962).

La règle du jeu à Paris, (Paris, Mouton, 1966), translated as *The Rules of the Game in Paris,* D. Coltman, trs., (Chicago, University of Chicago Press, 1969).

Rebellion and Authority (with Charles Wolf, Jr.), (Chicago, Markham, 1970).

The New Ego, (New York, Science House, 1971).

"The New Economic Togetherness: American and Soviet Reactions." Studies in Comparative Communism, VII (1974), 246-285.